C000115947

THE WORLDS OF JOHANN SEBASTIAN BACH

An Aston Magna Academy Book

THE WORLDS OF
JOHANN SEBASTIAN BACH

An Aston Magna Academy Book

Edited by Raymond Erickson

AMADEUS PRESS

AN IMPRINT OF HAL LEONARD CORPORATION

NEW YORK

Published in 2009 by Amadeus Press
An Imprint of Hal Leonard Corporation
7777 West Bluemound Road
Milwaukee, WI 53213

Trade Book Division Editorial Offices
19 West 21st Street, New York, NY 10010

Photo credits can be found on pages 311 to 313, which constitute an extension of this copyright page.

This publication has received generous financial support from Furthermore: a program of the J. M. Kaplan Fund.

Printed in the United States of America
Book design by Mark Lerner

Library of Congress Cataloging-in-Publication Data

The worlds of Johann Sebastian Bach / edited by Raymond Erickson.
     p. cm.
 Includes bibliographical references and index.
 ISBN 978-1-57467-166-7 (alk. paper)
 1. Bach, Johann Sebastian, 1685-1750. 2. Composers--Germany--Biography. I. Erickson, Raymond.
 ML410.B1W85 2009
 780.92--dc22
 [B]
                             2009005866

www.amadeuspress.com

In Memoriam Margaretha Lohmann Blumen

Contents

PART I   THE CONTEXT FOR BACH

PART II   BACH IN CONTEXT

Preface

The enduring appreciation of the music of Johann Sebastian Bach in the English-speaking world is a remarkable phenomenon. Born over three centuries ago, Bach is the oldest composer (along with Handel) to enjoy truly universal appeal. But unlike Handel, Haydn, Mozart, Beethoven, Wagner, Stravinsky, and most other great and popular composers, he lived a provincial life and never achieved in his lifetime the international reputation that they did. What is notable about Bach's reputation, in fact, is that it has grown continuously since his death in 1750, so that now he has become *the* central composer in the Western musical tradition.

That Bach would be so highly regarded in his native Germany is immediately understandable. That he would enjoy such status in the English-speaking world, however, is not. Bach, unlike Handel, had no significant connections with (and apparently no interest in) the English language or culture. His vocal music is almost all in German, a language not widely spoken in the U.S. and Britain. Already in his own time, his music was recognized as difficult and uncompromising, lacking popular qualities and the tunefulness of Handel, who like Mozart benefited from spending time in Italy, fount of vocal lyricism.

And yet there are in the United States alone some forty annual festivals devoted to the music of Bach—more than for any other composer, whether European or American, "classical" or otherwise. There are an American Bach Society, a Bach Institute, a journal named *Bach*, a Bach Ensemble, and various Bach choirs. There are American churches where Bach cantatas are performed every Sunday. The United States is home to a number of Bach autograph music-manuscripts and the one unequivocally authentic portrait of the composer (and perhaps another; see plate 1). No less important, Bach's personal family Bible, richly annotated in his own hand, found its way to the New World in the nineteenth century. All this suggests that a book that seeks to put Bach in the context of his own time might be welcomed by a broad English-speaking public ranging from music lovers to history buffs, from professional musicians to scholars of the humanities.

Although conceived several years later, this book was ultimately inspired by an earlier effort to view Bach in context during the anniversary year of 1985. Then, with the support of the National Endowment for the Humanities, the Exxon Education Foundation, and the Goethe Institute New York, the Aston Magna Foundation for Music and the Humanities sponsored the seventh of its thirteen cross-disciplinary "Academies" under my direction with the collaboration of then–Aston Magna Artistic Director John Hsu and Associate Academy Director Sally Sanford. The Academy brought together leading Bach scholars and interpreters as well as specialists in many other fields to consider broadly, for three weeks at the Mason Gross School of the Arts at Rutgers University in New Brunswick, the environment in which Bach's musical legacy was created. (With its approximately 120 events—lectures, lecture-demonstrations, master classes, play readings, baroque dance classes, discussion sessions, concerts—the Academy was arguably the broadest and most intense celebration of the three-hundredth anniversary of Bach's birth.)

In the spirit of the Aston Magna Academies, this volume (like its predecessor *Schubert's Vienna*) seeks to provide basic information from the perspectives of many disciplines, rather than focus on the kinds of abstract questions appropriate for more specialized disciplinary fora. The editor is therefore deeply grateful to the authors—distinguished specialists all, in their respective areas—for speaking through their writing to the interested general public as well as to their peers. It is hoped that their contributions have been enriched and interconnected through the more than two hundred images that embellish them, almost all chosen and provided with captions by the editor, many of which are not to be found in other books on Bach.

Within the last decade there have been some sensational breakthroughs in Bach research that came too late to be considered or discussed at length in the many publications appearing in connection with the Bach anniversary year of 2000. These advances are a consequence of the fall in 1989 of the Iron Curtain or, as the Germans say, the *Wende* (turn of events), which soon led to a still-ongoing, *systematic* perusal of archives, mainly in East Germany, not previously so studied. Among the fruits of the resulting harvest have been new documents incorporated into the fifth volume of the *Bach-Dokumente* (2007); the finding of the lost library of the Berlin Sing-Akademie (discovered in Kiev by Christoph Wolff and Patricia Kennedy Grimsted in 1999 and returned to Berlin in 2001)[1]—a collection that included the "Old Bach Archive" once in the hands of J. S. Bach himself (fig. 0.10, p. 14); and the discovery in 2005 of the first unknown vocal work by Bach to come to light in seventy years[2] (fig. 1.10, p. 90), in 2007 of the earliest Bach autographs (fig. 0.28a, p. 45),[3] and in 2008 of previously unknown textual documents in Bach's hand.[4] The possibility that the B Minor Mass may have had its premiere in Vienna's Roman Catholic St. Stephen's Cathedral—which, if true, would give an important new dimension to our sense of Bach's universality—is also being investigated. This is truly an exciting time for Bach scholars, performers, and aficionados.

Notes

1. For a detailed account of the rediscovery of the Berlin Sing-Akademie library, see Patricia Kennedy Grimsted, "Bach Is Back in Berlin: The Return of the Sing-Akademie Archive from Ukraine in the Context of Displaced Cultural Treasures and Restitution Politics," www.huri. harvard.edu/pdf/Grimsted_Bach_Back.pdf, which is also printed in *Spoils of War: International Newsletter*, no. 8 (Spring 2003). The Sing-Akademie collection contains over 5,100 scores, about ten percent of which are works by members of the Bach family.

2. Michael Maul, "'Alles mit Gott und nichts ohn' ihn'—Eine neu aufgefundene Aria von Johann Sebastian Bach," *BJ* 2005, 7–34; the aria is published in facsimile and transcription in Michael Maul, ed., *"Alles mit Gott und nichts ohn' ihn," BWV 1127* (Cassel and New York: Bärenreiter, 2005).

3. Michael Maul and Peter Wollny, eds. *Weimarer Orgeltablatur: die frühesten Notenhandschriften Johann Sebastian Bachs so wie Abschriften seines Schülers Johann Martin Schubart* (Kassel & New York: Bärenreiter, 2007) and Peter Wollny, "The 'Weimar Organ Tablature': Bach's Earliest Autographs," paper presented at the Bach-Network Conference, Oxford University, January 5, 2008.

4. Andreas Glöckner, "Johann Sebastian Bach und die Universität Leipzig. Neue Quellen (Teil I)," *BJ* 94 (2008): 159–201, esp. 187ff.

Acknowledgments

This volume could not have been accomplished without the support and assistance of many others. First, the authors, besides their extraordinary patience, have been willing to consider changes that would give the volume as a whole greater coherence and stylistic unity. The board of the Aston Magna Foundation, headed by Robert Strassler, has been unfailingly supportive and understanding, and the editor has benefited from the enterprise and efficiency of the foundation's executive director, Ronnie Boriskin, and her staff. The realization of the goal of a generously illustrated volume has been enabled by two crucial grants from Furthermore: a program of the J. M. Kaplan Fund. The editor has personally benefited from fellowships from the Alexander von Humboldt Foundation; a special residency at the National Humanities Center (Research Triangle Park, NC); a one-semester sabbatical, Faculty Incentive Award, and CUNY-Professional Staff Congress grant from Queens College, CUNY; and a William H. Scheide Research Award from the American Bach Society. His introductory essay (an updated and expanded version of his keynote address at the 1985 Aston Magna Academy) has had the benefit of readings by both specialists and non-specialists, among them Oliver Allen, Alexis Lalli, Michael Marissen, Robert Marshall, Francis Mason, Drora Pershing, Norman Rich, David Schulenberg, Daniel Stepner, and Robert Strassler, important since this book is aimed at both kinds of serious readers.

The management and staff of Amadeus Press have been very supportive of this volume. It was former music editor Reinhard Pauly who first proposed Amadeus Press as publisher for an Aston Magna Academy publication. More recently, the enthusiasm of publisher John Cerullo has energized the project, and I have benefited greatly from the advice and skills of Carol Flannery, editorial director; Jessica Burr, volume editor; and Sarah Gallogly, copy editor. To all I am most grateful.

Staff members of the dozens of institutions and studios visited and contacted in the search for illustrations have been universally helpful and cordial. In Germany, my thanks go to Ina Dressel (Stadtgeschichtlichesmuseum "Haus zum Palmbaum," Arnstadt); Dr. Janny Dittrich (Schlossmuseum, Arnstadt); Hellmut Hell and Norbert Ludwig (Musikabteilung and Bildarchiv, respectively, Staatsbibliothek Preußischer Kulturbesitz, Berlin); Bettina Raeder (Deutsche Oper, Berlin); Bernd Uhlig (Bernd-Uhlig-Fotografie, Berlin);

Thomas Döring, Christiana Pagel, and Frau Edelmann (Herzog-Anton-Ulrich-Museum, Braunschweig); Juliane Schmieglitz-Otten (Bomann Museum, Celle); Günther Hoppe and Inga Streuber (Historisches Museum und Bachgedenkstätte, Cöthen); Norbert Michels (Anhaltische Gemäldegalerie, Dessau); Bettina Erlenkamp (Sächsische Landesbibliothek–Staats- und Universitätsbibliothek, Dresden); Hans Ulrich Lehmann, Claudia Schnitze, and Frau Miller (Kupferstichkabinett, Dresden); Eckhart Leiseriung and Ragna Nicholaus (Sächsisches Hauptstaatsarchiv, Dresden); Uta Neidhardt, Cornelia Munzinger-Brandt, Gisela Müller, and Steffi Reh (Staatliche Kunstsammlungen, Dresden); Katrin Tauscher (Stadtsarchiv, Dresden); Jorg Schöner (Fotodesign BFF, Dresden); Jörg Hansen, Claus Oefner, and Gisela Vogt (Bachhaus, Eisenach); Reimar Lacher (Gleimhaus, Halberstadt); Rita Hoitz and Birgit Delius (Museum für Hamburgische Geschichte, Hamburg); Joachim Frank (Staatsarchiv, Hamburg); Christoph Kaufmann (Stadtgeschichtliches Museum, Leipzig); Dr. Eckard Michael and Michael Hospowsky (Museum für das Fürstentum Lüneburg); Beate Kaiser (Stadtarchiv, Mühlhausen); Peter Cramer (Museum Schloss Ehrenstein, Ohrdruf); Sibylle Michel (Stiftung Preussische Schlösser und Gärten Berlin-Brandenburg, Potsdam); Marian Schulz (Neuberin-Museum, Reichenbach); Lutz Unbehaun and Diana Turkenwald (Thüringer Landesmuseum Heidecksburg, Rudolstadt); Petra Ehrhardt (Anna Amalia Bibliothek, Weimar); Katrin Berger (Thüringisches Staatsarchiv, Rudolstadt); and Frauke van der Wall (Mainfränkisches Museum, Würzburg). Special thanks are due to George Sturm (Bärenreiter Music Corporation), Teri Noel Towe, Christina Newman, Erika Norwood, and William H. Scheide.

I also wish to acknowledge the help of Linda Schubert (Rand McNally), David Berger (Concordia Seminary Library, St. Louis), Tricia Smith (Art Resource, New York), and the staffs of the Beinecke Rare Book and Manuscript Library, Map Collection, and Music Library (especially Suzanne Lovejoy) of Yale University, the Center for the Humanities and Library of the Performing Arts of the New York Public Library, the Union Theological Seminary Library, the Libraries of Columbia University, and the Benjamin Rosenthal Library and Music Library (Joseph Ponte and Jennifer Owens) at Queens College. Others at Queens College who have been especially helpful were Kenneth Lord (Computer Science), Sergio Cruz (Office of Converging Technologies), Nancy Bareis (Photographic Services) and Dyanne Maue and Stephanie Goldson (Editorial Services). The libraries of Old Forge and Rhinebeck, both in New York State, as well as Bard College and Vassar College (especially Sarah Camino), have also provided facilities and a quiet place to work, when needed. I am also grateful to Gerd Harnischmacher, Deborah Schell, and William Richard for special favors that helped the project along. Finally, my research assistant John Temps was of invaluable assistance in the last stages of the project.

In addition, I have profited from discussions concerning various topics dealt with in this book with Hans-Joachim Schulze (Bach-Archiv, Leipzig), Martin Petzoldt (University of Leipzig), Arno Herzig (University of Hamburg), Hans-Günther Otten-burg (Technische-Universität, Dresden), and Claudia Schnitze (Kupferstichkabinett, Dresden). My thanks also to Anna Nekola, for the Neumeister text excerpted in the caption for fig. 2.12 (p. 126).

In conclusion, I wish to acknowledge two important people without whom this book would not have been. My wife, Carole De Saram, has understood how much this project has meant to me and has willingly endured several periods of separation when I have been involved in research away from home; possessed of a passion for history, a sensitivity to greatness in art, and a sharply honed faculty for critical judgment that has caused me to reconsider a number of issues, she has made important contributions to this book.

The other person is the dedicatee of this volume, the late pianist Margaretha Lohm-ann (1904–2000), an extraordinary musician and teacher whom my father found for me when I was but ten years old. A student of Sigismond Stojowski and Béla Bartók, she was best known in the Los Angeles area as a Bach performer and founder, over seventy years ago, of the Whittier College Bach Festival—one of the oldest continuing Bach Festivals in the United States—in which I cut my teeth on many a Bach work during my undergraduate years at the college. Although Margaretha Lohmann lived and breathed music, she also understood that making music does not simply require mastering an instrument, and the acuity of her intelligence and the breadth of her culture—summed up in her pithy motto that "everything helps everything else"—helped me to appreciate early on the importance of a liberal arts education for musicians and prepared me for future collaborations with my other most important musical mentor, Aston Magna's founding artistic director, the late Albert Fuller, with whom the first six Aston Magna Academies were developed. It is fitting that the last conversation I had with Margaretha Lohmann was a telephone call from a booth situated close to St. Thomas's Church in Leipzig, where her beloved Bach worked and is buried.

R. E.
Rhinecliff, New York
June 2008

Abbreviations

BC   *Bach-Compendium: analytisch-bibliographisches Repertorium der Werke Johann Sebastian Bachs.* Edd. Hans Joachim-Schulze and Christoph Wolff. Frankfurt and New York: C.F. Peters, 1985–.

BD   *Bach-Dokumente.* Ed. Bach-Archiv Leipzig. [Supplement to *NBA*, see below.] Kassel: Bärenreiter, 1963–. Vol. 1: *Schriftstücke von der Hand Johann Sebastian Bach.* Edd. Werner Neumann and Hans-Joachim Schulze. 1963. Vol. 2: *Fremdschriftliche und gedruckte Dokumente zur Lebensgeschichte Johann Sebastian Bachs 1685–1750.* Edd. Werner Neumann and Hans-Joachim Schulze. 1969. Vol. 3: *Dokumente zum Nachwirken Johann Sebastian Bachs 1750–1800.* Ed. Hans-Joachim Schulze. 1972. Vol. 4: *Bilddokumente zur Lebensgeschichte Johann Sebastian Bachs.* Ed. Werner Neumann. 1979. Vol. 5: *Dokumente zu Leben, Werk, und Nachwirken Johann Sebastian Bachs 1685–1800.* [New Documents: Supplement to Vols. 1–3] 2007.

BJ   *Bach-Jahrbuch.* Berlin, etc.: Evangelische Verlagsanstalt, 1904–.

BWV   "Bach-Werke-Verzeichnis" (Catalog of Bach's works). BWV numbers follow Wolfgang Schmieder, *Thematisch-systematisches Verzeichnis der musikalischen Werke Johann Sebastian Bachs.* Leipzig: Breitkopf und Härtel, 1950. 2nd, rev. and enlarged ed., Wiesbaden, Breitkopf und Härtel, 1990.

EM   *Early Music.* Oxford: Oxford University Press, 1973–.

LW   *Luther's Works: American Edition.* Edd. Jaroslav Pelikan and Helmut Lehman. 55 Vols. St. Louis and Philadelphia: Concordia Publishing House, 1955–86.

NBA   *Johann Sebastian Bach. Neue Ausgabe sämtlicher Werke.* Edd Johann-Sebastian-Bach-Institut, Göttingen, and Bach-Archiv, Leipzig. Kassel: Bärenreiter, 1955–.

NBR   *The New Bach Reader: A Life of Johann Sebastian Bach in Letters and Documents.* Edd. Hans T. David and Arthur Mendel; rev. and enlarged by Christoph Wolff. New York: W. W. Norton, 1998.

MGG   *Die Musik in Geschichte und Gegenwart: allgemeine Enzyklopädie der Musik.* Ed. Friedrich Blume. 16 Vols. Kassel: Bärenreiter, 1949–79. Online version at www.oxfordmusiconline.com.

New Grove   *The New Grove Dictionary of Music and Musicians.* Ed. Stanley Sadie. 2nd ed. 29 Vols. London and New York: Macmillan Publishers, 2001.

WA   *D. Martin Luthers Werke.* Kritische Gesamtausgabe. Weimar, 188ff. Reprint Graz, 1964ff.

Wolff, Essays   Christoph Wolff. *Bach: Essays on His Life and Music.* Cambridge, MA: Harvard University Press, 1991.

THE WORLDS OF JOHANN SEBASTIAN BACH

An Aston Magna Academy Book

The Legacies of J. S. Bach

Raymond Erickson

The area within which Bach lived and worked (save for three years in Lüneburg and trips to Lübeck and Carlsbad) can be enclosed by a rectangle of 90 by 70 miles (fig. 0.1). This little world was dwarfed in geographical and cultural extent by the far larger one traversed by his exact contemporary George Frideric Handel and other notable German musicians such as Georg Philipp Telemann. Nonetheless, it provided Bach with the training, life experiences, and challenges that stimulated his imagination and opened to him many other worlds, musical and otherwise. The ultimate result was a musical legacy that many feel is the most universal of any composer.

The following essay seeks to explain that universality in terms of traditions and circumstances that touched Bach in his small geographic world, for a distinguishing feature of Bach's music is its richly synthetic quality, drawing on virtually every realm of his personal experience. The "legacies" in the title, therefore, refer not to Bach's musical gifts to posterity but rather to those threads of tradition—be they intellectual, religious, family-related, musical, or social—that provided Bach with the raw materials he wove into his music, creating works of art so rich in meaning and inferences that to study them is to study Western civilization itself.

Bach's Life and Career

The Early Years:
Eisenach—Ohrdruf—Lüneburg—Weimar (1685–1703)

Johann Sebastian Bach was born in Eisenach, in that region of central Germany known as Thuringia, on March 21, 1685. He began his schooling in Eisenach, being first documented as a pupil in the fifth (*Quinta*) class, the second-lowest of six grade levels, at

St. George's Latin School. Since children there were required to attend school from
age six and since each level was normally repeated once, Bach had to have completed
the equivalent of the sixth (*Sexta*) or lowest level elsewhere in Eisenach—undoubtedly
at one of the so-called "German schools," where he learned the basics of reading and
writing in the vernacular.[1] At age nine he was promoted to the fourth class (*Quarta*),
but in 1695, after the conclusion of the first year, he went to live with his older brother
Johann Christoph in Ohrdruf, having lost his mother and father successively in 1694
and 1695. In Ohrdruf, he started his second year in the fourth class, and by 1699 he had
passed into the first (*Prima*), the highest level before the university. The boy Bach was

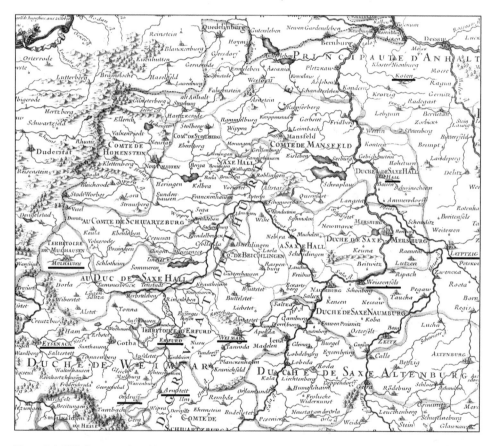

Figure 0.1. With the exception of Lüneburg to the north, all the towns and cities in which Bach lived and many
he visited—within a rectangle of only 90 by 70 miles—are found on this segment of a 1708 map of Saxony
by the French royal geographer Charles Jaillot. In the lower left quadrant are found, at left, "Eysenack" and
"Mulhausen" (to its north); southeast of Eisenach are "Ordruff" and "Arnstett," and east of Eisenach are Erfurt
("Erfurd"), birthplace of Bach's parents, and then Weimar. Just south of the middle of the map near the eastern
edge is "Leyptzig," whereas "Koten" is near the northeast corner (within the "PRINCIPAUTE D'ANHALT").
Dresden is off the eastern edge of the map to the southeast of Leipzig, whereas Weissenfels is southwest of
Leipzig (almost midway to Weimar) and "Hall" (Halle) is northwest of it. The map also conveys well the complex
patchwork of political units that made up Germany and the Holy Roman Empire in Bach's time.

an exceptional student, ranking first and second at his level after the 1695–96 and 1698–99 academic years, respectively, even though younger than most of his classmates.

In the spring of 1700, Bach, along with his older friend Georg Erdmann and several other boys, was forced to leave the Ohrdruf lyceum before the end of the school year. It has been thought this was because of the students' inability to arrange for the free meals that some benevolent families offered poor schoolboys.[2] For whatever reason, Erdmann and Bach made their way the goodly distance to Lüneburg (fig. 0.2), south of Hamburg, where they found places at the highly reputed St. Michael's School (a *Partikularschule*) attached to the eponymous church (fig. 3.3, p. 144) and paying jobs as singers with its select Matins Choir (*Mettenchor*) as well as with the *chorus simphoniacus*, a large school chorus such as also existed in Eisenach and Ohrdruf (fig. 0.3a–b). St. Michael's was noteworthy for its extraordinarily rich library of seventeenth-century vocal and choral

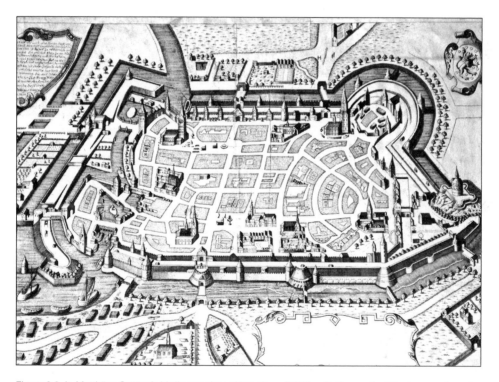

Figure 0.2. In Matthäus Seutter's bird's-eye view of Lüneburg (1730), with the south at the top, are the ruins of the former ducal fortress on the Kalkberg (the hill with the tower on the far right), St. Michael's Church and associated buildings (lower right), the marketplace with Town Hall and Ducal Palace (lower center, left of St. Michael's), and the main municipal church, St. John's (diagonally across town from St. Michael's in upper left). The Kalkberg fortress, its associated monastery of St. Michael's, and the importance of salt in Lüneburg's economy is documented from the tenth century. Ruled first by the Dukes of Saxony (Billings, then Welfs), then Dukes of Brunswick, the town enjoyed self-rule during the late fourteenth and fifteenth centuries—the period of its greatest wealth and importance—before gradually losing its independence. Thus, when Bach came to Lüneburg in 1700, Lüneburg was part of an absolutist state, the duchy of Brunswick-Lüneburg.

music.[3] There was also associated with St. Michael's a school for young nobility (*Ritterschule*, from 1732 *Ritterakademie*), the academic curriculum and instructional staff of which was the same as that of the Particular School (fig. o.4a–b).[4]

There are many questions concerning Bach's Ohrdruf and Lüneburg periods, which are very sparsely documented. For example, why would he travel far to the north of Bach-family territory, especially when it is now questioned that Elias Herda, the Ohrdruf cantor and former pupil at St. Michael's, was instrumental in obtaining places for Bach and his friend Erdmann?[5] Did Bach actually complete his last year of the standard curriculum at St. Michael's, which would have qualified him for university study? Extant payment records only record his presence in the Matins Choir for two months after his arrival (other records are missing), around which time his voice broke. Did Bach find other sources of support to enable him to complete his education if he could no longer sing in

Figure 0.3. The fifteen-year-old Bach arrived in Lüneburg just after one of the most sensational crimes of the time: the desecration in 1698, by a notorious band of thieves, of the precious "Golden Panel" in St. Michael's Church (a). Originally endowed by the Holy Roman Emperor and German King Otto II (r. 973–83), the priceless altarpiece, with its gold, precious stones, pearls, relics, and the like, was one of the city's most famous sights. The story of its pillaging and of the subsequent trial and executions was widely published, and the panel, stripped of its treasures, was left in view for all (including the chorister Bach) to deplore. The gruesome forms of execution to which the thieves were condemned (b) is a reminder of the harshness of justice in Bach's time, which was also carried out as public spectacle, often with participation of local musicians and choristers (see also fig. 9.5, p. 276).

Figure 0.4. In Bach's time there were two schools associated with St. Michael's Church in Lüneburg, both under the politically powerful "abbot" of St. Michael's. The first was an internal school, the *Ritterschule* (school for knights, seen here in a later view) (*a*), which, although founded only in 1656 upon the dissolution of the monastery of St. Michael's, continued a tradition dating to the tenth century of educating and boarding noble boys in the monastery. (In 1732 it was renamed *Ritterakademie*.) The other school (the *Partikularschule*) was non-residential or external, intended for commoners; founded ca. 1340, it had long enjoyed a superior academic reputation and in 1563 a new—if cramped and cold—building had been built for it. Despite the enormous social gulf between the noble and commoner pupils, both groups were now educated (separately) with the same academic curriculum in the same classrooms by the same teachers under the same administration, although they ate and lived apart—the twenty or so noble sons in the monastery, the more numerous commoner students in various homes.

The French influence at the Duke of Brunswick-Lüneburg's court at Celle spilled over into Lüneburg. The abbot of St. Michael's School (now *Landschaftsdirektor*) Ernst Wilhelm von Spörken had been educated at the French Academy in Hamburg, and several of the nine teachers were French. More visible evidence was the new three-winged ducal palace (*b*) on the north side of the market, designed in the baroque French style by Johann Caspar Borchmann, whom Duke Georg Wilhelm had sent to Paris for study. His wife Eleonore d'Olbreuse (plate 10) retired here after the Duke's death.

the Matins Choir? The sensational discovery in 2007 of the "Weimar Tablatures" (fig. 0.28a, p. 45), which are discussed below, has led to new insights into Bach's musical development and personal situation around this time, although not yet to firm answers concerning these questions.[6]

Career as Organist: Arnstadt (1703–7)—Mühlhausen (1707–8)—Weimar (1708–17)

Exactly when Bach left Lüneburg is unknown, but for the first half of 1703 he was back in Thuringia in the employ of Duke Johann Ernst of Saxony-Weimar, probably playing violin or viola and possibly substituting for the aging court organist whom he replaced a few years later.

Then, however, Bach began his real professional career. In July 1703, the eighteen-year-old was hired first as an organ consultant for, and subsequently as organist at, the New Church (the present "Bach Church") in Arnstadt (plate 5). A brand-new position with relatively light duties, it paid three times what Bach had earned in Weimar. In the winter of 1705–6, he received permission to go to Lübeck for a month "in order to comprehend one thing and another about his art" (as the town consistory report subsequently recorded).[7] In Lübeck was, of course, the great Dietrich Buxtehude, not only a famous organist and composer, but the organizer of large-scale oratorio-like concerts, famous all over Protestant Germany, offered under the rubric *Abendmusik* (Evening Music).[8]

Over time, the consistory of the Count of Schwarzburg-Arnstadt, to which Bach reported, had reason to be dissatisfied with him. He overstayed his leave in Lübeck by three months (missing the Christmas season), confused the congregation with his elaborate hymn accompaniments, got in a nasty fight with a student in the course of which he drew his dagger, was accused of inviting a young girl to the choir loft and "letting her make music there" (women were banned from performing in church), and was admonished for allowing the choir prefect to go into the wine cellar during the sermon.[9] Moreover, he refused to direct the children's choir in polyphony. Bach's stance in this matter is characteristic: he insisted that a professional choir director be engaged so that the music could be performed on a high artistic level; after all, he could not effectively direct singers in the choir loft immediately below the organ gallery[10] (fig. 3.5, p. 146).

In June of 1707 Bach therefore accepted an invitation to become organist at the most important church in Mühlhausen, the thirteenth-century church of St. Blaise (fig. 3.7, p. 147). One of the first things he did was to propose a major overhaul of the organ, which was approved despite the drain on the city budget from a major fire. Another positive development was his marriage to his second cousin Maria Barbara Bach of Arnstadt in the tiny village of Dornheim just outside her hometown. However, Bach soon became unhappy with the low quality of the musical forces in Mühlhausen and the lack of cooperation of the town musicians; he complained that even in the outlying villages the level of music-making was higher.[11] Moreover, he seems to have gotten along better with the pastor of Mühlhausen's other major church, St. Mary's, than with the pastor of St. Blaise.[12] So in June of 1708 Bach accepted a position in Weimar as court organist, asking the consistory in Mühlhausen to permit him to leave on the grounds that he saw "the possibility of a more adequate living and the achievement of my goal of a well-regulated church music" (by which he meant music for voices and instruments performed at a high level).[13] Nonetheless, Bach remained on good terms with Mühlhausen, being subsequently commissioned in 1709 and 1710 to compose and lead performances of a cantata celebrating the city council elections. He had already created such a work in 1708, *Gott ist mein König* (BWV 71) (fig. 0.5). It was not only one of his earliest cantatas, but also the first of only two published during his lifetime.[14] Worth noting here is that the term "cantata" was not used by Bach for most of the works that are commonly so

Figure 0.5. The grandly polychoral *Gott ist mein König* (BWV 71), with its colorful orchestration and solo/tutti vocal contrasts, was composed for the inauguration of a new town council and an eighty-three-year-old mayor in Mühlhausen's St. Mary's Church in 1708. It is the only complete Bach cantata published during the composer's lifetime—his works of this kind began to be published systematically only in the mid-nineteenth century. Bach did not himself designate such sacred pieces "Cantata," preferring terms such as "Konzert" (concerto), "Musik," or, in this case, "Motetto." The lack of recitatives and da capo arias shows that Bach was not yet influenced by the "reform cantata" inspired by the Italian opera (fig. 2.12, p. 126); a more likely inspiration was the music by Buxtehude Bach had heard in Lübeck during his Arnstadt period. The text of the work pays homage to the elders of the city but also makes a direct reference to "Joseph," for the Holy Roman Emperor Joseph I was the ultimate ruler of the free imperial city of Mühlhausen.

called today. Bach called *Gott ist mein König* a "motetto" and tended to reserve the term "cantata" for solo vocal works with orchestra but without choir.[15]

It was in Weimar that Bach had his last position as organist; it was also where he composed many of his greatest organ works, including the final (but uncompleted) form of the *Orgelbüchlein* (a series of forty-five short chorale preludes for organ [BWV 599–644], arranged in the order of the liturgical year; see chapter 7),[16] the Toccata, Adagio and Fugue in C Major (BWV 564), and the "Dorian" Toccata and Fugue (BWV 538). The latter part of the Weimar period is especially important for the expansion and transformation in his compositional style that resulted from his becoming acquainted with Vivaldi's concertos, brought or sent from Amsterdam in 1713 by Bach's musically gifted student, the short-lived Duke Johann Ernst (1697–1715). In 1714 Bach received the additional title and responsibility of concertmaster, with the duty and opportunity to compose and lead the performance of a cantata once a month. These cantatas, many with texts by the important Pietist-leaning Salomon Franck, are noted for their subjective but deeply moving quality—e.g., *Weinen, Klagen, Sorgen, Zagen* (Weeping, Lamenting, Worrying, Quaking) (BWV 12)—but also show increasing use of the recitative and aria forms used in Italian opera. This reflects the influence of the prolific, Thuringian-born poet and preacher Erdmann Neumeister (fig. 2.12, p. 126), who helped establish a new type of sacred cantata that was "no different from a piece out of an opera, being put together with recitative and arias."[17]

Figure 0.6. Among Bach's most extraordinary chamber music are the two sets of six works for unaccompanied violin (BWV 1001–6) and unaccompanied cello (BWV 1007–12), respectively. These are cast in the forms of the French dance suite (Bach uses the Italian term "partita" for the violin suites) or Italian sonata, but also carry on to its highest perfection the German tradition of multistopping and polyphonic textures (actual and implied) on a single stringed instrument. Of all these works, the most famous, shown here in Bach's autograph manuscript of 1720, is the monumental "Ciaccona" that concludes the Partita No. 2 in D Minor (BWV 1004). Despite the title, it is essentially a set of variations over a four-measure bass pattern (and its variants) on the model of the grand theatrical *passacailles* of French baroque opera. But the work is much more than that, being an integrated, encyclopedic traversal through French formal conventions and rhythms, virtuoso Italian embellishment and variation techniques, and German harmony and polyphonic string textures.

Bach apparently harbored hopes of advancing to the head of the Weimar musical establishment when the aging court music director (Hofcapellmeister), Salomo Drese, retired or died. However, Wilhelm Ernst gave the post to Drese's son Johann Wilhelm, who had had the advantage of studying in Italy. Bach, seeing no future in Weimar beyond what he had achieved, decided to accept an offer of Prince Leopold of Anhalt-Cöthen to come to Cöthen, which angered Wilhelm Ernst so much that he had Bach detained in the castle prison for a month before dismissing him in disgrace.

Court Music Director: Cöthen (1717–23)

In diminutive, quiet Cöthen, Bach held the most socially prestigious title he would ever have: that of court music director. Prince Leopold (plate 11), who had in the previous year assumed the rule of his realm, was a knowledgeable connoisseur of music and had hired a group of outstanding musicians (most of them recently let go by Friedrich Wilhelm I of Prussia). Moreover, because the prince was paying his new music director very well, Bach had good reason to be happy.[18] The only musical constraint was that the prince was a Calvinist, not an orthodox Lutheran, which meant that Bach's production of sacred cantatas and organ music stopped. On the other hand, Cöthen gave Bach occasion to write a sizable body of instrumental music, including at least some of the six Brandenburg Concertos (BWV 1046–51) and possibly some of the orchestral suites (BWV 1066–69), as well as the unaccompanied works for violin (BWV 1001–6) (fig. 0.6) and cello (BWV 1007–12). Moreover, especially from about 1720, he composed much keyboard music, often of a didactic nature: the little keyboard books for his son Wilhelm Friedemann (BWV 924–32) (fig. 0.7) and his second wife, Anna Magdalena (whom he married in 1721) (fig. 9.9, p. 283), the two- and three-part inventions (BWV 772–86 and 787–801), most of the so-called French Suites (BWV 812–17), and the Chromatic Fantasia and Fugue (BWV 903), to name the most familiar and important. Other works, such as the *Well-Tempered Clavier*, Book I (BWV 846–69) (fig. 10.4, p. 302), and the English Suites (BWV 806–11), were likely begun in Weimar and completed in Cöthen.[19]

Figure 0.7. This page from the *Clavierbüchlein* (Little keyboard book, 1720–1) for Bach's oldest and perhaps most gifted son, Wilhelm Friedemann, offers several useful insights. First, it shows Bach taking time from his duties as court music director to compose a simple keyboard exercise for his nine-year-old offspring. The initials "I.N.I." (for *In nomine Iesu*, "In the name of Jesus") at the top are a clear demonstration that Bach considered even the most modest musical effort, even in a secular context, an act of divine praise. Finally, one notes the meticulously detailed old-style fingering, which produces a natural unevenness that is basic to baroque articulation, although Bach is also known for his innovations in fingering techniques.

In a Leipzig letter of 1730 to his boyhood friend Georg Erdmann, Bach spoke of his happiness in Cöthen, as if he regretted having left it.[20] But leave it he did after only six years. Things had gone extremely well from Bach's perspective until 1722, when the music budget was cut. But even before then, religious tensions between the ruling Calvinist prince and his uncompromising, orthodox Lutheran mother (plate 12) had seriously threatened the religious freedom of Cöthen's Lutherans and therefore the quality of schooling available to the Lutheran families—something of great concern to Bach, who wanted his sons to have what he did not, a university education. And so Bach began to seek other opportunities: in 1720 he applied for an organist position in Hamburg; in 1721 he sent off the famous set of six concertos with a dedication to the Margrave of Brandenburg (fig. 1.13, p. 94), which the margrave never acknowledged; and in late 1722 he applied for the position of cantor of St. Thomas's school and director of city music in nearby Leipzig after his friend Georg Philipp Telemann had turned down the job. (The reason for leaving Cöthen that Bach gave in his letter to Erdmann—Leopold's marriage to an "unmusical" princess, who Bach claimed had turned the prince's attention away from music—is now judged as improbable. More likely the prince's interest in music cooled to "somewhat lukewarm" temperatures thanks to mounting financial and political pressures of which Bach may not have been aware.[21]) Nonetheless, Bach maintained his friendship with Prince Leopold, who allowed him to keep his title even after he left for Leipzig. On several occasions Bach returned to Cöthen to conduct his music, the last time being the prince's funeral in 1729.

Cantor of St. Thomas's School and Director of City Music: Leipzig (1723–50)

After considerable debate by members of the city council over whether they preferred a scholastically oriented cantor or a professionally ambitious music director who would make Leipzig a great center of music, Bach, who fell more into the second category, was hired.[22] He had made it clear that he was not interested in being a schoolroom teacher in the mold of previous cantors, and negotiated terms that allowed him to pay someone else to teach Latin. As cantor, Bach was merely the third-ranked official of St. Thomas's School (beneath the rector and conrector), but as city music director he was the city's first-ranked musician, an important figure not only in Leipzig but on the German musical scene.

Bach spent more than half his career in Leipzig (plate 14) (fig. 0.8), a flourishing commercial city without a resident lord that Lessing (fig. 5.3, p. 199), who studied there, called "little Paris." At the beginning, he focused his energies on creating a repertory of his own cantatas for the church year, although this was not required. Precisely how many cantatas he composed in Leipzig is not known (approximately two hundred is the

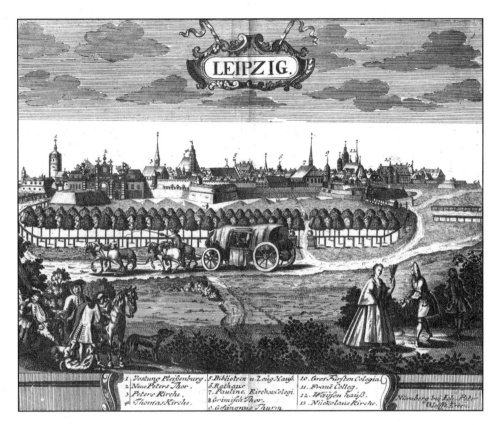

Figure 0.8. This view of Leipzig from the southeast shows the towers of (from left to right) the Pleissenburg fortress (1), St. Peter's Church (3), and St. Thomas's Church with its high roof (4). Just right of center is the town hall (6) and to its right the tall steeple of the University Church of St. Paul. The cluster of three towers to the right of the "9" are part of the front facade of St. Nicholas's Church, the middle tower having been elevated in 1732. The view hides the New Church, which was situated behind St. Thomas's, but nevertheless suggests how tree-lined avenues were found just outside the city walls. Note on the lower right the gentleman greeting the lady with a reverence (see also fig. 6.5, p. 211), a bow used not only in court dance, but in the etiquette of everyday life.

usual estimate), but it seems clear that he focused on cantata composition especially in the first two years and that most of the rest were created before 1729; in many cases he adapted earlier works in order to accommodate the new texts—a process musicologists call "parody."[23] A characteristic feature of many early Leipzig cantatas is a grand opening movement for chorus and orchestra incorporating the chorale melody and text on which the cantata is based.

From 1729 to the early 1740s his activity had a different emphasis: he directed the Collegium Musicum, made up of local professionals and talented university students, for which he also composed much chamber music, many concertos, and secular cantatas for weekly performances at Zimmermann's coffee house (fig. 3.19, p. 158); during the thrice yearly Leipzig trade fairs, there were additional presentations as well. It has been estimated that he organized at least five hundred concerts in all.[24]

During this period, Bach also showed a greater interest than ever before in leaving an enduring legacy, and began to publish with some regularity. As far back as 1726 (fig. 6.1, p. 207), the six partitas for keyboard (BWV 825–30) had begun to appear serially and then, in 1731, they were printed in one volume. The partitas were the first phase of a multi-stage project of keyboard publications consciously intended to set standards of musical sophistication and technical difficulty. Bach gave the enterprise the deceptively unpretentious title *Clavierübung* (Keyboard practice), which in its second part (1735), consisting of the Italian Concerto (BWV 971) and the French Overture for harpsichord (BWV 831), demonstrated Bach's awareness of the two most important national styles that exerted a dominant influence over German music. The concern with keyboard music continues throughout the 1730s, with Bach working on the second part of the *Well-Tempered Clavier* (BWV 870–93), and publishing in 1739 his largest collection of keyboard music, the *Clavierübung, Part III* for organ (fig. 2.6, p. 112; fig. 7.2, p. 231), with its two sets of chorale preludes (BWV 669–89), based on Luther's catechism hymns (see chapters 2 and 7) framed by the great "St. Anne" Prelude and Fugue (BWV 552).

The last decade of Bach's life brought to a high point of perfection this trend of synthetic, didactic, and consummately skillful work. Bach wrote virtually no new cantatas or organ music during this period, but 1741 saw the publication of the so-called Goldberg Variations (BWV 988) as *Clavierübung, Part IV*; 1744 the completion of the *Well-Tempered Clavier*, Book II; and 1747 the publication of *The Musical Offering* (BWV 1079), dedicated to Frederick the Great, whom Bach had visited in Potsdam earlier that year—an event looked at from several different perspectives in subsequent chapters. In addition, Bach worked on *The Art of Fugue* (BWV 1080), beginning in the early 1740s, preparing it for publication at the end of the decade (and apparently not really leaving it unfinished at his death as was long believed.).[25] The last major compositional effort, his hand somewhat shaky at the end, was the completion of the Mass in B Minor (BWV 232), the final *summa* of Bach's personal and musical credo (fig. 0.25, p. 38, and fig. 0.26, p. 39).

The Legacy of the Family

Bach's legacy to posterity is priceless and unique, but it was not created in a vacuum. Although he lost both parents before he was ten, he benefited from the extraordinary personal and professional support system that was the Bach family. Despite the disorienting loss of security that being orphaned surely occasioned, Bach knew even as a child what he had to do in life: by definition, to be a Bach meant to be a musician. His subsequent career therefore unfolded in a series of purposeful steps, each designed

Figure 0.9. Erfurt, the major city of Thuringia with a population of ca. eighteen thousand, was *the* Bach family center. Indeed, the Bach clan so dominated the musical scene that "Bach" was used at least once in city records synonymously for "town musician" ("Stadt Musikanten oder sogenannten Bachen"); members of the family also controlled many of the organist positions. Although the only professional activity in Erfurt associated with Johann Sebastian was his examination of an organ in 1716, perhaps he attended some of the regular gatherings of the Bach family in Erfurt.

to increase his potential for financial security and to fulfill a clear artistic objective of making music with appropriate forces, qualitatively and quantitatively.[26]

Because so much attention is paid to Johann Sebastian, the debt he owed to his family is often slighted. But because of his family's contributions to Thuringian musical life over many generations—he was in the fifth generation of descendants of Veit Bach—Bach had real advantages that made it possible for him to advance quickly in his professional life and to utilize his talent in the most varied ways. Bach himself knew this and took pride in his family, sitting down in 1735 to write a prose genealogy that, while not accurate in every detail, gives a good overview of the role his family played in the musical life of the region they inhabited.[27] Indeed, by his time the word "Bach" was sometimes used synonymously for "musician," as when the Count of Schwarzburg in Arnstadt allegedly said upon the death of one of Bach's uncles that he must get "another Bach"; similarly, a city council document from Erfurt (1716) (fig. 0.9 and fig. 3.15, p. 154) refers to "town musicians or so-called 'Baachen.'"[28]

By the time Johann Sebastian was growing up, the Bachs had integrated themselves into the civic, religious, and court establishments of the region, forming a mutually supportive network of contacts that helped foster and enhance the family's position in musical life. The dominance of the family was extended further by intermarriage with other musical families. We see this in Bach's own marriages. His first wife, Maria Barbara, was in fact a Bach, whereas his second wife, Anna Magdalena, was a Wilcke (or Wülcken), her father being a court musician at Weissenfels, where Bach and his music were much appreciated. Just how deeply entrenched the Bachs were in Thuringian musical life can be grasped by considering the dizzying array of family connections in some towns where Bach lived.

Eisenach

In Eisenach, a city of about six thousand when Johann Sebastian was born there in 1685, the Bach family went all the way back to Johannes (Hans) Bach (d. 1626), son of the baker Veit, who had established himself in Wechmar, about twenty miles to the east. Johannes, however, was an itinerant musician—the first real professional musician of the family—who worked in many towns in the area, including Eisenach. Johannes's grandson, Johann Christian (1640–82), although primarily based in Erfurt, which by then had become a major Bach family center, also spent some time in Eisenach.[29] But far more important were two other members of this fourth generation of Bachs in Thuringia. The first was Johann Christian's cousin Johann Christoph Bach (1642–1703), organist at Eisenach's main church of St. George as well as keyboardist at the court of the Duke of Saxony-Eisenach. He has been described as "probably the most important member of the family before Johann Sebastian."[30] Indeed, the latter, who

Figure 0.10. Bach's consciousness of himself as an important member of an important musical family found expression in the genealogy he wrote out in 1735. But later he also acquired (and sometimes performed in Leipzig) music by his forebears, from the family's first composer (Johann Bach, b. 1604) to, and especially, the brothers Johann Michael (his father-in-law) and Johann Christoph (his Eisenach "uncle"); how the manuscripts came to him is uncertain (surviving sources were copied in Arnstadt), but that his son Carl Philipp Emanuel inherited at least part of them is documented by the son's estate catalog (1790). The "Old Bach Archive" eventually came to the Berlin Sing-Akademie in the nineteenth century, but disappeared during World War II. In 1999 the Sing-Akademie library was found in Kiev, and it has since returned to Berlin. Among the works in the Archive is the funeral motet "Der Gerecht, ob er gleich" by Johann Christoph Bach of Eisenach, whom Johann Sebastian revered as a "profound composer." Shown is the figured-bass part used by the organist, giving just the left-hand notes, with the harmonies to be played with the right hand indicated by numbers and signs.

would later describe Johann Christoph as a "profound" composer and perform his works in Leipzig, no doubt received his earliest impressions of the organ with his "uncle" (really his first cousin once removed) at the instrument (fig. 0.10).

The other fourth-generation Bach was Johann Ambrosius (1645–1695), Johann Sebastian's father, from all accounts a superbly accomplished musician in the *Stadtpfeifer* (town-musician) tradition.[31] Born and trained in Erfurt, he was a violinist there, but in 1671 he moved, apparently with his small company of apprentices, to become

Figure 0.11. Johann Ambrosius Bach, a born Erfurter, was the son of a town musician who worked
in Arnstadt and Erfurt; he and his twin brother were
trained in the family trade by their father and an
uncle in Arnstadt, after which (1667) Johann Ambrosius moved back to Erfurt, where he married
the daughter of a recently deceased member of
the town council; this was not the only marriage
between the Bachs and the Erfurt middle class,
which helps explain the family's hold on music in
Erfurt. Family connections also helped effect an invitation to come to Eisenach in 1671. Johann Ambrosius's home city sought to entice him back in
1684, and if the Duke of Saxony-Eisenach had not
refused to release him, his son Johann Sebastian
would likely have been born in Erfurt the next year.
This portrait of Johann Ambrosius, commissioned
by the Eisenach court, is clear proof of the stature
Bach's father enjoyed.

Hausmann (head town musician) in Eisenach.[32] He was thus in charge of organizing
music for important civic occasions, major performances of music in the churches,
and weddings (supervising the nonprofessional and often difficult "beer-fiddlers" who
provided it); moreover, with the residency of Duke Johann Georg I (r. 1668–86) in
Eisenach beginning in 1672, he subsequently participated in court music as well. That
he was both ambitious and effective—he was made a citizen of Eisenach, a significant
honor, in 1674[33]—may be inferred from a chronicler who reported that "In 1672 the
new *Hausmann* made music at Easter with organ, violins, voices, trumpets and kettle-
drums, something never before known in the history of Eisenach."[34]

Music must have constantly resounded in Johann Ambrosius's home in the Fleischgasse—the fact he owned it being a further sign of his stature and relative prosperity in
a profession that did not pay especially well.[35] As the master of all the town musicians,
Johann Ambrosius was also responsible for training the apprentices. Thus Johann Sebastian must have grown up with music being taught, practiced, and performed on
many different instruments all around him. He would have recognized that his father
was somebody people respected and appreciated—in fact, the Eisenach city council
(no doubt under orders from the Duke) refused to let Johann Ambrosius go when
Erfurt tried to lure him back in 1684, and he was kept on despite drastic cutbacks in the
court musical establishment or *Capella* in 1692;[36] moreover, the court commissioned
an oil painting of the *Hausmann* (the only known portrait of an Eisenach town musician), which became the property of the Bach family a few generations later[37](fig. 0.11).
Johann Sebastian also could see in his father a kind of music director even if he lacked

Figure 0.12. Ohrdruf, with a few thousand inhabitants, was a Thuringian village so small that the map in figure 1.1 (p. 70) does not show it (although it is indicated in figure 0.1). However, it was the capital of the county of Gleichen (which itself was within the duchy of Saxony-Coburg-Gotha) and thus could justly claim, despite its diminutive size, the status of a *Residenzstadt* (i.e., a city with a ruler's residence). The residence itself, Schloss Ehrenstein (*b*), is here depicted in an image of 1747. In Bach's time Ohrdruf and the county of Gleichen were ruled by Johann Friedrich von Hohenlohe-Oehringen. The Hohenlohes inherited the county after the last count of Gleichen died. Currently under investigation is the role that the Hohenlohes may have played in Bach's decision to leave Ohrdruf in 1700.

Bach's older brother Johann Christoph was organist at St. Michael's Church (*a*), whose history goes back to the eighth century, although the structure known to Bach, which was destroyed by fire in 1753, dated from the early fifteenth century. St. Michael's was the principal church not only of the city but of the county.

the titles of music director (*Capellmeister*) or court music director (*Hofcapellmeister*), which the younger Bach would later aspire to hold.

With the necessary move of the orphaned Johann Sebastian, now ten, to Ohrdruf, the Bach tradition in Eisenach did not end. Bach's "uncle" Johann Christoph was followed as town organist and court harpsichordist by the Erfurt-born Johann Bernhard Bach (1676–1749). Johann Bernhard was succeeded by his son Johann Ernst (1722–1777), who in turn was succeeded by *his* son Johann Georg Bach (1751–1797).

Ohrdruf

In Ohrdruf, Johann Sebastian lived with his newly married, oldest brother Johann Christoph (1671–1721). It is likely that the younger sibling, preparing for a career in music, became aware of the limited earning potential of such a career, for the organist position of St. Michael's Church did not pay a living wage (figs. 0.12a–b). Johann Christoph, a gifted musician who had studied with the renowned Johann Pachelbel for three years in Erfurt, on numerous occasions pleaded with the town authorities for salary increases but eschewed the extramusical duties—such as teaching in the school or acting as a *Stadtschreiber* (town clerk)—that organists or other qualified city or court musicians often accepted for additional compensation. In 1700, however, Johann Christoph gave in and applied for part-time teaching to augment his income. Johann Sebastian left Ohrdruf for Lüneburg at about this time, undoubtedly aware of his brother's financial straits and his aversion to teaching school. It is interesting that from his first professional position in Arnstadt Bach demanded (and got) excellent compensation—always more than his predecessor and his successor in the position—and exhibited a strong dislike of giving academic instruction.

The two brothers may have been the first, but certainly were not the last Bachs with Ohrdruf connections. Johann Christoph's own offspring in particular continued the Bach presence in the town's musical life. Tobias Friedrich (1695–1768) served as organist in the Trinity Church from 1714 to 1717; Johann Bernhard Bach (1700–1743) succeeded his father at St. Michael's from 1721; Johann Christoph (1702–1756) served as cantor from 1728; Johann Heinrich (1707–1783), a student of Johann Sebastian in Leipzig, returned as assistant organist to his father before moving on to a cantor's position elsewhere; and Johann Andreas Bach (1713–1779) held organist posts both at the Trinity Church (1738–43) and St. Michael's (1743–79), also coming into possession of the so-called "Andreas Bach Buch," an important manuscript, partly copied by his father. This source and the "Möller Manuscript," both compiled by the Ohrdruf Johann Christoph Bach, along with the "Neumeister Chorales" (containing works attributed to Johann Sebastian as well as those by his father's cousins Johann Christoph (1642–1703) and Johann Michael (1648–94), Johann Pachelbel, and others), were the only evidence documenting the repertory known to young Johann Sebastian until the discovery of the Weimar Tablatures (fig 0.28a, p. 45).[38]

Arnstadt

Bach's next few years—in Lüneburg and Weimar—were spent out of Bach family territory, but in 1703 he returned, as a professional organ consultant and organist, to Arnstadt.

Arnstadt—its over three thousand inhabitants making it one of the larger towns in the region—was a natural place for Johann Sebastian to launch his career in a serious way, for it was truly a "Bach city." At least seventeen members of the family were born there between 1620 and 1792, and at least twenty-four are buried in its old cemetery. Arnstadt's Bach tradition began as far back as Caspar Bach (ca. 1570–ca. 1640), who had been a *Stadtpfeifer* there, as had been his sons Johann(es) (1602–1632) and Nicholas (ca.

Figure 0.13a. On August 4, 1705, Bach, walking by the Arnstadt city hall (*a*) at night, got into a row with the student Geyersbach over an insulting remark Bach had allegedly made to him (apparently about his bassoon playing). The situation soon turned physical—with Bach reaching for his dagger—and bystanders had to separate the two. The incident illustrates that Bach had respect only for the very competent and that the standard he aspired to meet was hardly achievable in the lowest-ranked church of a small town like Arnstadt. The town hall was also where Martin Feldhaus, mayor of Arnstadt and related to the Bachs by marriage, had his office. Feldhaus likely smoothed the way for Bach's appointment and generous salary in Arnstadt, but later was found guilty of mismanaging municipal funds.

That members of the Bach family were so dominant in Arnstadt's musical life that they provided replacements for each other is seen in a particularly striking way in a document (*b*) of August 9, 1703, recording the appointment of Johann Sebastian as organist in Arnstadt; it was revised on the sixth line at his departure in 1707 simply by crossing out "Johann Sebastian" and replacing it with "Johann Ernst" when Bach's cousin of that name succeeded him at the New Church.

1619–1637). However, another Arnstadt branch of the family played an even greater role, beginning with Heinrich (1615–1692), who from 1641 to 1692 served as *Stadtpfeifer* and as organist of the Church of Our Lady (*Liebfrauenkirche*). He was the father of Johann Christoph Bach, Johann Sebastian's Eisenach "uncle"; Johann Christoph, upon moving to Eisenach in 1665 after two years as Arnstadt court organist (which also carried responsibilities at the city's most socially important church, the Oberkirche or "upper church"), was succeeded in that position by his brother Johann Michael (1648–1694), who has recently been recognized as a more important composer of organ music than previously thought as well as a significant influence on Johann Sebastian.[39] Another brother, Johann Günther (1653–1683), assisted his father as organist but also worked as

Figure 0.14. Although not functional, the console of the then-new organ by Johann Friedrich Wender in the New Church in Arnstadt survives. The scale of the instrument is modest compared with the North German organs (fig. 8.3, p. 247), such as were played by Reinken and Buxtehude, yet its two manuals and twenty-one stops had been favorably evaluated by the young organist when he was hired by the town to test the organ; this led surprisingly quickly to the offer to assume the organist's position at the New Church, which he held from 1703 to 1707. Although Bach gave up his last organist position in 1717, his brilliance as a player and his encyclopedic knowledge of the instrument led to numerous performing and consulting opportunities throughout his life.

an instrument maker. The progeny of Heinrich's older brother Christoph (1613–1661) are at least as relevant here, for they included the Erfurt-born twins Johann Ambrosius, Bach's father and an Arnstadt *Stadtpfeifer* early in his career, and Johann Christoph (1645–1693), who remained a *Stadtpfeifer* in Arnstadt from 1671 until his death. His son Johann Ernst (1683–1739) was to become Johann Sebastian's successor as organist of the Arnstadt New Church (fig. 3.5, p. 146) and in fact was the latter's substitute during his overly long stay in Lübeck during the winter of 1705–6; in 1728 Johann Ernst became organist of the Church of Our Lady in Arnstadt.

Bach's appointment in Arnstadt is perhaps the best example of how he probably enjoyed advantages because of family connections. Still a teenager, he had held no official posts as organist and had had no time to develop a major reputation as a performer. Moreover, he had been living out of the area since 1700. Why, therefore, would he now be called upon—for the first time—to serve as an outside consultant to evaluate the new organ in the New Church in Arnstadt? And then why, five weeks later, would he be offered the position as organist presiding over that same instrument without being required to compete formally for the position and at a salary that was quite generous for the amount of responsibility (four services a week)[40] (figs. 0.13a–b and 0.14)?

Although there is no documentation to supply these answers unequivocally, Bach's extraordinary talents as organist must have been known to his family—not only to his brother and teacher Johann Christoph in neighboring Ohrdruf but likely to the entire clan, which met for reunions in Arnstadt. The local authorities, who had been served well by the Bachs in the past, might therefore have acted on a tip from a family member that *this* young Bach in particular would be someone worth attracting to Arnstadt. In addition, two other individuals of the extended Bach family could also have played significant roles. One was Arnstadt's court and senior parish church organist Christoph Herthum, who had succeeded his father-in-law Heinrich Bach in this position and was the godfather of the Ohrdruf Johann Christoph Bach. The other was the Arnstadt mayor Martin Feldhaus, who was related to the Bachs by marriage. Feldhaus, who several years later was removed from office and fined by the consistory for financial irregularities in office (including misuse of funds from the hospital, which had been one source of Bach's very generous salary), was certainly in a position to help young Bach's cause along. There is nothing to suggest that Bach himself was engaged in any suspicious dealings, but he probably made strong salary demands, as he was to do later on. In fact, however, it was the consistory, if anything, that was disingenuous, for the minutes describe the eighteen-year old incorrectly as "Court Organist at Weimar"; although he was probably active as an organist in Weimar just before coming to Arnstadt, he would likely have only served as substitute for the real court organist (whom he would replace in 1708). Perhaps the false title was a misunderstanding. Or perhaps the exaggeration was an intentional ploy to persuade the local ruler Günther Count of Schwarzburg-Arnstadt (plate 6), whose approval for the appointment was necessary and who was investing heavily in artistic activity and collecting to enhance his reputation, that Bach's appointment would increase Arnstadt's glory—and therefore his own.[41]

Religious Legacies

In Bach's world, which was only beginning to be touched by the secular currents of the Enlightenment, religion was an all-pervasive element. The local church, not the town hall, was where the records of births, deaths, marriages and the like were kept and where local communities gathered. There was no such thing as a secular school. Theology was the highest discipline at the universities. The rhythms of life through each year were largely determined by the ecclesiastical calendar—which fixed not only major holidays (which were largely religious), but opera and theater seasons at the courts and in the cities. Name days were celebrated, like birthdays, as secular celebrations, but the date was determined by the ecclesiastical feast day of the saint in question (despite Luther's suppression of saints' days as religious festivals).

Religion was also a basis for contention and intolerance. The Thirty Years' War (1618–48), the effects of which still lingered to some degree in Bach's time, had strong religious overtones to it. The Treaty of Westphalia that concluded the war in principle permitted freedom of religion—but only for Catholics, Lutherans, and Calvinists. Moreover, territories tended to be dominated by either Catholics or Protestants, a situation that did not nurture tolerance.[42] There were also sectarian movements within Germany's Protestant world, with the orthodox Lutherans, "reformed" Protestants (Calvinists), and Pietists contending with one another[43] (see chapter 2). And then there were "the others"—most significantly Jews, but also gypsies and, in trading centers like Leipzig, Russian Orthodox, Muslim Turks, and the like. All these were treated differently by local legal systems, their strange religious customs, as far as the local population was concerned, cause for fear or derision.

Lutheranism: Religion of the Bach Family

According to Bach's genealogy of 1735, Veit Bach came to Thuringia because of intolerance of Protestantism in the Habsburg territory that was his home. Thus, loyalty to Luther's legacy was a hallmark of the Bach family. Indeed, the evidence clearly points to Bach being a deeply religious man of firm orthodox Lutheran theological convictions (although he may have been influenced by the subjectively devotional aspects of Pietism, as reflected in some of the cantata texts he set, especially in Weimar).[44] Suffice it to say here that Bach knew his Bible—we know this because we have his personal copy with his marginal comments—and he knew his Luther—for he eventually owned two editions of Luther's complete works and additional copies of some texts.[45]

Bach learned his Lutheranism by being reared in a family that was distributed around many places of critical importance for the Lutheran movement: it was at the Wartburg Castle high above Eisenach—in which town Luther, like Bach, attended St. George's School—where Luther finished translating the New Testament into German; the Bach stronghold of Erfurt was the university town where Luther completed his master's degree; Luther had visited Arnstadt briefly and preached in Leipzig, and Saxony as a whole was so committed to Protestantism that, when the Elector Friedrich August I ("August the Strong") (fig. 1.2a, p. 77) and later his son Friedrich August II (plates 15 and 17) embraced Catholicism in order to be elected kings of Poland—as August II and III, respectively—the conversions were done in secret to avoid public outrage.

Nonetheless, the fact that the Saxon rulers were now Catholic may have had a momentous consequence for musical history, for when in 1733 Bach requested to be named court composer to Friedrich August II, he submitted as proof of his compositional skills the Kyrie and Gloria (BWV 232^I) of what would be the B Minor Mass. The fact that Bach, the firm orthodox Lutheran undoubtedly unsympathetic to Catholicism, chose to set texts of the Roman Catholic liturgy, may suggest a triumph of opportunism over

personal conviction. However, the Latin Kyrie and
Gloria, standard elements of the Catholic liturgy being celebrated at the official court liturgies in Dresden and other royal-electoral residences, were still
used in the Lutheran liturgy. There is one slight de-
viation from the standard Latin text—the addition
of the word "altissima" after the phrase "Domine fili
unigenite"—but this reflects a longstanding Leipzig
practice, both Roman Catholic and Protestant.[46]

The family was not the only means through which
Lutheranism was instilled in Bach, for religion was
the backbone of primary education in those times.

Figure 0.15. Johannes Amos Comenius, considered the father of modern
education, was a Moravian bishop. He
saw education for all classes and the
imparting of knowledge about everything—"pansophism" is the term used to
describe his educational philosophy—as
the key to religious unity and universal
peace. Author of over two hundred books,
he developed a curriculum based on the
Aristotelian principle that all knowledge
comes through sense experience and on
the belief that languages should be the
focal point of learning. His international
reputation and influence were so great
that he was even asked to consider the
presidency of Harvard College. Comenius also had a particular interest in the
education of native Americans.

Religion and Education

Bach received his formal education in three different
cities: Eisenach, Ohrdruf, and Lüneburg. Despite the
fact that these schools were located in three different political territories, their respective educational
systems had much in common. First of all, like much
of the world, they had all been transformed by the
pedagogical theories and writings of the seventeenth-
century Bohemian educational reformer Johann
Amos Comenius (often called "the father of modern
education")[47] (fig. 0.15). More specifically, one of
Comenius's disciples—to a point—was Andreas Reyher (fig. 0.16), who was rector of St. Michael's School
in Lüneburg before Duke Ernst the Pious of Saxony-
Gotha persuaded him to come to his residence city
of Gotha in 1641 and undertake major educational reforms in the duchy, which included
Ohrdruf.[48] Duke Ernst's and Reyher's reforms were spectacularly successful: universal
education from age five was instituted, the Latin Schools and especially the Gotha Gymnasium became renowned for their quality, and the lower classes (including girls) and
academically less gifted received an education in the so-called "German Schools" that was
shorter, Latin-free, and practical.[49] Because of Reyher and his employer it came to be said
that in Saxony-Gotha the farmers were better educated than the nobility elsewhere.

Reyher's curricula and educational policies, introduced in the 1640s and adopted
in the Ohrdruf lyceum in 1660, remained in force for nearly a century and a half.[50]

Figure 0.16. Andreas Reyher was an educational reformer with direct impact on the schooling Bach received in Eisenach, Ohrdruf, and Lüneburg. Although beginning from the base established by Comenius, Reyher developed a curriculum that was broader and more practical—including subjects such as geography and the life sciences—and less tied to theology. Hence, in his revision of Comenius's *Janua*, (fig. 0.17a), he not only sharply reduced the number of chapters, but began with the need for school (rather than the creation) and ended with death and burial, rather than a chapter on angels. His motto: "Children should be shown all there is to be shown." Reyher studied at the University of Leipzig and served as rector at the gymnasium in Lüneburg before embarking in 1642 on his wholesale educational reform of the duchy of Saxony-Gotha; he was so successful that it was said that the peasants of his patron, Duke Ernst ("the Pious") were better schooled than nobles elsewhere.

Thus Bach was introduced to the study of Latin through the *Vestibulum* of Comenius (fig. 0.17a–b) in Eisenach, continuing in Ohrdruf (and possibly Lüneburg) with the aid of texts written by Reyher and others. The stated primary purpose of all education was the instilling of piety, but there was also a practical side: the pupils in the German Schools received knowledge useful in daily life, whereas the Latin Schools offered a Comenius-Reyher pre-university curriculum that provided a unified and encyclopedic view of the world primarily through the study of languages and literature. The scriptures, so central to Lutheranism, provided fundamental texts for the study of Latin, Greek, and sometimes Hebrew as well as religion. Even arithmetic was related to the scriptures, for numbers and number symbolism were to be found there.[51] Moreover, music was an essential part of the curriculum on all levels, but not for its own sake: in particular, the singing of Luther's "catechism hymns," such as those that Bach set later in his *Clavierübung, Part III* (fig. 2.6, p. 112, and fig. 7.2, p. 231), reflected the religious purpose of all primary education. The emphasis on the catechism, with its question-and-answer format, goes directly back to Luther (fig. 2.4, p. 110, and fig. 2.5a–b, p. 111).

Once the basics of Latin were learned, a broader range of texts was introduced: for example, various writings of Cicero (excerpts rather than complete texts) were used at almost every level. Moreover, at the highest levels, genuine theology might be taught either in classes or privately by the rector, who often had a doctorate in the subject. One of the most frequently used texts for over a century in all of Lutherdom for this purpose was the *Compendium locarum theologicorum* of Leonard Hutter. This book (first published in 1610) brought together relevant references and excerpts concerning individual points of doctrine as found in the Lutheran dogmatic writings, especially the *Book of Concord* (discussed in chapter 2), and in the Bible.[52] Learning theology through this method facilitated the composition of sermons, cantata

Figure 0.17. The *Janua Linguarum Reserata* (1631) demonstrates how Comenius, renouncing the old grammatical approach to learning Latin, combined the teaching of Latin with religion and facts about the physical world. Becoming the Western world's most widely used textbook, it consisted of one thousand sentences in Latin and the local vernacular, topically arranged into one hundred chapters with titles like "On the Origin and Creation of the World," "On Cattle," "On the External Senses," and "On Sports and Pastimes." Since the text was used for several years, students would memorize the sentences, ultimately making ten passes through every sentence, each time concentrating on a different aspect (grammar, vocabulary, content, etc.). When the entire text had been studied, the student would ideally have acquired not only mastery of the Latin language but an encyclopedic body of edifying and useful knowledge.

For most students the *Janua* represented too great a challenge, so Comenius wrote the *Eurditionis scholasticae vestibulum* (or simply *Vestibulum*) as a primer: the principle of model sentences is the same, but they are fewer and simpler and deal with matters to which children might most easily relate: school, home, the city, etc. Bach's education employed both the *Janua*, in the revisions by Reyher, and the *Vestibulum*. Illustrated here is a London edition of 1650 that contains both the *Janua* and *Vestibulum*.

texts, and the like—for a common way of composing such texts was to synthesize different, but mutually reinforcing, scriptural passages or paraphrases on a common theme, a procedure, as will be shown, later criticized by advocates of Enlightenment thinking.

When Bach ended his formal education in Lüneburg by completing the *Prima*, he had acquired a better education than any of his siblings and almost all of his other relatives. To go to the university, for which he certainly qualified, was out of the question for financial reasons. But the strong religious and theological background he had acquired would enable him to pass the theological examination for the cantorate of St. Thomas's school over twenty years later.[53] Moreover, the extensive library he acquired over the years is testimony to his deep interest in and knowledge of religion and the scriptures.[54]

Calvinism, Pietism, and Enlightenment Rationalism

Because Bach's life revolved around religion, he made career decisions based on religious considerations and was not unaffected by the various philosophies of religion competing

Figure 0.18. In the second quarter of the eighteenth century, the undisputed leader of the movement to reform the German language and its drama and poetry was Johann Christoph Gottsched. Escaping conscription into the Prussian army (see chapter 1, note 3), he settled in Leipzig in 1723, where his teaching at the university, beginning in 1725, ultimately led to professorships in poetry (1730) and logic and metaphysics (1734), and three terms as rector from 1739. His international fame and influence was established by his *Versuch einer critischen Dichtkunst* (1730) (fig. 5.2, p. 197), but it began to wane before his death. He bitterly opposed the crowd-pleasing opera because it was not "natural" and did not follow classical principles. He wrote three texts used by Bach and numbered among his students J. A. Scheibe and Bach's student L.C. Mizler (fig. 9.8b, p. 281). Although he is criticized mainly for his literary positions, posterity has largely forgotten that he was a philosopher of great breadth of thought and also a strong advocate for women (see fig. 9.4, p. 274).

with orthodox Lutheranism in Protestant Germany (especially because they had different views of music's role in worship). Three in particular—taken up in greater detail in chapter 2—are relevant to an understanding of Bach: reformed Protestantism (Calvinism), Pietism, and the rationalism of the early Enlightenment. Prince Leopold in Cöthen has already been cited as a Calvinist, who therefore would not permit the kind of liturgical music Bach had composed in Weimar and would compose in Leipzig. The Pietists, on the other hand, shared with the orthodox Lutherans a belief in the centrality of the Bible, but they rejected elaborate liturgical ceremonies and correspondingly elaborate music. Pietism was an emotional branch of Protestantism and in fact was not without influence even in orthodox Leipzig; indeed, in the seventeenth century a number of theologians at the University were Pietists, and only after considerable debate were they finally ousted. Nonetheless, the stress on personal piety and devotion softened the perhaps too-intellectual orthodox Lutheranism, which, under the influence of Heinrich Müller, Johann Arnd(t), and Johann Gerhard—theologians whose works are found in Bach's library—put greater stress on personal transformation and piety than on intellectual understanding.

Rationalism, on the other hand, was not a religious sect, but a way of looking at the world and God's relationship to it; the rationalism developing in the Leipzig of Bach's time accepted the ability of human reason to reach at least some truths without the help of the scriptures. It was not anti-religious, yet, like Pietism, it caused some orthodox theologians of Leipzig concern.

One important representative of eighteenth-century German rationalism was Leipzig's most renowned philosopher and literary scholar, Johann Christoph Gottsched, who arrived in 1724 (the year after Bach) and soon rose to the top professional and administrative posts in the University (in 1738 he was elected rector for the first of several times) (fig. 0.18).

Gottsched saw classical principles as relevant to all literary fields (his impact on the theater, for example, is discussed in chapter 5). This included sermons, which he viewed as a type of public oratory, hence subject to the rules of the ancient rhetoricians. However, this put him into direct conflict with Leipzig's theologian-preachers, whom Gottsched attacked outright in his *Ausführliche Redekunst* (Comprehensive art of oratory) of 1736; as a result, he was summoned before the ecclesiastical council in Dresden in 1738, where he had to explain himself and was threatened with suspension from his university posts if he did not moderate his criticism (which he did).[55]

Sermons were an important part of the city's religious life. A Leipzig chronicle of 1717 reported that there were normally twenty-two orthodox Lutheran sermons delivered every week (fourteen of them on Sunday), and this does not count "the large number of practice sermons delivered by students of theology in their homiletics classes."[56] Gottsched was thus attempting to alter a massive and deeply entrenched tradition, disagreeing as he did with both the structure and rhetoric employed. He also complained of the length of sermons (typically an hour)—particularly the too-lengthy introductory sections of sermons, which were followed by a congregational hymn before the main part of the sermon was delivered. Bach's cantatas were often written in two parts, one to be performed before, the other after, the sermon.[57]

More significantly, however, he argued that, rather than seeking to persuade and convince the hearers of the truths in the Biblical text under consideration, preachers were merely quoting parallel passages taken from other scriptural or doctrinal writings. "They try to adduce so many Biblical quotations, that one can't see the sermon for the concordance," he wrote.[58] This represented, of course, an attack on the style of theological expositions represented by Hutter's *Compendium locarum theologicorum*, a work that, we have seen, Bach had studied—likely even memorized—in the course of his schooling.

The total reliance on scriptural texts to support other scriptural texts was also criticized by Gottsched. As a man of the Enlightenment with a strong faith in human reason, Gottsched felt sermons should utilize logic and human experience to make scriptural truths more evident and convincing. He felt that the Bible-based theology of the orthodox preachers and the natural (i.e., rationalistic) theology of the developing Enlightenment were complementary, not contradictory, means to revealed truth. Therefore, Gottsched was no enemy of religion. Son of a Lutheran minister and a

Figure 0.19. Christiane Eberhardine had married Friedrich August (August the Strong), the future Elector of Saxony, in 1693, but when he converted to Catholicism to become King of Poland (and she therefore Queen), she refused to be crowned and separated from him—earning her the love and respect of the Saxon Protestant population. After her death in 1727, the University of Leipzig student Hans Carl von Kirchbach organized a memorial service in the university church of St. Paul's. Apparently paying for the entire affair himself, he commissioned the *Trauer-Ode* from J. C. Gottsched and Bach, and gave the memorial oration before a distinguished audience that included the Leipzig city council and faculty of the university.

student of theology (among other things) at the University of Königsberg, he was a practicing orthodox Lutheran who regularly went to confession and communion and himself preached over one hundred times, in Leipzig and elsewhere.[59]

Bach's relationship to Gottsched was probably not close; nevertheless, they surely knew each other. Gottsched the poet did not provide any texts for the cycles of church cantatas that Bach wrote in his early years in Leipzig, although Bach did set to music Gottsched's texts for a lost wedding "serenata" (i.e., a cantata written for evening performance) and for a lost cantata honoring the visit of Elector Friedrich August II in 1738 (BWV Anh.13).[60] The only extant musical evidence of their collaboration is the so-called "Trauer-Ode" (BWV 198), written for a memorial service for the Electress Christiane Eberhardine in 1727 (fig. 0.19). This work, celebrated though it was, not only indicates that poet and composer did not work hand in glove, but also provides an example of how confident Bach was in his musical judgments.

Because of the solemnity and grandeur of the occasion, Gottsched chose to write a libretto in the form of a classical ode, "the most formal, ceremonious, and complexly organized form of lyric poetry,"[61] here nine eight-line stanzas of the same poetic structure. Apt as it might have been for oral delivery, it was not, in Bach's opinion, suitable for musical setting, so he (or, less likely, a poet working with him) radically revised the poem into a ten-section libretto suitable for recitative and aria settings, thereby destroying the original ode structure.[62] And indeed, Bach did not call the result *Trauer-Ode* (Gottsched's title for his text) but rather *Trauermusik* (the rubric *Musik* having the technical meaning in Bach's day of a work for voices and instruments in the modern

style). Furthermore, the modernity of the musical style was confirmed by a contemporary witness, who referred to "the Music of Mourning, which this time Capellmeister
Johann Sebastian Bach had composed in the Italian style."[63] Clearly Bach felt no obligation to force his music into the hallowed forms of antiquity (which he would have studied, of course). The mangling of his dignified text in this way could not have pleased
Gottsched, the arch-enemy of the Italian opera (which consisted largely of recitatives
and arias). Yet it should be pointed out that the young Gottsched, fifteen years younger
than Bach, had only begun his career, whereas Bach was clearly his senior in every
respect: it would not be until 1730 that Gottsched published the work that would make
him famous (the *Versuch einer critischen Dichtkunst*) (fig. 5.2, p. 197) and was named
extraordinary (i.e., adjunct) professor of poetry at the University of Leipzig.

Another representative of Enlightenment rationalism in Leipzig, and one with
whom Bach had to work on close terms, was Johann August Ernesti (1707–1781).[64] A
graduate of the University of Leipzig, where he studied philosophy and theology, he became rector of the Thomasschule at the age of twenty-seven, serving with distinction in
that position for twenty-eight years; in 1759 he was named professor of theology at the
university (he lectured in other fields as well). Ernesti approached scriptural texts the
way he would a text of Cicero, seeing them as historically conditioned documents that
could best be understood using the new philological methods. This impersonal, scientific approach was not, of course, the way Bach was trained to react to the scriptures; his
approach was more devotional, along the lines espoused in the writings of theologians
such as Gerhard and Müller.[65] Ernesti's continuous feuds with Bach are among the best
known aspects of Bach's life, for Ernesti, as a rationalist, could not perceive how the
intangible art of music could be *necessary* in education and life, whereas Bach could not
understand how it could be viewed as a mere ornament to these.

Jews and Judaism in Bach's World

A final aspect of the legacy of religious traditions as they might have affected Bach is a
subject that was avoided in Bach scholarship until recent years: Bach's relationship to
Jews and Judaism. This is important and germane because of Luther's own attitudes,
which hardened over time and surely created a particularly difficult atmosphere for
Jews living in Lutheran territories. The question therefore must be asked: what can or
should one infer from a composer who so dramatically set the Passion stories of the
New Testament, especially that of the anti-Judaising Gospel according to St. John?

The first thing to realize is that Bach probably had little or no direct personal or professional contact with Jews of his time. Johann Jacob Schudt, the Christian conrector
of a Frankfurt gymnasium, in his encyclopedic *Jüdische Merkwürdigkeiten* of 1715 (and

Figure 0.20. J. J. Schudt was the conrector of a gymnasium in Frankfurt am Main, a city not unlike Leipzig in its commercial character, but with a large Jewish community. In his *Jüdische Merkwürdigkeiten*, which went through several editions, he gives not only a comprehensive account of Frankfurt's Jewish community but also surveys the past and present situation of Jews throughout the world, region by region. Although he finds certain Jewish customs amusing and strange and is bent on converting Jews to Christianity, he also documents the persecution of Jews in Europe going back to the Middle Ages in a way that suggests sympathy for the loss of innocent life, regarding this nonetheless as divine retribution for Jewish resistance to conversion.

several subsequent editions) (fig. 0.20), reports on the past persecution of Jews in Thuringia (including the apparent annihilation of Arnstadt's Jews in the late Middle Ages);[66] he states that they are still not allowed residence after having been driven out in the fifteenth century, although one finds a few in places like Mühlhausen (a free imperial city).[67] In the Bach city of Erfurt (a loosely governed possession of the Roman Catholic elector of Mainz for centuries, so that there were both Protestant and Catholic churches there), no Jews are to be found, and during Bach's time only a few protected Jews could live in Dresden and Leipzig. In fact, Jews are banned from Electoral Saxony generally, according to Schudt, except for those from Poland and other places in Germany who participate in the Leipzig fairs that took place three times a year.

But one should not infer from this that Jews were really welcome in Leipzig even then.[68] They were admitted only upon presentation of a pass authorized by the elector (or his finance office) and then the passholder had to register within twenty-four hours or be subject to loss of pass plus fine or jail.[69] In 1727 this was slightly alleviated by August the Strong, who had in 1700 expressed his desire *not* to tolerate the "cursed and useless people" and in 1704 had forbidden assemblies of Jews for purposes of religious services.[70] Apparently it was feared that Christians might be attracted to the "false liturgies" of the Jews and their "superstitions," as the Leipzig city council expressed it. Needless to say, the building of public places of Jewish worship was not allowed.

Thus, Jews—hundreds of them each year, according to the still-extant registers that recorded their names and home cities—did make regular visits to Leipzig, but it is not likely they would have been in contact with the cantor of St. Thomas's School. Still, Bach would have likely seen them concentrated in the Brühl (see plan of Leipzig, fig. 3.18, p. 157), a few minutes' walk from his home in St. Thomas's School next to the eponymous church.

The question still remains: how did Bach, who had such high regard for Luther (see chapter 7), feel about the Jews, and did these feelings influence his music in any way? Luther, after all, was the author of a tract entitled *The Jews and their Lies* (1543), in which he saw the Jews as an immense danger to Lutheranism and what for him was religious truth. Luther's vision of the near future was apocalyptic—he saw the end of the world approaching—and one sign of that was (according to the traditional view of church history) the coming of the Antichrist and the consequent dissolution of Christianity from within under the influence of the Devil.[71] Luther saw the Jews as agents of Satan in this process, although it should be noted that he felt similarly about Muslims (the Turkish threat to European civilization was a realistic concern in those times), Anabaptists (who rejected infant baptism and other essentials of Lutheran belief), and "Papists" (for, in Luther's opinion, the Antichrist already controlled the papacy). The only way out, Luther believed, was for these threatening groups to undergo true conversion, although he seems in the end to have singled out the Jews especially: "A Christian has, next to the Devil, no more venomous, bitter enemy than the Jew."[72] Nonetheless, Luther hoped for the conversion of the Jews, "but if they refuse, we should neither tolerate nor suffer their presence in our midst!"[73]

As ominous and portentous as such utterances sound to the reader of today, it must be realized that Luther's attitudes are not racial: they are not concerned with Jews as a people but with those people who practiced Judaism. He was therefore not anti-Semitic but anti-Judaic, an attitude that was nourished by the (unfounded) rumors of large-scale Christian conversions to Judaism in the 1530s.

Luther's antipathy toward Jews was echoed later by many Lutheran writers. These include the Lutheran pastor and poet Erdmann Neumeister (fig. 2.12, p. 126) (some of whose texts were set by Bach), and Heinrich Müller (several of whose devotional works were in Bach's library) (fig. 2.11, p. 124).

And yet there is little evidence that Bach, whatever his personal feelings and prejudices might have been, tried to embody anti-Judaism in his music. This is likely because

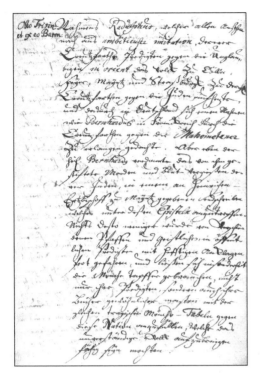

Figure 0.21. Although the University of Leipzig had a reputation for being intellectually conservative, it was not immune from the influence of the budding pan-European intellectual movement of the Enlightenment (*Aufklärung*). A document of 1714, entitled "Whether the Jews use Christian blood," authored by "the dean, senior and other professors of theology" using the rigorous, objective methods of the new scholarship, is a striking and unequivocal defense of the Jews against the centuries-old allegation that the blood of murdered Christian children was used for certain Jewish rituals; indeed, in the fourth line from the bottom on the page illustrated, this charge is denounced as a medieval "monk's fable." The document, addressed to August the Strong, could reflect a growing attitude of tolerance towards Jews in Leipzig—although they still were banned from living there—only a few years before Bach's arrival (see also fig. 5.3, p. 199).

there were other things that were more important to Bach—his own personal salvation, for example, and the salvation of his fellow Lutherans, to whom his music was directed for the honor of God. Moreover, Judaism posed far less of a threat to Bach's Lutheranism than Catholicism, which may explain Bach's setting of a few texts with clearly anti-Catholic passages.[74]

If there is one text that stands out as especially anti-Judaic it is the Gospel of John, which actually emanated from a community of Christian Jews late in the first century C.E., at a time of great antagonism between the Jewish authorities and expelled Jewish Christians. Not surprisingly, the poetic commentaries available to Bach that provided aria texts for settings of the passion story as recounted in St. John's Gospel sometimes also had anti-Jewish tendencies. However, Bach, while required to set the canonical passion text for the Good Friday liturgy, chose not to include chorale or aria texts with anti-Judaic content in his St. John Passion (BWV 245); moreover, none of the five cantata texts by Erdmann Neumeister that Bach set reflect that pastor-poet's anti-Jewish bias.[75]

To close this section, it is useful to mention an interesting episode that ties together Lutheran orthodoxy, Enlightenment ideals of scholarship and humanity, and Judaism, and suggests a change in intellectual climate in Leipzig in Bach's time. In 1714, August the Strong asked the theological faculty of the University of Leipzig to investigate and evaluate the centuries-old claims of the ritual murder of Christian children by Jews. Led by the Dean of Theology Gottfried Olearius, the entire faculty endorsed a strongly worded and precisely documented opinion that concluded that the accusation was a baseless "monks' fable" originating in the Middle Ages, one that had led to great tragedy, largely due to Christian venality and ignorance (fig. 0.21). This document was later published in 1751 by Christian Friedrich Boerner, who was a signer of the 1714 document and the senior Leipzig professor of theology during Bach's entire tenure there. The report marks the beginning of Enlightenment writing about Jews that would contribute to their eventual emancipation in Europe in the nineteenth century.[76]

The Legacies of Western Musical Traditions

Ancient and Medieval

The legacies of family and religion clearly played a role in shaping the career and personal *Weltanschauung* of Johann Sebastian Bach. However, they do not explain satisfactorily the universality of the composer's *music*, a body of work whose appeal has increased along with the temporal distance between his past and the modern listener's present.

Figure 0.22. A remarkable seventeenth-century polymath, Athanasius Kircher wrote thirty books, attempting a kind of *summa* of human knowledge from a Christian perspective. His *Musurgia universalis* (1650) is an encyclopedic account of music, treating its historical, mythological, theoretical, scientific, and practical aspects. In 1734, L. C. Mizler (fig. 9.8b, p. 281) wrote a dissertation on the thesis "That the science of music is also part of philosophical erudition"—dedicating it to (among others) his teacher J. S. Bach—in which Mizler uses Kircher to support his argument. Mizler was not the only one of Bach's milieu to utilize Kircher: the work of Buttstett (fig. 0.23) and Andreas Werckmeister (fig. 10.5, p. 303) is also indebted to this German Jesuit who lived in Rome.

One way to understand this is to assess the synthetic nature of Bach's musical art, one that, arguably, draws on more individual traditions of Western music, and thinking about music, than any other. As a consequence, Bach's music is a multifaceted mirror of Western civilization.

For example, one can look back to the ancient world and the Middle Ages and see legacies of those eras reflected in Bach's music and his ideas about music and composing. One of these ideas—emanating from the ancient Greek religious leader and philosopher Pythagoras and articulated by Plato in the soaring, mythic description of the creation of the world in his *Timaeus*—was that the world was created as a divinely ordered *harmonia* (ἁρμονία), that is, a concordant synthesis of diverse elements held together by simple mathematical relationships (1:1, 2:1, 3:2, 4:3) expressible in sound as consonant musical intervals (unison, octave, fifth, fourth).[77] This notion developed into what the Middle Ages called *musica mundana* (music of the spheres); while undermined as fact by the astronomical and other scientific advances of the late sixteenth and seventeenth centuries, it still had resonance in Bach's time[78] (fig. 0.22). In fact, recent research has revealed that the Pythagorean ratios seem to have played a role in the way Bach planned his works and collections, for example, in the proportional distribution of meter signatures and numbers of measures.[79]

Moreover, the Neoplatonic concept of *musica politica*, of a well-ordered state as a *harmonia* under the authority of an absolute ruler, was a metaphor with a long tradition.[80] Johann Friedrich Werckmeister, in his ceremonial oration honoring Bach's future employer Prince Leopold of Cöthen as the prince assumed personal rule in 1715, therefore drew on Leopold's love of music to suggest that music was both a cause and symbol of political stability and order in Anhalt-Cöthen: "How pleasant it is to hear the lovely Harmony of music, for one believes that he who performs it [also] considers how to rule justly and benevolently, and through it his true and devoted vassals are bound to him—so that he can rule over a state in which all its members harmonize sweetly."[81]

Since well-ordered music was therefore seen to be a reflection of a divinely ordered universe on microcosmic as well as macrocosmic levels, such music had a metaphysical and religious significance of a high order. That Bach subscribed to this view even in the context of the music of his time is seen in a little treatise on figured bass he prepared for his students in which Bach wrote:

> The thorough bass is the most perfect foundation of music, being played with both hands in such manner that the left hand plays the notes written down while the right adds consonances and dissonances, in order to make a well-sounding harmony to the Glory of God and the permissible delectation of the spirit; and the aim and final reason, as of all music, so of the thorough bass should be none else but the

Glory of God and the recreation of the mind. Where this is not observed, there will be no real music but only a devilish hubbub.[82]

Another ancient notion transmitted to the Middle Ages and beyond and fiercely defended by Bach was that music had to be an essential component of education.[83] Certainly his own schooling had reflected this view of music; but the challenge to it by the Enlightenment in the person of Johann August Ernesti, who became rector of the Thomasschule in 1734 and saw music as a nonessential subject, was, for Bach, one of the most troubling aspects of his experience in Leipzig. The traditional importance of music in education was rooted in the belief, going back to the ancients, that music had power to move the human soul—to instill human feelings and affect human behavior. In the single most important text on music, written in the sixth century and still studied a thousand years later, the late-Roman writer Boethius established these concepts for the European world:

> . . . music is associated not only with speculation but with morality as well. For nothing is more characteristic of human nature than to be soothed by pleasant modes or disturbed by their opposites. . . . Indeed no path to the mind is as open for instruction as the sense of hearing. Thus, when rhythms and modes reach an intellect through the ears, they doubtless affect and reshape that mind according to their particular character.[84]

Of course, these ideas came to Bach filtered through Luther's theology. But Luther refers to the mathematical basis of music, for he was familiar with the medieval traditions of music theory.[85] In fact, he felt music was so essential to education that all Lutheran ministers should be trained in music.[86] "I place music next to theology," he asserted, which recalls the fact that, in the Middle Ages, students prepared to learn theology and philosophy by studying, among other subjects, the mathematical basis of music.[87]

That medieval notions of the nature of music still survived in the immediate musical environment in which Bach grew up is attested to by a book in Bach's personal library, the *Ut Mi Sol, Re Fa La, Tota Musica et Harmonia Aeterna* (Erfurt, 1716) of Johann Heinrich Buttstett (figs. 0.23a–b), a Thuringian-born composer, organist, and music theorist in Erfurt who was distantly related to Bach by marriage and was, like Bach's brother and teacher Johann Christoph Bach, a student of Johann Pachelbel.[88] Early on Buttstett states that "music is derived from Arithmetic and Mathematics, whence its great powers come," alerting the reader that there will be an exposition of Boethian philosophical ideas, medieval music-theoretic concepts, and a point of view that is based on centuries-old presuppositions that Buttstett regards as eternally valid.[89]

Figure 0.23. The battle between an ancient view of music as a mathematically based art linked to a divinely ordained cosmic order and the new musical rationalism of the Enlightenment represented by Johannes Mattheson is reflected in a work by Bach's contemporary Johann Heinrich Buttstett. The title page (*a*) reads "UT, MI, SOL, RE, FA, LA, The Whole of Music and ETERNAL HARMONY, Or Newly Disclosed [Neu-eröffnetes], old, true, single and eternal FOUNDATION OF MUSIC contrasted with the Newly Constituted Orchestra [Neu-eröffneten Orchestre] . . . , in the first part of which will be refuted erroneous opinions of the Author [Johannes Mattheson] in the [*Neu-eröffnete*] *Orchestre* [Hamburg, 1703] concerning the species of the tones or modes of music. In the second part the true Foundation of Music will be shown: not only will Guidonian solmization be defended, but also the usefulness of this will be indicated by the introduction of a tutor; then it will also be asserted that some day one will make music in heaven with the very same tones that are used here on earth. . . . Erfurt [, 1716]."

The frontispiece (*b*) of J. H. Buttstett's *Ut, Mi, Sol, Re, Fa, La* makes clear the author's belief, shared by Bach, in music as a reflection of divine order and the worthiness of praising God through music. The six-pointed star made of two superimposed triangles and trinitarian flames, which symbolize the godhead, finds reflection in the two named musical triads. The legend, aimed at the earthly reader, asks, "Where were you when the morning star and all children of God praised me?" Bach, however, was much more open than Buttstett to new ideas about music: the modern Italian and French music rejected by the latter was warmly embraced by Bach.

From ancient times through the Middle Ages came the Bible, translated into Latin for the medieval world by St. Jerome, and later into German most famously by Luther. In his personal copy of the Luther Bible—edited, with extensive commentary, by Abraham Calov—Bach wrote at the beginning of 1 Chronicles 25, which describes the vocal and instrumental music of the Temple: "This chapter is the true foundation of all church music pleasing to God"[90] (fig. 0.24). Bach saw himself in a historic line of those who served God through music, and in particular through elaborate music using both voices and instruments, as described in the Old Testament; he thus regarded the passage as a defense against those (such as Calvinists and Pietists) who would do away with the sophisticated church music of the type he composed and espoused.

Many aspects of Lutheran liturgy, for which Bach wrote his sacred music, go back to medieval Roman Catholicism. The principal Sunday services, with their rites of Word and Eucharist (communion) preserved much of the basic structure of the Roman Catholic Mass.[91] The liturgical year—with its fixed and variable feasts that determined the textual content of the several cycles of cantatas that Bach, in an awesome display of creative energy, composed 1723–28—developed in late antiquity and the Middle Ages; likewise, his much earlier *Orgelbüchlein* is organized according to the annual liturgical order of the chorale (i.e., Lutheran hymn) tunes used as

Figure 0.24. There are two points of connection between Bach and the orthodox, sometimes polemical seventeenth-century Lutheran theologian Abraham Calov. First, Bach acquired a copy of Calov's multivolume bible with commentary; since 1938 this work, with numerous annotations by Bach, has resided at Concordia Seminary (St. Louis, MO). On the page illustrated, concerning 1 Chronicles 26, which describes the music in the ancient Temple, Bach writes, "This chapter is the true foundation for all church music that is pleasing to God," thus demonstrating his self-identification with the Old Testament musicians in whose train he felt himself to follow. Second, Bach bought at auction (fig. 7.4, p. 236) a set of Luther's complete works that had once belonged to Calov, the set presumably used in the preparation of the latter's biblical commentary.

the basis for the organ chorale preludes. The cycle of Sundays offered an annual review of the life of Christ—Christmas, Epiphany, Lent (culminating in the Holy Week observance of the Passion of Christ, the central focus of Lutheran theology), Easter, Ascension, Pentecost, and Trinity Sunday—preceded by Advent and followed by the Sundays after Trinity. In addition there were other feasts, including Marian feasts, that were assigned to specific days of the year.

Bach's modest attitude about his own work was characteristic of the Middle Ages, when those who created works of art were considered not artists but artisans and the later eighteenth-century concept of "genius" had not yet been introduced.[92] After all, Bach came from a family of town musicians, who operated in guild-like fashion with master-apprentice relationships; although he took the other possible career route—that of organist—he still credited simple hard work for the success he achieved.[93]

In matters of compositional technique, legacies of the Middle Ages had sufficient staying power to reach Bach, even though the rules of composition and even notions of consonance and dissonance had undergone radical transformation. The most important of these links was the continuing practice of building a musical work on an existing sacred melody or *cantus firmus*. For the Middle Ages, the most common source for such melodies was the body of what is commonly called Gregorian chant.[94] For the Lutheran Bach, the melodies were taken from the rich treasury of German Lutheran hymns, many of which were, however, based on an older Latin chant (for example, *Nun komm, der Heiden Heiland* is derived from the Catholic hymn chant *Veni Redemptor gentium*). In the early history of cantus firmus composition, the pre-existing melody was usually found in long notes in a lower voice; later on it could be found elsewhere, especially in the topmost voice, where it was usually embellished. Subsequent composers, Bach included, continued to use both techniques. Thus the Credo of the B Minor Mass (BWV 232) opens with a movement based on a Gregorian chant intonation for the words *Credo in unum Deum*, the notes of which are in long note values to give it a traditional, even archaic quality, although it is used as the subject of an accompanied fugue in baroque style (fig. 0.25). A host of long-established cantus firmus techniques are found in Bach's cantatas and chorale preludes for organ as well.

Finally, Bach followed the long tradition, dating back to medieval times, of seeing sacred and secular as two aspects of one whole rather than two mutually exclusive spheres. If a thirteenth-century polytextual motet might combine a vernacular love lyric with a Marian hymn and a popular song could be given a religious text (or vice versa)—practices that may remind us of how the secular aspects of everyday life are also incorporated into the sculptural and window imagery of medieval cathedrals—so could Bach build much of his Christmas Oratorio (BWV 248) and a number of his Leipzig church cantatas out of what were originally secular cantatas. At one point in the mid-twentieth century, Bach's commitment to sacred music was questioned partly on this basis by one of the world's most eminent musical scholars, yet Bach gave plenty of evidence that *all* of his music was written for the glory of God.[95] Bach even wrote abbreviated prayers at the beginning or end of secular works such as the *Clavierbüchlein* for Wilhelm Friedemann Bach (fig. 0.7, p. 9), a sign of his sincere, unwavering faith.

It should perhaps not surprise us that Bach felt connected with medieval intellectual, liturgical, and musical legacies. After all, most of the churches Bach experienced were in fact medieval structures, palpable physical links to the Middle Ages.[96]

Figure 0.25. When in the late 1740s Bach decided to take the *Missa* (i.e., Kyrie and Gloria, BWV 232¹) he had dedicated to the new Elector Friedrich August II (soon also to be King August III of Poland) and add to it the remaining parts of the Ordinary of the Roman Catholic Mass to produce what we call the Mass in B Minor (BWV 232), he had therefore to set to music the text of the fourth-century Nicene Creed or Credo (as well as the texts of the Sanctus, Benedictus, and Agnus Dei). In the opening movement of the Credo (*Credo in unum Deum*, "I believe in one God"), the convinced Lutheran Bach seems to have aimed for a kind of universality, for not only does he compose the voices (and two solo violins) in an archaic (Roman Catholic) imitative Renaissance style in long notes—a texture that could stand on its own—but uses as the subject of imitation a well-known Lutheran chant intonation of the text clearly derived from a medieval Catholic melody. These elements are then placed over a marching basso continuo line that is completely baroque, producing the kind of synthetic musical structure that reflects Bach's comprehensive musical knowledge and consummate craftsmanship.

The Renaissance

Bach absorbed and reflected ideas and ideals from the Renaissance as well. This era was shaped by a rediscovered confidence in humankind, and it was then that the profession of composer was first recognized. Surely one of the most marked features of Bach's music, for all his modesty and personal piety, is a ringing, essentially humanistic, confidence in what he accepted as his God-given powers, not to mention his uncompromising professionalism. Furthermore, we know that Bach did possess a genuine self-confidence that enabled him to define his artistic goals clearly, demand highly favorable salary terms, and have the courage to abandon situations he felt were not in his best interest—even if in Weimar it meant paying for his boldness with time in jail.

Renaissance humanism put emphasis on what distinguishes humankind from the rest of creation: language and speech. This resulted in concern for eloquence and persuasiveness and in the intensive study of the ancient rhetoricians—the discovery of Quintilian's great treatise on oratory in 1416 and the publication of Aristotle's *Rhetoric* in Latin were major events—and even letter-writing became an art form. As a natural result of this, there also developed a concern for making music reflect the content of a text (something not of general concern to medieval composers) that has continued down to the present day.[97] And so in music there were developed expressive devices and a rhetorical approach for representing in music the images and—increasingly as the Baroque approached—*feelings* embedded in the texts, devices without which the music of Bach's time would also be unthinkable.

There is for example, the simple device of "word painting," whereby the music "paints" an image of a word of phrase: thus the word "ascend" will likely be set to a rising musical line. Bach does precisely this on "Ascendit in coelum" (He ascended into heaven) in the Credo of the B Minor Mass (BWV 232), to take but one obvious example. Sometimes the representation was numerical, as when Bach, again in the B Minor Mass, sets as *duets* the texts "Christe eleison" (Christ, have mercy) and "Et in unam Dominum Jesum Christum" (And in one Lord, Jesus Christ)—both referring to the *second* Person of the Blessed Trinity—with the latter instance also involving imitation at the *unison* as additional musical symbolism (*one* Lord); simple number symbolism is perhaps also inferrable when the bass melody of the "Crucifixus" of the Credo is stated a fateful and unlucky thirteen times[98] (fig. 0.26). The expressive use of chromaticism, of using pitches outside the standard scale for a given mode or key, is a further Renaissance technique, especially for the representation of sadness (again, as Bach uses it in the "Crucifixus" of the B Minor Mass, most notably in the repeating, descending bass pattern that was associated with sadness).

Figure 0.26. The "Crucifixus" ("He was crucified and was buried") of the Mass in B Minor (BWV 232) is an example of musical "parody," of adapting preexisting music to a different text. In this case, the opening of the 1714 Weimar cantata "Weinen, Klagen, Sorgen, Zagen" (Weeping, lamenting, worrying, quaking) (BWV 12), with its repeating, chromatically descending bass line formula (a musical symbol of lament), provides the basis. In fact, about half of the twenty-seven movements of the Mass have been shown to be parodies, and some scholars think the same could be demonstrated for most if not all of the work. Parody developed as a sophisticated compositional approach in the Renaissance, yet just a century ago scholars of Bach and Handel were scandalized to discover that these composers often based their religious music on secular originals, as is the case with Bach's Christmas Oratorio (BWV 248) and some of the most beloved choruses from Handel's *Messiah*.

0.27a

0.27b

Figure 0.27. (*This page and facing*) Hunting was the sport of lords, although often there was little that was sporting about it. Reflecting the hierarchical society that fostered them, hunts were ranked "high" and "low" (and, in some places, "middle"), and elaborate regulations, such as were published in Weissenfels in 1728 (*d*), governed them. The higher types of hunt, restricted to the ruling class, targeted large animals such as deer, wild boars, and bears. The lower forms involved smaller game and even then were rarely permitted to the lower classes—indeed, illicit hunting carried severe penalties. (One exception: bird-catching, to which Papageno in Mozart's *The Magic Flute* still bears witness.)

The *parforce* hunt, especially popular in France and England, involved an equestrian chase with dogs of a single animal, with the direction and progress of the hunt communicated by specific calls of the "parforce horn" (*b*); like all brass instruments of the time, horns had no valves and different pitches are achieved mainly by varying air pressure. The Germans were especially fond of the *eingestellte Jagd* or "enclosed hunt," in which animals were forced into an enclosed area, such as is being prepared in 0.27a; once within, the animals could be picked off by the hunting party safely esconced in a protected pavilion within the area.

On February 23, 1713, as part of an multi-day birthday celebration, Duke Christian of Saxony-Weissenfels (plate 7) and his guests were entertained by a "combat hunt" (*Kampf-Jagd*), in which animals fought each other to the death for the amusement of onlookers—similar, perhaps, to the combat hunt in the courtyard of the Electoral Palace in Dresden depicted in (*c*). Such activities were regularly mounted in the courtyard of the Neu-Augustusburg palace. The banquet that followed in the house of the Duke's master of the hunt on the Weissenfels hunting grounds featured, as musical entertainment, Bach's "Hunt" Cantata (BWV 208) under the composer's direction. (The cantata may have been introduced with what became the first movement of Brandenburg Concerto No. 1, which conjures up vividly the spirit of the hunt.) The cantata's text, by the Weimar court poet Salomon Franck, praised Christian as "a woodland Pan" and "Saxon hero . . . who makes the country so happy that forest and field and everything else live and laugh." Nonetheless, it is known that the Duke's subjects greatly resented—especially at harvest time—the burdens that Christian's passion for hunting imposed on them, including the preparing of enclosures, rounding up and guarding game, and serving the large entourage that accompanied the duke to the many hunting areas of his realm.

But if Bach maintained these traditions of word painting and expressive
chromaticism, he also became interested
in the more conservative "classical" style
of Renaissance vocal music associated
with the Italian composer Palestrina
(an icon of Renaissance Catholic church
music) and the late-Renaissance Roman
school, which influenced a number of his later works.[99] Bach was also cognizant of the
polychoral style that was a hallmark of late-Renaissance Venice and was brought to
Saxony by the former Electoral Music Director Heinrich Schütz, who was born exactly
one hundred years before Bach. We see the use of multiple choruses in the motets and
in the Sanctus of the B Minor Mass (in which the six vocal lines are variously grouped
polychorally as two three-voice choruses), and the opening movement of the St. Matthew Passion (BWV 244) (which also has a double orchestra).[100]

Another tradition stemming from the Renaissance is the symbolic use of instruments. This was notably associated with the Medici festivals of sixteenth-century
Florence (to which German nobility were invited), in which elaborate tableaux called
intermedi between acts of a play were presented; these often involved large ensembles
of instruments that were sometimes used symbolically: flutes and oboes for pastoral
scenes, sackbuts (trombones) for the underworld (although not found in Bach, this
last usage survives in Mozart's *Don Giovanni* and even Verdi's *Requiem*), and so on. In
Germany, every self-respecting lord hired trumpeters and a drummer for ceremonial
purposes, and Bach uses the trumpet in works conveying the dignity and power of

lordship, e.g., in the aria "Großer Herr, O Starker König" from the Christmas Oratorio (BWV 248). Similarly, horns conjured up images of the hunt, so vigorously suggested in Brandenburg Concerto No. 1 (BWV 1046) and the "Hunt Cantata" (BWV 208), the latter also having oboi da caccia, "hunting oboes." But hunting was reserved for lords (fig. 0.27a–d), so the horn is also appropriately featured in the "Quoniam . . . tu solus altissimus" (You[, Lord,] are most high) of the Credo of the B Minor Mass. Furthermore, Bach seems to have extended associations of this sort to solo voices, as it has been argued, for example, that Bach sometimes used an alto soloist to represent the Holy Spirit.[101]

Bach, of course, was personally engaged with that most important development during the period of the European Renaissance, the Protestant Reformation. Luther's views on music were in many respects medieval, as we have seen, but a kind of spiritual humanism is embodied in Luther's belief in the priesthood of all believers and his concern for the sensitive use of the German language in Lutheran music (most notably the chorales that underlie so many of Bach's organ works and sacred vocal compositions).[102]

The Baroque

Finally, Bach was very much of his own Baroque age, when artistic expression, fundamentally Italian in origin, tended to the representation of the strongest and most profound human sentiments. Baroque arts aimed to be dramatic, and they projected a sense of power, whether heavenly, ecclesiastical, absolutist, or civic. Although Bach never wrote an opera, the baroque art form par excellence established in the early seventeenth century, he did use operatic forms and techniques, above all in his passions and cantatas, to achieve drama and power in his music.[103]

Baroque Germany was not an exporter of cultural standards; rather, it thirstily lapped up the innovations imported especially from Italy and France. In this tradition, Bach took up with gusto the Italian sonata and concerto and the French dance suite, reformulating them in his own, particularly German way: no Italian could or would have written *his* Italian Concerto (BWV 971). But Bach also brought native German traditions to a new pinnacle, for example, that of the extroverted North German school of organ composition and performance.

How Bach came to know these legacies of various national schools of musical composition is important for understanding his development as a musician and composer, for he apparently never studied composition formally; rather, he learned by hearing, by performing, by copying, and by arranging music of other composers—and, of course, by composing and revising his own music.

The Organ

Let us first take up Bach's development as an organist, for that is how he began his career.[104] Nothing is known about Bach's receiving formal music instruction in Eisenach, and, in the authoritative and generally accurate obituary of Bach written in 1754 by Sebastian's son Carl Philipp Emanuel and his student Johann Friedrich Agricola, it is implied that it was not until Bach went to Ohrdruf to live with his brother Johann Christoph, a student of the famous South German organist Johann Pachelbel, that he undertook systematic keyboard studies.[105] However, it seemed clear that the boy had extraordinary talent and a voracious appetite for music—even to the point of his illicitly copying out by candlelight a manuscript belonging to his brother of keyboard pieces by Johann Jacob Froberger, Johann Caspar Kerll, Johann Pachelbel, and other leading seventeenth-century keyboard composers of central and south Germany.[106] Moreover, the Weimar tablatures contain a work by Buxtehude copied by Bach at about age thirteen—the oldest known musical document in Bach's hand—demonstrating the boy's early interest in the North German organ tradition, which may have stimulated his interest in going to Lüneburg.

In Lüneburg, Bach certainly had contact with, and may have had lessons from, Georg Böhm, a university-educated, Thuringian-born organist who had spent about five years in the sophisticated metropolis of nearby Hamburg before obtaining a position at Lüneburg's St. John's Church. Böhm lived not far from St. Michael's Church, where Bach sang in the Matins Choir; but because the organ at St. John's was in very bad repair it is thought that Böhm probably was limited in what he could demonstrate and teach Bach on the organ. Most important is that Böhm was the likely link to the Hamburg-based Johann Adam Reinken, the most famous organ virtuoso in northern Germany—a long-held belief now documented by an organ tablature, copied by Bach at Böhm's home and dated 1700, of Reinken's massive fantasia on the chorale *An Wasserflüssen Babylon*.[107] One can only imagine the powerful impression the flamboyant and apparently arrogant Reinken made on the teenager. But in Bach Reinken had a kindred spirit, for in 1720, the old master (who may not have been as old as tradition has held him to be), after hearing Bach improvise for an hour on that same chorale, was moved to tell him, "I thought this art was dead, but I see that it lives in you."[108] Moreover, Reinken, as a founder of the Hamburg opera, could offer Bach exposure to the larger world of North German musical life (see chapter 8).[109] It is also significant that about this time Bach arranged as harpsichord pieces (recomposed might be a better term) some trio sonatas (or parts thereof) from Reinken's *Hortus musicus* of 1687, which was a compliment to the older master that he paid no other German organist-composer.

In the Lüneburg period and later during his overextended Lübeck visit to Buxtehude, Bach naturally became acquainted with a different style of organ, for the North

German organs were larger and more colorful than those he had known in Thuringia (fig. 0.14, p. 19, and fig. 8.3, p. 247).[110] In Lüneburg, the organ at St. Michael's had three manuals and thirty-two registers, but surely making an even bigger impression was the magnificent four-manual organ at Hamburg's St. Catherine's Church (Katharinen-kirche) over which Reinken presided. North German organs also had more expansive pedal boards that allowed for virtuoso pedal parts to be written. Bach was so impressed with the thirty-two-foot pedal stop on the St. Catherine's organ (such a stop produces tones two octaves below the written pitches) that he later recommended such stops for other organs.[111]

Nonetheless, there still is no unequivocal proof that Bach took lessons, or played the organ for services, or even practiced in Lüneburg (although all are possible, even likely). Equally uncertain is the possible influence of other organists there, such as Johann Jakob Löwe at St. Nicholas's and the apparently not very competent Friedrich Christoph Mohrhardt at St. Michael's, whose distinguished father Peter composed organ music that some have found stylistically similar to early Bach.[112] Bach had a more certain if indirect connection (likely through Böhm) with the eminent Christian Flor, who preceded Böhm at St. John's; one of Flor's suites is found in the Möller Manuscript, most likely a work Bach came to know in Lüneburg. When Bach returned to Thuringia, he doubtless brought with him much music he had collected during his sojourn in the north (fig. 0.28a–b).

In the late twentieth century there came to light a new source for Bach's early organ music: a collection of eighty-two chorale preludes compiled at the end of the eighteenth century by the organist Johann Gottfried Neumeister. Thirty-eight of the works are attributed to Bach, thirty-three of them previously unknown.[113] It has been argued that this source points to the strong influence on Bach, most likely already in his Ohrdruf years, of Johann Michael Bach, represented by twenty-five pieces in the collection; he was a younger brother of the Eisenach Johann Christoph and father of Bach's future first wife, Maria Barbara. The pieces exhibit a stylistic range that reflects both Thuringian and North German influences, although without obbligato pedal parts; the works have therefore been dated 1695–1705.

The organ offers an especially good way to understand how Bach was influenced by native German musical traditions—but, as noted above, much German music during Bach's time reflected the powerful cultural influences of France and Italy.

France

It is quite possible that Bach learned something about French music in Ohrdruf. For example, the well-traveled Johann Jacob Froberger was one of the composers likely represented in the manuscript belonging to Johann Christoph that, according to the

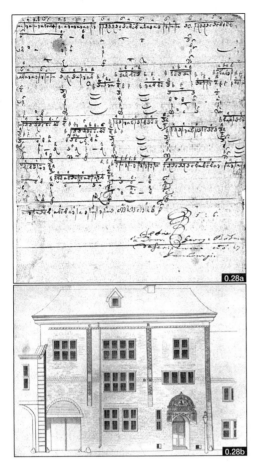

Figure 0.28. Despite a tragic fire in 2005, the systematic search of the Anna Amalia Library in Weimar led to the spectacular discovery that year of the earliest known Bach autographs. The manuscripts are in keyboard tablature rather than in regular music notation and contain large-scale, virtuoso fantasias on Lutheran chorales by J. A. Reinken and Dietrich Buxtehude. A comment in Bach's hand indicates that he copied the Reinken work, a monumental setting of *An Wasserflüssen Babylon* (*a*), in 1700 at the home of the organist Georg Böhm in Lüneburg; furthermore, the paper has been identified as that owned by Böhm. Böhm lived at Neue-Sulze 8 (*b*), close by St. Michael's Church and School. The Buxtehude work, on "Nun freut euch, lieben Christen g'mein," was apparently copied in Ohrdruf (1698 or 1699), when Bach was only thirteen or so. The fact that Bach, a Thuringian from central Germany, was already familiar with the work of the two great North German composers is early evidence of his insatiable musical curiosity and probably represents only a fraction of the North German music he then knew. It is likely that other (lost) music Bach copied in Lüneburg found its way into the Möller Manuscript and Andreas Bach Book, which belonged to Bach's older brother in Ohrdruf, Johann Christoph.

obituary, Bach copied illicitly by moonlight. However, since Bach apparently lost access to both Johann Christoph's manuscript and his own copy, and since there are no extant copies of Froberger's music in Bach's hand, it is difficult to assess the direct influence of the older composer on Bach.[114] Nonetheless, the German keyboardist Froberger was probably the single most influential transmitter of the latest styles of both Italian and French keyboard music in the generation before Johann Sebastian, and Johann Christoph would undoubtedly have come to know Froberger's music at least in the course of his studies with Pachelbel. Although Froberger spent more time in Italy than in France, it was his harpsichord suites in the French style that had the broadest impact and were known all over Germany.

On the other hand, the keyboard suites by Georg Böhm that found their way into the Möller Manuscript and the Andreas Bach Book most likely were brought back by Bach from Lüneburg, and are evidence of Böhm's cultivation of the French harpsichord idiom, which was principally embodied in stylized dances. As described more fully in chapter 6, France was the dance center of Europe; French court and theatrical dance, patronized lavishly by Louis XIV, was adopted everywhere and its music adapted to various performance media. Therefore, Bach's understanding of this special harpsichord style—later to be adapted in his own keyboard suites—would seem to date from the Lüneburg period at the latest. French harpsichord music was characterized by a keyboard texture—the *stile brisé* or broken style—that was not strictly polyphonic (as in choral music and in ensemble music for melody instruments), but rather involved a varying number of notes from moment to moment, reflecting the natural capabilities of chord-playing instruments such as keyboards, lutes, guitars, etc.

Bach did not learn the French harpsichord style solely through fellow Germans, however.[115] The Möller Manuscript has five suites by royal organist Nicolas Antoine Le Bègue, and the Andreas Bach Book has one suite by the brilliant virtuoso Louis Marchand (fig. 8.17, p. 260)—both famous French keyboard composer-performers of the time.[116] Moreover, as residents of Lüneburg, Böhm and Bach both apparently had opportunity to hear the French orchestra of the Duke of Brunswick-Lüneburg in its visits to the newly built palace on the Lüneburg market square. (The traditional view that Bach heard this orchestra in the capital city of Celle, a not inconsiderable distance away, is now doubted, but see caption to fig. 1.1, p. 70.) Most likely the music they heard was dance music from French ballets and operas, in the style established by Jean-Baptiste Lully, the most imitated French composer of the era, performed with the uniform bowing that was the hallmark of the Lully tradition. Typically the dance movements would have been preceded by an overture (*ouverture*) in the French style, which term was then applied to the entire work:[117] hence the title assigned to the four *Ouvertures* (suites) for orchestra by Bach (BWV 1066–69). Finally, although Bach probably did not see French opera, it is important to note not only that dance music played a central role in it (the French being more interested in the poetry, dance, and spectacle than in singing per se) but also that in the late seventeenth and early eighteenth centuries French opera was presented at many German courts,[118] and performances of Italian operas incorporated French dance.

If it was in dance music specifically that the French made their greatest impact on German music, French organ music also attracted Bach's insatiable musical curiosity. He therefore copied out the *Première Livre d'Orgue* by the organist of the cathedral at Rheims (where the French kings were crowned), Nicolas de Grigny (1672–1703),[119] even though French organs differed greatly from their German counterparts. Moreover, French keyboard music—whether dance suites or organ pieces—was characterized by the use of a meticulously notated style of ornamentation that Bach incorporated into his overall style (the Möller Manuscript contains a table of ornaments originally published by François [Charles] Dieupart that Bach apparently got from Böhm [fig. 0.29]).[120]

Figure 0.29. French harpsichord music is characterized by two features also found in Bach's keyboard music. The first is the so-called *stile luthé*, which is modeled on the loose polyphony of lute music, in which one or two notes sound at one moment and a full chord at another. The second is a specific style of ornamentation. The important table of ornaments in the *Pièces de clavecin* (Harpsichord pieces) by Jean-Henri d'Anglebert (Paris, 1689) was copied by Bach into a manuscript ca. 1710 along with Nicolas de Grigny's first book of organ pieces and keyboard suites by Charles Dieupart. The ornament table in the *Clavierbüchlein* for Wilhelm Friedemann, often reproduced in modern editions of Bach's keyboard music, was based on d'Anglebert's model.

Evidence from the Cöthen and Leipzig periods suggests, in addition, that Bach became acquainted with harpsichord and chamber music by François Couperin.[121]

The Italian Legacy

Although the French offered Bach important models, the Italians provided an even broader spectrum to be emulated. Italy was the true home of the Baroque, and the well to which musicians—like painters, sculptors, and architects—went to draw inspiration. It is difficult to know whether it was financial inability or lack of desire to travel to foreign lands that kept Bach in central Germany; however, very few of the Bach family ever went far from their Thuringian nests. Moreover, of his many children, several of whom had university educations, only one traversed the Alps, and continued from there to England: the youngest of his progeny, Johann Christian.

Had he been able to travel, Bach's career could have been more spectacular—like that of his exact contemporary Handel; in this regard it is worth reiterating that when Bach was rejected for the music directorship in Weimar in 1717, the successful candidate had been sent to Italy by the court many years before to prepare him for precisely such a position.[122]

Be that as it may, Italy had experienced a major musical revolution in the late sixteenth and early seventeenth centuries that sent ripples—perhaps a tidal wave is a more apt image—throughout Europe. So many of the genres familiar to concertgoers today were born in the fast-moving developments of that time: sonata, concerto, partita, aria, cantata, oratorio, and, perhaps most symptomatic of the age, opera. New musical techniques were also developed that underlie Bach's musical art: recitative (which Bach began to use in Weimar) and figured bass (fig. 4.6, p. 187), to name the most important.

Of course, not everything was revolutionary and new. Genres like toccata, canzona, ricercare, even aria have their roots in the Renaissance, and the strict style of Renaissance polyphony continued to be taught and practiced as the *stile antico* (old style) in conscious differentiation from the *stile moderno* (new style) represented by the innovations.

There were several waves of Italian influence, each putting its stamp on musical art. Bach took a special interest in the early seventeenth-century keyboard music of Girolamo Frescobaldi, the brilliant virtuoso organist at St. Peter's in Rome, with whom Froberger had studied—as became evident in Froberger's freewheeling toccatas on the Frescobaldian model that circulated widely in Germany. But Bach later on also owned a copy of Frescobaldi's *Fiori musicali* (Rome, 1635), demonstrating that composer's mastery of the rules of strict counterpoint. This work may have been an inspiration for Bach's *Art of Fugue* and certainly for the *ricercari* of *The Musical Offering* of 1747 (BWV 1079), the term *ricercare* being an old-fashioned one dating back to the late sixteenth and early seventeenth centuries.

Italian music of various kinds was floating around Thuringia, Lüneburg, Hamburg, and Weimar during Bach's formative years. The Möller Manuscript and the Andreas Bach Book contain, in addition to German and French music, arrangements of trio sonatas by Tomaso Albinoni, two capriccios of Carlo Francesco Pollarodo, and a Bach fugue based on a theme by Giovanni Legrenzi (BWV 574).[123] Similarly, Bach came to know eventually the works of the most influential of all baroque composers for the violin, Arcangelo Corelli, who provided the models for many of Bach's chamber music sonatas; the so-called "Corelli Adagio style," whereby a simple melodic line was elaborately embellished by the performer, found expression by Bach in written-out form, such as the opening movement to the Sonata in E Major for violin and obbligato harpsichord (BWV 1016).[124] Other examples include the thirteenth of the Goldberg Variations (BWV 988) and the slow movement of the Italian Concerto (BWV 971).

The solo concerto and concerto grosso, with their timbral contrasts of larger and smaller sound, were of particular interest to Bach. Around 1709–10 he copied, or possibly arranged, at least one concerto of Albinoni published in 1700—although only a partial continuo part survives (BWV Anh. 28).[125] Moreover, in 1709, the violinist Johann Georg Pisendel, who had studied with the Italian composer Giuseppe Torelli, visited Bach in Weimar on his way to Leipzig, where he would stun the local musicians with his artistry playing a Torelli concerto,[126] so it is likely that Bach acquired some knowledge of the Torelli concerto style at this time.[127] But the most significant experience of all was Bach's encounter with the concertos of Vivaldi, specifically those of *L'estro armonico*, Op. 3 (1711), which young Prince Johann Ernst of Saxony-Weimar sent or brought back from Holland in 1713.[128] Here was the hottest new music from Italy, employing not only a new structural procedure, the ritornello form, but also new ways of generating musical materials.[129] The impact on Bach was profound. This is because he saw in Vivaldi's concertos a way of structuring music that could be applied to a wide variety of situations. And so it is that the Vivaldian ritornello principle became ubiquitous in Bach's music from that point on, used not only in most fast movements of many concertos for orchestra instruments (like Vivaldi's), but also the innovative concertos for keyboard and strings (BWV 1052–59), the Italian Concerto for solo harpsichord, the "preludes" of the so-called "English" suites (BWV 806–11), the "Gloria in excelsis Deo" of the B Minor Mass, the B Minor Prelude for organ (BWV 544), and even some of the large opening movements of his Leipzig cantatas, to name but a few examples.[130]

In the last two decades of his life, Bach looked to Italy again, but for different kinds of inspiration. Not being able to go to Italy, he used in part the rich resources of Dresden which, because the elector was Roman Catholic, had extensive holdings of Catholic church music and intensively cultivated musical relationships with Italy and Vienna.[131] Bach therefore studied, arranged, and performed the Renaissance music of the sixteenth-century composer Palestrina on the one hand and on the other gave the first performance in Germany of Giovanni Battista Pergolesi's *Stabat Mater* of 1735–36 in his own German-language arrangement (BWV 1083).[132] The latter was post-baroque music, adumbrating the age of Mozart to come, and is evidence of Bach's never-ending search for worthy music of all kinds.

"Bach the Progressive"

Bach's interest in Pergolesi prompts at least brief consideration of his relationship to the new musical trends of his time. While there is no question that he was a traditionalist and a conservative in many ways, intellectually and musically, he was also very much "tuned in" to what was going on around him.[133] It has been mentioned how the young Bach traveled to meet the most important contemporary musicians, how he eagerly absorbed the new Italian music of Albinoni and especially Vivaldi. Although he never wrote opera, he apparently made sure he was in Dresden in 1731 to hear Johann Adolf Hasse's *Cleofide*, which featured Hasse's wife Faustina Bordoni, the brilliant soprano.[134] The obituary by C. P. E. Bach and Agricola tells of how Bach asked son Wilhelm Friedemann, "Well, Friedemann, should we go again and hear the lovely Dresden ditties?" suggesting Bach's delight in contemporary Italian opera[135] (see chapter 8).

Many of the Dresden stars, Hasse (fig. 8.13, p. 256) and Faustina among them, visited Leipzig and perhaps performed at the Collegium Musicum concerts. At any rate, much new music, and not only music of Bach, was performed at these concerts, so that the repertoire was not conservative. Moreover, it is important to remember that Bach championed new methods of tuning keyboard instruments; was known for his innovative fingerings (using the previously underemployed thumb, thereby helping move keyboard *playing* into the modern age); and took such interest in the new fortepiano that he served as an agent for such instruments. In addition, although there is nothing specifically "pianistic" about the keyboard ricercari or the continuo part of the Trio Sonata from *The Musical Offering* (BWV 1079), he may have considered that these pieces might be played on the fortepiano, given Frederick the Great's large collection of them.[136] The Trio Sonata also demonstrates Bach's willingness to adopt the characteristics of the *galant* style then all the rage in Berlin.[137]

Bach the Synthesizer

The foregoing has attempted to show the extraordinary range of influences on Bach the musician. What remains is to emphasize the unique way in which Bach was able to absorb all of these musical ideas and models, and, with supreme confidence and technical mastery, create at every turn new syntheses that are uniquely his.

Here are a few examples to illustrate the point: the opening chorus of Cantata 78, *Jesu, der du meine Seele*, combines the techniques of the passacaglia with its repeating bass line, the concerto ritornello principle, and a Lutheran chorale. The third and final movement of the Brandenburg Concerto No. 5 combines the concerto grosso idea (that is, textural contrast between a small group of soloists and the larger supporting orchestra), the da capo aria form (used in operas, cantatas, and oratorios), fugue, the French gigue and Italian giga, and a keyboard part that uniquely has two distinct roles: virtuoso soloist (with the music fully written out) and, in the ritornello sections, continuo player (where only the bass line is given and chords are improvised from the musical shorthand known as "figured bass"). The Suite (*Ouverture*) for Flute and Strings (BWV 1067) combines the French orchestral suite developed at Louis XIV's Versailles with the textural contrast and soloistic element of the Italian concerto. The Goldberg Variations (BWV 988), in addition to putting extraordinary technical demands on the performer (reminiscent of Reinken's hand-crossings and the keyboard pyrotechnics of Rameau and Domenico Scarlatti[138]) and requiring a two-manual harpsichord with its ability to provide concerto-like textual contrast, is built on the late-Renaissance/early Baroque aria principle (repetition of a harmonic pattern for each strophe/variation) over which is laid a series of complex canons, a French overture and gigue, Corellian Adagio-style embellishment, a range of emotions from the most profoundly saddening to joie de vivre, and, as the last variation, a quodlibet—i.e., a medley of popular tunes such as the Bachs liked to improvise at their annual family gatherings as exemplified by the texted Quodlibet (BWV 524).[139]

Bach's urge to synthesize, to set standards, to sum up various aspects of musical art reaches its most profound expression in the last decade of his life. Writing mainly for himself rather than to fulfill commissions or obligations of his offices, he created a series of imposing works that stand as the *ne plus ultra* within their realms: *The Well Tempered Clavier*, Book II (BWV 870–93), which explores an enormous range of old and new keyboard styles and forms in its preludes and fugues while also systematically utilizing every major and minor key; the Goldberg Variations, the most monumental of all variation sets; and *The Art of Fugue* (BWV 1080), a universe unto itself of the contrapuntist's art, perhaps somewhat abstract and didactic, yet awesome in the inexorable and systematic way the master reveals his total technical command of imitative counterpoint.

But it is the B Minor Mass (BWV 232), Bach's last great compositional effort, in which he synthesizes most profoundly the legacies that were his inheritance as man and musician. It is for this reason that an eminent Bach scholar who happens to be a Japanese Buddhist—yet another concrete sign of Bach's universality—can still call this work "the greatest musical art work for all times and peoples."[140] The B Minor Mass exemplifies, and is, a *harmonia* as lasting as Plato's metaphor of the cosmos in the *Timaeus*. Using the formal mold of the most traditional and timeless of musical genres—the Mass— and the most traditional and timeless language—Latin—Bach combines a vast array of disparate elements with results that are ineffable, sublime, and *catholic* in the sense of universal and all-embracing. Numerous musical textures and techniques—vocal solos and duets, choral and polychoral writing, *stile antico* and *stile moderno*, basso ostinato, canon and fugue, word-painting and simple number symbolism, a cappella and concertato textures, basso seguente and basso continuo, instrumental symbolism—are integrated with numerous musical genres—concerto, fugue, aria, French dance idioms, passacaglia—and musical traditions—the late Roman Renaissance, the baroque Dresden Mass, the Neapolitan love song—all reflecting Bach's encyclopedic familiarity with the music of his time and of ages before.[141] The work itself was not conceived originally as a complete whole, and so Bach, in addition to composing some sections as completely new pieces, also borrowed ideas from other composers (as in the opening Kyrie) and reworked pieces of his own, in the end producing a work that, in spite of its staggering dimensions and diversity of its sources and styles, completely satisfies. In this, his final paean of praise to the Lord he sought to serve through music, Bach brings chorus and orchestra together, augmented by trumpets and drums, to plead for peace (*Dona nobis pacem*); in so doing, he employs the music previously composed for the text of "We give you thanks" (*Gratias agimus tibi*). It is not unreasonable to infer from this intentional juxtaposition that Bach wished to give thanks for his life and talent as he also yearned for the eternal peace he expected would soon be his.

Bach, who was dying and going blind as he composed this work, undoubtedly knew he would never have a chance to perform it. But in its universality—in its unity and diversity—the Mass in B Minor epitomizes on the one hand the legacies of which Bach was the receiver and, on the other, the greatness of his legacy to posterity.

Notes

1. Rainer Keiser, "Johann Sebastian Bach als Schüler einer 'deutschen Schule' in Eisenach?" *BJ* 80 (1994): 177–84.

2. See also Hans-Joachim Schulze, "Johann Christoph Bach (1671–1721)," 72f. The matter is also discussed by Küster, *Der junge Bach* (Stuttgart: Deutsche Verlags-Anstalt, 1996), 97–109, but his interpretation is disputed by Schulze in a review of Küster's book in *BJ* 83 (1997): 203–5. Apparently, the custom of *Freitische* ("free tables") was a voluntary but common form of charity, whereby a family would provide a meal once a week or more to poor schoolboys; however, this meant that to be assured of regular meals the entire week, the pupils would have to make arrangements with several families. If sufficient sustenance could not be arranged, the youths might have to drop out of school "*ob defectum hospitiorum*" ("on account of a lack of hospitality," as the Ohrdruf school records recorded it), either to work or to try their luck in another town.

3. A catalog of the inventory is given in Max Seiffert, "Die Chorbibliothek der St. Michaelis-schule in Lüneburg zu Seb. Bachs Zeit," *Sämmelbände der Internationalen Musik-Gesellschaft* (1907–8): 593–621. It is not known, however, if Bach had contact with this collection.

4. A pamphlet published by the Lüneburg Michaelisakademie in 2000 contains a historical sketch of St. Michael's School with particular attention to the Bach period by Dr. Eckhard Michael, director of the Museum des Fürstentums Lüneburg; it also contains an essay by Heinz Henschke, "Lage und Ausstattung der Michaelisschule," which includes drawings showing the layout and exterior of the school. I am grateful to Dr. Michael not only for a copy of this pamphlet but also for other assistance and information.

5. *Weimarer Orgeltabulatur. Die frühesten Notenhandschriften Johann Sebastian Bachs sowie Abschriften seiner Schülers Johann Martin Schubart*, ed. with a preface by Michael Maul and Peter Wollny (Kassel, etc.: Bärenreiter, 2007), xxxii, n. 37.

6. *Ibid.*, xxi–xxxiii, passim.

7. *NBR*, 46 (*BD* 2, no. 16, pp. 19–21).

8. Wolff, "Buxtehude, Bach, and Seventeenth-Century Music in Retrospect," *Essays*, 41–55. Kerela J. Snyder, *Dietrich Buxtehude, Organist in Lübeck*, rev. ed. (Rochester, NY: University of Rochester Press, 2007).

9. *NBR*, 43–48 (*BD* 2, nos. 14, 16, 17, pp. 15–23).

10. Konrad Küster, *Der junge Bach*, 144f.

11. *NBR*, 57 (*BD* 1, no. 1, pp. 19–21). This request to be released from his duties, addressed to the Mühlhausen town council, is the oldest extant textual document in Bach's hand. See also Küster, *Der junge Bach*, 160–65.

12. Martin Petzoldt, *Bachstätten aufsuchen* (Leipzig: Verlag Kunst und Touristik, 1992), 133–37; Küster, *Der junge Bach*, 161f.

13. *NBR*, 56f. (*BD* 1, no.1, pp. 19f.).

14. The second published cantata celebrated the new city council in Mühlhausen in 1709, but is lost. Bach also wrote a number of cantatas in Leipzig for the same purpose, among them BWV 119, 193, 120, 29, and 69. For others text but no music survives.

15. Bach's use of the term "motet" here is nonetheless unusual, for later he applied it mainly to works in which instruments more or less double vocal lines rather than enjoy musical independence from the voices. It has been proposed that perhaps Bach was following the terminology used in Buxtehude's *Abendmusik*, which Bach heard in Lübeck. See Daniel R. Melamed, *J. S. Bach and the German Motet* (Cambridge: Cambridge University Press, 1995), chapters 1 and 2, esp. 29–31.

16. Russell Stinson, *Bach: The Orgelbüchlein* (New York: Schirmer Books, 1996), 2ff., points out that the manuscript is largely empty, although with titles of, and space for, a total of 164 chorale preludes, which he then lists along with their liturgical association.

17. Erdmann Neumeister, *Geistliche Cantaten über alle Sonn-, Fest- u. Apostel-Tage* (Halle, 1705 [or 1704]), cited in Elke Axmacher, "Erdmann Neumeister—ein Kantatendichter J. S. Bachs," *Musik und Kirche* 60 (1990): 294–303, esp. 296.

18. On the Cöthen musical establishment or *Capelle*, see Friedrich Smend, *Bach in Köthen* (Berlin: Christliche Zeitschriftenverlag, ca. 1951), 21–23. Günther Hoppe, "Leopold von Anhalt-Köthen und die 'Rathische Partei.' Vom harmvollen Regiment eines '*Musik* liebenden als kennenden *Serenissimi*,'" *Cöthener Bach-Hefte* 6 (1994): 114b, expresses some skepticism concerning Leopold's commitment to music as such, and regards the Prince's patronage as merely one means to enhance the prestige of his court.

19. On the keyboard works generally, see David Schulenberg, *The Keyboard Music of J. S. Bach*, 2nd edition (New York: Routledge, Taylor and Francis, 2006).

20. *NBA*, 151 (*BD* 1, no. 23, p. 67).

21. Problems facing Prince Leopold that may have contributed to Bach's decision to leave Cöthen are treated in Günther Hoppe, "Leopold von Anhalt-Köthen und die 'Rathische Partei,'" and chapter 1.

22. Hans-Joachim Schulze, "'. . . da man nun die besten nicht bekommen könne . . .'" *Bericht über die Wissenschaftliche Konferenz zum III. Internationalen Bach-Fest der DDR. Leipzig, 18./19. September 1975* (Leipzig: VEB Deutscher Verlag für Musik, 1975), 71–77 exploded the myth that Bach was considered a "mediocre" candidate and prompted a reevaluation of the entire matter of Bach's selection and subsequent relations with the city council in terms of local politics. Ulrich Siegele, "Bachs Stellung in der Leipziger Kulturpolitik seiner Zeit," *BJ* 69 (1983): 7–50; 70 (1984): 7–43; and 72 (1986): 33–67 subsequently characterized the city council as politically divided between two parties, which he designates the "Cantor" and "Music Director" parties. See also chapter 1, note 20.

23. Michael Tilmouth and Richard Sherr, "Parody (i)," *New Grove*, 2nd ed., 19: 145–47; Paul Brainard, "Bach's Parody Procedure and the St. Matthew Passion," *Journal of the American Musicological Society* 22 (1969): 241–60; Hans-Joachim Schulze, "Bachs Parodieverfahren," *Die Welt der Bach Kantaten* 2 (Stuttgart: Metzler and Kassel: Bärenreiter, 1999): 167–87.

24. Christoph Wolff, *Johann Sebastian Bach: The Learned Musician* (New York and London: W. W. Norton & Co., 2000, and Oxford and New York: Oxford University Press, 2002), 355.

25. Christoph Wolff, "Bach's Last Fugue: Unfinished?" and "The Compositional History of the Art of Fugue," *Essays*, 259–64 and 265–81, respectively.

26. See his letter to the Mühlhausen city council, *NBR*, 57 (*BD* 1, no. 1, p. 19f.) and the Leipzig "Short but Most Necessary Draft for a Well-Appointed Church Music, with Certain Modest Reflections on the Decline of the Same," *NBR*, 145–55 (*BD* 1, no. 22, pp. 60–64). The latter has been the subject of great controversy regarding the size of the choir used in Bach's own performances of his Leipzig church music. See, for example, Joshua Rifkin, "Bach's Chorus: A Preliminary Report," *The Musical Times* 123 (1982): 747–54; Christoph Wolff, "Bach's Chorus: An Amplification," *EM* 17 (1999): 172; Andrew Parrott, *The Essential Bach Choir* (Woodbridge, Suffolk, UK and Rochester, NY: Boydell Press, 2000); Martin Geck, "Bach's Art of Church Music and His Leipzig Performance Forces: Contradictions in the System," *EM* 31 (2003): 558–71; and Andreas Glöckner, "Alumnen und Externe in den Kantoreien der Thomasschule zur Zeit Bachs," *BJ* 2006, 9–36.

27. The text of the genealogy is given in *NBR*, 283–94 (*BD* 1, no. 184, pp. 255–61). A family tree is given in *NBR*, 285. For an interpretation of Bach's motivation in writing the family genealogy see Mary Dalton Greer, "From the House of Aaron to the House of Johann Sebastian: Old Testament Roots for the Bach Family Tree," *About Bach*, ed. Gregory G. Butler, George B. Stauffer, and Mary Dalton Greer (Urbana: University of Illinois Press, 2008), 15–34.

28. For the first statement, see *NBR*, 33 (*BD* 2, no. 3, p. 5). For the second citation see Günther Kraft and Richard Schal, "Erfurt," *MGG* 3: 1481 and 1485f., Abb. 6 and Otto Rollert, "Die Erfurter Bach," *Johann Sebastian Bach in Thüringen* (Weimar: Thüringer Volksverlag, 1950), 208. For information on the most important members of the Bach family, see Christoph Wolff and Walter Emery, *The New Grove Bach Family* (New York and London: W. W. Norton, 1983) and individual biographies in *New Grove*, 2nd ed.

29. Regarding the Bach family and Erfurt, see Günther Kraft and Dieter Härtwig, "Erfurt," *New Grove*, 2nd ed., 8: 289; and Helga Brück, "Die Erfurter Bach-Familien von 1635–1805," *BJ* 82 (1996): 101–32.

30. Wolff, "Johann Christoph Bach," *New Grove*, 2nd ed., 2: 306.

31. Fritz Rollberg, "Johann Ambrosius Bach, Stadtpfeifer zu Eisenach von 1671–1695," *BJ* 24 (1927): 133–52. Claus Oefner, "Eisenach zur Zeit des jungen Bachs," *BJ* 71 (1985): 43–54. Rainer Kaiser, "Johann Ambrosius Bachs letztes Eisenacher Lebensjahr," *BJ* 81 (1995): 177–82.

32. Werner Braun, "Theodor Schuchardt und die Eisenacher Musikkultur im 17. Jahrhundert," *Archiv für Musikwissenschaft* 15 (1958): 296.

33. Hans-Joachim Schulze, "Johann Christoph Bach (1671 bis 1721), 'Organist und Schul Collega in Ohrdruf,' Johann Sebastian Bachs erster Lehrer," *BJ* 71 (1985): 62, n.36.

34. Wolff, "Bach," *New Grove*, 2nd ed., 2: 299. German text in Küster, *Der junge Bach*, 45.

35. The present "Bachhaus" in Eisenach at Frauenplan 21 is not the home in which Bach lived, although it does give a general impression of the style of house Bach might have known. The former Fleischgasse, where the Bach family actually lived, is now called Luthergasse. Martin Petzoldt, *Bachstätten aufsuchen*, 52–55, esp. 54.

36. H-J. Schulze, "Johann Christoph Bach," 64.

37. Conrad Freyse, "Das Porträt Johann Ambrosius Bach," *BJ* 46 (1959): 149–55.

38. Hans-Joachim Schulze, *Studien zur Bach-Überlieferung im 18. Jahrhundert* (Leipzig: Peters, 1984), 30–56. Selected compositions from these sources are published in Robert Hill, ed., *Keyboard Music from the Andreas Bach Book and the Möller Manuscript* (Cambridge, MA: Department of Music, Harvard University, 1991) (Harvard Publications in Music 16). A third source, copied later but important for understanding Bach's development in the period 1695–1705 is the Neumeister Collection (see following note).

39. Wolff, "The Neumeister Collection of Chorale Preludes," *Essays*, 118 states that "the connections between Johann Michael's and Johann Sebastian's chorale preludes cannot be overestimated." The former's are published in Johann Michael Bach, *Sämtliche Orgelchoräle, mit einem Anhang (Orgelchoräle des Bach-Kreises, hauptsächlich aus der Neumeister-Sammlung)*, ed. Christoph Wolff (Neuhausen-Stuttgart: Hänssler, 1987; Stuttgart: Carus-Verlag, 1998). A facsimile edition of the collection of eighty-two chorale preludes is *The Neumeister Collection of Chorale Preludes from the Bach Circle (Yale University Manuscript LM 4708)* (New Haven: Yale University Press, 1986). The thirty-eight chorales attributed to J. S. Bach, edited by Wolff, are in *NBA* IV/9 (Kassel: Bärenreiter, 2003). Supporting Wolff's attribution to J. S. Bach of these works is Russell Stinson, "Some Thoughts on Bach's Neumeister Chorales," *Journal of Musicology* 11 (1993): 455–77, whereas Peter Williams, review of Wolff's edition above, *The Organ Yearbook* 17 (1986): 123f., takes a somewhat more skeptical stance.

40. Regarding Bach's duties in Arnstadt, see *NBR*, 41 (*BD* 2, no. 8, pp. 11f.) Küster, *Der junge Bach*, 135–38, and Petzoldt, *Bachstätten aufsuchen*, 17.

41. The count's, later prince's, collections (see caption to Plate 6), along with the notable puppet collection of Princess Augusta Dorothea of Schwarzburg-Arnstadt, are briefly described in the guidebook *Museen der Stadt Arnstadt* (Arnstadt: Museum der Stadt, 1984).

42. There were anomalous situations. For example, the Luther- and Bach-family city of Erfurt, strictly speaking, was a possession of the Roman Catholic elector of Mainz (who in the past had sometimes been a Wettin), and Catholics and Protestants coexisted there. Even in strictly orthodox Lutheran Leipzig, however, it was possible to attend a Catholic Mass on Sunday in the Pleissenburg fortress during the years of Bach's tenure, since the elector of Saxony was Catholic.

43. Herbert Zimpel, "Der Streit zwischen Reformierten und Lutheranern in Köthen während Bachs Amtzeit," *BJ* 65 (1979): 97–106, treats such a situation in Cöthen.

44. Anneliese Bach, "Salamo Franck als Verfasser geistlichen Dichtungen," *Johann Sebastian Bach in Thüringen*, 135–39. Lothar Hoffmann-Erbrecht, "Bachs Weimarer Textdichter Salomo Franck" *Ibid.*, 120–34. Alfred Dürr, "Über Kantatenformen in den geistlichen Dichtungen Salomon Francks," *Die Musikforschung* 3 (1950): 18–26. Peter Wollny, "Cantata Arias and Recitatives," *The World of the Bach Cantatas*, ed. Christoph Wolff, 1: *Johann Sebastian Bach's Early Sacred Cantatas* (New York and London: W. W. Norton and Co., 1995), 171–83.

45. Robin A. Leaver, "Bach und die Lutherschriften seiner Bibliothek," *BJ* 61 (1975): 124–32.

46. See George B. Stauffer, *Bach: The Mass in B Minor* (New York: Schirmer Books, 1997; New Haven and London: Yale University Press, 2003), 79f.

47. Martin Petzoldt, "*Ut probus & doctus reddar.* Zum Anteil der Theologie bei der Schulausbildung Johann Sebastian Bachs in Eisenach, Ohrdruf und Lüneburg," *BJ* 71 (1985): 13 and 19f. On Comenius in relation to Bach see Martin Petzoldt, "Zwischen Orthodoxie, Pietismus und Aufklärung. Überlegungen zum theologiegeschichtlichen Kontext Johann Sebastian Bachs," *Johann Sebastian Bach und die Aufklärung*, ed. Reinhard Szeskus (Leipzig: Breitkopf und Härtel, 1982), 67f., 72f., 75–77, 80, 88f., and 93.

48. See Kurt Schmidt, "Gothas Stellung in der Bildungsgeschichte des 17. Jahrhunderts," in Heinrich Anz, ed., *Gotha und sein Gymnasium. Bausteine zur Geistesgeschichte einer deutschen Residenz* (Gotha and Stuttgart: Verlag Friedrich Andreas Perthes, 1924), 42–52; Martin Petzoldt, "Zwischen Orthodoxie, Pietismus und Aufklärung," 67–78, 89, and 93; and "*Ut probus & doctus reddar*," 17–20.

49. A *Gymnasium* is a pre-university secondary school. Traditionally, gymnasia have been very strong in the humanities, with the most advanced classes sometimes on the university level.

50. Martin Petzoldt, *Bachstätten aufsuchen*, 152–54. For Reyher's influence in Ohrdruf see also Petzoldt, "Zwischen Orthdoxie, Pietismus und Aufklärung," 67, and *Bachstätten aufsuchen*, 155f.

51. A book that concerns itself with numbers and number relationships in the Bible is Caspar Heunisch, *Hauptschlüßel über die hohe Offenbarung S. Johannis* (The principal key to the high revelation of St. John) (Schleusingen, 1684; repr. Basel: A. Heiber, 1981), which Bach later owned. It was known in Ohrdruf in Bach's time inasmuch as a copy is preserved there with a handwritten dedication to the Ohrdruf superintendent by the author; moreover, a copy was in Bach's library when he died. See Martin Petzoldt, "*Ut probus & doctus reddar*," 18.

52. The *Compendium* (modern edition Berlin: Wilhelm Hertz, 1855) is organized into thirty-four doctrinal areas (e.g., "Concerning Holy Scripture," "Concerning the One and Triune God," "Concerning Christ," etc. The 541 questions that are posed are distributed in three levels of difficulty for each question. Thus the text could be used for several years of instruction, each time at a more sophisticated level, as shown in the chart on 338f. in Paul Nebel, "Leonhart Hutter's *Compendium Locorum Theologicorum*," *Neue Jahrbücher für Pädagogik* 5 (1902): 327–61. For Hutter and Bach, see Reinhard Kirste, "Theologische und spirituelle Ermöglichungsansätze für Bachs Werk unter besonderer Berücksichtigung des Verständnisses von Wort und Geist bei Leonhart Hutter und Johann Arnd," *Bach als Ausleger der Bibel*, ed. Martin Petzoldt (Berlin: Evangelische Verlagsanstalt, 1985), 77–95; 72–74, 77, 80, and 88f.

53. Martin Petzoldt, "Bachs Prüfung vor dem Kurfürstlichen Konsitorium zu Leipzig," *BJ* 84 (1998): 19–30.

54. Robin A. Leaver, *Bachs theologische Bibliothek. Eine kritische Bibliographie. Mit einem Beitrag von Christoph Trautmann./Bach's Theological Library. A Critical Bibliography. With an essay by Christoph Trautmann* (Neuhausen-Stuttgart: Hänssler-Verlag, 1983). Johannes Wallmann, "Johannes Sebastian Bach und die 'Geistlichen Bücher' seiner Bibliothek," *Pietismus und Neuzeit* 12 (1986): 162–81. *Ex Libris Bachianis II. Das Weltbild Johann Sebastian Bachs im Spiegel seiner theologischen Bibliothek* (exhibition catalog), Ausstellung zum Heidelberger Bachfest 1985 (Heidelberg: Kurpfälzischen Museum der Stadt Heidelberg, 1985).

55. Walter Blankenburg, "Aufklärungsauslegung der Bibel in Leipzig zu Zeit Bachs. Zu Johann Christoph Gottscheds Homiletik," *Bach als Ausleger der Bibel*, ed. Martin Petzoldt (Berlin: Evangelische Verlaganstalt, 1985), 99–101.

56. Ernst Sicul, *Neo annalium Lipsiensium continuatio* II, cited in Günther Stiller, *Johann Sebastian Bach and Liturgical Life in Leipzig*, translated by Herbert J. A. Bouman, D. F. Poellot, and H. C. Oswald and edited by Robin A. Leaver (St. Louis: Concordia Publishing House, 1984), 52f. Sicul also comments that in addition there is a Roman Catholic and Pietist sermon to be heard every Sunday. There was also a Huguenot community that gathered privately for worship, as they were not allowed to worship publicly.

57. Examples of cantatas in two parts are BWV 17, 20, 38, 39, and 45. It was Leipzig practice to have the Nicene Creed, or Luther's Credo hymn *Wir glauben all in einem Gott*, or both,

sung after the Gospel but before the sermon, which began with a second reading from the Gospel of the day. The sermon was followed by prayers of petition and intercession as well as announcements, after which the second part of the cantata was sung. (Stiller, *Johann Sebastian Bach and Liturgical Life in Leipzig*, 122–25.) On certain Sundays and festivals, cantatas or excerpts were performed during communion; BWV 180 apparently was used frequently for this purpose and acquired the name "Communion Cantata" (*Ibid.*, 82–85.) See also chapter 2, "Lutheran Mass Forms."

58. Johann Christoph Gottsched, *Ausgewählte Werke*, ed. Joachim Birke (Berlin: W. De Greyter, 1968–), 7:125.

59. Regarding the religious participation of both Gottsched and Bach as members of the parish of St. Thomas in Leipzig, see Günther Stiller, "Johann Sebastian Bach und Johann Christoph Gottsched—eine beachtliche Gemeinsamkeit," *Musik und Kirche* 46 (1976): 166–72.

60. Regarding the 1738 work, see *NBR*, 197–199 (*BD* 2, nos. 424f., pp. 326–8; *BD* 1, no. 122, p. 198); p. 198 reproduces the title page of the printed cantata text by Gottsched. See also Hans Joachim Kreutzer, "Dichter und Dichtungen der weltlichen Kantaten Bachs," in *Die Welt der Bach Kantaten* II, ed. Christoph Wolff with a foreword by Ton Koopman (Stuttgart and Weimar: J. B. Metzler and Kassel: Bärenreiter, 1997), 129–33. Note, however, that the date for BWV 198 is incorrectly given as 1729 (rather than 1727).

61. Alex Preminger, ed., *The Princeton Encyclopedia of Poetry and Poetics* (Princeton: Princeton University Press, 1974), 585.

62. A detailed analysis of these changes is Armin Schneiderheinze, "Über Bachs Umgang mit Gottscheds Versen," *Bericht über die Wissenschaftliche Konferenz zum III. Internationalen Bach-Fest der DDR* (Leipzig: Deutscher Verlag für Musik, 1975), 91–98.

63. Christoph Ernst Sicul, *Das thränende Leipzig* (Leipzig, 1727). Translated excerpt in *NBR*, 136 (*BD* 2, no. 232, p. 175).

64. For Ernesti's career, see *Allgemeine Deutsche Biographie* (Berlin: Duncker and Humblot, 1968; repr of 1st ed. of 1877) 6: 235–41.

65. Bach's library included Gerhard's *Schola Pietatis* (5 vols.) and, by Heinrich Müller, the *Evangelisches Praeservativ wider den Schaden Josephs, Evangelische Schluss-Kette und Krafft-Kern oder Gründliche Auslegung der gewöhnlichen Sonn- und Fest-Tags-Episteln, Göttliche Liebes-Flamme . . . mit schönen melodeyen von Nicolao Hassen gezieret, Geistliche Erquickstunden oder Dreyhundert Haus- und Tisch-Andachten*, and *Rath Gottes*, among others.

66. The title is hard to render in English. *Merkwürdigkeiten* can be translated "distinctive qualities" but also can carry the implication of otherness, strangeness, and foreignness. Schudt demonstrates a profound interest in Jews, and even sympathy for the injustices they have suffered, yet he is also driven by a desire for the conversion of Jews to Christianity.

67. Johann Jacob Schudt, *Jüdische Merckwürdigkeiten* (Frankfurt and Leipzig: Samuel Tobias Hocker, 1715), 354ff, and (Frankfurt: Samuel Tobias Hocker, 1717), 241ff.

68. Perhaps the first Jew to receive permission to live in Leipzig in the eighteenth century was Baruch Levi of Hamburg, who arrived in 1710. Such permissions were not obtainable from the city government, only from the court in Dresden.

69. This is what happened to a Samuel Seligmann, servant of one of the Jewish electoral court actors. See Adolf Diamant, *Chronik der Juden in Leipzig* (Chemnitz and Leipzig: Verlag Heimatland Sachsen, 1993), 7.

70. Diamant, *Chronik der Juden in Leipzig*, 5–8, and Schudt, *Jüdische Merckwürdigkeiten* (Frankfurt, 1717), 241f.

71. Heiko A. Oberman, *The Roots of Anti-Semitism in the Age of Renaissance and Reformation*, translated from the German by James I. Porter (Philadelphia: Fortress Press, 1984), 105. This is a thoughtful, thorough, and sensitive treatment of a difficult and important subject.

72. "On the Jews and their Lies, 1543," *LW* 47 (*The Christian in Society* 4), trans. Martin H. Bertram, ed. Franklin Sherman (Philadelphia: Fortress, 1971), 278 (= *WA* 53: 530).

73. "Eine Vermahnung wider die Juden," *WA* 51:196 (not translated in *LW*).

74. For example, one passage of the Weimar cantata *Gleich wie der Regen und Schnee vom Himmel fällt* (BWV 18) reads: "Protect us in fatherly fashion from the gruesome death and depravity, rage, and madness of the Turk and the Pope," cited, along with a similar example from the Leipzig cantata BWV 126, by Yoshitake Kobayashi, "Die Universitalität in Bachs h-moll Messe," *Musik und Kirche* 57 (1987): 15. Michael Marissen, "The character and sources of the anti-Judaism in Bach's cantata 46," *Harvard Theological Review* 96/1 (2003): 63–99, argues (not completely convincingly) that *Schauet doch und sehet* (BWV 46) is directed against the Jews.

75. See Michael Marissen, *Lutheranism, Anti-Judaism and Bach's St. John Passion: With an Annotated Literal Translation of the Libretto* (New York: Oxford University Press, 1998), who also takes up the historical question, "Who killed Jesus?" He also cites earlier studies on this topic by Renate Steiger, Dagmar Hoffmann-Axthelm, Walter Meinrad, and Lothar Steiger. On the sources for Bach's libretto of the St. John Passion, see Alfred Dürr, *Die Johannes-Passion von Johann Sebastian Bach: Entstehung, Überlieferung, Werkeinführung* (Munich/Kassel: Bärenreiter, 1988), 44–71.

76. Arno Herzig, "Das Gutachten der Leipziger theologischen Facultät von 1714 gegen die jahrhundertealte Blutschuldlüge," *Judaica Lipsiensia. Zur Geschichte der Juden in Leipzig*, ed. by the Ephraim Carlebach Stiftung (Leipzig: Edition Leipzig, 1994), 28–32. Jakub Goldberg, "Die sächsisch-polnische Verbindung und die polnischen Juden," *Sachsen und Polen zwischen 1697 und 1765. Beiträge der wissenschaftlichen Konferenz vom 26. bis 28 Juni 1997 in Dresden* (*Saxonia*. Schriftenreihe des Vereins für sächsische Landesgeschichte e.V., Band 4/5) (Dresden: Sächsisches Druck- und Verlagshaus, 1998), 247–54. The opinion was published in *Auserlesene Bedenken der Theologischen Facultät zu Leipzig. In drey Theile verfasset von D. Christian Friedrich Boernern* (Leipzig: Bernhard Christoph Breitkopf, 1751), 613–22. The present author is preparing a study of the opinion and its background to appear in *The Musical Quarterly*.

77. Plato, *Timaeus* 35b–36e.

78. See, for example, Athanasius Kircher, *Mursurgia universalis, sive Ars magna consoni et dissoni* (Rome, 1656; rpt. Hildesheim and New York: Georg Olms Verlag, 1970), 47 and 549–52; Johannes Kepler, *Harmonices mundi* (Linz, 1619), discussed in Eric Werner, "The Last Pythagorean Musician: Johannes Kepler," *Aspects of Medieval and Renaissance Music: A Birthday Offering to Gustave Reese*, ed. Jan LaRue (New York: W. W. Norton & Co., 1966), 867–82 (Kepler believed that the rotating planets each produced a sounding musical tone); and Andreas Werckmeister, *Musicae mathematicae Hodegus curiosus, oder Richtiger musicalischer Weg-Weiser* (Frankfurt and Leipzig, 1686; rpt. Hildesheim and New York: Georg Olms, 1972), which is strongly influenced by Kepler.

79. Don Franklin, "Das Verhältnis zwischen Taktart und Kompositionstechnik im Wohltemperierten Klavier I," *Bach: Das Wohltemperierte Klavier I. Tradition, Entstehung, Funktion, Analyse*, ed. Siegbert Rampe (Zirnberg: Musikverlag Katzbichler, 2002), 147–58, demonstrates that meter signatures are proportionately distributed in *The Well-Tempered Clavier*. See also his "Composing in Time: Bach's Temporal Design for the Goldberg Variations,"

Bach Studies from Dublin, ed. Anne Leahy and Yo Tomita (Dublin: Four Courts Press, 2004), 103–28. Ruth Tatlow has discovered Pythagorean proportional relationships of numbers of measures among collections, between works, and between movements and groups of movements. See her "Collections, Bars and Numbers: Analytical Coincidence or Bach's Design?" *Understanding Bach* (Web Journal of Bach Network UK) 2 (2007): 37–58. A book-length study, tentatively titled *Bach's Numbers Explained*, is in preparation. No claims are made by either scholar that these proportional distributions have symbolic meaning.

80. See, for example, Robert Isherwood, *Music in the Service of the King* (Ithaca and London: Cornell University Press, 1973), chapter 1, and Volker Scherliess, "Musica Politica," *Festschrift Georg von Dadelsen zum 60. Geburtstag*, ed. Thomas Kohlhase und Volker Scherliess (Neuhausen-Stuttgart: Hänssler Verlag, 1978), 270–83.

81. German text in Günther Hoppe, "Leopold von Anhalt-Köthen und die 'Rathische Partei,'" 114b.

82. *NBR*, 16f. (*BD* 2, no. 433, p.334). The text is a paraphrase by Bach of a passage in Friedrich Erhardt Niedt's *Musikalische Handleitung* (Hamburg, 1700). Cf. F.T Arnold, *The Art of Accompaniment from a Thorough-Bass* (2 vols.; New York: Dover Publications, 1965) 1: 213–36, esp. 214 and 223. "Thoroughbass" refers to the bass line (often designated "[basso] continuo") of a baroque musical score giving the lowest note of the harmony, over which the performer improvises appropriate harmony; often such a bass line would have indications (by means of numbers, sharp/flat/natural signs, etc.) to indicate what pitches should sound over a given bass note. In such cases, a thorough bass was also a "figured bass." The use of thorough- or figured bass is one of the most characteristic features of baroque music, being introduced in Italy about 1600 (see fig. 4.6, p. 187). For the philosophical implications of the Niedt-Bach definition of figured bass, see Walter Blankenburg, "J. S. Bach und die Aufklärung," *Johann Sebastian Bach*, ed. Walter Blankenburg (Darmstadt: Wissenschaftliche Buchgesellschaft, 1970), 100–10.

83. Plato, *The Republic* 398b–405a and 410a–412b; Aristotle, *Politics* 1337b4–38b8 and 1338a11–42b34. These excerpts are printed in Oliver Strunk, *Source Readings in Music History* (New York: W. W. Norton, 1950), 4–12 and 13–24, respectively, and in *idem*, rev. ed., Leo Treitler, general editor (New York and London: W. W. Norton, 1998) 1 (ed. Thomas J. Mathiesen): 9–19 and 24–34, respectively.

84. *Fundamentals of Music. Anicius Manlius Severinus Boethius*, translated, with introduction and notes by Calvin M. Bower, edited by Claude V. Palisca (New Haven and London: Yale University Press, 1989), 2f.

85. Thus Luther refers to the study of music as a liberal art along with "the whole of mathematics," for in the medieval university music was one of four mathematical disciplines of the *quadrivium*, the others being arithmetic, geometry, and astronomy. "To the councilmen of all the cities in Germany that they establish and maintain Christian schools," tr. Albert T. W. Steinhaeuser, rev. Walther I. Brandt, *LW* 45: 369 and 369n4 (= *WA* 15: 46). See also "A sermon on keeping children in school," *LW* 46: 252 (= *WA* 30.2: 579).

86. *WA*, Tischreden 5: 557, no. 6248.

87. See *LW* 49: 428 and *What Luther Says. An Anthology*, Ewald M. Plass, comp. (St. Louis, MO: Concordia Publishing House, 1959), nos. 3090f.

88. Walter Blankenburg, "Der Titel und das Titelbild von J. H. Buttstetts Schrift *Ut, mi, sol, re, fa, la—Tota Musica et Harmonia aeterna oder Neueröffnetes altes, wahres, einziges und ewiges fundamentum musices* (1717)," *Die Musikforschung* 3 (1950): 64–66; however, the date of 1717 should be 1716. Two pieces by Buttstett (a fugue and a prelude) are included in the

Andreas Bach Book. See Hans-Joachim Schulze, *Studien zur Bach-Überlieferung im 18. Jahrhundert,* 44–47.

89. Buttstett, *Ut, mi, sol, re, fa, la,* 6.

90. Bach's annotations are produced in facsimile in Howard H. Cox, ed., *The Calov Bible of J. S. Bach* (Ann Arbor: UMI Research Press, 1985), facs. 110.

91. Günther Stiller, *Johann Sebastian Bach and Liturgical Life in Leipzig,* 108–31, esp. 116–29.

92. Edward E. Lowinsky, "Musical Genius—Evolution and Origins of a Concept," *The Musical Quarterly* 50 (1964): 321–40 and 476–95.

93. Bach is alleged to have said, according to his first biographer, J. N. Forkel, "I have had to work hard; anyone who works just as hard will get just as far." Cited in *NBR,* 20, and Ulrich Siegele, "'Ich habe fleißig sein müssen. . . .' Zur Vermittlung von Bachs sozialem und musikalischen Charakter," *Musik und Kirche* 61 (1991): 73–8, esp. 72. See also *BD* 2, no. 409, p. 299.

94. The term "Gregorian" is unhistorical since Pope Gregory the Great (r. 590–604), from whom the melodies were long thought to stem, had nothing to do with "Gregorian chant."

95. Friedrich Blume, "Outlines of a New Picture of Bach," *Music and Letters* 44 (1963): 214–27. The "new picture" proposed by Blume did not find support among Bach scholars, who have overwhelmingly rejected Blume's doubts about Bach's religiosity. See, for example, Friedrich Smend, "Was bleibt? Zur Friedrich Blumes Bach-Bild," *Der Kirchenmusiker* 13 (1962): 178–89.

96. This is more fully discussed in chapter 3.

97. See, for example, Z. Philip Ambrose, "*Weinen, Klagen, Sorgen, Zagen* und die antike Rhetoric," *BJ* 66 (1980): 35–46.

98. This example is particularly convincing because the movement is a parody, i.e., is adapted from an earlier work, namely Cantata 12 (1714), in which the bass melody is stated twelve times. There is no reason Bach had to extend the number of repetitions to thirteen, so it may well have been a conscious decision to modify the original in this way. However, some scholars and musicians have argued for a much more far-reaching use of number symbolism, finding highly abstract and complicated manifestations of it everywhere in Bach's music, although there is no hard evidence that number symbolism in fact played a role in Bach's compositional procedures except in rather obvious instances. The chief proponent for the presence of number symbolism in the twentieth century was Frederick Smend, whose arguments were critically evaluated in Ruth Tatlow, *Bach and the Riddle of the Number Alphabet* (Cambridge: Cambridge University Press, 1991). Helga Thoene proposed that number symbolism (and other hidden features) are to be found in Bach's unaccompanied music for violin. See her "Johann Sebastian Bach. Ciaccona—Tanz oder Tombeau. Verborgene Sprache eines berühmten Werkes," *Cöthener Bach-Hefte* 6 (1994), 14–81 and "'Ehre sey der Gott gesungen,' Johann Sebastian Bach, Die Violin-Sonata G-Moll, BWV 1001: Der verschlüsselte Lobgesang," *Cöthener Bach-Hefte* 7 (1998): 3–114. Thoene's theories are challenged in Raymond Erickson, "Sacred Codes, Dance, Bach's Great Ciaccona," *Early Music America Magazine* 8/2 (Summer 2002): 34–43 and "Towards a Twenty-first Century Interpretation of Bach's Ciaccona," *The American Bach Society Newsletter* (Spring, 2003), 1, 5, and 10. On the possible influence of *ratios* on Bach's compositional process, see note 79.

99. Christoph Wolff, *Der stile antico in der Musik Johann Sebastian Bachs. Studien zur Bachs Spätwerk* (Wiesbaden: Franz Steiner Verlag, 1968).

100. The Sanctus may also reflect other aspects of the text of Isaiah 6:1–3, for the prophet speaks of *two* seraphim, each having six wings, just as Bach's six vocal lines are divided into two choruses. Moreover, the flying of the angels, also cited by Isaiah, is possibly described

musically by the soaring triplet figures joined to the exclamations "*Sanctus!*" See George Stauffer, *Bach: The Mass in B Minor*, 151f.

101. Renate Steiger, "SUAVISSIMA MUSICA CHRISTO. Zur Symbolik der Stimmlagen bei J.S. Bach," *Musik und Kirche* 61 (1991): 318–324, suggests that Bach sometimes assigned voice ranges according to the symbolism proposed by the theologian Johann Saubert in his *Seelen Musik* (1629): alto as Holy Spirit, bass as belief or faith, discant (soprano) as prayer, and tenor as holy Christian life (see p. 320). In particular, she discusses the association between alto voice and Holy Spirit in BWV 75/10 and 172/5. Ernst Koch, "Die Stimme des Heiligen Geistes, Theologische Hintergründe der solistischen Altpartien in der Kirchenmusik Johann Sebastian Bachs," *BJ* 81 (1995): 61–82, extends Steiger's argument, adducing additional examples from cantatas, the Christmas Oratorio, St. Matthew Passion, and other works, and also asserts that this symbolism is supported in the writings of Heinrich Müller that Bach had in his library.

102. Oskar Söhngen, "Die Musikanschauungen der Reformatoren und die Überwindung der Mittelalterlichen Musiktheologie," *Musa-Mens-Musici. Im Gedenken an Walther Vetter* (Leipzig: VEB Verlag für Musik, [1969]), 51–62 discusses the "new" view of music with respect to religion and theology in Protestant thought of the Renaissance (including Calvin and Zwingli as well as Luther). Johann Michael Schmidt, "Theologie und Musik—Luther und Bach," *Musik und Kirche* 56 (1986): 276–86 considers the medieval roots of Luther's utterances on music, but also argues that he took music out of the (medieval) world of numbers and brought it closer to the (Renaissance) world of language.

103. See, for example, Karl-Heinz Viertel, "Johann Sebastian Bachs Verhältnis zur Oper seiner Zeit," *Bericht über die wissenschaftliche Konferenz zum III. Internationalen Bach-Fest der DDR* (Leipzig: Deutscher Verlag für Musik, 1975), 91–98.

104. Bach's career as organist is treated comprehensively in *J. S. Bach as Organist: His Instruments, Music, and Performance Practices*, ed. George Stauffer and Ernest May (Bloomington: Indiana University Press, 1986).

105. *NBR*, 299 (*BD* 3, no. 666, p. 81). On the sort of repertoire Johann Christoph Bach, Bach's Ohrdruf teacher, studied with Pachelbel and likely passed on to his younger brother, cf. Christoph Wolff, "Johann Valentin Eckels Tabulaturebuch von 1692," *Festschrift Martin Rulnke zum 65. Geburtstag*, ed. Klaus-Jürgen Sachs (Neuhausen/Stuttgart: Hanssler, 1986), 374–86.

106. Described in the obituary of C. P. E. Bach and J. F. Agricola, in *NBR*, 299 (*BD* 3, no. 666, pp. 81f.)

107. Published in facsimile and transcription in *Weimarer Tabulatur*, edited, with a foreword and transcriptions, by Michael Maul and Peter Wollny (Kassel et. al: Bärenreiter, 2007).

108. An assessment of Reinken's influence on Bach is Christoph Wolff, "Bach and Johann Adam Reinken: A Context for the Early Works," *Essays*, 56–71. Ulf Graperthin, "Reincken, Johann Adam," *Die Musik in Geschichte und Gegenwart*, 2nd ed., ed. Ludwig Finscher (Kassel, etc.: Bärenreiter and Stuttgart and Weimar: J. B. Metzler, 2005) Personenteil 13: 1506, challenges the date of Reinken's birth, normally accepted as 1623, proposing instead 1643.

109. For a survey of North German musical culture, especially that of Hamburg and Lübeck, see Karl Heller, "Norddeutsche Musikkultur als Traditionsraum des jungen Bach," *BJ* 75 (1989): 7–19.

110. For the respective qualities of Thuringian and North German organs, see Hartmut Haupt, "Bach Organs in Thuringia," *J. S. Bach as Organist*, 425–30, and Harald Vogel, "North German Organ Building of the Late Seventeenth Century: Registration and Tuning," *Ibid.*,

31–40. Bach's career as recitalist and organ consultant is detailed in Ulrich Dähnert, "Organs Played and Tested by Bach," *Ibid.*, 3–24.

111. English and Italian organs (and those based on Italian models in southern Germany and Austria) had no or few pedals. Each geographic region in Europe had its own style and tradition of organ building and consequently organ compositional style.

112. According to Erdmann Werner Böhme, *(Materialien über) 150 Lüneburger Musiker-Namen (1532–1864) nach Akten aus dem Stadtarchiv Lüneburg* (typescript, Lüneburg, 1950), citing W. Junghans, "J. S. Bach als Schüler der Partikularschule zu St. Michaelis in Lüneburg" (Programm des Johanneum zu Lüneburg, Stern, 1870), Christoph Mohrhardt, son of Peter, was organist at St. Michael's 1690–1707. (However, Horst Walker, *Musikgeschichte der Stadt Lüneburg: vom Ende des 16. bis zum Anfang des 18. Jahrhunderts* [Tutzing, 1967], 303, gives "Peter Morhard" as organist at St. Michael's from 1662 to 1685 and his son Friedrich Christoph from 1685 to 1707.)

113. See note 39.

114. Froberger did not consistently employ a fixed order of movements in his dance suites.

115. Another direct influence is Johann Kaspar Ferdinand Fischer, whose instrumental music shows the influence of Lully and from whom Bach borrowed musical ideas for *The Well-Tempered Clavier*.

116. Two even more famous French composers are also represented, but in transcriptions of operatic orchestral music: the Möller Manuscript contains a chaconne from *Phaeton* by Jean-Baptiste Lully, Louis XIV's music czar; the Andreas Bach Book has a suite from the opera *Alcide* by Marin Marais, Louis's viola da gamba player.

117. The "French overture" form consisted of two sections: the first, grand and noble, usually with sharp, "dotted" rhythms, and the second, fast and fugal. Sometimes the first section (or an abbreviated version of it) returned at the end. Probably the most familiar example of a French overture is the overture to *Messiah* by Handel.

118. A study of opera at a typically modest Thuringian court is "Die frühdeutsche Oper am Schwarzburg-Rudolstädtischen Hofe unter Philipp Heinrich Erlebach (1657–1714)," *Musik-theatralische Formen in kleinen Residenzen*, ed. Friedhelm Bruzniak (Cologne: Studio, Medien und Verlag Dr. Ulrich Tank, 1993), 32–54.

119. The full title is *Première Livre d'Orgue contenant une Messe e les Hymnes des principalles Festes de l'année* (Organ Book, Vol. 1, containing a mass and hymns of the principal feasts for the year). Modern edition by Charles-Léon Koehlhoeffer (Paris: Heugel, 1986). Bach's transcription is discussed in Kirsten Beißwanger, "Bachs Eingriffe in Werke fremder Komponisten. Beobachtungen an den Notenhandschriften aus seiner Bibliothek unter besonderer Berücksichtigung der lateinischen Kirchenmusik," *BJ* 77 (1991):126–58, esp. 139–43.

120. Hans-Joachim Schulze, *Studien zur Bach-Überlieferung*, 42. In England Dieupart was known by the first name of Charles. Bach's continuing concern with French ornamentation is inferrable from his copying, in Weimar, the famous table of ornaments by Jean Henri d'Anglebert.

121. The 1725 Clavierbüchlein for Anna Magdalena Bach contains a harpsichord piece, *Les Bergeries*, by Couperin.

122. On the Italian journey of Johann Wilhelm Drese (May 1702 to January 1703), see Küster, *Der junge Bach*, 190f. and 200–202. Konrad Küster, "Der Herr denket an uns BWV 196: Eine frühe Bach-Kantate und ihr Kontext," *Musik und Kirche* 66 (1996): 84–96, argues that Cantata 196 shows Bach's awareness of current Italian music before Duke Johann Ernst brought the music of Vivaldi to Weimar. Küster proposes that music that J. W. Drese brought back from Italy played a role here.

123. *Keyboard Music from the Andreas Bach Book and the Möller Manuscript*, ed. Robert Hill, xxiv–xlvi. See also Robert Hill, "Die Herkunft von Bachs 'Thema Legrenzianum,'" *BJ* 72 (1986): 105–7.

124. This written-out right-hand part of this same movement gives an idea of the elaborate way Bach might have improvised a continuo realization, of which there are several accounts. See *NBR* 328 (*BD* 2, no. 419 [not 432 as indicated in *NBR*]), 362 (*BD* 3, no. 680, p. 111), 397 (*BD* 3, no. 801, p. 285), and 399 (*BD* 3, no. 803, p. 289).

125. Hans-Joachim Schulze, *Studien zur Bach-Überlieferung*, 28. It is possible that the Albinoni concerto was brought back from a study-trip to Italy in 1702–3 by Johann Wilhelm Drese, who had been sent there by the court to become acquainted with the latest Italian trends. Drese later succeeded his father as Weimar Capellmeister, a post that Bach coveted. Cf. Konrad Küster, *Der junge Bach*, 190.

126. An eyewitness account of Pisendel's Leipzig performance of Torelli is quoted in Andreas Glöckner, "Bachs Leipziger Collegium Musicum und seine Vorgeschichte," *Die Welt der Bach Kantaten* 2, 108f.

127. However, the earliest surviving transcription by Bach of a Torelli concerto (BWV 979) dates from 1713. See Jean-Claude Zehnder, "Giuseppe Torelli and Johann Sebastian Bach," *BJ* 77 (1991): 33–95, esp. 34f.

128. Johann Ernst's travels and the dating of the Bach transcriptions for organ and harpsichord of concertos by Vivaldi and other composers (BWV 592–96 and 972–87) are discussed in Schulze, *Studien zur Bach-Überlieferung*, 156–63.

129. The ritornello form was not invented by Vivaldi, but he made it his own. Simply stated, a movement in ritornello form consists of an opening and closing statement of the "ritornello" (that is, music that "returns"); the body of the movement then consists of passages where the soloist(s) dominate (usually playing music thematically unrelated to the ritornello) and passages played by the orchestra that draw on ritornello material. A clear example of this by Bach is the first movement of the Brandenburg Concerto No. 5, which also has a cadenza immediately preceding the final ritornello. For a discussion of what Bach learned from Vivaldi, see Christoph Wolff, "Vivaldi's Compositional Art, Bach, and the Process of 'Musical Thinking,'" *Essays*, 72–81, and Michael Talbot, "The Concerto Allegro in the Early Eighteenth Century," *Music and Letters* 52 (1971): 8–18, 159–72.

130. Gregory G. Butler, "J. S. Bach's Reception of Tomaso Albinoni's Mature Concertos," *Bach Studies* 2, ed. Daniel Melamed (Cambridge: Cambridge University Press, 1995), 20–46, argues on formal and stylistic grounds that certain movements of Brandenburg Concertos nos. 1 and 6 (among other works) may show the influence of Albinoni's oboe concertos, Op. 7 of 1715; if true, this would suggest that the Bach works originated between 1715 and 1721 (the year of the dedication of the Brandenburg Concertos). Butler thinks that Bach may have encountered Albinoni's Op. 9 (1722) at Weissenfels in 1725.

131. On sacred music at the Dresden court see Wolfgang Horn, *Die Dresdner Hofkirchenmusik 1720–45. Studien zu ihren Voraussetzungen und ihren Repertoire* (Kassel, etc.: Bärenreiter and Stuttgart: Carus, 1987). The impact of primarily Italian Catholic church music on Bach during the 1730s and 1740s is the focus of Christoph Wolff, *Stile antico*. Kirsten Beißwanger, "Bachs Eingriffe in Werke fremder Komponisten," discusses Catholic church music by Antonio Caldara, Francesco Durante, Sebastian Knüpfer, Antonio Lotti, Johann Christoph Pez, et al. copied and or reworked by Bach.

132. Karl Gustav Fellerer, "J. S. Bachs Bearbeitung der *Missa sine nomine* von Palestrina," *BJ* 24 (1927): 123–32; Emil Platen, "Eine Pergolesi-Bearbeitung Bachs," *BJ* 47 (1961): 35–51; and

Alfred Dürr, "Neues über Bachs Pergolesi-Bearbeitung," *BJ* 54 (1968): 89–100. See also Christoph Wolff, *Stile antico*, passim, and Barbara Wiermann, "Bach und Palestrina. Neue Quellen aus Johann Sebastian Bachs Notenbibliothek," *BJ* 88 (2002): 9–23.

133. Robert Marshall, "Bach the Progressive," *The Musical Quarterly* 62 (1976): 313–57, was a seminal article drawing attention to this previously neglected aspect of Bach's creative work. See also Christian Ahrens, "Joh. Seb. Bach und der 'neue Gusto' in der Musik um 1740," *BJ* 72 (1986): 69–79, which is concerned primarily with the style of *The Musical Offering*.

134. See chapter 8, table 3 and note 39.

135. The quote appears in Johann Nikolaus Forkel *Über Johann Sebastian Bachs Leben, Kunst, und Kunstwerke* (Leipzig, 1802; rpt. Berlin:, 1974), ed. with an afterword by Walther Vetter (Kassel: Bärenreiter, 1970), 86 (*NBR*, 461). This is one of the earliest and still very important biographies of Bach, inasmuch as it contains much material received directly from Bach's sons Carl Philipp Emanuel and Wilhelm Friedemann. However, it was largely superseded by the *Johann Sebastian Bach* by Philipp Spitta (2 vols.; Leipzig, 1873–80; rpt. of English ed.[London, 1884] New York: Dover Publications, 1952). For an evaluation of Spitta's work, see Christoph Wolff, "New Perspectives in Bach Biography," *Essays*, 3–13. Wolff's *Johann Sebastian Bach: The Learned Musician* (see note 24) is now the standard full-length biography of Bach.

136. Christoph Wolff, "Bach und das Pianoforte," *Bach und die italienische Musik—Bach e la musica italiana*, ed. Wolfgang Osthoff und Reinhard Wiesend (Venice, 1987), 197–210. (Centro Tedesco di Studi Veneziani—Quaderni, Vol. 36.) (This work was not available to the author.)

137. For a provocative hypothesis regarding Bach and the fortepiano see also Eva Badura-Skoda, "Komponierte J. S. Bach 'Hammerklavier-Konzerte?'" *BJ* 77 (1991): 159–71.

138. David Yearsley, "The Awkward Idiom: Hand-Crossing and the European Keyboard Scene around 1730," *EM* 30 (2002): 225–35, sees Domenico Scarlatti as the likely inventor and propagator of this virtuosic technique that became very popular in the eighteenth century. He suggests that Bach may have become acquainted with Scarlatti's keyboard innovations through S. L. Weiss (fig. 8.14), who was a mutual friend of both.

139. Other reflections of Bach's extraordinary ability to synthesize successfully disparate elements are Robert Marshall, "Bach's Universality," *The Music of Johann Sebastian Bach. The Sources, the Style, the Significance* (New York: Schirmer Books, 1989), 59–79 (which offers a closer analysis of the opening movement of BWV 78), and Werner Felix, "Beobachtungen zu Formensynthese und Gattungsintegration in Schaffen Johann Sebastian Bachs," *Musik und Kirche* 60 (1990): 61–81.

140. Kobayashi, "Die Universalität in Bachs h-moll-Messe," 17. His formulation is a rephrasing of the statement of Hans Georg Nägeli (1818) that the Mass is "the greatest musical art work of all times and peoples."

141. Most of these aspects, and some others as well, are cited in George B. Stauffer, *Bach: The Mass in B Minor*.

PART I

~

The Context for Bach

CHAPTER I

The Historical Setting:
Politics and Patronage

Norman Rich

I: The Holy Roman Empire

A major difficulty in dealing with German history in the Bach era is to decide what is meant by Germany, for at that time Germany did not exist as a political entity. "Germany" was merely a convenient designation for that large agglomeration of three-hundred-odd states where a majority of the inhabitants spoke German in one or more of its many dialects, for as yet there was not even a standardized German language. Most of these states were members of that venerable European institution, the Holy Roman Empire (plates 2 and 3), but that empire was never conceived as an exclusively German institution. In imperial political theory, the empire laid claim to universal dominion over all peoples, regardless of nationality, just as the Roman Catholic Church laid claim to universal spiritual dominion.

To non-Germans, the Holy Roman Empire is best known by the gibe attributed to Voltaire (among others) that it was neither holy, Roman, nor an empire. Historians of the empire contend that this clever but simplistic epithet did more to undermine its authority than any number of lost battles. It reinforced the belief of "enlightened" political theorists that the empire was an antiquated anachronism doomed to die of its own obsolescence, an institution serving no useful purpose, not worthy of support or serious study.

The name of the empire, like the empire itself, was the product of many centuries of historical development. It was called "Roman" because, with the restoration of the imperial title in Western Europe through the coronation of Charlemagne in the year 800, the people of that era could not conceive of an empire that was not Roman. The title was subsequently formally adopted by Charlemagne's successors in the belief that it added to their authority and prestige. The designation "Holy" was added in the twelfth century by the Hohenstaufen Emperor Frederick I (Barbarossa) during the empire's long struggle with the Roman papacy to match or overtrump the claims to divine authority of the Holy Roman Church.

In the fourteenth century, after the loss of most of its non-German territories, the empire came to be called the Holy Roman Empire of the German Nation, but the empire never claimed to be, nor was it ever regarded as, a German state representing German national interests. The very fact that the empire laid claim to universal temporal dominion made it impossible for emperors to think of the empire as an exclusively German institution.

Imperial Institutions

The history of the empire's institutions is infinitely more complicated than the history of its name. Over the centuries these developed into an incredibly complex amalgam of laws and customs, rights and exemptions, that defy generalization or schematization. This complexity was compounded by the diverse nature of the various components of the empire, which was made up of secular and ecclesiastical states of widely varying size and strength—duchies and counties, prince-bishoprics, self-governing and imperial abbeys, imperial and free cities, small knightly holdings—all of which developed their own traditions and institutions. Because of a steady overlapping of jurisdictions, inheritances, partitions, and alienations, the states themselves were always changing and without fixed frontiers.

There were divisions and subdivisions within a single state or region. In Brunswick (German: Braunschweig), for example, there was a Brunswick-Lüneburg, with its capital at Celle; a Brunswick-Wolfenbüttel, with capitals at the cities of Wolfenbüttel and Brunswick; a Brunswick-Calenberg, with its capital at Hanover. Among the many Saxonys, there was an electorate, a grand-duchy, a Saxony-Anhalt, a Saxony-Coburg, a Saxony-Weimar, a Saxony-Weissenfels. There were any number of Hessens. There were imperial cities such as Augsburg, Nürnberg, and Mühlhausen, which were under the direct rule of the emperor; Hanseatic cities, which were members of that great commercial network, the Hanseatic League; and there was Leipzig in Electoral Saxony, not a free or imperial city, but one to which the electors had granted considerable autonomy in the running of its internal affairs. There were imperial abbeys, which like imperial cities were under the direct rule of the emperor. There were bishops and archbishops, who might rule an entire cluster of ecclesiastical states. At one time the archbishop of Cologne was also prince-bishop of Regensburg (Ratisbon), Hildesheim, and Lüttich

(Liège); likewise an archbishop of Mainz, who was also prince-bishop of Bamberg and Würzburg, possessed in addition Thuringian Erfurt and its surrounding territory. From the thirteenth century, many members of the House of Habsburg were elected Holy Roman Emperor, but as rulers of the Habsburg Austrian lands they bore the title of archduke, and as rulers of Bohemia and Hungary they bore the title of king.[1]

The most important of the empire's institutions that survived the Middle Ages was the election of the emperor, deriving from the custom of German tribal chieftains of electing their leaders. The original electors were the major secular and ecclesiastical princes of the empire, and over the years the elections were a frequent source of conflict and confusion. In 1356 Emperor Charles IV of the House of Luxembourg secured acceptance by the imperial estates[2] of a Golden Bull (an official document with a golden seal, or *bulla*) to regulate imperial elections, avoid the evils of disputed elections, and prevent the intervention of foreign powers, in particular the papacy. Henceforth, elections were to be in the hands of an electoral college of seven electors (*Kurfürsten*): three ecclesiastical princes (the archbishops of Mainz, Trier, and Cologne) and four secular princes (the king of Bohemia, the duke of Saxony, the margrave of Brandenburg, and the count Palatine of the Rhine)—hence the title *elector* of Saxony, *elector* of Brandenburg, etc. The number and membership of the electoral college were to vary slightly over the centuries, but the Golden Bull was seen from the first as a fundamental law of the empire.

Even the most powerful emperors were weakened by the electoral procedure, for the Golden Bull did not end disputes or foreign intervention. The French in particular were to seek the imperial title for their own kings or their satellites, and to secure the votes needed for election candidates found themselves obliged to make political and economic concessions or outright bribes to the electors and their constituencies. Over the years the practice of demanding concessions from candidates became institutionalized and the concessions themselves were called by the appropriate name of Electoral Capitulations (*Wahlkapitulationen*). As the electoral system gave the great princes of the empire the means to curb the power of the emperor and prevent his establishment of effective control over themselves, they had every motivation to maintain it. Thus, while many secular princes of the empire were making the succession in their realms hereditary, the office of emperor remained elective.

The Post-Medieval Period to the Thirty Years' War

The great age of the medieval German empire came to an end with the death of the Hohenstaufen emperor Frederick II in 1250. There followed a lengthy interregnum and the election in 1273 of a minor German prince named Rudolf of Habsburg, who was

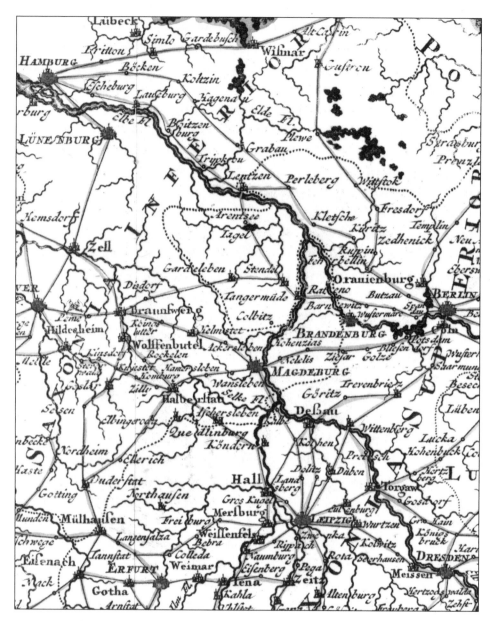

Figure 1.1. With the exception of Carlsbad in Bohemia to the south and Ohrdruf near Arnstadt, this portion of an eighteenth-century map depicting the main roads shows all of the principal places associated with Bach. Most of these are in the lower quarter of the map, namely (from left) Eisenach, Mühlhausen, Arnstadt ("Arnstat"), Weimar, Weissenfels, Leipzig, and Dresden. Cöthen ("Kothen") is north of Leipzig, and Berlin is farther north in the middle near the eastern edge. Clearly evident is the course of the Elbe River diagonally from lower right (Dresden) to upper left (Hamburg). Lüneburg is southeast of Hamburg whereas Lübeck is northeast of it. The map also makes clear how ambitious and even dangerous it was for the young organist Bach to travel over two hundred miles from Arnstadt to Lübeck in 1705–6 to hear Dietrich Buxtehude. But it also reveals the intriguing likelihood that Bach passed through Celle (the capital of Brunswick-Lüneburg) on the way to Lüneburg in 1700; there he might have heard the famous French orchestra that likely also came to Lüneburg during his time there. Or perhaps he stopped there in connection with obtaining a place in Lüneburg's St. Michael's School and its Matins Choir (*Mettenchor*), since apparently the Celle court authorities exercised influence in such matters.

elected precisely because he was weak and unable to impose imperial authority on the princes of the empire.

Early in the sixteenth century, however, it seemed for a time as though the imperial ideal of uniting all Western Christendom under a single Christian emperor might at last be realized. This possibility arose as the result of the fruition of a remarkable series of dynastic marriages arranged by members of the House of Habsburg and the resulting dynastic union of a large part of Europe and the Spanish possessions overseas under a single Habsburg ruler, Charles, who became king of Spain in 1516 (as King Charles I) and Holy Roman Emperor in 1519 (as Emperor Charles V). Joined under Charles was the heritage of Ferdinand and Isabella (Spain, a large part of Italy, and the Spanish conquests overseas), the dukes of Burgundy (the duchy and free county of Burgundy and the Low Countries), and the Austrian Habsburgs (the Austrian crown lands, Bohemia, and Hungary).

While falling heir to (or otherwise acquiring) such abundance, Charles also inherited the traditional foreign and domestic problems of each of his dominions: the imperial conflict with the papacy, the hostility between Burgundy and France, the rivalry of his various states with each other, and the resistance of the estates within all his dominions to imperial/royal/ducal authority. At the heart of the opposition to Charles V and the Habsburgs was France, now surrounded by Habsburg or imperial territory, which was to wage a campaign for another century and a half to break out of Habsburg encirclement.

During the reign of Charles V, a new divisive force developed to confound the ideal of Christian unity. This was the Protestant Reformation and the adoption of the Lutheran faith and other forms of Protestantism by a large number of European princes, whether for reasons of genuine religious idealism or because the repudiation of the Roman faith allowed them to confiscate the property of the Church and assume supreme spiritual as well as secular authority over their subjects. Because Charles remained a loyal Catholic, a majority of Protestant princes, fearing that he would use his power to reimpose the Roman faith on their states, also joined the ranks of his opponents.

Charles and the empire faced yet another danger. In 1453 the Muslim Turks had captured Constantinople, and from there they extended their empire over much of the Near East, North Africa, and the Balkans. In 1526 they defeated a Hungarian army at the Battle of Mohacs, which brought them control over a large part of Hungary, and in 1529 they laid siege to Vienna. With his power diffused in so many areas of Western Europe, Charles found it necessary to purchase a truce with the Turks through an annual payment of thirty thousand ducats—but this truce gave the empire little more than a respite. The Turkish threat remained.

This assortment of anti-imperial, anti-Habsburg, and anti-Catholic forces was to produce a succession of unlikely coalitions that included at one time or another Catholic France, Catholic Poland, Orthodox Russia, Protestant Denmark and Sweden, the Protestant (and some Catholic) princes of Germany, the Muslim Turks—and the papacy. However improbable and fragile these coalitions might be, they proved too strong for Charles to overcome. Toward the end of his reign he even found it necessary to grant official recognition to the Lutheran Protestants (although to no other Protestant sect) within the empire. By the religious Peace of Augsburg of 1555, the rulers of the states of the empire were ceded the right to determine the religion of their subjects on the basis of the principle *cuius regio, eius religio*, an extraordinarily cruel formula that required the citizens of a state to adopt the religion of their ruler. In 1556 Charles, weary of a life of ceaseless and inconclusive struggle, abdicated and divided his empire between his son Philip and his brother Ferdinand, thereby creating a Spanish and an Austrian branch of the house of Habsburg.

The Thirty Years' War and the Treaties of Westphalia

A century after the election of Charles V, another Habsburg emperor, Ferdinand II (r. 1619–37), made yet another attempt to bring the states of the Holy Roman Empire under effective imperial control. The opportunity to do so came with the revolt in 1618 of Protestant noblemen in Bohemia (under Habsburg rule since 1526) and their ejection of Ferdinand's representatives from a window of Prague's Hradčany Castle (the famous Defenestration of Prague). In 1619 they deposed Ferdinand as king of Bohemia and elected in his stead a German Protestant prince, Friedrich V, elector of the Palatine, head of the German Calvinists and Protestant Union, and son-in-law of King James I of England. These events in Bohemia set off a conflict that has become known in history as the Thirty Years' War, a war that has been depicted as a religious war, but fundamentally was a political one.

The Thirty Years' War was the most terrible thus far in German history in its geographical compass, the size of the rival armies, and the extent of its destruction, which turned a large part of Germany, including Bach's homeland of Saxony, into a wasteland. Perhaps even worse than the material destruction—the burning of towns and villages, the devastation of the countryside, the plunder of churches and any other buildings left standing—was the spiritual destruction, the gradual extinction of feelings of humanity among soldiers and civilians alike, who engaged in mass murder, torture, and rape on a scale not seen heretofore.

The 1648 Treaties of Westphalia, which brought the Thirty Years' War to an end, were far more than peace treaties: they were nothing less than a new imperial constitution and were specifically described as being "a perpetual, universal, and fundamental law of the Reich." In all matters affecting the domestic and foreign affairs of the Empire, the emperor was now required to seek the consent and agreement of the estates, whereas the individual estates were conceded the right to conclude alliances with each other and with foreign powers. Thus in effect the Westphalian treaties recognized the de facto independence of the three-hundred-odd states of the Reich, an independence now backed by international guarantees that ended any possibility of establishing a strong, centralized, imperial government. At the same time, however, the treaties guaranteed the continued existence of that confederation of German states known as the Holy Roman Empire.

In matters of religion, the Westphalian peace recognized Calvinism as well as Lutheranism as a religion of the Reich (but no other form of Protestantism), and relaxed the brutal principle of *cuius regio, eius religio* by conceding the right of private worship and freedom of conscience. The most ingenious provisions dealing with religion were those designed to prevent the champions of one faith from imposing their will on others. The Catholic and Protestant religions were to be represented by two equal bodies in the *Reichstag* (the parliament of the imperial estates), and no religious legislation affecting the empire as a whole could be considered until they had reached agreement between themselves. With that, a system was established requiring the settlement of all future religious differences through negotiation, without resort to arms.

The great winners in Westphalia were France and Sweden, which made substantial territorial and strategic gains at the expense of the Empire and were made guarantors of the Westphalian treaties. They thereby secured the right to intervene in the Empire's affairs whenever they suspected any violation of those treaties—a right that could easily be transformed into an excuse to send their armies into Germany at any time to defend or promote their own interests.

The Development of Absolutism

In the Holy Roman Empire itself, the big winners were the German princes, their sovereignty and independence from imperial control now guaranteed by international treaty, who had long been expanding their authority at the expense of their own estates. This process was to culminate in their establishment of a system of government that historians have chosen to call absolutism—an absolutism tempered by inefficiency and corruption, and, not infrequently, by the incompetence or sloth of individual rulers, but a system that nevertheless gave the German princes a large measure of control over their country's policies. Exempt from this kind of absolutism were the free imperial cities (such as Mühlhausen and Lübeck) and the imperial monasteries, which for the most part continued to be governed by their own elected officials—who could be authoritative enough in their own right.

The power of the princes had already been greatly enhanced in the course of the Reformation, as Catholic as well as Protestant rulers were given the right to determine the religion of their subjects and Protestant princes gained both power and wealth through the expropriation of ecclesiastical property. The princes acquired still more power during the Thirty Years' War and its aftermath, when crisis situations enabled them to break down restraints on their authority previously exercised by their estates and by custom and tradition. In the postwar years, the princes continued to exercise the powers accumulated in wartime, their authority and independence now buttressed by the Treaties of Westphalia.

In 1654 the imperial estates themselves sanctioned the continued maintenance of standing armies through legislation requiring that the residents of a state pay for the maintenance of existing fortresses and for the soldiers needed to garrison them. This legislation was enacted to enable state governments to contribute to the common defense of the empire and, more immediately important, to provide them with armed forces to cope with the immense tasks of restoring order in lands wracked by wartime devastation and social upheaval. These standing armies did indeed play a critical role in the restoration of order and, later, in wars against the Turks and the French. But they also provided German princes with the means of consolidating their power at home and suppressing domestic discontent.

For large and small states alike, however, the fundamental ingredient of absolutism was money: money derived from the powers of taxation accumulated in wartime, from the exploitation of state-owned properties (mines, forests, fisheries), from government monopolies on the sale of commonly used items (salt) or luxury products (coffee, tobacco), from border or transit tolls, from the sponsorship of new industries to stimulate a country's economy. Some German rulers were able to supplement their income through foreign subsidies/bribes in return for their political/military support, and many indulged in the ignominious but immensely profitable practice of selling their subjects as soldiers to foreign governments, a practice known best to Americans through the Hessians in the armies of King George III.[3]

This money paid for the government apparatus through which the princes exercised their power, an apparatus that often functioned badly so that the absolutism of many German princes was anything but absolute. But even in states with corrupt and inefficient bureaucracies, there was still enough money to allow the vast array of Germany's great and petty princes to lead lives of ostentatious luxury and to seek glory and prestige through the splendor of their courts and their patronage of the arts.

Saxony

Patronage of the arts, often on a lavish scale, was a prominent feature at the courts of the many states in the region of Saxony, where Bach was born and lived most of his life. The states of Saxony are also prime examples of the incredible political complexity of the Holy Roman Empire (fig. 0.1, p. 2). This complexity was caused in part by the failure of many German princes to adopt the principle of primogeniture, whereby all their lands go undivided to an eldest son, and their adherence to the old Germanic custom of dividing their lands among all their surviving sons. Such divisions necessarily weakened the states involved and contributed to political instability within the empire.

In the Golden Bull of 1356 setting up an imperial electoral college (see above), the duke of Saxony had been named one of the seven electors of the Holy Roman Empire. Although the Golden Bull had stipulated that the empire's secular electorates should remain indivisible and pass by primogeniture, that principle was abandoned by two brothers of Saxony's ruling House of Wettin, Ernst and Albrecht, whose partition of their heritage in 1485 established the Ernestine and Albertine branches of the Wettin dynasty. The lands that carried with them the electoral title went to Ernst, the elder brother.

In Protestant annals, the most famous of the Ernestine electors was Duke Frederick (surnamed "The Wise"), who during the turbulent days of the Protestant Reformation gave sanctuary to Martin Luther in his Wartburg castle above the city of Eisenach and subsequently made Electoral Saxony a stronghold of the Lutheran faith.

Disaster struck the Ernestine Wettins under the rule of Friedrich's grandson, Johann Friedrich, who had joined a league of Protestant princes to counter the efforts of Emperor Charles V to crush Protestantism in Germany. Although the Albertine Wettins, too, had converted to Protestantism, Duke Moritz, the head of the Albertine branch, had found it expedient to side with the emperor. This political decision paid off handsomely, for in 1547 Charles defeated the Protestants at the Battle of Mühlberg (an equestrian portrait of the emperor on the field of Mühlberg is one of Titian's finest paintings) and electoral Saxony was awarded to the Albertine Moritz. Some years later, angered by the intervention of the emperor on behalf of Saxony's Catholics, Moritz went over to the Protestants—who would subsequently hail him as a champion of German religious liberty.

Only a few territories were left to the unfortunate Johann Friedrich, and on these were founded the Ernestine duchies of Saxony-Gotha, Saxony-Weimar, Saxony-Meiningen, and Saxony-Altenburg. In 1672 a new duchy of Saxony-Eisenach was carved out of Saxony-Weimar, and it was in this duchy that Bach was born thirteen years later.

The policies of Elector Johann Georg (r. 1611–56) during the Thirty Years' War proved disastrous for his Saxon subjects. When, after some hesitation, he took the side of the Protestants, his lands were devastated by imperial troops under Wallenstein, but on going over to the emperor his lands were devastated yet again, this time by the Protestant Swedes. No state of the Holy Roman Empire suffered more than electoral Saxony, which emerged from the conflict with its economy in ruins, its population reduced by one-half, its political influence in the empire weakened by the vacillating policies of its ruler. At his death in 1656, Johann Georg weakened his state still further by assigning electoral Saxony's duchies of Saxony-Weissenfels (where Bach was later honorary music director), Saxony-Merseburg, and Saxony-Zeitz to his three younger sons.

There were no further partitions of electoral Saxony during the reign of the three successors of Johann Georg, all named Johann Georg, and under their rule the Saxon economy slowly recovered. In 1694 the last of these Johann Georgs was succeeded by his brother Friedrich August I, better known as August the Strong, and it was during his reign that Bach came to the electoral Saxony city of Leipzig in 1723.

An enthusiastic patron of the arts, Friedrich August (fig. 1.2a) was to preside over a flowering of the arts in Dresden that transformed this small provincial city into a cultural capital of European stature.

But the new elector was also inordinately ambitious. Not content with the rulership of Saxony, he converted to Catholicism to become eligible for election to the crown of Catholic Poland upon the death of King Jan III Sobieski. Thanks to the support of the Habsburg Emperor Leopold I and lavish bribes to the Polish electors, his candidacy was successful and on September 15, 1697, he was crowned King of Poland as August II (fig. 1.2b).

Eager to extend his Polish dominions (see plates 2 and 3) at the expense of Sweden, he brought Saxony into the Great Northern War, only to be defeated and forced to abdicate the Polish crown. Thanks to the victory of his Russian allies over Sweden in 1709, he was reinstated in Poland, but with his power sorely diminished by the influence of Russia and the resistance of the Polish magnates to his absolutist pretensions.

Friedrich August I died in 1733 and was succeeded by his son, Friedrich August II (plate 15), who emulated his father in his patronage of the arts. Pressured by his father, he too converted to Catholicism to become eligible for election to the crown of Poland. With his candidacy contested by the French, he brought Saxony into the War of the Polish Succession. Once again, the Saxon pretender was saved by the arms of Russia, and in 1734 he was crowned in Cracow as King August III (plate 17), a success Bach was to commemorate in a cantata giving sole credit to the elector for this victory (see p. 100). The power of the new king was even more severely circumscribed than that of his father by the influence of Russia and the Polish nobility. In Saxony, the elector left the conduct of affairs largely in the hands of his ministers, notably Heinrich von Brühl (fig. 1.3), whose name appears on the document naming Bach royal court composer.

Figure 1.2. Becoming Elector of Saxony unexpectedly in 1694, Friedrich August I ("the Strong") was a forceful but not always successful ruler. Hardworking and ambitious, and depicted here (a) in an engraving by Berni-geroth after a painting by Antoine Pesne, he promoted Saxony's economy partly by establishing the famous Meissen porcelain factory, and enhanced Saxony's cultural position through his lavish patronage of the arts. This included an architectural transformation of the capital Dresden as well as the establishment and expansion of numerous royal-electoral collections open to the public, notably that of the famous "Green Vault" with its unrivaled masterpieces of the jeweler's art. Although traditionally he has not fared well in the judgment of historians, he was open to the progressive ideas of the Enlightenment.

August the Strong also sought to increase the stature of Saxony by having his son Friedrich August II (after secretly converting to Catholicism in 1712) marry Maria Josepha, daughter of Emperor Joseph I. His ploy was successful, and after the 1719 Vienna wedding there were four weeks of extravagant celebrations in Dresden (fig. 1.4a, p. 80; fig. 6.8b, p. 214; fig. 6.11, p. 220) that intentionally recalled the spectacular fêtes produced by Louis XIV, whom August sought to emulate. Here (b) a *Te Deum* of thanks is performed in the Catholic chapel of the residential palace, the former opera theater, by members of the Royal-Electoral Chapel, the ancestor of today's Dresden Staatskapelle orchestra. The court musical establishment had been reorganized after August's conversion to Catholicism into a small "Lutheran Court Music" and the much more favored "Royal-Polish and Electoral-Saxon Capella and Chamber Music." The vocal Capella eventually included some of the most famous operatic stars in Europe, while the instrumental "Chamber Music" grew into the finest orchestra of its time. The lack of a proper opera house and of a Catholic church edifice worthy of the king-electors was resolved by the new opera house in the Zwinger (fig. 3.28, p. 165) and, some years later, the Catholic Court Church (*Hofkirche*) (see plate 18).

Saxony was not spared further conflict, for it became involved in the War of the Austrian Succession (1740–48), in the course of which the electorate was repeatedly invaded and occupied by rival armies. It is remarkable that Bach's life and work appear to have been so little affected by these conflicts (but see fig. 1.5).

Anhalt

The principality of Anhalt, where Bach was to be employed before coming to Leipzig, is another example of the Holy Roman Empire's political complexities. Part of Saxony until 1212, it was divided and subdivided, reunited in 1570 under Prince Joachim Ernst, but

Figure 1.3. Heinrich, Count von Brühl, who rose under King August III to be Saxony's first prime minister, was a Thuringian-born diplomat and courtier whose determined ambition took him to the pinnacle of power at the Dresden court, where he became the indispensable counselor to the king-elector and kept titles he had accumulated on the way up (along with their incomes). It was said that he, not the king, ruled Poland and Saxony. It was Brühl who cosigned the document naming Bach royal court composer in Dresden in 1736. Moreover, he proposed his own music director, Gottlob Harrer, as Bach's successor, even before Bach's death, a proposal that the Leipzig city council was unable to refuse (although Harrer satisfied the desired requirements). This is a good example of how Leipzig, although in many respects able to run its civic affairs independent of outside influence, was not immune to the Dresden court's influence on occasion.

divided yet again in 1603 among his five sons into the principalities of Anhalt-Dessau, Anhalt-Bernburg, Anhalt-Plötzkau, Anhalt-Zerbst, and Anhalt-Cöthen.[4] Prince Leopold of Anhalt-Cöthen was to give his principality its small measure of fame through his patronage of Bach. The fame of Anhalt-Zerbst, on the other hand, was achieved through the dynastic marriage market. In 1744 a princess of Anhalt-Zerbst, Sophia Augusta, married the heir to the crown of Russia, who was crowned Czar Peter III in 1762. Six months after his accession, however, he was deposed and murdered. He was succeeded by his wife, who had taken the name of Catherine at the time of her marriage and is known in history as Catherine the Great.

Post-Westphalian Conflicts and Crises

The Peace of Westphalia did not bring lasting peace to the Empire or to Europe. In the century after Westphalia, the states of the Empire were to be engaged in a long succession of wars: with the Turks in the southeast, with the Swedes in the north, with the French in the west, and with each other. Apart from the wars with the Muslim Turks, these were no longer religious wars, much less national or patriotic wars. They were dynastic wars, fought on behalf of claims to particular states or territories on the basis of marriage ties and legal technicalities. Further—and this point cannot be emphasized too strongly for contemporary readers—they were also wars for the sake of war, waged by kings and princes to win immortal fame, to be celebrated as new Alexanders or Caesars, as reincarnations of Mars or Hercules.

The wars of the later seventeenth and eighteenth centuries have been described as more "civilized" than the Thirty Years' War, a change ascribed to the creation of standing armies, the improvement in their discipline, rules and conventions to protect the civilian population, and a decline in religious fanaticism. However, the post-1648 wars were fought on a larger scale than ever before, the battles were brutal and bloody, and the troops could behave with a savagery quite as fierce as in earlier conflicts.

There was nevertheless one decisive difference between the Thirty Years' War and later conflicts. Grim as these were, none of them caused such widespread devastation, nor did they prevent a general economic recovery or a renewed cultivation of the arts. Indeed, in the years after the Treaties of Westphalia there was to be a veritable flowering of the arts in the states of the Holy Roman Empire.

The event that did most to inspire and create conditions for this flowering was the Christian victory over the Turks in 1683 during the second Turkish siege of Vienna. The victory of 1683 proved to be a turning point in the Turkish wars and the beginning of an imperial counter-offensive that was to free the Empire from the Turkish menace and give the Habsburgs control over Hungary and Transylvania (now part of present-day Romania). Wars with the Turks were to continue, but they were now fought at the periphery of the Habsburg lands (fig. 1.4a–d).

By the early eighteenth century, the Swedish threat, too, had been eliminated. In 1709 a Swedish army, which had penetrated far into the vastness of Russia, was annihilated by Peter the Great in the Battle of Poltava. The Swedes never recovered from this defeat, which proved to be the beginning of the end of Swedish dominance in the Baltic.

There remained the threat of France, which, usually in alliance with the Turks and Sweden, was to wage a steady succession of wars against the empire from the 1660s well into the eighteenth century. The treaties ending the last of these, the War of Spanish Succession (1701–14), inaugurated a comparatively lengthy period of peace for the empire, a peace interrupted in 1733 by a war with France over the Polish succession that was to end with the empire's permanent loss of the duchy of Lorraine.

In 1740 the empire was confronted with yet another threat, this time from one of its own members, King Frederick II (the Great) of Brandenburg-Prussia, who launched

Figure 1.4 (*This page and facing*)   **THE TURKISH MODE AT THE DRESDEN COURT**   Although August
the Strong hardly distinguished himself leading imperial and Saxon troops against the Turks in Hungary in
the 1690s, he liked to present himself as a great conqueror of the infidel, creating thereby a veritable Turkish
fashion at court. Moreover, Poland bordered the Osmanish Empire, with which it had diplomatic relations. In
1697 August appeared as the Great Sultan in a festival procession, and in 1719 he transformed the Italian
Garden outside the Dresden city walls into a "Turkish Garden" with a "Turkish Palace" (*a*), where the serv-
ers wore Turkish garb, paintings of women of the court in Middle Eastern dress were hanging on the walls,
and the Polish Kapelle (the musicians who traveled with the King to Poland), also attired *à la Turque*, shared
music-making duties with the band from the king-elector's "Janissary Corps" (made up of tall Saxons in white
and red Muslim dress (*b*). The Corps did not exist continually, but was utilized on special occasions to make
an impression, such as at the 1719 wedding celebrations, visits to or by foreign rulers, or for accompanying
the King to the Leipzig fair.

   Part of the fascination of the East for Europe was the fearsome cruelty, indulgent sensuality, and sheer
exoticism that Muslim culture suggested to their minds. Although the Moor in (*c*) is not fearsome, he does
lend an exotic touch to this Meissen porcelain piece, carrying the coffee (fig. 9.6, p. 279), an everyday reminder of the alluring East.

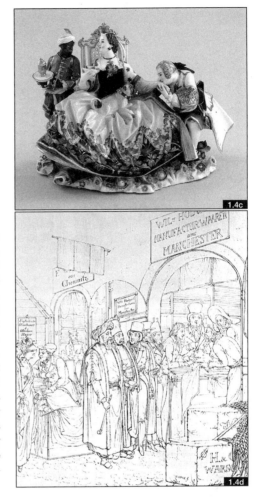

Although certainly considered alien in Bach's world, Turks and Moors were not absent from it. Some were captured in war or received as gifts from Turkish rulers. August the Strong counted among his several mistresses Fatima, a Turk, who bore him two daughters, and Bach's student Johann Caspar Vogler married the daughter of a Turk captured in the siege of Vienna (1683) [H. J. Schulze]. When Turkish converts were baptized, such as occurred from time to time in Leipzig, it was cause for festive celebration. But unconverted Turks also did business in Saxony during Bach's time there and later, as indicated by an early nineteenth-century drawing (d) of some Muslims at the Leipzig fair, still the object of curiosity by boys and perhaps of snide remarks by some of the adults, but nonetheless adding color and an international flavor to the scene.

the equivalent of an imperial civil war with his invasion of the Habsburg province of Silesia. He therewith inaugurated almost a quarter-century of intermittent but devastating warfare—the Wars of the Austrian Succession (1740–48) and the Seven Years' War (1756–63) (fig. 1.5).

Considering the immense investment in blood and treasure by all the powers involved in the wars waged in the century and a half after Westphalia, the size of the armies they were able to field, and the extent of the belligerents' original war aims, these wars did surprisingly little to alter the political configuration of the Holy Roman Empire or its constituent states. The net result of the Empire's wars with France was the definitive loss of Alsace (including the imperial free city of Strassburg) and the duchy of Lorraine, while the wars with Frederick II of Prussia ended with the Habsburg loss of Silesia, a severe but not annihilating blow.[5]

Figure 1.5. Leipzig naturally opposed outside efforts to weaken its position and imperial privileges as a trade-fair city. Especially dangerous was Brandenburg-Prussia, which sought by import-export bans, increased tolls, and even attacks on convoys to undermine Leipzig. This competition even contributed to the Second Silesian War between Frederick the Great's Prussia and Saxony's ally Austria, when Leipzig suffered a month-long occupation by Prussian troops under Prince Leopold of Dessau, shown here accepting on November 30, 1745 the surrender of the city, which had to pay a huge indemnity. That Leipzig residents suffered real hardship is implied in a 1748 letter from Bach to his cousin Johann Elias, in which he refers to "the time we had (alas!) the Prussian Invasion." Fortunately, Bach would not live to see even greater destruction and deprivation at Frederick's hands in the Seven Years' War (1756–63). (Anon. engr., 1745)

The Survival of the Holy Roman Empire: Its Political and Cultural Role

The Holy Roman Empire survived because its Habsburg emperors could draw on the resources of their own domains to defend it, but did not have enough power to transform the Empire into a Habsburg centralized state. It survived because, while safeguarding its member states from Habsburg/imperial control, it protected those states from one another. It survived because the majority of its secular and ecclesiastical states were small and weak, and, without defensive resources of their own, they depended on the empire for their survival and rallied to its defense in times of crisis. Finally, it survived because other powers, notably England, saw the empire as a guardian of their own interests and essential to the maintenance of a European balance of power. Nonetheless, with the awakening of German national self-consciousness, it was subjected to far more intense and bitter criticism by German patriots, who deplored its failure to provide Germany with strong, centralized government, and its consequent inability to defend the country against foreign predators or play a dominant role in European affairs.

Goethe, while acknowledging the empire's political value, reserved his highest praise for the very quality most vilified by eighteenth-century German nationalists, namely, its guardianship of the sovereignty and independence of Germany's wide variety of great and small states. He observed how much German culture owed to the "manifold diversity" of these states, which he saw as patrons and incubators of the arts. "Would they remain what they are if they should lose their sovereign status and be incorporated as provincial entities (*Provinzstädte*) into some kind of greater German Reich?"[6]

The maintenance of this manifold diversity was surely the empire's greatest contribution to Germany's cultural development. The states of the empire had been incubators of the arts long before the Thirty Years' War, and they were to resume that role as their economies recovered during the postwar years despite the frequent disruptions of later conflicts. In contrast to relatively centralized states such as England and France, where artists converged on the capitals of London or Paris, there were literally dozens of German secular, ecclesiastical, and monastic states, as well as imperial and free cities, to serve as sources of cultural patronage.

And they performed that function. Princes of the empire's largest states regarded patronage of the arts as second only to exploits on the battlefield as an avenue to fame. But for the petty German princes, who lacked the power and resources to win glory on the battlefield, patronage of the arts was the sole route to fame, and they vied with one another in attracting the greatest architects, painters, and musicians from every part of Europe to their courts. The majority of these princes, moreover, were genuine lovers of the arts, some of them accomplished artists in their own right, especially in the field of music. Many of them spent extensive time traveling and living in other parts of Europe, and in their role as patrons they sent their most promising native artists abroad for further training. Thanks to this regular cultural interchange, the arts in Germany became increasingly cosmopolitan despite the oppressively parochial nature of most German politics. At these princely courts, artists were not only provided with patronage but with an audience, a society whose members shared similar tastes and cultural values and where the artists themselves were exposed to constant challenge.

Among the most lavish patrons of the arts were the princes of the Church—the bishops, archbishops, and abbots of the great German monasteries, who employed architects and hundreds of painters, sculptors, and masons in building "palaces of faith" and who maintained composers and musicians to add another dimension to their glorification of God (fig. 3.8, p. 148). In Roman Catholic churches, the choir and the organ rivaled the high altar as religious focal points on which to lavish the decorative skills of artists and

Figure 1.6. August III (r. 1733–63) was not a great ruler but he was a great lover of the arts, his tastes having been refined by travel, especially in Italy and France, during the years 1711–19. Here he is greeted as Prince-Elector Friedrich August II by Louis XIV at Fontainebleau in 1714, as depicted by the Saxon court painter Louis de Silvestre *fils* (1675–1760). However, unlike his father, who looked primarily to France as a model, the future elector had more Italianate tastes, and so Italian opera played a significant role in his wedding of 1719 and during his reign, when Court Music Director J. A. Hasse (fig. 8.13, p. 256) made Dresden a European capital of Italian opera. It was to August III, who succeeded his father August the Strong in 1733, that Bach dedicated the *Missa* (Kyrie and Gloria) of what would become the Mass in B Minor) (figs. 0.25 and 0.26, pp. 38–39)"); this accompanied his request to be named Saxon court composer, a title granted in 1736 but without any ensuing commissions.

craftsmen. In most Protestant churches, on the other hand, which stressed simplicity in art and architecture, music was the principal vehicle for the expression of faith and spiritual emotion, although there were Protestant sects (Calvinists, Pietists, Mennonites) that rejected elaborate music on the grounds that it distracted from worship and prayer.

There is a widely accepted view that the Versailles court of Louis XIV was the model for the courts of Germany and that France exercised a predominant influence over German eighteenth-century art and architecture. This was not the case, especially for South German courts in the early decades of the eighteenth century, when wars with France stirred up a positive hostility to all things French and the French language and dress were actually banned at the court of Vienna. In any event, the etiquette and dress of

Figure 1.7. The visits of royalty (or royalty-to-be) to cities and courts were celebrated with extravagant enter-tainments, often of a theatrical nature. Such was the case when the Saxon electoral prince Friedrich August II visited Medici Florence in 1712: the Accademia de Nobili entertained the future King August III and his party with a production of "Mercury of Fame and of Flora." The caption of this illustration in a festival book (Florence, 1712) indicates the participation of trumpeters, fauns playing oboes, and a chorus of shepherds and cupids, as well as the *dramatis personae* that included Mercury with genii, Fame, Flora, and priests of the Temple of Virtue supported by forest creatures, shepherds, and nymphs.

the Viennese court derived from the court of the dukes of Burgundy, where ceremony had been developed into a fine art, and Vienna, not Versailles, was the prime model for most other German courts.

As noted earlier, however, the Habsburg taste and that of most other German princ-es was cosmopolitan, and the Saxon court in Dresden is a good example. August the Strong, in his attempt to emulate Louis XIV, appointed as concertmaster of the Dresden court orchestra in 1708 the Flemish-born, French-trained violinist and dancing master Jean-Baptiste Volumier and also imported French actors and dancers; on the other hand, Volumier was succeeded in 1728 by the J. G. Pisendel, a student of Torelli and Vivaldi. However, the electoral prince Friedrich August II, who traveled to both France and Italy on his grand tour (figs. 1.6, 1.7), was partial to Italian culture and persuaded his father to establish an Italian opera company, though it lasted only from 1717 to 1719 (fig. 3.28, p. 165). Later, from 1731 to 1764, the leadership of Court Music Director Johann Adolf Hasse (fig. 8.13, p. 256), fresh from spectacular successes in Naples, guar-anteed Dresden's reputation as one of Europe's leading centers of Italian opera.[7]

If any foreign artistic influence can be said to have predominated, then it was that of Italy. In their foreign travels, German princes generally lingered longest in Italy, bringing back with them a taste for Italian art and music. Italy was a major source for their recruitment of artists and musicians, and it was usually to Italy that they sent their own artists for further training and experience.[8]

By the early eighteenth century, German artists, while absorbing a variety of foreign influences, were demonstrating talents that brought them to the forefront of their professions and enabled them to secure commissions previously entrusted to foreigners. These artists were the beneficiaries, and in many cases the products, of a long and proud tradition of artisanship cultivated by the German guilds, which maintained meticulous standards in the training and performance of their apprentices. Practitioners of the visual arts thus had available to them a labor force capable of carrying out their plans: stone carvers; masons who could build vaults and arches; painters and sculptors; and workers in stucco, which could be used to make artificial marble, colored to fit into an overall decorative scheme, or molded into sculptures and decorative motifs.

The towering figure of Bach tends to obscure the achievements of his contemporaries in other fields and the fact that in the realm of music, too, there was a profusion of talent in the Baroque era. As was the case with visual artists, German musicians benefited from a heritage of skilled craftsmanship, which for them included the making of musical instruments as well as training in composition and performance. Further, they also profited from the patronage available through the vast array of states and religious institutions in the Holy Roman Empire.

II: Bach and the Politics of Patronage

Although an appreciation of Bach must necessarily focus on his music, the record of his career itself is of great historical interest because of the valuable insights it offers into the institution of patronage in eighteenth-century Germany. For Bach was the recipient of virtually every kind of patronage available to musicians of his era: as a scholarship student at a church school; as a municipal and court organist; as musician, composer, and orchestra director at princely courts; as composer, organizer of sacred music, and musical director of a major city; and finally, as director of a collegium musicum, a group of musicians playing in coffee houses and at civic festivals who were supported by popular audiences, an institution that was to develop into the civic orchestras of the nineteenth century.

In our contemporary view it would seem that, for a burgher like Bach, service to a town or church council composed of men of comparable social standing would be more agreeable and dignified than service to a prince, to whom he would be both subject and servant. In the eighteenth century, however, service at a court carried with it an exalted status and social distinction, and throughout his life Bach was to seek and take pride in his titles as court musician.

Nor was service at a court necessarily more unpleasant or demeaning than service to a church or city council. As Bach was to discover in all the towns in which he was employed, urban authorities could be as exacting and capricious as any prince, and there were many more of them whose wishes had to be observed and whose personal foibles had to be dealt with. Conditions of work for churches and towns were also generally more regimented than at a princely court, as can be seen in their contracts of employment and service. Music at court, on the other hand, was a luxury. Musicians would not be employed at all if the ruler did not enjoy music or if their work did not conform to his desires and tastes, and he frequently spent immense sums to secure the services of a famous or favorite artist. In churches and towns, on the other hand, musicians were required to fulfill specific functions and their employers tried to secure maximum service at minimum cost, although they too might indulge an artist whose talents shed fame on their institutions.

The great risk in service at a court was that everything depended on the person of the prince, or the dominant influences around him. A sadistic ruler could obviously make life unbearable for those who served him, and, if an understanding patron were succeeded by a ruler indifferent or hostile to the arts, the artists at his court might soon find themselves unemployed. Fortunately for the more talented artists, the competition for their services was usually sufficiently great to enable them to find employment elsewhere.

Lüneburg, Arnstadt, Mühlhausen

In 1700, when barely fifteen years of age, Bach was awarded what we today would call a scholarship at St. Michael's School (Michaelisschule) in Lüneburg, an important and still charming Hanseatic town in the North German duchy of Brunswick-Lüneburg (fig. 0.2, p. 3). In Lüneburg, he was given important opportunities to extend his musical horizons, among them the opportunity to hear music performed in the French manner by the court orchestra of Celle, the capital of Brunswick-Lüneburg.

The powerful French influence at the court of Celle was provided by Eleonore d'Olbreuse, the daughter of a French Huguenot refugee, who had come to Celle as Duke Georg Wilhelm's mistress (under a face-saving contractual agreement) in 1665 (plate 10). Although the duke himself favored Italian music, he yielded to Eleonore's influence to bring outstanding French musicians and dancers to Celle, where his orchestra rapidly gained the reputation of being one of the best in Germany. Bach was thus not only introduced to French music, but to French music performed at a high level of professional competence.[9]

In August 1703, after a brief stint in the duchy of Weimar as a member of the court capella, Bach received his first independent post as organist at the New Church (Neuekirche) in the charming little Thuringian town of Arnstadt in the minuscule county (*Grafschaft*) of Schwarzburg-Arnstadt (plate 4). Although his appointment was made in the name of Count Anton Günther, Count of Schwarzburg (plate 6), Bach worked under the direction of a church council (*consistorium*), responsible for performing on the organ on Sundays, feast days, and all occasions of public worship, and for keeping the organ in good repair.

Already at Arnstadt, although only eighteen at the time of his appointment, Bach was to display an independence to-

Figure 1.8. Weimar would enjoy its greatest fame as the center of German literary classicism in the later eighteenth century. In Bach's time it was not so important, the entire duchy of Saxony-Weimar having fewer than fifty thousand inhabitants and Weimar itself about forty-seven hundred, about a third of whom worked at the palace. Weimar had an awkward arrangement of co-regentship that meant that from 1709 Bach and his fellow musicians had to serve two masters who did not get along: the dukes Wilhelm Ernst, who had been reigning since 1683, and his twenty-six-year-old younger nephew Ernst August. Although the capella members were paid out of a joint account, Wilhelm Ernst was very supportive of Bach in the early years, ensuring that his salary was equal to that of the court music director; at the end of Bach's Weimar period, however, it was Ernst August who maintained Bach's special salary supplements.

ward authority that was to characterize his entire life. A notable example of this is when he overstayed by three months, to the great annoyance of the Arnstadt authorities, his four-week leave to go and hear the great Dietrich Buxtehude in Lübeck.[10] Moreover, Bach might have succeeded that master as musical director of St. Mary's Church (*Marienkirche*) (fig. 3.6, p. 147), had he been willing to accept the patronage tradition there. That meant marrying Buxtehude's thirty-year old daughter, Anna Margareta. Apparently Bach was unwilling to do this, perhaps because he was already committed to his second cousin Maria Barbara, whom he would soon marry.

In June 1707, Bach was appointed organist at St. Blaise's Church (Blasiuskirche, fig. 3.7, p. 147) in the free imperial city of Mühlhausen, where he was responsible to a municipal, not a church, council made up of six burgomasters and forty-two councilmen.[11] Here the problem of satisfying a large corporate body was complicated by a rift between orthodox Lutherans and Pietists, who emphasized faith and devotion at the expense of ritual in their religious practices. Bach clearly found the situation in Mühlhausen uncomfortable and artistically unsatisfying, for after only a year in Mühlhausen he was eager to accept the offer of a position at the Lutheran court of Weimar, capital of the small duchy of Saxony-Weimar.[12]

The Weimar Years

The tradition for learning and the arts was well established in Weimar, where Bach had been employed briefly in 1703 as violinist in an orchestra of Duke Johann Ernst, a devoted patron of the arts and a talented amateur musician. The ruler of Weimar at the time of Bach's arrival in 1708, the then forty-six-year-old Duke Wilhelm Ernst, kept up the traditions of his house (fig. 1.9). He founded the famous Bibliotheca Historica in Weimar, the first collection of historical documents and works of history published since the invention of printing, and laid the basis for the equally famous ducal collection of ancient coins and medals. He shared his family's enthusiasm for music, and at the time of Bach's appointment he maintained a capella of about a dozen full-time singers and instrumentalists.

Wilhelm Ernst was also a deeply religious man, who considered it his duty to ensure the spiritual welfare of his subjects, in particular the members of his court. All court officials and servants, including the court musicians, were required to attend one or more church services daily and to participate in them by reading aloud from the Bible and conducting prayers. To make certain that his subjects listened attentively to church

Figure 1.9. Wilhelm Ernst, Duke of Saxony-Weimar, was the senior ruler of the duchy from 1694 until his death in 1728. A despotic absolutist who brooked no opposition from his subjects and employees (including Bach), he nonetheless often acted out of a well-meaning paternalism that found expression in sumptuary laws, the requirement that his guards attend church services, highly controlled manufacturing enterprises, and a concern for education. In 1715 he appointed Johann Mathias Gesner, later Bach's superior as rector of St. Thomas's School in Leipzig, conrector of the Weimar Gymnasium.

sermons, the duke examined them minutely on the subject and meaning of
these pious discourses. The court itself
was run with puritan austerity, and the
duke personally supervised the conduct
of its personnel. Punctually at eight in
the evening during the winter and only
an hour later in the summer, all court
activity ceased, the kitchens and cellars
were closed, all lights were extinguished,
and the servants were sent to bed. The
duke's moral solicitude did not stop
with his court but was extended to the
citizens of his duchy, for whom he laid
down regulations in 1715 for the dress of
the various classes, their food, and the
music to be performed at weddings and
secular festivals (fig. 1.10).

Because Duke Wilhelm Ernst val-
ued music as a means of glorifying the
Lord, Bach occupied a distinguished
and favored place at the Weimar court.
But in Weimar as in Mühlhausen he
did not escape the unpleasantness of in-
fighting among his patrons. The trouble
in Weimar stemmed from the fact that
the duchy had not adopted the rule of
primogeniture and that Wilhelm Ernst
was obliged to share the rulership with
his nephew, Ernst August, who came of
age in 1709 (fig. 1.11). From that time, the
rivalry between uncle and nephew created difficulties for all members of the
ducal court, even though the two rulers
maintained separate domestic establish-

Figure 1.10. The first original vocal composition by
Bach to have been discovered in seventy years (in
2005) is the soprano aria *Alles mit Gott und nichts
ohn' ihn* (Everything with God and nothing without
Him) (BWV 1127), the opening line being a translation
of Duke Wilhelm Ernst's Latin motto *Omnia cum deo
et nihil sine eo*. The cleverly constructed twelve stanzas contain the acrostic WJLHELM ERNST (embodied in the first letter of the third word of each stanza).
Although probably performed in the Weimar castle's
"Himmelsburg" chapel (fig. 3.10, p. 150), this work is
a rare piece of secular vocal music from Bach's Weimar period. Since there is no documentation linking
the poet, Johann Mylius of Buttstadt, to Bach, then
(1713) the Weimar court organist, it is not known why
Bach was chosen to compose the text, a birthday gift
from Mylius to the Duke. Although the birthday was
celebrated in Weimar while the Duke was away, the
text was published and Bach, coincidentally or not,
was promoted to concertmaster the next year with
composing obligations.

ments. For Bach, who had only taken up his post in Weimar in 1708, the situation was
especially complicated because Ernst August's love of music resulted in attempts to
lure his uncle's musicians, including Bach, to his own establishment. To prevent their

ERNEST AUGUSTE,
Duc Regnant de
Saxe Weimar,
&c. &c. &c.

Figure 1.11. Ernst August, Duke of Saxony-Weimar, was the junior coruler (from 1709) during Bach's tenure in Weimar. He is treated more sympathetically than his uncle Wilhelm Ernst by Bach biographers because of his greater affinity with the composer. This notwithstanding, Ernst August was also a cruel and ambitious man with a yearning for power and fame. In order to be named general, for example, he formed several regiments of troops for the Emperor, forcing his subjects—who, if they merely stole fruit, could be executed by strangulation—into hazardous military service. In the end, Ernst August turned out not to be a friend of music either, for in 1735 he dissolved the court musical establishment. Perhaps this was brought on by huge earlier expenditures for over twenty park-palaces, hunting lodges, and fortifications, not to mention the cost of maintaining over eleven hundred hunting dogs and several hundred horses.

defection, Wilhelm Ernst forbade his musicians to attend the court of his nephew. With characteristic independence, Bach not only evaded this order but provided the music for Ernst August's wedding in 1716.

The same year, following the death of the music director at the Weimar court, Bach applied for the position and was clearly disappointed when Duke Wilhelm Ernst, after first offering it to Telemann, bestowed it on the deceased music director's son, whom Bach regarded as an inferior talent. That rebuff, together with the unpleasantness caused by the ducal rivalry, may have decided Bach to resign his position in Weimar and accept an offer from Prince Leopold, ruler of the tiny principality of Anhalt-Cöthen, to serve as conductor of his court orchestra. But an infuriated Duke Wilhelm Ernst at first refused to release Bach and went so far as to place him under detention for almost a month "for too stubbornly forcing the issue of his dismissal" before letting him go.[13]

Bach's connection with the court of Cöthen appears to have begun at the time of Duke Ernst August's marriage in January 1716 to the widowed Duchess Eleonore Wilhelmine of Saxony-Meiningen, the sister of the reigning Prince Leopold of Anhalt-Cöthen. Described by her contemporaries as a woman of exceptional intelligence and cultivation, she shared her husband's delight in music. She stood godmother to the last of Bach's children by Maria Barbara and it was she who presumably brought Bach to the attention of her brother, Prince Leopold.

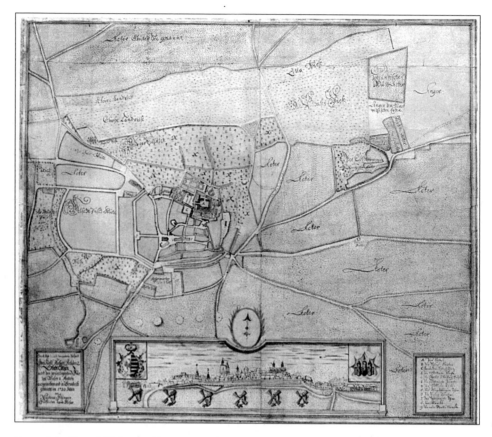

Figure 1.12. Plan of Cöthen, residence of the Prince Leopold of Anhalt-Cöthen. Anhalt-Cöthen was one of several principalities in the larger dominion of Anhalt (fig. 0.1, p. 2, upper right), which was located between Saxony to the south and more influential Prussia to the north. Cöthen itself was a small, provincial town, as this plan by Nicolaus Hitzinger (ca. 1730) certainly shows, but for Bach it meant becoming *Hofcapellmeister* (court music director), the highest office he ever enjoyed, and working for someone he truly liked and appreciated.

Anhalt-Cöthen

In contrast to Weimar, Cöthen is almost unknown to students of German culture or to tourists. It is not listed at all in the 1980 *Schatzkammer Deutschland*, and a 1909 Baedecker mentions it only as containing a technical institute and several sugar and chemical factories. Eduard Vehse, the redoubtable early nineteenth-century chronicler of the German courts, described Anhalt-Cöthen as one of the most forlorn regions of Germany, and he quotes a contemporary visitor's observation that, "apart from hymnals and Bibles, there were no other books to be found."[14] Indeed, the epithet "Kuh-Cöthen" (cow-Cöthen) was dismissively applied to the place (fig. 1.12, plate 9).

Yet Cöthen, too, had had rulers who in the past had raised their tiny state to a position of some cultural significance. Prince Ludwig, the first of the Cöthen branch of the house of Anhalt, who died in 1650, was an educated and well-traveled man. He was the founder of the *Fruchtbringende Gesellschaft*, a society dedicated to establishing a "pure" form of the German language and to refining German customs and manners. In connection with his interest in language, he became a patron of the eminent philologist Wolfgang Ratich, for whom he built a printing press in Cöthen capable of printing books in six languages.

Unlike Bach's previous patrons, the rulers of Cöthen were members of the Calvinist branch of the Protestant church, but Prince Leopold's father, Emanuel Leberecht, had not been bigoted in matters of religion. He had married a Lutheran, Gisela Agnes von Rath, a member of the lesser nobility and thus far below her husband in rank. For love of her (and perhaps prodded by her), he built a Lutheran church in Cöthen and granted Lutherans freedom of religion, a display of religious toleration that aroused the wrath of his more rigid Calvinist subjects. He also allowed his wife to found a Lutheran school in Cöthen that was later attended by Bach's children.

Upon the death of her husband in 1704, Gisela Agnes served as regent until her son came of age in December 1715. A cultivated, intelligent, but determined woman, she relaxed the severe Calvinist discipline that had prevailed heretofore at the Cöthen court, but at the same time she practiced a strict economy, which included cutting off the funds for the small orchestra assembled by her husband (plate 12). Leopold, her oldest son, was only ten years old when his father died but already showed signs of unusual musical talent. By 1707 he had become sufficiently skilled as a bass viol player to persuade his mother to employ three musicians for performances of chamber music. In that same year, however, the staunchly Calvinist king of Prussia, Friedrich I, to whom Emanuel Leberecht had entrusted the guardianship of his son, arranged that the prince be sent to the Ritterakademie (school for the nobility) in Berlin, presumably to ensure that he received a proper Calvinist education.[15]

In Berlin, Prince Leopold's interest in music was nourished by performances of the excellent orchestra maintained by Friedrich I, an interest cultivated further during a three-year Grand Tour that took him to the Netherlands, London, Vienna, and the art capitals of Italy. In the Netherlands, he took particular interest in the works of the seventeenth-century French composer Jean-Baptiste Lully. As was the case with so many German princes, however, he was especially enthralled by Italy and spent a large part of his Grand Tour in that country, learning Italian and collecting Italian artifacts and musical scores.

Upon his return to Cöthen in 1713, Prince Leopold immediately set about assembling an orchestra of his own. It was an opportune time for doing so, for Friedrich Wilhelm, the notorious Prussian soldier-king who had just succeeded to the crown of Prussia, dissolved the Berlin orchestra, having no use for what he considered the frivolities of his father. Prince Leopold proceeded to enroll seven members of the Berlin troupe in his own orchestra, which he enlarged to eighteen when he came of age three years later.

Figure 1.13. Because a past ruler had ensured that
Brandenburg would be inherited undivided through
primogeniture, Christian Ludwig ruled no territory
but was Margrave of Brandenburg, a title first established 1157 to designate the ruler of the Mark
or March (i.e., a frontier territory) of Brandenburg in
northeastern Germany. In 1252 the Margrave was
designated an imperial elector, and in 1415 the
electorate of Brandenburg passed to the Hohenzollern family, which ruled it until 1918. When Prussia
was inherited by the elector Johann Sigismund in
1618, the territorial basis of a potential great power
was achieved. This led to the declaration of the
Kingdom of Prussia in 1701 by Elector Friedrich III
(= King Friedrich I of Prussia, r. 1701–13), which included the electorate of Brandenburg with the capital at Berlin. He was succeeded by King Friedrich
Wilhelm I (r. 1713–40), in whose palace his younger
brother, the Margrave Christian Ludwig, lived and
on whose largess the Margrave depended.

Thus, when Bach took over the position of music director at the court of Cöthen, he
found a body of skilled and well-trained musicians at his disposal.

In Prince Leopold, Bach had a patron who not only loved music but evoked Bach's
praise for his musical understanding (plate 11). The prince also appears to have been
an accomplished musician in his own right. As conductor of the court orchestra, Bach
enjoyed a high social status at Cöthen, and his salary of four hundred thalers a year was
higher than all but one official in the government.

Despite this supportive environment, however, Bach appears to have grown restless
in Cöthen, especially after the death in 1720 of his first wife, Maria Barbara. Later that
same year he applied for the position of organist at the St. Jacobi Church in Hamburg, a
position he did not win because he was unable, and unwilling, to donate to the church
the substantial sum that was evidently expected of the successful candidate.

In March 1721, two years after being asked for some of his compositions by the margrave
of Brandenburg (the half-brother of Friedrich I of Prussia and uncle of the soldier-king
Friedrich Wilhelm I), Bach sent him a collection of pieces for various instruments (the
Brandenburg Concertos, BWV 1046–51) with a letter of dedication expressing the hope
that he would continue to enjoy the margrave's favor and that he might again be employed
in his service (fig. 1.13). "Nothing is so close to my heart as the wish that I may be employed
on occasions more worthy of Your Royal Highness."[16] Bach's wish remained unfulfilled.
The margrave did not employ him or even acknowledge receipt of the concertos.[17]

Late in the year 1722 Bach applied for and was eventually awarded the position
of cantor at St. Thomas's School in Leipzig, which had fallen vacant with the death

of Johann Kuhnau on June 5, 1722. Bach's hesitation in applying may have been due to more than his reluctance to move to a socially inferior position. His situation at Cöthen had become more agreeable following his marriage in December 1721 to Anna Magdalena Wilcke (or Wülcken), one of the professional singers employed by Prince Leopold. After her marriage to Bach, the prince increased her annual salary from two hundred to three hundred thalers, making her one of the highest-paid members of his court. There is also considerable reason to doubt that the prince's marriage to an "un-musical" princess, or any other unpleasantness Bach had experienced at Cöthen, had played a major role in his decision to leave. Music-making continued at Cöthen after Bach's departure, his relations with the prince remained as friendly as before, and he returned at least three times, twice with Anna Magdalena, to perform with his former orchestra. He proudly retained his title of court music director to His Royal Highness, the Prince of Anhalt-Cöthen, and was called upon to provide the music for the prince's funeral in March 1729, four months after his death.

Why then did Bach leave Cöthen? In his meticulously detailed biography of Bach, Philipp Spitta wrote that "the post of cantor to the town-school of St. Thomas at Leipzig was not a brilliant one," although "those who were familiar with its conditions knew that it had certain valuable advantages." Spitta's description of conditions at St. Thom-as's School, however, make the position sound thoroughly unattractive. The school had been in decline since early in the century, the number of students had dropped pre-cipitously, the teaching staff was riddled with dissension and jealousy, the scholars had fallen into slovenly and undisciplined habits, the school building was unhealthy, and the headmaster (rector), Johann Heinrich Ernesti, who had held the post for almost forty years, had stoutly resisted all pressures and proposals for reform.[18]

Yet the fact remains that some of Germany's most eminent musicians applied for the position, including men who had lived for some time in Leipzig and could have had no illusions about the job. For them the attractions of the city of Leipzig itself must have outweighed any reservations they may have had about the school. This must surely have been true of Bach as well. As he had acknowledged to his friend Erdmann, he wanted to provide his sons with better educational opportunities. But he must also have wanted a position for himself where there would be broader scope for his own talents and where the composition and performance of music for the church would again be central to his professional obligations.[19]

Leipzig

At the time of Bach's arrival, Leipzig had become one of Europe's most flourishing intel-lectual and commercial centers (fig. 0.8, p. 11; fig. 3.18, p. 157; plate 14). The great Leipzig trade fairs, held three times a year since the Peace of Westphalia, were at the height of their popularity and prosperity, and the quantity and quality of the goods displayed there evoked the general astonishment of visitors. These fairs earned enormous profits for the city and for the government of Saxony, and during the fair weeks Leipzig became the equivalent of Venice as a rendezvous for the princes and nobility of northern Germany.

In the late seventeenth century, Leipzig supplanted the imperial free city of Frankfurt am Main as the center of the German book trade (the publishing business in Frankfurt had been badly hurt by imperial censorship). With the decline of Frankfurt, the publishing houses in Leipzig began the development that would make them among the most distinguished in the world, an eminence they retained until the twentieth century. Leipzig became a major literary center as well with the founding in 1727 of a Leipzig literary society (the Deutsche Gesellschaft or German Society) by Johann Christoph Gottsched (fig. 0.18, p. 25, and fig. 5.2, p. 197) dedicated to eliminating the pompousness and bombast prevalent in German literature at that time.[20] Although called the "inventor of boredom" by one of his contemporaries, Gottsched has nevertheless been credited with reforms of the German language that were to give Leipzig the reputation of being the cradle of German literature. Leipzig had also become a major center for the publication of music from every part of Europe, and for Bach the ready availability of musical texts must have been another of the city's more prominent attractions.

As mentioned earlier, at the time of Bach's arrival in Leipzig, the ruler of Saxony was Elector Friedrich August I (1694–1733), better known as August the Strong, whether for his prodigious physical strength or for his sexual prowess. Lady Mary Wortley Montagu tells the story of how he declared his love for one of his many mistresses by bringing one hundred thousand crowns in one hand and a horseshoe in the other "which he snapped asunder before her face, leaving her to draw the consequences of such remarkable proofes of Strength and Liberality."[21]

Both August the Strong and his son Friedrich August II ruled Leipzig from their capital at Dresden but left a large measure of authority to a municipal council made up of the city's most powerful and prosperous citizens. This council controlled not only the city's politics and commerce but all aspects of its artistic life, from the design of buildings and parks, to the selection of artists and musicians, to the sequence of church services and the music to be performed during the trade fairs.

The cantorate—the third-ranked position at St. Thomas's School—may not have been "brilliant," but it was sufficiently important to be the subject of a typical game of power politics between rivals on the Leipzig city council that sought to secure the appointment of their respective candidates. As is well known, Bach was not the first or even the second or third choice of the Leipzig authorities for the position. Given that

Bach is now regarded as the supreme musician of his era, the question has long been raised as to why he seems to have been so lightly regarded by the Leipzig selection committee. The members of the committee, however, were basing their judgments on the current reputation of the applicants and their (differing) ideas of the position. Bach was less well known than the candidates who ranked above him in the committee's selection process. Further, he lacked the teaching credentials deemed essential by a powerful faction of the city council that emphasized the importance of the teaching over the musical side of the position; moreover, he was an organist, not an established composer of opera such as other councilmen desired. In view of these factional differences, the remarkable thing is that in the end the only candidates to be seriously considered were those whose reputations were based on their qualifications as musicians.

The first choices of the committee were Georg Philipp Telemann (who turned down the position before Bach applied for it), Johann Friedrich Fasch, and Johann Christoph Graupner. All three were more famous than Bach, all three had the advantage of having studied and performed music in Leipzig, and all were well known to the selection committee. Telemann and Graupner, however, were unable to obtain a release from their positions and were handsomely compensated by increases in salary. Fasch, who had recently accepted the position of music director to the princely court of Anhalt-Zerbst, informed the selection committee that he would be unable to assume the burden of teaching in addition to his other duties. The entire business of Fasch's candidacy remains vague, however, because the records of his negotiations with Leipzig have been lost.

Meanwhile, Bach's music at his trial audition had so impressed the city authorities that he was now favored over other candidates and was unanimously elected by the selection committee.[22] In April 1723 Bach secured his release from Prince Leopold (with "highest recommendation for service elsewhere"),[23] and on May 22 two carriages and four wagons brought his family and their possessions to their new lodging at St. Thomas's School.

Bach's responsibilities as cantor of St. Thomas's School and director of music for the city of Leipzig are detailed in chapter 9. In these official capacities, Bach reported to three separate authorities: the ecclesiastic consistory, the Leipzig city council, and the rector and board of directors of the school. The officials of all three authorities, major and minor, insisted on full recognition of their vested rights and authority. They were in constant conflict among themselves and their orders were frequently inconsistent and contradictory. Small wonder that Bach found his new position far from easy.

Bach's first years at St. Thomas's School were made relatively agreeable by his good relationship with its rector, Johann Heinrich Ernesti, who, as noted earlier, had been at his post almost forty years and had successfully resisted all proposals for change or reform. But he did not attempt to impose his ideas on Bach or otherwise interfere in his musical performances. Bach had a far closer and more satisfactory relationship with Johann Matthäus Gesner, who succeeded Ernesti in 1729. Gesner was a firm believer in the importance of music in the school curriculum and an ardent admirer of Bach. Much as he cherished the arts of classical antiquity in all other respects, Gesner wrote, "the accomplishments of our Bach" could not be matched by any number of Orpheuses. Bach's situation at the school changed for the worse when Gesner left Leipzig in 1734 to become professor of poetry at Göttingen and was succeeded as rector by Johann August Ernesti (no relation to the previous Ernesti), a champion of the educational theories associated with the Enlightenment. He advocated a modernization of the curriculum, with emphasis on such "useful subjects" as science and mathematics, leaving little room for music, which he regarded as an actual impediment to the study of more practical matters (fig. 1.14).

Bach's clashes with Ernesti are among the more unsavory episodes of his career, but he had been engaged in conflicts with authority since his first appointment in Arnstadt, and in Leipzig his quarrels with officialdom had begun virtually from the time of his arrival. Bach was far from blameless in these quarrels. He caused what appears to have been quite unnecessary friction in defending his prerogatives in dealing with the governors of the University of Leipzig as well as with the Leipzig city council. But the most serious controversies of his tenure arose over musical performances, his dislike of teaching and working with mediocre students, and his anger over the lack of support provided by secular and ecclesiastical officials.

At its meeting of August 2, 1730, the city council complained of Bach's frequent absences without permission, his failure to provide adequately for his teaching duties, and other unspecified lapses. Worse still, Bach had not even deigned to answer the council's charges and explain his conduct. What he did instead was to present the council with a memorandum, "A Short but Most Necessary Draft Proposal for the Proper Performance of Music for the Church, with Some Modest Observations on its Decline." There followed a detailed description of what was needed for an adequate performance, and a complaint about the inadequacy of the musicians at his disposal. Far too many boys with no talent for music had been admitted to the school, with the result that musical performances had deteriorated. Further, instead of increasing the school's few merit scholarships, the council had withdrawn them altogether. Bach concluded with an evaluation of the musical abilities of the school's pupils: "Total: 17 usable, 20 not yet usable, and 17 unfit."[24]

To bolster his prestige in dealing with the Leipzig authorities, Bach clung to the title of honorary court music director conferred on him by Prince Leopold of Anhalt-Cöthen, and after the death of Leopold he was awarded a similar title by Duke Christian

Figure 1.14. Johann August Ernesti was rector of St. Thomas's School (1734–59), succeeding Bach's friend and supporter Johann Matthäus Gesner at age twenty-seven. For his installation Bach composed the now lost cantata *Thomana saß annoch betrübt* (BWV Anh. 19). Arriving in Leipzig in 1728, Ernesti changed his career goals from preacher to educator, and came under the protection of the Leipzig mayor Christian Ludwig Stieglitz, who made him conrector at St. Thomas's School in 1731. Under his leadership St. Thomas's School flourished academically. Subsequently, Ernesti assumed a chair of theology at the University of Leipzig, where he had long lectured on classical Greek and Latin writers, as exemplified by his edition of Tacitus pictured here. His influence on education in the region was long-lived through his Saxon School Regulations, which remained in force from 1773 to 1847. The disputes between Bach and Ernesti (who did not see music as essential to the curriculum) have often obscured Ernesti's genuine distinction and accomplishments.

of Saxony-Weissenfels. Finding that this title availed him little, he appealed to his immediate ruler, the elector of Saxony, to be awarded a more prestigious title.

In an obsequious letter of July 27, 1733, to Elector Friedrich August II, typical of communications with sovereigns of that era, Bach complained that he had been the innocent victim of one injury after another in his present position, but all such affronts would end if he were awarded a royal title and issued a document to that effect. In deepest devotion, he was sending his sovereign an "insignificant example" of the skill he had achieved in *musique*, hoping that His Majesty would look upon it with his "Most Gracious Eyes" and his "World Famous Clemency." Such a gracious fulfillment of his humble prayer, Bach concluded, "will bind me to unending devotion, and I offer myself in most indebted obedience to show at all times . . . my untiring zeal in the composition of music for the church as well as for the orchestra, and to devote all my powers to the service of Your Highness."[25] The "insignificant example" of his musical skill was the Kyrie and Gloria (BWV 232^I) that would later be combined with other movements to form what we now call his B Minor Mass (BWV 232), one of the supreme musical works of all time.

Bach, that fervent Lutheran, was obviously not deterred by the Catholicism of his sovereigns from appealing for their support or from seeking appointment to their court in Dresden. It is even possible that what became the B Minor Mass, with a Latin rather than German text, was intended as a compromise religious statement.

Nothing came of Bach's petition of July 17, although he wrote three cantatas (BWV Anh. 12, 213, and 214) later that same year to honor the new elector and members of his family and two more in 1734, the first (BWV 205a) to celebrate the elector's coronation in Cracow as King August III of Poland, a second (BWV 215) to commemorate the anniversary of his election to the Polish crown and his victory in the War of the Polish Succession. In all, Bach is known to have written a dozen cantatas in honor of the Dresden court, performed mainly by Bach's Collegium Musicum in Leipzig.

That second cantata (*Preise dein Glücke, gesegnetes Sachsen*, BWV 215), performed on October 5, 1734 in front of the "King's House" (fig. 3.20, p. 159) in the marketplace with six hundred torch-bearing Leipzig university students present, is another example of the adulation of royalty typical of this absolutist era, in this case praise for a king who owed his political and military success in Poland in large measure to the support of Russia, which had borne the brunt of the fighting. The cantata text, by a Leipzig schoolmaster named Johann Christoph Clauder, called upon "blessed Saxony" to praise its good fortune, because God supports the throne of its king, enhances its prosperity, and ensures the security of its borders. Through Friedrich August II's election as king of Poland, all the northern lands had been pacified, and through the fiery spirit of his arms he had also dealt with the power of the French, who had so often threatened "our fatherland" with fire and sword. The text may be ludicrous, but the music is splendid and we are told by a contemporary observer that His Majesty listened to it "most graciously."[26]

Bach was finally awarded the title of court composer in November 1736 in response to a second petition, but he was never offered a position at the Dresden court—or even a commission. As mentioned above, August III already had as his music director one of Europe's most eminent composers of Italian opera, Johann Adolf Hasse. Hasse possessed the additional advantage of being married to Faustina Bordoni, widely celebrated as the most accomplished as well as the most beautiful singer of her day. Against such an array of reputations Bach was unable to compete. He remained for the rest of his life in Leipzig, where all the annoyances to which he was exposed did not prevent him from continuing to produce some of the greatest music ever conceived by the human spirit.

Notes

1. All the Holy Roman Emperors during Bach's lifetime were Habsburgs except Charles VII (1742–45), the Wittelsbach elector of Bavaria, who took advantage of the extinction of the male line of the Austrian Habsburgs to claim the imperial title in the name of his wife, the younger daughter of Emperor Joseph I (1705–11). In 1736 the Habsburg heiress, Maria Theresa, had married Francis Stephen of Lorraine, who was elected to succeed Charles VII as Emperor Francis I in 1745. With Maria Theresa's marriage to Francis, the House of Habsburg became the House of Habsburg-Lorraine. Already in 1738, however, the French had compelled Francis to exchange the duchy of Lorraine for Milan, whereby Lorraine was permanently lost to the Holy Roman Empire. See note 5.

2. By "estates" is meant the political classes of the Empire—electors, other princes, and imperial cities—represented in the imperial assembly or Reichstag; after 1663 the Reichstag met at Regensburg.

3. Another example, directly relevant to Bach's world, is that many European rulers, knowing the passion of King Friedrich Wilhelm I of Prussia for tall soldiers, gave him such as presents (which were, of course, reciprocated with other gifts). Thus August the Strong sent twelve of these *lange Kerls* to Prussia in 1720 and, in 1717, presented the "soldier-king" with six hundred Saxon dragoons (hand-picked by a Prussian general), in return for which he received over one hundred pieces of rare porcelain. The exchange reflects both Friedrich Wilhelm I's disinterest in the arts—he disbanded the orchestra (some members of which ended up in Bach's orchestra in Cöthen, see below) and gave away much of what had been the finest porcelain collection in Europe—and August II's enthusiasm for collecting. August had a special passion for porcelain: he established the Meissen porcelain manufactory in 1710. Samuel Wittwer, "*Liaisons Fragiles*: Exchange of Gifts Between Saxony and Prussia in the Early Eighteenth Century," *Fragile Diplomacy: Meissen Porcelain for European Courts ca. 1710–63*, exhibition catalog, ed. Maureen Cassidy-Geiger, Bard Graduate Center for Studies in the Decorative Arts, Design, and Culture (New York and London: Yale University Press, 87–109, esp. 89–91). Worth noting is that if Johann Christoph Gottsched had not fled Prussia, because his height would have led to his induction into the army, Leipzig, where he eventually settled, would have been bereft of its single most important intellectual force during the Bach period. —Ed.

4. Bach's activity was not limited to the courts at which he had official positions, such as Anhalt-Cöthen. For example, he composed a birthday cantata for the Prince of Anhalt-Zerbst in 1722. See Barbara Reul, "'O vergnügte Stunden / da mein Hertzog funden seinen Lebenstag': Ein unbekannter Textdruck zu einer Geburtstagskantate J. S. Bachs für den Fürsten Johann August von Anhalt-Zerbst," *Bach Jahrbuch* 85 (1999): 7–17.

5. Alsace and Strassburg were permanently lost to France through the Treaty of Ryswick of October 30, 1697, ending the War of the League of Augsburg against Louis XIV; Lorraine was permanently lost through the Treaty of Vienna of November 18, 1738, ending the War of the Polish Succession, which placed Lorraine under the rule of Louis XV's father-in-law but provided for its annexation to France after his death; Silesia was permanently lost to Austria through the Treaty of Hubertusburg of February 15, 1763, which ended the Seven Years' War.

6. Cited in Wolfgang Braunfels, *Die Kunst im Heiligen Römischen Reich Deutscher Nation*, 8 vols. (Munich: C. H. Beck, 1979–), 1: 14.

7. On the Italian influence in Baroque Dresden, see *Elbflorenz. Italienische Präsenz in Dresden 16.–19. Jahrhundert*, ed. Barbara Marx (Dresden: Verlag der Kunst, 2000), especially Michael Walter, "Italienische Musik als Repräsentationskunst der Dresdener Fürstenhochzeit von 1719," 177–202, which discusses fig. 3.28a–b (p. 165).

8. French influence grew appreciably after Frederick the Great's invasion of Silesia in 1740, when Prussia took the place of France as the principal enemy of the Habsburgs. French was the native language of Francis of Lorraine (Emperor Francis I), the beloved husband of the Habsburg heiress Maria Theresa; Francis never learned to speak adequate German.

9. By the time of Bach's arrival, the atmosphere at the court of Celle was clouded by melodrama and tragedy. The daughter and heiress of Duke Georg Wilhelm and Eleonore d'Olbreuse, Sophie Dorothea, had married her cousin, Georg Ludwig, heir to the duchy of Brunswick-Calenberg, which in 1692 was elevated to the status of an imperial electorate and took the name of its capital city, Hanover. Neglected by her husband, she had become involved in a passionate love affair (to judge from her letters) with a dashing Swedish nobleman named Philipp von Königsmarck. They evidently planned to elope, but on the night of July 1, 1694, Philipp disappeared under circumstances that remain controversial, though there can be little doubt that he was murdered.

   With the evidence of his wife's infidelity revealed by her letters, Georg Ludwig divorced her (on the grounds of desertion, to preserve the good name of their children) and had her confined in the castle of Ahlden, only four miles from Celle, where she languished until her death thirty-two years later. Her husband and children had a better and more illustrious fate. In 1713 Georg Ludwig, now elector of Hanover, succeeded to the crown of Great Britain as King George I (through his mother Sophia, a granddaughter of King James I). Georg Ludwig's son by Sophie Dorothea succeeded his father as King George II of Great Britain, and their daughter, also called Sophie Dorothea, married the "soldier-king" of Prussia, Friedrich Wilhelm I. This second Sophie Dorothea was to be the mother of Frederick the Great and his talented sister, Wilhelmine of Bayreuth, who were thus the grandchildren of the illegitimate union of Georg Wilhelm of Brunswick-Lüneburg and Eleonore d'Olbreuse.

10. *NBR*, 46–48 (*BD* 2, no. 16f., pp. 19–21). I have altered some of the *NBR* editors' English translations.

11. As an imperial city, Mühlhausen was ruled in principle by the emperor; that it was "free" meant that the emperor allowed it essentially to govern itself.

12. *NBR*, 57 (*BD* 1, no. 1, pp. 19f.).

13. *Ibid.*, 80 (*BD* 2, no. 84, p. 65).

14. Eduard Vehse, *Geschichte der deutschen Höfe*, 44 vols. (Hamburg, 1851–59) 17: 305.

15. This guardianship was instituted to ward off the possibility that the succession of his children by Gisela Agnes would be challenged because she had not been his equal in rank. On Gisela Agnes, see Thorsten Heese, "Gisela Agnes von Anhalt-Köthen, geb. von Rath—die Fürstmutter des Bach-Mäzens," *Cötherer Bach-Hefte* 10 (2002):141–80.

16. *NBR*, 92f. (*BD* 1, no. 150, pp. 216f.) The dedication was written in French.

17. The immaculate condition of Bach's autograph score when it was discovered in Berlin after his death, the Prussian soldier-king's notorious parsimony in dealing with his family, and the fact that only six musicians provided the music for the margrave's funeral in 1734 have led to the assumption by some that the concertos were never performed in Berlin because the margrave lacked an orchestra capable of playing them.

This assumption is challenged by scholars who have discovered that the king allowed his uncle the margrave to remain in residence at the Prussian court and endowed him with two landed estates that gave him an annual income of almost fifty thousand thalers. The music-loving margrave thus had ample funds to maintain an excellent orchestra, and he was reputed to have spent a substantial part of that income on music and musicians. Further, there is no evidence that the Bach concertos were *not* performed at the margrave's court. The immaculate condition of the Bach score proves nothing, because individual instrumental parts would have been made for purposes of performance. And the fact that only six musicians performed at the margrave's funeral does not mean that these were the only musicians in his household.

In the end, however, we are left with the question as to why the margrave never acknowledged receipt of the works that now bear his name. We are also left with the fact that Bach's autograph with the dedication to the margrave was not found until many years after Bach sent it to Berlin, nor were the concertos listed in the inventory of the margrave's music library, which after his death was divided among five members of the Prussian royal family. The score subsequently came into the possession of Bach's former student Johann Philipp Kirnberger, who had entered the service of the Prussian court and presumably discovered them in the Prussian archives. Kirnberger left the greater part of his music library, including the Bach concertos, to Princess Amalia of Prussia (1739–1807), whose own extensive musical collection eventually became part of the Prussian Royal Library. Philipp Spitta, *Johann Sebastian Bach. His Work and Influence on the Music of Germany, 1685–1750* (repr. of 1884) English translation of German 3-vol. original (1873–1881) (London: Novello and New York: Dover Publications, 1951) 2: 128; Heinrich Besseler, "Markgraf Christian Ludwig von Brandenburg," *BJ* 43 (1956): 18–35; Malcolm Boyd, *Bach: The Brandenburg Concertos* (Cambridge: Cambridge University Press, 1993), 9–11 and 17f.

18. Spitta, *op. cit.* 2: 181, 200–213.

19. Numerous other theories have been put forward for Bach's decision to leave Cöthen: his unhappiness about the running feud between Prince Leopold and his mother; the prince's reversion to a strict Calvinism, which obliged Bach to have his son baptized according to Calvinist ritual; the failure of the prince to keep up the strength of his court orchestra. The baptism of Bach's son in the court chapel of Cöthen, however, was surely regarded by Bach as a sign of princely favor, for Prince Leopold, his brother, and his sister (the grand duchess of Weimar) stood as godparents to the child, who was named after the two princes, Leopold Augustus. The most convincing argument that conditions at Cöthen played an important role in Bach's decision to leave was his probable concern about the health of Prince Leopold, sickly since birth, and the possibility that Leopold would be succeeded by his brother, who was not a music lover. As the position of an artist at a princely court depended so much on the tastes of his patron, the poor health of Prince Leopold must have been a serious concern indeed. See Günther Hoppe, "Köthener politische, ökonomische und höfische Verhältnisse als Schaffensbedingungen Bachs" and "Leopold von Anhalt-Köthen und die 'Rathische Partei.' Vom harmvollen Regiment eines 'Music liebenden als kennenden *Serenissimi*," *Köthener Bach-Hefte* 4 (1986): 13–64 and 6 (1994): 94–125.

20. On Gottsched, see also note 3.

21. *The Letters and Works of Lady Mary Wortley Montagu*, 3 vols. (London, 1837) 1: 312.

22. There is an enormous literature on the problem of Bach's selection. Ulrich Siegele, on the basis of research in the city archives, places Bach's appointment in the context of a struggle between the representatives of the Dresden court (the Absolutists) and the city estates, in

which Bach figures as the candidate of the Absolutists. See "Bachs Stellung in der Leipziger Kulturpolitik seiner Zeit," *BJ* 69 (1983): 7–50, 70 (1984): 7–43, and 72 (1986): 33–67. His arguments are summarized in an article in English, "Bach and the domestic politics of Electoral Saxony" in *The Cambridge Companion to Bach*, ed. John Butt (Cambridge: Cambridge University Press, 1997), 17–34, which suffers from a poor translation. More recently a translation of an abridged version of Siegele's original articles appeared as "Bach's Situation in the Cultural Politics of Contemporary Leipzig" in Carol K. Baron, ed., *Bach's Changing World: Voices in the Community*, (Rochester: University of Rochester Press, 2006), 127–73. Siegele's conclusions are admittedly speculative, but I found his political theories dubious and his interpretations overblown and frequently at odds with the sparse but reliable existing evidence.

23. *NBR*, 101 (*BD* 2, no. 128, p. 93).
24. *Ibid.*, 145–158 (*BD* 1, no. 22, pp. 60–64).
25. *Ibid.*, 156–158 (*BD* 1, no. 27, p. 74). See also *NBR*, 161 (BD 1, no. 166, pp. 233f.).
26. *Ibid.*, 164–67 (*BD* 2, no. 352, p. 250). *BD* gives only the last paragraph of a larger excerpt translated in *NBR*; the full German text, from the so-called "Riemar Chronicle," is in Gustav Wustmann, *Quellen zur Geschichte Leipzigs* I (Leipzig, 1889), 259f.

CHAPTER 2

Religion and Religious Currents

Robin A. Leaver

Bach was a Lutheran Christian, both professionally and personally. With one exception, all his church and court appointments were within the ethos and polity of the Lutheran church. And when he served as capellmeister (music director) of the Calvinist court at Cöthen, Bach and his family continued to worship at the local Lutheran church of St. Agnes; the compositions he wrote for the Cöthen court, celebrating the new year and birthdays, sounded very Lutheran, and indeed they were later adapted for specific Lutheran use. All Bach's other appointments in Arnstadt, Mühlhausen, Weimar, and Leipzig, required him to serve various liturgical needs of the Lutheran church.

Bach was born into a famous family of musicians that had served Lutheran churches and courts in Thuringia for generations. He was baptized as a Lutheran, as were each of his twenty children. He attended Lutheran schools in Eisenach, Ohrdruf, and Lüneberg, and later in life, when cantor of the Lutheran St. Thomas school in Leipzig, was a teacher not only of music but also of the basic theology of Luther's Small Catechism. Over the years he assembled a significant library of theological and devotional books, almost exclusively written by Lutheran authors, that almost any pastor of the time would have been pleased to have owned.

It is this Lutheran heritage, its contexts and contours, as Bach received it and was shaped by it, that forms the subject matter of this chapter.

The Lutheran Reformation

In many respects Luther was a reluctant reformer. His principal concern was not to destroy the unity of the Catholic Church by creating another, but to reform it from within. The action that marks the beginning of the Reformation was the posting of his *Ninety-five Theses* on October 31, 1517, the Eve of All Saints. In later Lutheranism this action

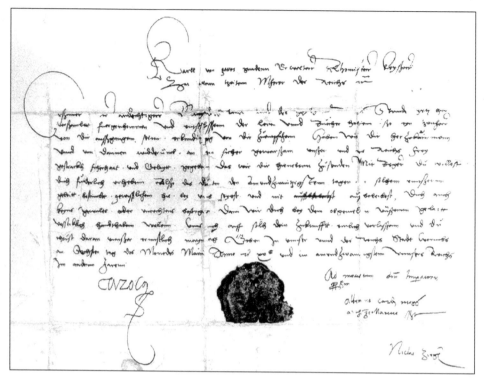

Figure 2.1. Although Luther had just been excommunicated by Rome for challenging papal authority and certain church doctrines and traditions, the Saxon elector Frederick the Wise persuaded the Holy Roman Emperor Charles V to command Luther's presence at the Diet of Worms—a German assembly of secular and ecclesiastical authorities—so that Luther could at least defend his positions. In the summons reproduced here, dated March 6, 1521, the emperor requests "Dear, honored, and pious Dr. Martin Luther" to present himself within three weeks with "information concerning the doctrine and the books which have come from time to time from him." Enclosed with the summons was a document guaranteeing Luther safe passage to the Diet.

was to assume particular importance: following the 150th anniversary of 1667, the event was celebrated annually in Saxony in various liturgical forms that included specially composed music, such as Bach's Reformation cantatas (BWV 79 and 80—the latter in its later manifestations). Luther's placarding was not the protest of a rabble-rouser but one theology professor's measured call to his colleagues for a discussion of the contemporary issue of indulgences. That he nailed the theses to the door of the palace church in Wittenberg means no more than that he posted them on the university notice board, where they would be seen by all the faculty and students as they attended daily Mass. The first thesis—"When our Lord and Master Jesus Christ said 'Repent,' he willed the entire life of believers to be one of repentance"[1]—is expounded and clarified in the other ninety-four. These *Ninety-five Theses* enshrine the crux of the Reformation debate since they bring into focus the two sides of the issue. "Repentance" is *poenitentia* in Latin, and was usually interpreted as meaning "to do penance," that is, to accept the authority of the Church. Behind the Latin is the Greek term *metanoia*, which in its New Testament context means a complete turnaround, a change of life and lifestyle, an understanding that implies the acceptance of the authority of Scripture. The debate continued over the next four years, with pressure being put upon Luther to obey the decrees of the Church, and the Reformer responding that he would do so only if those decrees accorded with scriptural teaching. At the Diet of Worms in 1521 (fig. 2.1) Luther was given the opportunity to recant; he stood his ground and was therefore condemned as a heretic and an outlaw. For the next eighteen months or so he was kept out of circulation for his own safety, so it was not until 1523 that he began the practical reforms that would eventually become normative for what was to be the Lutheran church. He did not believe, however, that he had created a new church but that the Catholic Church of his day had become apostate by abandoning both biblical theology and the practice of the Church of the first few centuries of the Christian era. Although the Lutheran Reformation was concerned about particular abuses, its primary concern was with fundamental theology.

Lutheran Theology

After the protestation that the Lutheran princes and rulers made to the Diet of Speyer in April 1529—an action that earned them the appellation "Protestant"—a more systematic exposition of the theological issues was presented at the Diet of Augsburg the following year, on June 25, 1530. This was the document that became known as the Augsburg Confession, the primary confession of the Lutheran church (fig. 2.2a–b). It had two major sections: the first (Arts. I–XXI) expounded fundamental theology with regard to the nature of God, the essence of sin, the uniqueness of Christ, the meaning of forgiveness and grace, the church and the sacraments, and so forth; the second (Arts. XXII–XXVIII) dealt with the correction of abuses, such as the restoration of the cup to the laity at communion, the marriage of priests, the rectification of the misuse of the Mass, the reinterpretation of the practice of confession, and various ecclesiastical matters including the abrogation of monastic vows and the curtailment of the power of bishops. All of these articles were argued according to biblical principles rather than from the decrees and formulations of the church. The document became the theological touchstone for emerging Lutheranism, with major cities and areas signifying their acceptance of Reformation theology by their subscription to the Augsburg Confession, as did the city and university of Leipzig in 1539. Two hundred years later the jubilee of the presentation of the Confession was celebrated in Leipzig (as elsewhere in Lutheran Germany) over three days, June 25–27, 1730, with a cantata by Bach being performed as part of the worship on each day.[2] The libretti, by Picander,[3] employ appropriate celebratory verses from the Psalms and portions of Luther's rhymed vernacular version of the Te Deum, and conclude with suitable

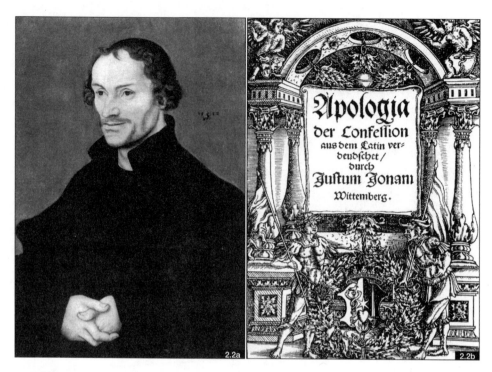

Figure 2.2. The humanist scholar and early Protestant leader Philipp Melanchthon, painted in 1532 by Lukas Cranach the Elder (a), was born Philipp Schwartzend, but changed his last name to its Greek equivalent while a student—a reflection of his commitment to classical learning. In fact, in 1518, about the time he became friends with Martin Luther, he became the University of Wittenberg's first professor of ancient Greek. His dual interests in Luther's Protestant movement and educational reform came together in his *Unterricht der Visitatoren* (Instructions for Visitors), which offered an elementary school curriculum that was imposed in Saxony by law in 1528, thereby establishing the first true Protestant school system, although its influence went far beyond Saxony.

At the Diet of Augsburg in 1530, it was Melanchthon, not the banned Luther, who was the leading representative of Protestantism, and it was he who wrote the Augsburg Confession, of central importance not only for Lutheranism, but also for all subsequent Protestant statements of belief. The following year, seeking to find a middle ground for conciliation between hard-line positions of Catholics and Luther alike, he wrote the *Apologia of the Confession*, pictured in (b) in the German translation from the original Latin by Justum Jonam. Melanchthon was sometimes accused of being too soft on the Catholic Church, but he never backed down on Lutheranism's fundamental doctrines of justification and scriptural authority.

chorales. The recitatives and arias are meditations on what it means to believe and live by the doctrines of the Augsburg Confession, though it is never explicitly named: references to the "Word," that is, the Word of Scripture, also embrace the Augsburg Confession, which was understood as a summary of biblical theology. Thus movement 5 (an aria) of the first cantata states (echoing the Beatitudes of Matthew 5):

Blessed are we through the Word,
Blessed are we through faith,

Blessed are we here and there,

Blessed, when we remain true.

Blessed, when we are not hearers,

but also doers.

Movement 5 (a recitative) of the third cantata is in the form of a prayer (with mixed metaphors):

Give, Lord, your Word that Christians may profit from

the rock-solidness of the Evangelists

and search your vineyard home,

that the refined honey of your Word

may refresh weary souls.

Stand by your little flock

and let no heresy

destroy the purity of the church . . .[4]

There is a strong allusion here to Art. VII of the Augsburg Confession, which defines the church as "the assembly of all believers among whom the gospel is purely preached and the holy sacraments are administered according to the gospel."[5]

Figure 2.3. Formerly in St. Nicholas's Church in Leipzig, this 1601 painting, "The Handing Over of the Augsburg Confession" by Andreas Herneisen, summarizes essential beliefs, practices, and events of early Lutheranism. On the right is represented the Diet of Augsburg (1530), when Emperor Charles V rejected the Augsburg Confession and the Apology of the Augsburg Confession (fig. 2.2b). On the left are depicted, along with the Devil, those Luther had singled out as enemies of Lutheranism: a Muslim, a Jew, and an Anabaptist. The sacraments of baptism (left center) and holy communion (lower center), central to Lutheranism, are also represented.

The Augsburg Confession defined Lutheran theology in contradistinction to Roman Catholic theology and served the emerging church as its primary confession of faith (fig. 2.3). During the decades following Luther's death in 1546 Lutheran unity was threatened by a number of internal theological controversies. After much disputation a united theological position was achieved by the Formula of Concord (1577). Within a few years an anthology of Lutheran confessions was published as *Concordia: Christliches widerholtes einmütiges Bekenntnis nachbenannter Kurfürsten, Fürsten und Stände Augsburgischer Konfession und derselben zu Ende des Buchs unterschriebener Theologen Lehre und Glaubens* (Concordia: Christian, reiterated, and unanimous confession of the doctrine and faith of the undersigned electors, princes, and estates who embrace the Augsburg Confession and of their theologians), issued in Dresden in 1580,[6] usually referred to in English as the *Book of Concord*.[7] It included such documents as the unaltered Augsburg Confession of 1530, Melanchthon's "Apology" of the Augsburg Confession of 1531 (fig 2.2), Luther's Schmalkald Articles and his Small and Large Catechisms, and the Formula of Concord. In view of the growing influence of Calvinism in Germany, Saxon Visitation Articles[8] were issued in 1593 to deal with the problem of the Crypto-Calvinism of some "Lutherans." These Visitation Articles were then commonly appended to the *Book of Concord*.[9] This anthology of confessional documents encompassed fundamental Lutheran theology to which all pastors, teachers, and musicians of the church had to subscribe. Thus before Bach could be officially appointed to the position of Thomaskantor in Leipzig in 1723 his theoretical knowledge was evaluated by two theology professors of the university[10] and he had to make two written declarations that he believed without reservation the substance and detail of the *Book of*

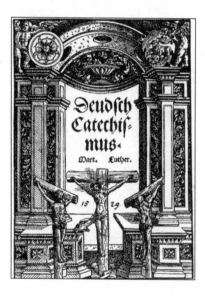

Figure 2.4. In 1528–9, Martin Luther undertook a visitation of schools in Saxony and discovered a serious lack of knowledge of Christian doctrine among both children and adults. To remedy this, he produced in 1529 two catechisms, both of which were included in the *Book of Concord* and both of which find resonance in Bach's *Clavierübung*, Part III. The *Deudsch Catechismus* (Wittenberg, 1529) pictured here, literally "German Catechism" but commonly called the "Large Catechism," was intended for the use of pastors and provided lengthy explanations of the Ten Commandments as well as discussions of the Apostles' Creed and Lords Prayer. In the preface, Luther minced no words in denouncing those pastors and heads of households alike who had failed to be true spiritual educators.

Figure 2.5. Recognizing that his *Deudsch Catechismus* was too formidable and detailed for instruction of the common people (and perhaps even the clergy), Luther produced within months of the Large Catechism a "Small Catechism," which proved to be enormously popular because of its direct, clear, and concise style. Treating the Commandments, Apostles' Creed, Lord's Prayer, baptism, confession, communion, morning and evening prayers, grace before meals, and the like, the book was widely adopted as a school textbook but also inspired many other catechisms. This ultimately resulted in a 1580 Saxon law making Luther's Small Catechism the only officially sanctioned one. The illustration (Leipzig, 1547 edition) gives the first article of the Creed: "I believe in God the Father almighty, Creator of heaven and earth," continuing, "What is that? Answer," at which point the elucidation begins.

Concord: once positively, endorsing Lutheran doctrines, and once negatively, denying non-Lutheran beliefs.[11] This double subscription was necessary because each theological position of both the Formula of Concord and the Saxon Visitation Articles of 1593 was defined both positively and negatively. This theological examination demonstrates that Bach had more than a perfunctory knowledge of the primary tenets of Lutheran theology.[12]

The *Book of Concord* embraced the theological parameters of the Lutheran church, which all pastors and teachers should understand and be able to expound. But the anthology also contained shorter summaries, as well as longer expositions, that were more accessible to the laity. For example, the articles of the Formula of Concord were given in two forms: in summary (*Epitome*) and fully expounded (*Solid Declaration*). Similarly, both catechisms of Luther were included: the Small Catechism (fig. 2.5), for all to learn, especially children, and the Large Catechism (fig. 2.4a–b), for pastors to study in

Figure 2.6. The *Clavierübung III* chorale preludes associated with Luther's Large Catechism employ two manuals and pedal; those related to the Small Catechism, only the manuals. "Diese sind die heilgen zehen Geboth" (These are the holy ten Commandments) is an example of a "Large" chorale prelude; the melody of the hymn is on the middle stave, where, as the inscription "Canto fermo in Canone" at the head of the piece indicates, it is treated in canon (at the octave). That is, a second statement of the melody (beginning in the third full measure of the middle stave of the second system) rigorously imitates (an octave higher) the first statement of the melody begun two measures earlier. Since *canon* means "law," no doubt Bach intended a musical pun here, linking the rigorous musical law of the canon with the Mosaic law expressed in the Ten Commandments.

connection with their catechetical teaching. Such catechizing was usually included within Sunday vespers, as well as on certain weekdays, when Luther's catechism chorales were frequently sung.[13] In his collection of organ pieces, published in 1739 as *Clavierübung III*, Bach included two chorale preludes for each of these catechism chorales, reflecting the two catechisms of Luther: one "large" for two manuals and pedal, and one "small" for manuals alone, the "epitome" of the larger setting[14] (fig. 2.6 and fig. 7.1, p. 230).

Lutheran Preaching and Music

The sermon was the primary vehicle by which Lutheran theology was taught and expounded for the church. In Catholic practice of the sixteenth century the sermon was an irregular feature of the Mass and what preaching there was frequently centered on

Figure 2.7. One of Luther's most important accomplishments was to make the scriptures more accessible to ordinary people by translating the Bible into German, although his was not the first attempt. For his source, he did not use the Latin Vulgate, the standard version in the West produced by St. Jerome in the fourth century; rather, for the New Testament, he went back to Greek texts, enlisting the help of Melanchthon and others during his period of hiding from authorities in the Warburg Castle near Eisenach (fig. 7.5, p. 239) and publishing the translation in 1522. A German translation of the Old Testament from the Hebrew appeared together with the New Testament in 1534, the title page of which is reproduced here.

the lives of the saints. For Luther and his followers substantial preaching of scriptural content became an integral part of all worship, but especially at the Sunday evangelical Mass (fig. 2.8). Luther abolished daily Masses, which were replaced by reformed daily offices of matins and vespers. Preaching was a feature of these services, especially vespers at which whole books of the Bible—Old Testament and New Testament books being assigned to different days of the week—were gradually and sequentially preached through, a practice that might require longer than a year to complete one biblical book (fig. 2.7). Sunday and festival preaching became centered on the epistles and gospels of the church year, which remained substantially unaltered from those associated with the Roman Mass, except that they eventually were chanted only in the vernacular. The pattern was for the sermon at the Sunday morning eucharist (*Hauptgottesdienst*) to be an exposition of the gospel of the day or celebration, and for the sermon at the Sunday afternoon vesper service to be on the respective epistle. Thus these biblical pericopes (assigned texts), with their homiletic exposition, were as effectively catechetical as were the specific catechisms of Luther, since they covered fundamental biblical theology and Christian practice, centered as they are on the life and work of Christ.

In the same way that he had provided a Small and Large Catechism, Luther also produced a collection of small-scale sermons on the church year pericopes and another of larger-scale sermons: the *Hauspostille*, first published in 1544, was an anthology of sermons on the gospels intended for lay use in the home, and the *Kirchenpostille*, published in sections between 1520 and 1544, comprised extended sermons on both the epistles and gospels of the church year. These *postille*[15] were reprinted numerous times in every subsequent generation, the *Hauspostille* becoming a primary book for domestic devotion and the *Kirchenpostille* a source and model for preachers. Following the example of Luther, a veritable flood of published church year sermons ensued: virtually every prominent theologian of later Lutheranism authored similar anthologies. Bach had quite a selection of such volumes in his personal library, including two different editions of Luther's *Hauspostille*, as well as the church year sermons of by a number of later Lutheran theologians and pastors.[16]

That a church musician should have such homiletic sources in his library is not really surprising since the Lutheran church music tradition had a close connection with these pericopes, particularly the Sunday gospels. Georg Rhau, the Wittenberg musician/publisher, issued motet settings[17] of the gospels for the major festivals of Christmas, Circumcision (i.e., the New Year), and Easter by Johannes Galliculus, Johannes Lupi, Cristóbal de Morales, and Balthasar Resinarius in his *Officia paschali . . .* (1539) and *Officiorum . . . nativitate* (1545). These polyphonic settings of the gospel pericopes developed into two significant genres.

Gospel Motets

First was the gospel motet (*Evangelienmotette*), sometimes referred to as Scripture-verse-motet (*Spruch-Motette*), a through-composed setting of one or more verses (occasionally the complete pericope) of the Sunday or festival gospel. For example, between 1556 and 1571 Orlandus Lassus published seventeen gospel motets, and complete church year cycles were issued by Leonhard Päminger (1573–80), Andreas Raselius (1594–95), and Sethus Calvisius (1595–99). During the seventeenth century the gospel motet was expanded into the church concerto,[18] which further evolved into the church cantata by the early eighteenth century. According to Bach's *Nekrolog* (obituary) written by Carl Philipp Emanuel Bach and Johann Friedrich Agricola, he composed "Five full annual cycles of church pieces [= cantatas], for all the Sundays and holidays [of the church year]."[19] Like sermons preached on the gospels in the annual cycle of Sundays and festivals, Bach's cantatas were expositions of the same pericopes, but in musical rather than verbal form. Each annual cycle of cantatas therefore approximates to the various volumes of sermons on the church year pericopes published by Lutheran preachers. Although only three of Bach's reported five cycles can now be reconstructed with any certainty, one wonders whether Bach thought of them as approximating to Luther's *Kirchenpostille*. There is a parallel between them: Luther's "sermon" on any given Sunday in this anthology is frequently made up of several different sermons he had preached at various times. Similarly, Bach wrote different cantatas over the years for the same Sunday or festival. Further, if he did think of his church cantata output as his musical *Kirchenpostille*, did he also consider his cycle of chorale cantatas (mostly written between 1724 and 1725) as his musical *Hauspostille*, in the sense that they were composed on the church year chorales known and loved by the laity?

Historiae, Passions, and Oratorios

The second genre to develop from polyphonic settings of gospel pericopes was that of the "Historia," that is, through-composed settings of the biblical narratives of fundamental events in the life of Christ that were featured in the church year gospels: Nativity, Passion, Resurrection, and Ascension, with Passions predominating. Rhau's anthology *Selectae harmoniae de passione Domini* (1538) included Passions by Antoine de Longaval (or Longueval) and Johann Walter. The St. Matthew and St. John Passions of Walter were almost universally sung as the gospel for Palm Sunday and Good Friday respectively until well into the eighteenth century. But with these simple "histories" there developed simultaneously more extended settings, beginning with motet passions[20] and continuing through concerted settings to the larger works of Bach that include his Christmas, Resurrection, and Ascension oratorios (BWV 248, 249, 11) as well as his three known Passions (BWV 244, 245, 247).[21] The *Nekrolog* also records that Bach composed "Five Passions, of which one is for double chorus."[22] The fact that there were five,[23] the same number as the cycles of cantatas, would seem to imply that the two were connected. Again there is a parallel with Luther's church year *postille*: the *Hauspostille* had an appendix of thirteen passion sermons, under the heading "Passio oder Historie vom Leiden Christi Jesu unseres Heilands" (Passion or history of the suffering of Christ Jesus our Savior), and the *Kirchenpostille* offered several passion sermons, including Luther's significant Good Friday sermon of 1519.

Whether or not Bach consciously made the connection between his church compositions and Luther's *postille*, the way in which he developed theological themes by musical means is closely analogous to the art of preaching.[24]

Lutheran Patterns of Worship

Lutheran Mass Forms

Lutheran preaching was heard within the context of liturgical worship. Luther's primary liturgical reforms are found in two documents: the Latin *Formula missae* (1523)

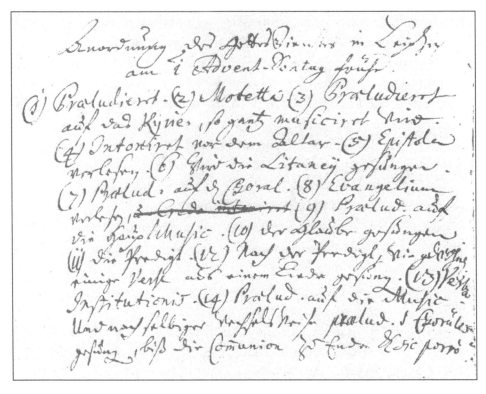

Figure 2.8. Still new in his position, Bach jotted down the order of service for the first Sunday of Advent on his score of the advent cantata *Nun komm, der Heiden Heiland* (BWV 61), a work based on Luther's eponymous chorale and composed in Weimar (1714) that Bach revived on that occasion (November 28, 1723). Indicated in order are preluding [on the organ]; motet; preludizing on the Kyrie [the latter then being performed with voices and instruments]; intonation in front of the altar; Epistle reading; singing of the litany; preluding on [followed by singing of] the chorale; Gospel reading; preluding on the principal music, i.e., cantata 61; singing of the Credo; sermon; singing of several hymn stanzas; words of institution [of the Eucharist]; and preluding on, followed by performance of, the "Musik" [i.e., second part of the cantata]; thereafter, alternate preluding and singing of chorales during Communion, "and so on."

and the vernacular *Deutsche Messe* (1526). Neither liturgy was intended to be mutually exclusive, and the many territorial Lutheran church orders of the sixteenth century were essentially conflations of the two liturgical forms, with some local minor variations. In the evangelical (i.e., Lutheran) Mass, later referred to as the *Hauptgottesdienst*, the earlier part of the service generally followed the Latin of the *Formula missae* and the later communion the *Deutsche Messe* (fig. 2.8). The traditional structure of the Mass was retained but the service was radically reinterpreted theologically: instead of considering it to be a *sacrificium*, an offering to God, Luther understood it as a *beneficium*, a gift from God. All references to the Mass as a sacrifice were deleted, which included the Offertory and most of the Canon. The *Verba testamenti*, the Words of Institution (or consecration), were retained, but Luther regarded them as proclamation rather than prayer, and therefore directed that they should be sung by the celebrant, in contrast to their being mostly inaudible as they were in the Roman Catholic Canon of the Mass.

Musical settings of the ordinary continued to be sung, but a Lutheran *Missa* quickly came to comprise a paired Kyrie and Gloria without the remainder of the main parts of the ordinary. Bach's five *Missae* (BWV 232[I] [later incorporated into the B Minor Mass], 233–36) are therefore representative of this tradition. The Latin Credo, in either plainsong or polyphonic/concerted settings, was an occasional feature in Lutheran practice, but the congregation would always sing the hymnic form of the Creed, Luther's *Wir glauben all an einen Gott*, whether or not the traditional Latin Credo was sung. That Bach used settings of the Nicene Creed by Palestrina and Bassani in the early 1740s, as well as his own *Symbolum Nicenum* (BWV 232, also later incorporated into the B Minor Mass), perhaps suggests that such concerted settings were becoming more frequent around this time. Luther considered the *Sanctus* as *musica sub communione*, that is, sung during the distribution of communion; it could either be in Latin or in his rhymed vernacular version, *Jesaja dem Propheten das geschah*. Most Lutheran church orders, including that of Saxony 1539–40, directed that the traditional *Sursum corda* (Lift up your hearts), leading to the Preface and Sanctus, should be only sung on the major festivals of the church year. Hence polyphonic or concerted settings of the *Sanctus*, such as those by Bach (BWV 232 [later incorporated into the B Minor Mass], 237–41) were performed in the traditional liturgical sequence on these occasions. The Agnus Dei, either in Latin or German (usually *Christe, du Lamm Gottes*) were options, along with vernacular eucharistic hymns, that could be sung during the distribution of communion. By the eighteenth century it had become customary to include concerted music as *musica sub communione*. This could take the form of the second part of the cantata of the day, or even a second cantata performed within the same service.

Lutheran Office Hours

Early in 1523 Luther experimented with a vernacular daily office, morning and evening, comprising biblical lections, preaching, and psalm-singing. But the Wittenberg churches soon reverted to the traditional form, substantially unchanged, of matins and vespers, a pattern followed by other Lutheran church orders. Matins was associated primarily with Latin schools attached to the churches, but vespers became a more widely attended service, with prominent celebrations on Saturdays, the eves of festivals, and Sunday afternoons. The main elements were psalmody (which encouraged the composition of large-scale Psalm motets),[25] a biblical reading (the epistle of the day on Sundays and festivals), a sermon, the *Magnificat*, and a concluding *Benedicamus*. On Sundays and some weekdays there was also catechetical teaching. The singing of the vespers canticle, the *Magnificat*, took two forms. It could be sung in German to the *Tonus peregrinus* by the congregation, or sung in Latin by the choir—in all the eight psalm tones during the course of a year.[26] But on major festivals the canticle would be sung in a polyphonic or concerted setting, such as Bach's *Magnificat* (BWV 243).

The Lutheran Chorale

A fundamental element of Lutheran worship was the congregational chorale, the unique contribution of Luther and his Wittenberg colleagues to Protestantism in general. In restoring the practice of the combined song of the gathered congregation at worship, Lutheran theologians reinstituted a sound that had not been heard within Western Christendom for around a thousand years. Lutheran chorales—constituted from translated Latin hymns, rewritten religious folksongs, as well as original texts and melodies—were simultaneously liturgical and catechetical vehicles of worship and theology. In encouraging others to write such hymns in 1523 Luther explained his purpose: "I intend to make vernacular psalms for the people, that is, spiritual songs so that the Word of God even by means of song may live among the people."[27] In time there were specific chorales that were sung as vernacular versifications of the Ordinary of the Mass (Kyrie: *Kyrie, Gott Vater in Ewigkeit*; Gloria: *Allein Gott in der Höh sei Ehr*; Credo: *Wir glauben all an einen Gott*; Sanctus: *Jesaja dem Propheten das geschah*; Agnus Dei: *Christe, du Lamm Gottes*, or *O Lamm Gottes, unschuldig*), as well as for each of the main sections of Luther's Catechisms (Ten Commandments: *Dies sind der heilgen zehn Gebot*; Creed: *Wir Glauben all an einen Gott*; Lord's Prayer: *Vater unser im Himmelreich*; Baptism: *Christ unser Herr zum Jordan kam*; Confession: *Aus tiefer Not schrei ich zu dir*; Lord's Supper: *Jesus Christus unser Heiland, der von uns*). Church year chorales were also developed as *Graduallieder* (Gradual songs), to be sung in the position of the old Gradual chant between the epistle and gospel at the *Hauptgottesdienst*. In the early Wittenberg hymnals these were hymns of the season, but as the basic corpus expanded specific chorales were assigned to every Sunday and festival of the church year.[28]

Bach's Use of Chorales

Many of the principal chorales of this corpus were used by Bach for his cycle of chorale cantatas composed mainly in Leipzig between 1724 and 1725. But earlier he had intended to create a cycle of primarily church year organ chorale preludes when he was in Weimar (1713–16). This was his *Orgelbüchlein* (BWV 599–644), a manuscript that was never fully completed (fig. 2.9). These chorale preludes are short and concise, suitable for their purpose of introducing the melody to be sung by the congregation. But he also composed other, more extended chorale preludes during his Weimar years, though they are usually referred

Figure 2.9. In his *Orgelbüchlein*, an incomplete collection of chorale preludes for organ ordered according to the liturgical year, Bach puts the melody of the Lutheran hymn in the treble, generally in quarter notes, while the more rhythmically active accompaniment supports it below. The example is the setting of "Lobt Gott, ihr Christen, allzugleich" (Praise God, you Christians, all together) (BWV 609). However, it was not Bach's only use of that melody. Two simpler settings (BWV 375f.) appear in the didactic collection of Bach's 374 four-voice chorale settings edited by Kirnberger and C. P. E. Bach (fig. 7.1, p. 230), whereas BWV 732, one of the so-called "Arnstadt" chorales (although its origin is uncertain), is more freewheeling in style.

to as the "Leipzig" chorales, since he reworked them in Leipzig sometime during the years 1744–48, the same period when he added a further prelude to the *Orgelbüchlein*. There are signs that the original versions of the "Leipzig" chorales may have been assembled as a companion collection to the *Orgelbüchlein*. The *Orgelbüchlein* is mostly structured according to the annual cycle of Sundays, and Bach clearly intended to provide a working repertoire for the whole church year. Bach's organizing principle of his "Leipzig" chorales is not as obvious as those in the *Orgelbüchlein*, and there has been much debate about what he may have had in mind. Their lack of a cohesive overall structure suggests that these chorale preludes are together but a torso of another incomplete project, rather like the *Orgelbüchlein*, only in this case there is no original manuscript from which the composer's intentions can be known. But the general purpose of such a collection is not difficult to determine. In his liturgical orders Luther indicated that during the distribution of communion the congregation should sing suitable eucharistic hymns. The practice that developed from this—which predates the use of concerted music as *sub communione*, noted above—was the alternation of the singing of eucharistic hymns with organ "preluding." Thus, while chorale preludes elsewhere in the service needed to be concise, those played during the distribution of communion could be somewhat lengthy because time was available while the congregation received both elements of bread and wine of the sacrament.

It therefore seems a strong possibility that the "Leipzig" chorales were salvaged from an intended larger collection of "Weimar" communion preludes arranged, at least in part, according to the major feasts of the church year: one is specifically headed *sub communione* (BWV 665);[29] there are three preludes each for Advent (BWV 659–61), Trinity (BWV 662–64), and Pentecost (BWV 651, 652, 667). If the hypothesis is correct, then it is likely that Bach originally intended to include three such preludes for Christmas and Easter, but these were presumably never composed. Again, if the original "Weimar" intention of the "Leipzig" chorales was for them to function as *musica sub communione*, then there is yet another parallel with significant works of Luther (similarities with his settings of the catechism chorale preludes in *Clavierübung III*): the *Orgelbüchlein* preludes correspond to the Luther's Small Catechism and *Hauspostille*, and the larger "Weimar/Leipzig" settings to the Large Catechism and *Kirchenpostille*.

Music and Worship: Concord and Discord

Some of the Reformers of the sixteenth century were exceedingly suspicious of the role of music in the service of the church, such as Calvin, who limited its use to unaccompanied congregational metrical psalmody, and Zwingli, who eliminated all forms of music from worship. Luther's approach was different. For him music was a *donum Dei*—a gift from God, not a human creation—that had to be understood in theological terms. Hence he often alluded in his writings to the interconnections between music and theology.[30] For example, in a letter to the composer Ludwig Senfl, dated October 4, 1530, he wrote: "I plainly judge, and do not hesitate to affirm, that except for theology there is no art that could not be put on the same level with music, since, except for theology, [music] alone produces what otherwise only theology can do, namely, a calm and joyful disposition."[31] His preface to Georg Rhau's *Symphoniae iucundae* (1538) includes the following:

> I would certainly like to praise music with all my heart as the excellent gift of God which it is and to commend it to everyone. . . . [Music] transcends the greatest eloquence of the most eloquent, because of the infinite variety of its forms and benefits.

We can mention only one point (which experience confirms), namely, that next to the Word of God, music deserves the highest praise.[32]

For Luther there were practical implications of this theological understanding of music that impacted on both church and school: "Music I have always loved. He who knows music has a good nature. Necessity demands that music be kept in the schools. A schoolmaster must be able to sing; otherwise I will not look at him. And before a young man is ordained into the ministry, he should practice music in school."[33]

Both clergy and musicians taught in the schools as well as exercising their ministry in the churches. In the schools clergy were expected to have some knowledge and practical experience of music, and church musicians were given the responsibility of teaching basic theology. Thus part of Bach's duties in St. Thomas's school, Leipzig, was to teach Luther's Small Catechism. Here is the reason why it was necessary for musicians as well as clergy to be theologically examined and to formally subscribe to the *Book of Concord* before being confirmed in their appointments. This close connection between clergy and musicians, and between theology and music, was largely unbroken until the eighteenth century, though it increasingly came under pressure from various sources.

Pre-Pietism

One of the early debates within post-Luther Lutheranism was the adiaphoristic controversy, so-called from the Greek term *adiaphora*, meaning "things indifferent." In the theological debate the issue revolved around the question: are rites and ceremonies adiaphora or essential for one's salvation? The controversy erupted as a result of the imposition of the Leipzig Interim of 1548, by which Lutherans were required to re-introduce the Roman rites and ceremonies they had abolished. There were those Lutherans—"Philippists," followers of Philipp Melanchthon—who believed such things to be adiaphora, who were opposed by others—"Gnesio-Lutherans," real Lutherans—who argued that they could not be considered adiaphora because of the theological presuppositions on which they were based, doctrines that undermined the Lutheran understanding of justification by faith.[34] Ultimately the issue was dealt with in Art. X of the Formula of Concord (1577), which included the following:

> We should not regard as free and indifferent, but rather as things forbidden by God that are to be avoided, the kind of things presented under the name and appearance of external, indifferent things that are nevertheless fundamentally opposed to God's Word (even if they are painted another color). Moreover we must not include among the truly free adiaphora or indifferent matters ceremonies that give the

appearance or (in order to avoid persecution) are designed to give the impression that our religion does not differ greatly from the papist religion or that their religion were not completely contrary to ours. . . .[35]

Thus the confessional stance of Orthodox Lutheranism was established as against Catholicism.[36] But the influence of Calvinism during the seventeenth century meant that the question of adiaphora was given a new interpretation. The Antitheses of the Formula of Concord, Article X, Epitome, began:

> We reject and condemn as incorrect and contrary to God's Word: 1. When anyone teaches that human commands and prescriptions in the church are to be regarded in and of themselves as worship ordained by God or a part of it. 2. When anyone imposes such ceremonies, commands, and prescriptions upon the community of God with coercive force as if they were necessary, against its Christian freedom, which it has in external matters. . . .[37]

There were Calvinists and Crypto-Calvinists who argued that specific Lutheran liturgical ceremonies, as well as the tradition of elaborate church music, were among "human precepts and institutions" that, if they were adiaphora, could, and therefore should, be abandoned. But Orthodox Lutherans responded that while liturgical forms and their associated music were, strictly speaking, adiaphora—in the sense that none were required to be observed as qualifications for salvation—nevertheless, they were founded upon and expressed distinctive Lutheran theology. Therefore, to abandon them would be to deny God's Word and turn the freedom of grace into the constraints of law. Further, if these Calvinists had read to the end of the Antitheses of Art. X, they would have seen that their position was specifically negated by the Formula of Concord:

> We reject and condemn as incorrect and contrary to God's Word . . . the teaching . . . 4. Likewise when such external ceremonies and indifferent matters are abolished in a way that suggests that the community of God is not free at all times, according to its specific situation, to use one or more of these ceremonies in Christian freedom, as is most beneficial to the church.[38]

The continuing influence of Calvinism meant that during the earlier seventeenth century Lutheran theologians were perhaps somewhat more circumspect in their praise and use of music. Thus, while not conceding anything of substance to the Calvinist position, they nevertheless were careful to warn against the misuse of music in

worship. But in this, as in other matters, they could find support in the writings of
Luther. For example, toward the end of his preface to Rhau's *Symphoniae iucundae*
(1538), he wrote:

> Take special care to shun perverted minds who prostitute this lovely gift of nature
> and of art with their erotic rantings; and be quite assured that none but the devil
> goads them on to defy their very nature which would and should praise God its
> Maker with this gift, so that these bastards purloin the gift of God and use it to wor-
> ship the foe of God, the enemy of nature and this lovely art.[39]

This is essentially the perspective of the sermons of Christoph Frick (1631), Konrad
Dietrich (1632), Johann Konrad Dannhauer (1642), and Martin Geier (1672), though
there was an increasing tendency to stress that outward formalism in worship and its
music is in itself inadequate if it is not undergirded by an inner spirituality on the part

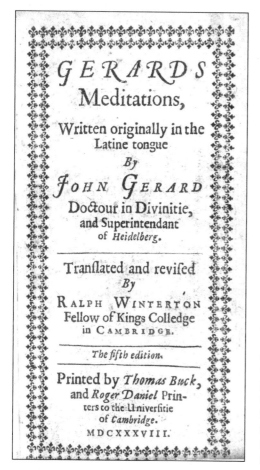

Figure 2.10. Johann Gerhard was the leading Lutheran theologian of his time and Bach owned a
copy of his five-volume *School of Piety*. Deeply
influenced by Johann Arndt, who was also represented in Bach's personal library, Gerhard's
magnum opus was the *Loci Theologici* (9 volumes,
1610–22), an exposition of orthodox Lutheran theology that argued for the infallibility of the Bible
against that of the pope. This title page of the
1638 London edition of his *Meditationes Sacrae*
(1603/4–6), indicates the international influence of
this book first published in 1606; furthermore, Gerhard's continuing power as a moral and theological
force is evidenced by the fact that even the dancing master Gottfried Taubert, in his *Rechtschaffener Tanzmeister* (1717) (fig. 6.7, p. 213), cites him
in a chapter entitled "How galant dance helps a
good marriage."

Figure 2.11. Heinrich Müller, a theologian, preacher, and professor from Rostock, seems to have exercised special influence on Bach, since several works of his were in the composer's library. Müller wrote that "the preacher should preach from the heart into the heart, for what does not come from the heart will not penetrate other hearts." There is a very sensual, subjectively emotional, and physical—hence very baroque—quality to his prose: "Preachers are the sows of the community. They should give healthy, sweet milk; therefore, they must previously have tasted themselves the food of divine word, have chewed it, have digested it, and lived it." The text here begins: "I wander around in error and find no way out," symbolically illustrated by the labyrinth in the background (see also fig. 3.13, p. 153).

of each of the worshipers.[40] This internalization of spirituality was in large part created by the reaction to the destruction and disease engendered by successive waves of battles across Germany during the interminable Thirty Years' War (1618–48). When the outward world was falling apart the tendency was to retreat into the security of the inner world. Thus this awful period gave rise to a more intimate spirituality that was sustained by such books as Johann Gerhard's *Meditationes sacrae ad verum pietatem excitandam* (Sacred meditations to awaken true piety), first published in 1606 (fig. 2.10), the same author's *Schola pietatis* (School of piety), first published in 1622–23, and Johann Arndt's *Wahres Christenthum* (True Christianity), issued in six books between 1606 and 1609.[41] A similar spirituality was also expressed in the new hymns written by such poets as Martin Rinckart and Paul Gerhardt, and the new melodies supplied by such composers as Johann Crüger and Johann Georg Ebeling.[42]

The theologian Theophilus Großgebauer took a more critical position, in all essentials that of Calvinism, in his *Wächterstimmen* (Warning voices), published in Rostock in 1661. He argued, on theological grounds, for the elimination of virtually all music that was not in essence congregational. Großgebauer was answered by Heinrich Mithobius, in his *Psalmodia Christiana* (Jena, 1665), who expounded the Orthodox Lutheran understanding of the place and purpose of *figural* music in worship.[43] Other Rostock theologians, such as Joachim Lütkemann and Heinrich Müller, had also criticized liturgical music, but, unlike Großgebauer, did so from within confessional Lutheran parameters.

Plate 1. Although there is only one portrait of Bach universally acknowledged as authentic, a large fragment of a portrait held by family tradition to be that of Bach came to light in America in 2000. It has been argued by Teri Noel Towe that this is the long-lost likeness of Bach owned by Bach's last student, Johann Christian Kittel; the portrait is described by Ernst Ludwig Gerber in his *Lexikon der Tonkünstler* [Dictionary of Musicians] of 1812. The recently discovered fragment (*a*), which bears no identifying information, apparently came to the United States around 1870 with Edward Weydenhammer, whose descendants own the portrait. If authentic, it is the oldest image of Bach, and possibly shows him in the livery of honorary music director of the Weissenfels court, which title he held from 1729 to 1736. The likeness can be conveniently compared here with the 1748 portrait of Bach (*b*) by the official Leipzig portraitist Elias Gottlob Haussmann (1695–1774), owned by William H. Scheide of Princeton, New Jersey. This is generally believed to be a copy of the artist's less well-preserved portrait of 1746, which is in Leipzig.

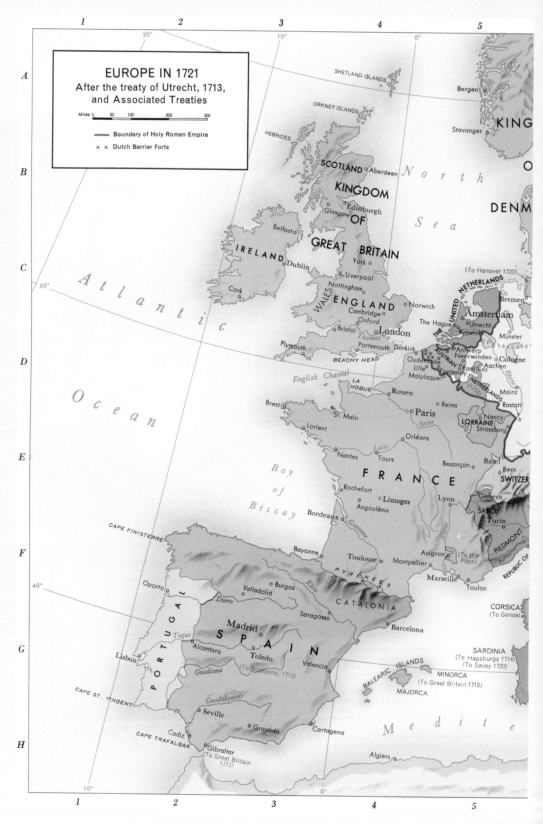

Plates 2 and 3. This map of Europe in 1721 shows the boundaries of the Holy Roman Empire as well as the larger geopolitical units within and without it. Clearly shown is how much August the Strong expanded his realm by election as king of Poland-Lithuania—to his approximately 1.4 million Saxon subjects were now added eight million Poles. Also evident is the pressure that could be brought to bear on the Polish-Saxon rulers by Brandenburg-Prussia and Russia especially.

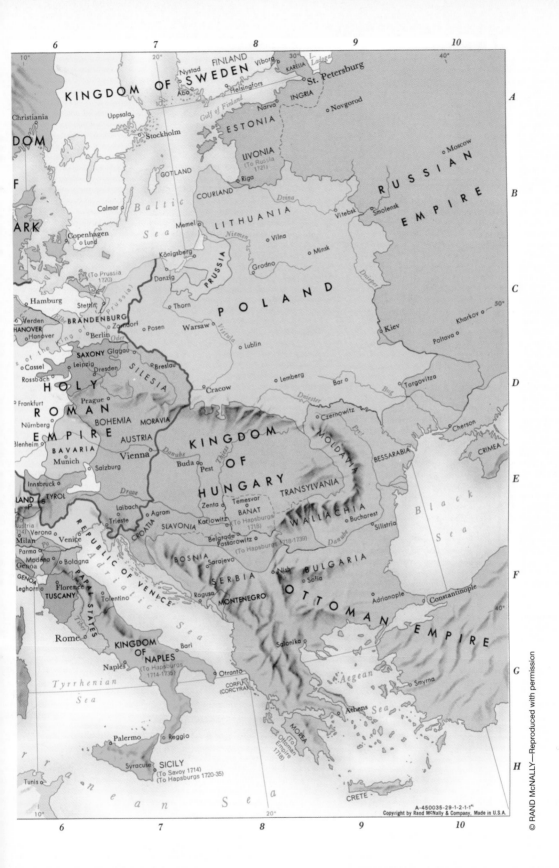

Plate 4. The counts of Schwarzburg ruled parts of Thuringia, but since medieval times they had been vassals of the Wettins of Weimar, who ruled the area to the immediate east. Their territory or county, like the realms of most ruling families, was made up of a patchwork of areas out of which were assembled separate political units, depending on how many lines of the family existed at a particular time. In 1599 the county was divided into the secondary counties of Schwarzburg-Rudolstadt (the northern enclosed area on the map) and Schwarzburg-Sondershausen (the southern areas); these were separated by land belonging to the Schönborn electorate of Mainz (including Erfurt). However, in 1681, Sondershausen was subdivided into the tertiary counties of Sondershausen and Arnstadt. The latter was ruled by Anton Günther II (plate 6) during Bach's time there (1703–7), and when the count, later prince, died in 1716, the territory of Schwarzburg-Arnstadt reverted to Schwarzburg-Sondershausen until 1918.

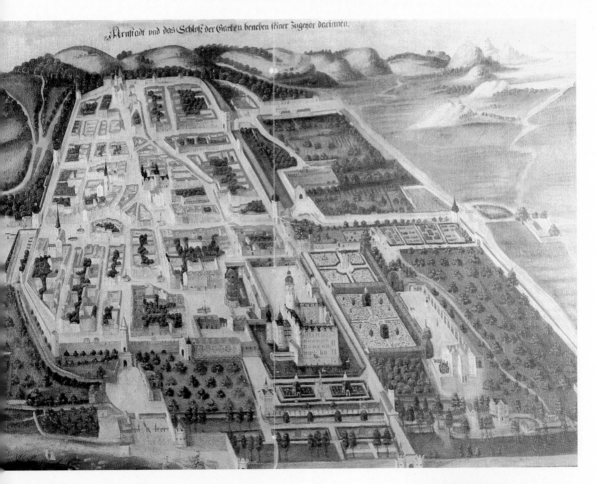

Plate 5. Documented since the year 704, Arnstadt is the oldest town in Thuringia. In this painting (ca.1580) by Wolf Kelner, which looks west, Arnstadt's three churches are visible: the Upper Church (or Franciscan Church), south of the market square (i.e., center far left), was where the ruling and other leading families worshiped; second in rank was the Church of Our Lady, top left, up the street from the central market; and the New Church (just below and to the right of the market, northwest of the Upper Church), the lowest-ranked church, where Bach presided over a new organ he had been engaged to evaluate (fig. 0.14, p. 19). This view shows the church as St. Boniface's, which the New Church (now Bach Church) replaced after a fire in 1581. It is possible, even likely, that Bach participated in musical activities at the castle (lower center), which no longer exists, but there is (as yet) no documentation to prove it.

Plate 6. Count Anton Günther of Schwarzburg-Arnstadt moved to the no longer extant Schloss Neideck in Arnstadt in 1683, two years after the county of Schwarzburg had been divided between him and his brother. (Schwarzburgs ruled Arnstadt, Thuringia's oldest town, from 1332 to 1918.) His court personnel numbered 120 and his court chapel almost two dozen. Anton Günther enhanced the cultural profile of his court by building an important coin collection, a painting gallery, and an extensive library, and also established Arnstadt as a center of glass cutting and of faience manufacturing. However, during Bach's time there (1704–7), life was made difficult by conscription of local men to fight against Louis XIV and a tense relationship with more powerful Weimar: in 1705, Weimar Duke Johann Ernst III occupied Arnstadt, as occurred again in 1711 under Bach's then junior Weimar employer Duke Ernst August. This probably was in reaction to the elevation of the Schwarzburg brothers in 1697 to the title of prince by Emperor Joseph I, a title they dared not exercise until several years later.

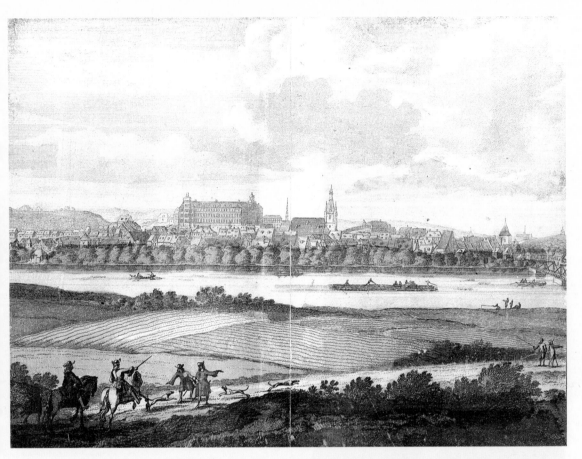

Plate 7. (*Facing page*) Duke Christian of Saxony-Weissenfels (b. 1682; r. 1712–36), was a longtime patron of Bach, beginning with the "Hunt Cantata" (BWV 208) of 1713, the composer's first secular cantata (fig. 0.27, p. 40). The duke was saddled with an inherited deficit but also so reckless with his expenditures that his budgets came to be controlled and audited by the electoral court in Dresden. Extant records give the annual salaries of the court musicians, revealing that the soprano "Mme. Pauline" received a third more than the music director, Johann Philipp Krieger. Bach was probably appointed honorary court music director in 1729, the year he performed his lost cantata BWV 210a for the Duke, who was visiting the New Year's Fair in Leipzig. There was apparently no stipend attached; presumably he received compensation for each of his services to Christian's court.

Plate 8. Weissenfels, view to castle. Perched on the "white cliff" that gave the city its name, the Neu-Augustusburg palace was built in the late 1660s for Duke August in a representational baroque style to designs of the architect of Weimar's Wilhelmsburg, Moritz Richter, and his like-named son. This may explain why both palaces feature a French-influenced, three-wing, three-story design, and is representative of a surprisingly close relationship between Albertine Weissenfels and Ernestine Weimar. Weissenfels became a ducal residence because of the 1632 division of electoral Saxony among the four sons of Elector Johann Georg I. Thereby, three secondary duchies came into existence until their ruling lines became extinct, 1746 in the case of Saxony-Weissenfels, ruled 1712–36 by Bach's patron Duke Christian. The father of Bach's second wife, Anna Magdalena, was court trumpeter in Weissenfels, and the daughter was also employed for a while as a singer there.

Plate 9. In this 1720 view of Cöthen from the west, the towers from left mark the Hallesche Tor, the Reformed Church of the Calvinist community (the largest building), the Lutheran church of St. Agnes (to which Bach belonged), and the princely palace with its two towers (fig. 3.13, p. 153). Further to the right (south) is the New Town with its promenades. Watercolor with pen and brown and gray ink by Jean Baptiste Monjou.

Plate 10. Duchess Eleonore Desmier d'Olbreuse was born into a noble Huguenot family. In 1665 she entered into a morganatic marriage with her lover and the new ruler of Brunswick-Lüneburg, Duke Georg Wilhelm, who had contractually promised his younger brother he would not marry. Only when it was confirmed that the duchy would go to the brother upon Georg Wilhelm's death was the latter able to marry Eleonore officially in 1676. Despite her husband's and the duchy's Lutheranism, Eleonore remained true to her reformed faith, and the ducal capital Celle became not only a magnet for French Calvinists escaping Louis XIV's repression but also a major center of French culture in Germany. For a while it even had a purely French musical establishment, led by a Catholic who could easily travel back and forth and thus keep the Celle musicians *au courant* with the latest musical developments in France. The Electress Sophie von Hanover's remark that "The court at Celle, it is said, is entirely French . . . one doesn't see Germans there any more" may have been exaggerated, but it does speak to the court's unusual character, which apparently made a big impression on the young Bach (see also fig. 0.4b, p. 5).

Plate 11. Leopold of Anhalt-Cöthen, godfather and namesake for Bach's last, but short-lived child of his first marriage, was plagued by religious disagreements with his Lutheran mother, fights over money and power with his brother, political and economic pressures from Prussia, and a sickly constitution. Nonetheless, Bach appreciated and long remembered him for his love and understanding of music. The prince, educated in Prussia and by a grand tour during which he experienced and accumulated much music in the French and Italian styles, also put considerable resources into a high-quality group of musicians resident at the court, over which Bach presided from 1717 to 1723 as court music director. Even after Bach left Cöthen for Leipzig, he was allowed to keep his title and returned several times to present music in honor of the prince—the last occasion being the rather perfunctory funeral for the prince in March 1729 (he had died on November 19, 1728). Portrait by Johann Christoph Müller, 1724.

Plate 12. Gisela Agnes von Rath. Since 1704 widow of the tolerant Prince Emanuel Leberecht and regent for their minor son, Bach's later patron Prince Leopold, Gisela Agnes aggressively furthered the interests of Lutheranism in Calvinist Cöthen. In 1694 the groundstone of a Lutheran church (the Agneskirche) was laid. The foundation documents specified that Agnes (and her Lutheran successor-patrons) could name the preacher and teachers of the parish, a right later challenged by her son. When her son assumed power in 1716 there began a serious feud between them as Leopold was determined to assert his precedence. In the end, she retired to her castle, Schloss Nienburg. It is interesting that there is no documentation linking Bach and Gisela Agnes. However, not only did Bach have a close friendship with the prince he would not have wanted to jeopardize, but Gisela Agnes, who in her later years tended to Pietism, may simply not have had sufficient interest in Bach or in what was most important to him.

Plate 13. The musically gifted Frederick II ("the Great"), seen here as prince before assuming the throne as the third king of Prussia (r. 1740–86), was studying keyboard and composition already at seven. His experience as a teenager during a 1728 visit to Dresden, when he heard his first opera—Hasse's *Cleofide* (fig. 8.11, p. 254)—as well as the flutist Johann Joachim Quantz, made especially powerful impressions that found resonance early in his reign through the new royal opera house (fig. 3.32, p. 169) and the luring of Quantz away from Dresden (with an eightfold salary increase). As prince, Frederick maintained residences and a capella at Ruppin and Rheinsberg, and J. S. Bach's son Carl Philipp Emanuel participated as keyboardist in performances there before becoming first harpsichordist to the new king in 1741. Frederick, of course, was aware of the father's reputation, so it was at his repeated requests that Bach finally went to Berlin in 1747, a trip delayed, ironically, because of Frederick's military aggression, resulting in (among other consequences) the occupation of Leipzig (fig. 1.5, p. 82).

Plate 14. The traveler approaching Leipzig in the eighteenth century would have seen not only landmark buildings originating in the Middle Ages and Renaissance but also an impressive number of new gardens and promenades that had recently been built outside the city walls. In this view, the numbered buildings are: 1. The Pleissenburg fortress; 2 and 3. St. Peter's Gate and Church; 4. The Provisions Warehouse; 5. Bose's Garden; 6. St. Thomas's Church; 7. The Gewandhaus; 8. The New Church (formerly the Barfuss or Franciscan Church); 9. The City Hall (*Rathaus*); 10. St. Paul's Gate and Church in the university area; 11. The Grimma Gate; 12. St. Nicholas's Church; 13. St. John's or Cemetery Church; 14. The Hospital; 15. The Orphanage. The city was granted a rare degree of autonomy by the Wettin ruling family in Dresden because of Leipzig's particular importance as a city of trade and business, located at the crossroads of north-south and east-west routes. Three times a year the city was host to major international trade fairs, which attracted thousands of traders and their entourages from near and far, some of whom attended Bach's Collegium Musicum concerts.

Plate 15. This representational equestrian portrait of the prince-elector Friedrich August II by the French-born Saxon court painter Louis de Silvestre was painted ca. 1718 in the course of the prince's long grand tour (1711–19), which included an audience with Louis XIV (fig. 1.6, p. 84). He had been sent away from Saxony, under the care of Catholic tutors, by his father August the Strong; the purpose was to distance him from his Lutheran mother and August's estranged wife, Christiane Eberhardine, who had made her son promise not to give up the Lutheranism in which she raised him. But the abandonment of the traditional Saxon faith was necessary if the prince was to acquire the throne of Poland and to develop a close relationship with the imperial court in Vienna, so Friedrich August II did convert and eventually became August III of Poland. An indecisive and uninterested ruler, he nevertheless made important contributions to the Saxon cultural patrimony through his refined artistic sensibilities and extravagant acquisitions, especially to the royal painting collection.

Plate 16. "The Water Palace of Neptune," a scenic design by Johann Oswald Harms for a festival honoring Friedrich III in Hamburg in 1701. Harms was a leading scene designer and decorator of his time, and worked at the Hamburg opera (fig 8.4, p. 247) during Bach's Lüneburg period (1700–3). Something of the spectacular effects baroque scenography enabled may be seen in this design, with its illusion of water, floating swans and the like. It is quite possible that Bach sampled the operatic fare offered in the city, although there is no documentary proof that he did. Nonetheless, the pastor of St. Catherine's Church (where Johann Adam Reinken was organist) was a supporter of the opera, as was Reinken.

Plate 17. The court artist Johann Samuel Mock here depicts the new king of Poland, August III, as he made his way into Warsaw on November 25, 1734, passing through a triumphal arch erected for the occasion. Thereafter he was welcomed by the city's president and given the keys to the city. The scene, however, belies the fact that in 1733 Stanisław I Leszczyński (a former Polish king beloved by Poles) had in the same city been reelected king a month before August III's election; this then led to the War of Polish Succession (1733–6), which definitively secured the crown for the Saxon only in 1736. Both August II and August III became electors of Saxony by inheritance (as Friedrich August I and II, respectively), but could be elected king by the Polish nobility only after converting to Catholicism. Since August III was more interested in the arts than in governing, his reign has generally been considered a disaster for Poland.

Plate 18. Born in Venice and dying in Warsaw, Bernardo Bellotto was also known outside Italy by the name of his famous uncle and teacher Canaletto, whose tradition of painting realistically faithful views Bellotto brought to eastern Europe. Appointed Saxon court painter in 1748, he painted many scenes of Dresden and environs as it existed in the years soon after Bach's last known visit in 1747. In this, the most famous of his seventeen views of the city (1748), one sees from the right side of the Elbe River the electoral capital as transformed into a kind of German baroque Rome during the reigns of August II and III. Dominating on the right is the new Catholic court church (*Hofkirche*) by the Italian architect Gaetano Chiaveri, whereas left of center is its recently built Protestant antipode, the Church of Our Lady (fig. 3.29, p. 166; plate 20). Behind the Catholic church to left and right can be seen parts of the Renaissance electoral palace; just left of the church is the steeple of the Kreuzkirche, with its centuries-old and still-existing choir school. In front of the Church of Our Lady, close to the water, is a baroque palace complex belonging to Count Heinrich von Brühl, including his library and art gallery in separate buildings. Spanning the Elbe is the Augustus Bridge by M. D. Pöppelmann.

Plate 19. The most celebrated feature of the Würzburg Residenz (fig. 3.17, p. 156) is the ceremonial stair-case (*Treppenhaus*). Begun in 1737, it was decorated in 1752–3 by the great Venetian painter Giovanni Battista Tiepolo, whose gigantic ceiling fresco apotheosized the new Prince-Bishop Karl Philipp von Greiff-enklau, depicted in a painted portrait held by Fame. Suggesting his fame was universal is a depiction of the four continents Africa, Asia, America, and Europe, a popular theme in the eighteenth century. Neumann's early training in engineering enabled him to build the vast area of the ceiling without interior supports; in fact, this part of the building withstood the bombing attack in World War II that badly damaged the sur-rounding area.

Plate 20. The Frauenkirche (Our Lady's Church), which symbolized Dresden's faithfulness to Lutheranism despite the conversion of the Wettin rulers, was especially beloved by the population. A pile of ruins between World War II and the *Wende* in 1989, its meticulous restoration culminating in its rededication in 2006 was an occasion of the greatest joy not only in Dresden but all over Germany. However, the decision to put in a modern, electronic-action instrument, instead of a tracker-action organ similar to the brand-new one by Gottfried Silbermann that Bach played in a recital in 1736, caused a contretemps of international proportions. The building's central design, good acoustics and pulpit's central location—all serving to facilitate preaching—reflect positions advanced by the eighteenth-century architectural writer Leonhard Christoph Sturm (see also fig. 9.1a, p. 268).

For example, in his sermons Heinrich Müller promoted a mystic spirituality without which, he argued, worship was merely an outward duty instead of the expression of inward desire (fig. 2.11). The content and contours of Müller's spirituality take on particular importance with regard to Bach when it is realized that the composer had no fewer than five volumes of Müller's sermons in his personal library, and that one of them supplied concepts and vocabulary for the libretto of his St. Matthew Passion (BWV 244).[44] It therefore seems certain that this pre-Pietist spirituality was a major factor in Bach's spiritual formation.

Pietism

Pietism in this context denotes the movement within the Lutheran church that began around 1675, reached its peak during the first half of the eighteenth century, and had a continuing significance throughout the nineteenth century and beyond. But Lutheran Pietism continues to be misunderstood and misrepresented. If the Pietists had been concerned only with "piety," then the Orthodox-Pietist controversy within Lutheranism would not have reached the proportions it did. The Pietists could not make an exclusive claim to "piety," indeed, there is an unbroken succession of devotional writings (*Erbauungsliteratur*) within Lutheranism that begins with Luther himself. One example is the Bride-Bridegroom imagery, based on the Song of Solomon, found in various places of Luther's writings, especially in the treatise *The Freedom of a Christian* (1520), an imagery that is continued in many devotional handbooks, collected sermons, and cantata libretti of later Lutheran orthodoxy. But the Pietists had much broader concerns than an intensification of spiritual life.[45]

At root Pietism was a holiness movement that involved a reevaluation of confessional Lutheran theology. The six-point agenda was set by Philipp Jakob Spener[46] in his pamphlet *Pia Desideria* (Pious desires),[47] originally published as an introduction to Arndt's *Wahres Christenthum* in 1675:

1. Christians ought to read from the Bible daily and to study passages at weekly home meetings with neighbors and friends.
2. Every Christian, not only the minister, is called to lead a holy life.
3. The Christian must be known by his actions, not merely by his knowledge of doctrine.
4. Theological controversy and confessional polemics, now prevalent in the Church, must be reduced.
5. Theology students ought to take part in *collegia*, or Bible study meetings for devotional study.

    6. Sermons ought to illustrate how to lead a Christian life, not present a rhetorical argument.[48]

The primary difference between Orthodoxy and Pietism within Lutheranism was essentially ecclesiological rather than a question of the nature and content of devotional life. The creation of the *collegia pietatis* for weekly Bible study and prayer, in the pursuit of holiness of life, marked a modification of the doctrine of the church: they were *ecclesiola in ecclesia*, little churches in the Church. This went much further than the definition in Art. VII of the Augsburg Confession: " [The] one holy, Christian church . . . is the assembly of all believers among whom the gospel is purely preached and the holy sacraments are administered according to the gospel."[49] The Church is therefore the visible community of faith at worship, within which the Word is read and expounded, and at which the sacraments of baptism and eucharist are observed. The following article (Art. VIII) explains that the visible community may include "false Christians, hypocrites, and even public sinners,"[50] but their presence does not undermine the doctrine of the church or invalidate the efficacy of the sacraments. But the Pietists essentially disagreed with this confessional position and called for holiness of life on the part of individual Christians as a means of purifying the corporate church. This purification, however, was not effected through participation in liturgical worship Sunday by Sunday, but rather in the activities of the *collegia pietatis*, the small groups

Figure 2.12. The worlds of Bach and the theologian and poet Erdmann Neumeister, who probably never met each other, nonetheless intersected. Born near Weissenfels, the strictly orthodox Lutheran studied at the University of Leipzig. From 1715 to 1755 he was pastor of Hamburg's St. Jacobi Church, where Bach auditioned in 1720. While in Leipzig, Neumeister wrote some cantata texts that combined scriptural verses, poetic stanzas, and sometimes a chorale, but he is more famous for his cantata libretti, beginning in 1704, that consist of texts to be set as recitatives and arias, like "a piece out of an opera," such as Bach used for his cantatas 18, 24, 28, 59, and 61. These texts are free from the vitriolic polemics other Neumeister libretti display, especially against Pietists. One of the latter reads, in part, "They talk a lot about piety / But they are only Pietists / . . . Therefore, protect yourself from the devil's prophets / As from toads and vipers."

that met for Bible study and prayer. Members of the *collegia pietatis* comprised those who had experienced the "new birth" of conversion, who were thus designated "true Christians." Their reasoning concluded that if the *collegia pietatis* were made up of true Christians, then these small groups constituted the true church; and further, if they were the true church, then the outward manifestation of public worship within Lutheranism would be purified when the practice of the local parish churches resembled more closely that of the *collegia pietatis*.

While the Pietist movement promoted personal piety there was no essential conflict. For example, as a student in Leipzig Erdmann Neumeister (fig. 2.12) was attracted by the preaching and teaching of August Hermann Francke, Spener's successor as the leader of Pietism[51]. But when Francke went on to argue that Luther's Reformation was incomplete, that Lutheran worship practices should be purged and simplified—the elimination of such things as eucharistic vestments, exorcism at baptism, elaborate liturgical music (which was considered to be worldly ostentation), the promotion of simple, devotional hymnody, etc.—Neumeister became antagonistic and wrote many polemical tracts against Pietism.[52] He opposed not the piety of the Pietists but rather their attempt to change the theological foundations of Lutheranism, to dismantle Lutheran liturgical practice, and to destroy the Lutheran tradition of church music. Neumeister was the architect of the reform cantata that employed *secco* recitative and the *da capo* aria, both self-consciously borrowed from opera, a development that Pietists dismissed as inappropriate "Theatralische Kirchen-Musik."[53] Although strictly Orthodox in theology Neumeister breathed a warm devotional piety in his hymns[54] and cantata libretti,[55] sentiments that are frequently but mistakenly labeled "Pietist." Similarly, the theological framework of Bach's vocal works was Orthodox while at the same time exhibiting a warm devotional piety that was akin to that of the Pietists. But Bach cannot be called a Pietist in a formal sense because his commitment to elaborate liturgical music ran counter to the ideals and practice of the movement.

At various points of his life Bach is found to be working in an Orthodox environment and leaning more towards Orthodoxy rather than Pietism, as the following examples illustrate. In Arnstadt, when Bach was employed as organist between 1703 and 1707, the clergy he worked with were strongly Orthodox. One of them, Johann Christoph Olearius, a pioneer Lutheran hymnologist, was an advocate of the sixteenth-century chorales of Luther and others as against the newer hymns of Pietism. Indeed, Olearius wrote an anti-Pietist hymn text, a parody of Luther's *Ach Gott, vom Himmel, sieh darein*, that was included in the *Neu-Verbessertes Arnstädtisches Gesangbuch* (Newly improved Arnstadt hymnal) of 1700, as well as the later edition of 1705.[56] When Bach was the organist of St. Blaise's Church in Mühlhausen (1707–8)—a town noted for its Pietist sympathies[57]—he appears to have had some close relationship with Georg

Christian Eilmar, the Orthodox pastor of St. Mary's Church, rather than with Johann Adolph Frohne, superintendent of the Mühlhausen churches and pastor of St. Blaise's, the church he served (fig. 2.13). There is no doubt that Eilmar was a strongly Orthodox pastor, but Spitta's conclusion that Frohne was a Pietist has recently been called into question.[58] Although the two pastors were in frequent contention, it is argued that Frohne remained Orthodox in his theology and ecclesiology. Notwithstanding this modern point of view, Frohne's contemporaries, including Eilmar, regarded him as expressing Pietist views, especially with regard to his understanding of spiritual priesthood.[59] Eilmar was not only Orthodox but also specifically and uncompromisingly anti-Pietist, the author of such publications as *Der Anatomie der Pietistischen Fledermaus* (The anatomy of the pietistic bat) (1704) and *Pietisterey als das gröste Hindernis wahrer Gottseligkeit* (Pietism as the greatest hindrance to true Godliness) (1705). Thus Bach may well have been drawn to the pastor of St. Mary's Church because of his opposition to the Pietists who, among other things, sought to eliminate elaborate music from the churches. Eilmar, who was

Figure 2.13. Georg Christian Eilmar was pastor of St. Mary's Church, the official municipal church in Mühlhausen. Although Bach was organist at the other principal church, St. Blaise (*Divi Blasii*), he had a closer personal relationship to Eilmar than to Johann Adolf Frohne, who was pastor of St. Blaise's and, as Mühlhausen superintendent, head of the town's ecclesiastical establishment. Eilmar was godfather to Bach's firstborn child, Catharina Dorothea, and prompted the composition of one of another of Bach's earliest cantatas, *Aus der Tiefe rufe ich, Herr, zu dir* ("Out of the depths I cry to you, O Lord") (BWV 131). Bach's personal empathy with Eilmar seems to have had a theological basis, insofar as Bach was undoubtedly in sympathy with Eilmar's virulent opposition to Pietism, which was a threat to the "well-ordered church music" to which Bach was committed.

godfather to Bach's firstborn child, Catharina Dorothea,[60] apparently commissioned Bach to write the cantata *Aus der Tiefen rufe ich* (BWV 131), which was performed in St. Mary's rather than St. Blaise's. The theological faculty and clergy of the churches in Leipzig were almost uniformly Orthodox who expressed strong anti-Pietist sentiments from time to time. Johann Benedict Carpzov II, professor of theology and pastor of St. Thomas's Church, was a relentless opponent of both Spener and Francke in the final decades of the seventeenth century, and his nephew, Johann Gottlob Carpzov, archdeacon

Figure 2.14. A well-traveled cleric who visited Holland and England as preacher of the Saxon electoral ambassador, Johann Gottlob Carpzov settled in Leipzig in 1708, remaining there as deacon, then archdeacon, of St. Thomas's Church and as a lecturer at the university (where he became a doctor of theology in 1724) before becoming superintendent in Lübeck (1730), as pictured here. He was an important defender of Lutheran orthodoxy, especially as regards interpreting the Old Testament, defending it against modern intellectual currents represented by Hobbes, Spinoza, and others. He also rejected the notion that in the second century, the Jews had altered the Hebrew script and thereby had falsified the text of the Old Testament because of polemical arguments with Christians. Carpzov had a personal relationship with Bach and his family, baptizing two of Bach's children (1727 and 1730).

of St. Thomas's between 1714 and 1730, whose family had connections with the Bachs in Leipzig,[61] similarly opposed Pietism (fig. 2.14). Most of the authors in Bach's personal theological library, known from the inventory drawn up after his death, were theologically Orthodox; a few were Pietists but many of their writings that Bach owned were not typically "Pietist."[62]

Again it needs to be stressed that the differences between Orthodoxy and Pietism were found in their respective theology and ecclesiology rather than in their spirituality, which was frequently expressed in similar terms. Thus the important and influential Pietist hymnal, *Geistreiches Gesangbuch* (Halle, 1704), edited by Johann Anastasius Freylinghausen, included some hymn texts written by the Orthodox poet/theologian Erdmann Neumeister. Similarly, many of the melodies that Bach edited for Georg Christian Schemelli's *Musicalisches Gesangbuch* (BWV 439–507) (Leipzig, 1736) were either taken from Freylinghausen's *Gesangbuch* or composed in a similar style.[63] But whereas the Pietists tended to favor the exclusive singing of such melodies, Bach apparently did not intend that they should replace the traditional chorale.[64]

Rationalism

Although the *Aufklärung* (enlightenment) in Germany did not reach its zenith until after Bach's death, it had already begun to influence intellectual life in the early decades of the eighteenth century. Christian Thomasius is usually credited as being its progenitor in the late seventeenth century. He was the son of the Leipzig philosopher Jakob Thomasius, Leibniz's teacher. As lecturer in law in Leipzig—the first university lecturer to use German rather than Latin—Christian Thomasius advocated a pragmatic rationalism tempered by humanitarianism. But his unorthodox religious views brought him into conflict with the theological faculty, who engineered the cessation of his lectures. Like his contemporary in Leipzig, the Pietist August Hermann Francke, he eventually became a professor at the newly founded university of Halle (1694) (fig. 2.15). In the early decades of the eighteenth century, while the Leipzig theological faculty remained essentially Orthodox, other faculties became less rigid with regard to a moderate rationalism. For example, Thomasius was offered the chair of law in 1709, but declined to accept, and Johann Christoph Gottsched, whose views owed much to Leibniz and especially Christian Wolff,[65] lectured in philosophy and poetry from 1723, becoming professor of logic and metaphysics in 1734.

Bach could not have avoided the influence of Wolffian philosophy in Leipzig. First, he composed the music for at least three libretti by Gottsched: a wedding cantata in 1725 (BWV Anh. I 196; music lost); the *Trauer-Ode* (BWV 198) in memory of Christiane Eberhardine, electress of Saxony and queen of Poland (fig. 0.19, p. 27); and a homage cantata (BWV Anh. I 13; music lost). Second, Johann Adolph Scheibe, a former student of Bach, published a musical journal in Hamburg between 1737 and 1745 under the title *Der critische Musikus*, in which music was discussed in a way similar to Gottsched's treatment of poetry in *Versuch einer critischen Dichtkunst vor die Deutschen* (An attempt of a critical art of poetry for Germans) (Leipzig, 1730; 4th ed., 1751; fig. 5.2, p. 197).[66] The sixth issue (May 14, 1737) contained an attack on Bach's compositional style, and in the composer's defense Johann Abraham Birnbaum published the tract *Unparteyische Anmerckungen über eine bedenckliche Stelle in dem sechsten Stück des Critischen Musicus* (Impartial comments on a questionable passage in the sixth number of the *Critische Musicus*) ([Leipzig], 1738), a document that may well have been written under Bach's direction. Throughout the controversy the categories of Gottsched, inspired by Wolff, were employed.[67] Third, Lorenz Christoph Mizler, music theorist and mathematician, who had also studied theology, law, and medicine, began lecturing on music in Leipzig in 1737, and published the monthly journal *Musikalische Bibliothek* between 1736 and 1754 (fig. 9.8b, p. 281). He also founded the exclusive Societät der Musicalischen Wissenschaften (Society of musical sciences), of which Bach became a member in 1747. Mizler and Bach were colleagues, though the exact nature of their relationship remains unclear. Mizler's writings are full of Wolffian categories with many citations from Gottsched's *Versuch einer critischen Dichtkunst*.[68]

The metaphysics of both Leibniz and Wolff, while "rationalist," were nevertheless theocentric. For them the universe was rational, mathematically ordered, and a totally integrated whole, the observable creation of the good God. Much of their metaphysics

Figure 2.15. August Hermann Francke and Christian Thomasius were both forced to leave the conservative University of Leipzig because of their anti-traditional views. They then became the dominant intellectual leaders at the revolutionary and innovative University at Halle, founded in 1695, where German, not Latin, was the language of instruction. Francke—theologian, philologist, and Germany's leading Pietist—was committed to social action and founded the Francke Institute, with orphanage, school, infirmary, and even a publishing house. The philosopher Thomasius, who went through a radically Pietist period around the turn of the century, separated theology from philosophy; his followers were soon entrenched in philosophy departments all over Germany. In electoral Saxony, where a High Consistory had forced Leipzig professors to renounce Thomasius's teachings in 1697, August the Strong counteracted the order, liberalizing Leipzig's intellectual climate and opening it to the influence of the Enlightenment.

could therefore be embraced by the concept of *theologia naturalis* (natural theology) as understood by the Orthodox dogmaticians of the seventeenth century. But *theologia naturalis* was always treated in contradistinction to *theologia revelata* (revealed theology), in the sense that the natural theology of reason afforded only an incomplete knowledge of God in comparison to the revealed theology of Scripture.[69] Thus while this distinction remained clear there was little difficulty in employing such theocentric metaphysics to explore and explain the natural world, including the human arts and sciences. It was therefore possible to embrace a dialectic of philosophical explanations of the natural with theological acceptance of the spiritual, the exercise of reason with regard to God's creation and the exercise of faith with regard to God's revelation. Thus Bach and his contemporaries may well have espoused aspects of Wolffian philosophy without compromising Orthodox Lutheran theology.[70]

Between 1736 and 1738, Bach carried on a dispute with the rector of St. Thomas's School, Johann August Ernesti, over the right to appoint prefects.[71] Prefects were responsible for directing performances in the absence of the cantor, who until then had appointed them. Bach objected to the rector appointing these prefects not only because this usurped his authority but also because Ernesti disparaged music.[72] The dispute may also have had another subplot. Ernesti was a philologist who published many editions of classical authors (fig. 1.14, p. 99). Over the years he developed an approach to Scripture that was somewhat different from that of the dogmaticians of Orthodoxy, a view that was exploited by later rationalists. Most books of dogmatic theology—including the handbook used in the Thomasschule, Leonard Hutter's *Compendium locorum theologicorum* (Wittenberg, 1610)[73]—began with the doctrine of Scripture as the Word of God and the source of theology. The Bible was thus revered as the unique revelation of God. Ernesti argued that the Bible should not be regarded as different from other books and should be studied in the same way that classical literature was critically scrutinized, and be interpreted more from its grammatical sense than its doctrinal content.[74] To judge from Bach's setting of biblical texts in his vocal works, the general content of his extensive theological library, and the marginal notes (fig. 0.24, p. 36) he entered into the Bible commentary, edited by Abraham Calov, he owned,[75] he shared the older view of Scripture rather than the philological approach of Ernesti, which may well have been an additional factor in the dispute between the two men.[76]

The twin forces of Pietism and Rationalism, each with its own different presuppositions, produced a similar effect in the later eighteenth century: the simplification of worship and a decline in church music, though the cantatas of Bach were heard from time to time in the Leipzig churches, at least during the immediate decade following his death in 1750.[77]

Coda

Johann Sebastian Bach was not an independent artist seeking self-expression through his music but was essentially a craftsman, like his predecessors, with a specific task to perform: making music for the worship of the church throughout the year and on special occasions, as well as suitable music for important civic observances. Although much of the music he provided was his own, he was not employed to compose music but rather to direct it. Thus it is understandable that when Bach was first appointed in Leipzig he should work extremely hard during these early years to establish a basic corpus of music, both his own and by others, that could be re-performed as necessary in later years, freeing him for other endeavors. The fact that his compositional activity for the church was concentrated in one primary period is no indication that Bach subsequently lost his faith, as some have proposed, any more than composing one cantata a month throughout his twenty-seven years in Leipzig necessarily would prove his religiosity.[78]

There is no doubt that Bach was a man of faith, a church musician who took theology seriously, as is demonstrated by the underlinings and marginal notes he added to his personal copy of Abraham Calov's *Deutsche Bibel.* The title pages of each of the three volumes have Bach's monogram on the bottom right-hand corner with the year "1733." The personal marginal notes witness to Bach digging deeper into his theological roots and investigating the biblical foundation of his profession of church musician exactly at a time when his activity in composing Lutheran church music had become less intense. Therefore the reduction of compositions for the church at this time cannot be seen as a marker of his loss of commitment either to his faith or his vocation. Further, instead of *Die Kunst der Fuge* (BWV 1080) being among the last compositions that Bach worked on, as early biographers and others believed, it is now known that the final sections of the B Minor Mass occupied the last year or so of his life. Rather than being solely occupied with the "absolute" music of fugal counterpoint, Bach was involved with creating a structure of liturgical music, monumental in concept and execution, that is as much a theological statement as it is a musical one. But Bach's Lutheran world-view conditioned not only his specifically religious music but also his non-text compositions that are usually designated "secular." As has been pointed out, works such as the six Brandenburg Concertos (BWV 1046–51) and the *Musical Offering* (BWV 1079) are as much "theological" and "religious," though certainly less overt, as are the cantatas and Bach's other compositions for liturgical worship.[79]

The complex religious contexts and cross-currents within which Bach lived and worked, instead of simply being the external environment of his professional and personal activities, were in fact more fundamental: they formed the substance of his internalized world-view that undergirded all of his compositional output.

Notes

1. *LW* 31: 25.
2. No scores or parts of the three cantatas (BWV 190a, 120b, and Anh. 4a) have survived, though the music of some of the movements is known from its use in other works. The libretti were published in 1731; see *BC* B 27–29.

3. Picander was the nom de plume of Christian Friedrich Henrici, many of whose texts, both sacred and secular, Bach set during his Leipzig period.

4. See Werner Neumann, *Sämtliche von Johann Sebastian Bach vertonte Texte* (Leipzig: VEB Deutscher Verlag für Musik, 1974), 333–34.

5. *The Book of Concord: The Confessions of the Evangelical Lutheran Church*, ed. Robert Kolb and Timothy J. Wengert (Minneapolis: Fortress, 2000), 42 (German text).

6. A Latin version was issued in Leipzig in 1584: *Concordia. Pia et unanimi consensu repetita confessio fidei et doctrinae Electorum, Principum et Ordinum Imperii atque eorundem Theologorum, qui Augustanam Confessionem amplectuntur.*

7. See note 4 above.

8. A "Visitation" was an official ecclesiastical inspection, and "Visitation articles" were the questions addressed to clergy and theologians.

9. German, Latin and English versions of the Visitation Articles can be found in *Triglott Concordia: The Symbolical Books of the Ev. Lutheran Church* (St. Louis: Concordia, 1921), 1150–1157.

10. *NBR*, 92–93 (*BD* 2, no. 134, pp. 99–100). A facsimile of the document is given facing page 177.

11. *BD* 3, no. 92a, pp. 630–31.

12. The last, and least satisfactory, chapter, "Johann Sebastian Bach: A Musician Not a Theologian," in Joyce Irwin's *Neither Voice nor Heart Alone: German Lutheran Theology of Music in the Age of the Baroque* (New York: Lang, 1993), is misleading on a number of grounds but especially because the background of confessional Lutheranism is never explored. There was no dichotomy between "a musician" and "a confessional churchman" (p. 143), since to be a church musician at this time one had to be a confessional Lutheran. A more balanced approach is found in Jaroslav Pelikan, *Bach Among the Theologians* (Philadelphia: Fortress, 1986).

13. See Robin A. Leaver, *Luther's Liturgical Music: Principles and Implications* (Grand Rapids: Eerdmans, 2007), Section II, "Musical Catechesis" (chapters 4–11).

14. See Robin A. Leaver, "Bach's 'Clavierübung III': Some Historical and Theological Considerations," *The Organ Yearbook* 6 (1975): 17–32.

15. The Latin term is derived from the phrase *post illa verba textus* ("after the words of the text"), meaning phrase-by-phrase expositions of the biblical pericopes.

16. See Robin A. Leaver, *Bachs theologische Bibliothek/ Bach's Theological Library* (Stuttgart: Hänssler, 1983) and "Bach's Understanding and Use of the Epistles and Gospels of the Church Year," *Bach: The Journal of the Riemenschneider Bach Institute* 6/4 (October 1975): 4–13.

17. Through-composed settings in four or more vocal parts, without sections assigned to individual voices.

18. "Concerto" was the common term for music scored for both voices and instruments. In this sense, Bach's cantatas are "concertos," and in fact he used the term in this way.

19. *NBR*, 304 (*BD* 3, no. 666, p. 86).

20. Through-composed settings of passion narratives in four or more vocal parts.

21. These are based on the Gospels of Matthew, John, and Mark, respectively.

22. Ibid.

23. On the identity of the "five" passions, see Robin A. Leaver, "The Mature Vocal Works and Their Theological and Liturgical Context," *The Cambridge Companion to Bach*, ed. John Butt (Cambridge: Cambridge University Press, 1997), 100.

24. Various studies have explored this connection, including Martin J. Naumann, "Bach as Preacher," *The Little Bach Book*, ed. Theodore Hoelty-Nickel (Valparaiso: Valparaiso University Press, 1950), 14–25; Hanns Lilje, "Johann Sebastian Bach als musikalischer Prediger der Lehre Luthers," *Luther*, 23 (1953): 20–25; Robin A. Leaver, *J. S. Bach as Preacher: His Passions and Music in Worship* (St. Louis: Concordia, 1984); Wolfgang Böhme, ed., *Johann Sebastian Bach: Prediger in Tönen* (Karlsruhe: Evangelische Akademie Baden, 1985); Robin A. Leaver, "The Liturgical Place and Homiletic Purpose of Bach's Cantatas," *Worship*, 59 (1985): 194–202; Martin Petzoldt, "Passionspredigt und Passionsmusik der Bachzeit," *Johann Sebastian Bach: Matthäus Passion BWV 244*, ed. Ulrich Prinz (Kassel: Bärenreiter, 1990), 8–23; Lothar Steiger and Renate Steiger, "Die Passionstheologie der Bachzeit, der Predigttypus und der Text der Johannes Passion," *Johann Sebastian Bach: Johannes Passion BWV 245*, ed. Ulrich Prinz (Kassel: Bärenreiter, 1993), 8–43.

25. Such as Schütz's *Psalmen Davids* of 1619. Heinrich Schütz was born exactly one hundred years before Bach.

26. A psalm tone is a cantillation-like melodic formula for chanting psalms going back to the early Middle Ages. There were eight such formulas (with variants), one for each of the medieval modes (sometimes designated by the Greek terms Dorian, Hypodorian, Phrygian, etc.). Although each of these regular psalm tones had a single "reciting tone" or pitch on which most of the text was sung, the *Tonus perigrinus* ("wandering") was the exception with two such tones.

27. *LW* 53: 221.

28. See Detlef Gojowy, "Kirchenlieder im Umkreis von J. S. Bach," *Jahrbuch für Liturgik und Hymnologie* 22 (1978): 79–123.

29. This is the first of two preludes on *Jesus Christus unser Heiland* that Luther specifically designates a distribution hymn in his *Deutsche Messe*, the second being BWV 666. Among the "Leipzig" chorale preludes are two on the melodies of eucharistic hymns that were also commonly sung during the distribution of communion: *Schmücke dich, O liebe Seele* (BWV 654), and *O Lamm Gottes unschuldig* (BWV 656)—a German version of the *Agnus Dei*.

30. The literature includes: Hermann Abert, *Luther und die Musik* (Wittenberg: Luther-Gesellschaft, 1924); Oskar Söhngen, *Theologie der Musik* (Kassel: Stauda 1967); Lothar Steiger and Renate Steiger, *Sehet! Wir gehn hinauf gen Jerusalem: Johann Sebastian Bachs Kantaten auf den Sonntag Estomihi* (Göttingen: Vandenhoeck and Ruprecht, 1992), 11–14; Walter E. Buszin, "Luther on Music," *Musical Quarterly* 32 (1946): 80–97, which is based on Karl Anton, *Luther und die Musik* (Zwickau: Hermann, 1916, 3rd ed., 1928); Paul Nettl, *Luther and Music* (Philadelphia: Muhlenberg, 1948); Carl Schalk, *Luther on Music: Paradigms of Praise* (St. Louis: Concordia, 1988); and Leaver, *Luther's Liturgical Music*, esp. chapters 1–3. On the connections between Luther's theology and Bach, see Friedhelm Krummacher, "Luthers Musikbegriff und die Kirchenmusik Bachs," *Luther: Zeitschrift der Luther-Gesellschaft* 56 (1985): 136–51; Leaver, *Luther's Liturgical Music*, esp. Chapters 17–18; and Robert L. Marshall's chapter in this volume.

31. *LW* 49: 428.

32. *LW* 53: 321, 323.

33. *Luthers Werke: Kritische Gesamtausgabe*, ed. J. F. K. Knaake, et al. (Weimar: Böhlau, 1883–), *Tischreden*, No. 6248.

34. An overview of the complexities of the debate can be found in *Triglott Concordia*, 107–12.

35. Formula of Concord, Art X, Solid Declaration, *Book of Concord*, 636.

36. See John T. Pless, "The Relationship of Adiaphora and Liturgy in the Lutheran Confessions," *And Every Tongue Confess: Essays in Honor of Norman Nagel on the Occasion of His Sixty-fifth Birthday*, ed. Gerald S. Krispin and Jon D. Vieker (Dearborn: Nagel Festschrift Committee, 1990), 195–210.

37. *Book of Concord*, 516.

38. Ibid.

39. *LW* 53: 324.

40. The basic literature includes Christian Bunners, *Kirchenmusik und Seelenmusik: Studien zu Frömmigkeit und Musik im Luthertum des 17. Jahrhunderts* (Berlin: Evangelische Verlagsanstalt, 1966); Robin A. Leaver, *Music in the Service of the Church: The Funeral Sermon for Heinrich Schütz (1585–1672)* (St. Louis, Concordia, 1984); Irwin, *Neither Voice nor Heart Alone*; Geoffrey Webber, "Organ or Orphanage?: Religious Controversy Surrounding the Role of Organ Music in German Lutheran Worship in the Baroque Era," *BIOS: Journal of the British Institute of Organ Studies* 16 (1992): 29–38.

41. Copies of Gerhard's *Schola* and Arndt's *Wahres Christenthum* were in Bach's personal library; see Leaver, *Bachs theologische Bibliothek*, Nos. 45 and 51.

42. See Bunners, *Kirchenmusik und Seelenmusik*; and Ingeborg Röbbelen, *Theologie und Frömmigkeit im deutschen evangelische-lutherischen Gesangbuch des 17. und frühen 18. Jahrhunderts* (Berlin: Evangelische Verlagsanstalt, 1957).

43. Mithobius's book was written at the request of Heinrich Scheidemann; see Pieter Dirksen, *Heinrich Scheidemann's Keyboard Music: Transmission, Style and Chronology* (Aldershot: Ashgate, 2007), 201–2.

44. Leaver, *Bachs theologische Bibliothek*, nos. 8, 19, 20, 41 and 42. See also Elke Axmacher, "Ein Quellenfund zum Text der Matthäus-Passion," *BJ* (1978): 181–91 and *"Aus Liebe will mein Heyland Sterben": Untersuchungen zum Wandel des Passionsverständnis im frühen 18. Jahrhundert* (Stuttgart: Hänssler, 1984).

45. See further Robin A. Leaver, "Bach and Pietism: Similarities Today," *Concordia Theological Quarterly* 55 (1991): 5–22.

46. Bach owned a copy of Spener's *Gerechter Eifer wider das Antichristische Pabsthum* (Frankfurt, 1714) (Leaver, *Bachs theologische Bibliothek*, No. 48), an anthology of mostly Reformation-day sermons that share the common anti-Catholic sentiments of Orthodoxy rather than the specific concerns of Pietism.

47. Philipp Jakob Spener, *Pia Desideria*, trans. and ed. Theodore G. Tappert (Philadelphia: Fortress Press 1964).

48. Cited Dianne M. McMullen, "The *Geistreiches Gesangbuch* of Johann Anastasius Freylinghausen (1670–1739): A German Pietist Hymnal," Ph.D. diss. (University of Michigan, 1987), 224.

49. *Book of Concord*, 42 (German).

50. Ibid.

51. Bach owned an edition of Francke's sermons, though there is some uncertainty as to which collection Bach owned; see Leaver, *Bachs theologische Bibliothek*, no. 35.

52. One of Neumeister's anti-Pietist writings was issued under the pseudonym "Orthodoxophilus" (lover of Orthodoxy): *Idea Pietismi, oder kurtzer Entwurff von der Pietisten Ursprung, Lehr und Glauben: durch ein Send-Schreiben in gebundener Rede gezeiget* (Frankfurt, 1712).

53. See Jürgen Heidrich, *Der Meier-Mattheson-Disput: Eine Polemik zur deutschen protestantischen Kirchenkantaten in der ersten Hälfte des 18. Jahrhunderts* (Göttingen: Vandenhoeck & Ruprecht, 1995).

54. See Miersemann, "Lieddichtung im Spannungsfeld zwischen Orthodoxie und Pietismus: Zu Erdmann Neumeisters Weißenfelser Kommunionbuch," *Der Zugang zum Gnaden-Stuhl Jesu Christi," Weißenfels als Ort literarischer und künstlerischer Kultur im Barockzeitalter: Vorträge eines interdiziplinaren Kolloquiums vom 8–10 Oktober 1992 in Weißenfels, Sachsen/Anhalt*, ed. Roswitha Jacobsen (Amsterdam: Rodopi, 1994), 177–216. Some of his other hymns, however, were specifically anti-Pietist, such as his additions to Luther's *Erhalt uns, Herr, bei deinem Wort* that the piety of our hearts should be free from the essence of Pietism ("Kein pietistisch Wesen"); see *ibid.*, 181, and Eduard Emil Koch, *Geschichte des Kirchenlieds und Kirchengesangs der christlichen, insbesondere der deutschen evangelischen Kirche*, 3rd ed. (Stuttgart: Belser, 1866–76), 5: 374.

55. Over the years Bach composed music for at least five of Neumeister's libretti, Cantatas 18, 24, 28, 59, 61, and possibly 79; see Robin A. Leaver, "The Libretto of Bach's Cantata 79: A Conjecture," *Bach: The Journal of the Riemenschneider Bach Institute* 6/1 (January, 1975): 3–11). When Neumeister was pastor of St. Jacobi Church, Hamburg, he attempted to get Bach appointed as the organist in 1720; see *NBR*, 89–91.

56. Koch, *Geschichte des Kirchenlieds und Kirchengesangs* 5: 358; see also Andreas Lindner, "Der Kampf um das reformatorische Liedgut in der ersten Hälfte des 18. Jahrhunderts: Johann Martin Schamelius," *"Geist-reicher" Gesang: Halle und das pietistische Lied*, ed. Gudrun Busch and Wolfgang Miersemann (Tübingen: Niemeyer, 1997), 260.

57. Among Bach's predecessors in Mühlhausen were the father and son, Johann Rudolf and Johann Georg Ahle, musicians who composed sacred music in a popular style favored by some Pietists.

58. See Martin Petzoldt, *Bachstätten aufsuchen* (Leipzig: Verlag Kunst und Touristik, 1992), 133–37; and Konrad Küster, *Der junge Bach* (Stuttgart: Deutsche Verlags-Anstalt, 1996), 161–65. But compare Alfred Dürr's more recently expressed opinion, regarding the reasons for Bach's decision to leave Mühlhausen in June 1708: "[Bach's] resignation letter contains the much-quoted sentence: 'Even if I desire always to perform regular church music to the glory of God and according to your [the council's] will . . . it is not possible without unpleasantness.' This 'unpleasantness' is an apparent reference to the fierce struggle between Pietism and Orthodoxy in Mühlhausen; Bach's superior, the pastor Johann Adolph Frohne (1652–1713), seems to have shared the Pietists' dislike of playing figural music during services (according to the opinion of Philipp Spitta, which has not yet been credibly disproved)." Entry on "Bach, Johann Sebastian," in *Dictionary of German Biography (DGB)*, ed. Walther Killy and Rudolf Vierhaus, with Dietrich von Engelhardt et al. (Munich: K. G. Saur, 2001–6) 1: 237; originally published in German as *Deutsche biographische Enzyklopädie (DBE)* (Munich: Saur, 1995–2000).

59. See Valentin Ernst Loescher, *Vollständiger Timotheus verinus*, 2 vols. (Wittenberg, 1718–21), translated as *The Complete Timotheus Verinus*, trans. James L. Langbartels and Robert J. Koester (Milwaukee: Northwestern, 1998). In the second volume Loescher details the controversy between Frohne and Eilmar and indicates that Frohne was essentially a Pietist; *The Complete Timotheus Verinus*, 2: 92 and 108; see also Johann Georg Walch, *Bibliotheca theologica selecta litterariis adnotationibvs instrvcta*, 4 vols. (Jena: Cröcker, 1757–65), 2: 765–66.

60. *BD* 1:37.

61. Carpzov's daughter, Benedicta, was godparent to Bach's daughter Sophia Benedicta in January 1730; see *BD* 2, no. 273, p. 200. Benedict/Benedicta was a common name in the Carpzov family.

62. See Leaver, *Bachs theologische Bibliothek*, passim.

63. For the background see the McMullen dissertation cited in note 48 above; and Dianne M. McMullen, "Melodien geistlicher Lieder und ihre kontroverse Diskussion zur Bach-Zeit: Pietistische kontra orthodox-lutherische Auffassungen im Umkreis des Geist-reichen Gesang-Buches (Halle 1704) von Johann Anastasius Freylinghausen," Busch and Miersemann, eds., *"Geist-reicher" Gesang*, 197–210.

64. See Robin A. Leaver, "Congregational Hymn and Soloistic Aria in the Music of Johann Sebastian Bach," *The Hymnology Annual: An International Forum on the Hymn and Worship*, ed. Vernon Wicker (Berrein Springs, MI: Vande Vere Publishing, 1993) 3:109–19.

65. See Joachim Birke, *Christian Wolffs Metaphysik und die Zeitgenössische literatur- und musiktheorie: Gottsched, Scheibe, Mizler* (Berlin: De Gruyter, 1966), 21–48. Wolff lectured at the University of Leipzig 1703–7.

66. Birke, *Christian Wolffs Metaphysik*, 49–66.

67. *NBR*, 337–53 (*BD* 2, no. 400, pp. 286–8; no. 409, pp. 296–306; no. 413, pp. 309f.; no. 420, pp. 322f.; no. 436, pp. 336; no. 442, pp. 360–3; no. 512, p. 404). See also John Butt, "Bach's Metaphysics of Music," *Cambridge Companion to Bach*, 46–59, 256–59.

68. Birke, *Christian Wolffs Metaphysik*, 67–82.

69. See, for example, Abraham Calov, *Theologia naturalis et revelata* (Leipzig: Reitzsch, [1646]).

70. For example, Valentin Loescher, a moderate Orthodox theologian (see note 59 above), on some matters favorably cited Leibniz against other philosophers in his *Praenotiones theologicae* (Wittenberg: Gerdesius, 1708). On Bach's connections with Enlightenment ideas, see Walter Blankenburg, "Johann Sebastian Bach und die Aufklärung," *Bach-Gedenkschrift 1950*, ed. Karl Matthaei (Zurich: Atlantis, 1950), 25–34; *Johann Sebastian Bach und die Aufklärung* [Bach-Studien 7], ed. Reinhard Szeskus (Leipzig: Breitkopf & Härtel, 1982), esp. 66–108; Martin Petzoldt, "Zwischen Orthodoxie, Pietismus und Aufklärung: Überlegungen zum theologiegeschichtlichen Kontext Johann Sebastian Bachs"; John Butt, "'A Mind Unconscious that it is Calculating'? Bach and the Rationalist Philosophy of Wolff, Leibniz and Spinoza," *Cambridge Companion to Bach*, 60–71, 259–61. Arnold Schering's study, "Bach und das Symbol. 3. Studie: Psychologische Grundlegung des Symbolbegriffs aus Christian Wolffs 'Psychologia emperica,'" *BJ* 34 (1937): 83–95, is weakened by the fact that his chosen musical examples are now known to have been composed by Bach ten years before the appearance of Wolff's *Psychologia empirica*.

71. See *NBR* 172–85, 189–96 (*BD* 1, nos. 32–35, pp. 82–91; nos. 39–41, pp. 95–106; *BD* 2, no. 382, pp. 268–74; no. 406, p. 293; *BD* 3, no. 820, pp. 312–15) It is unfortunate that the *NBR* confuses the two Ernestis. Although the correct name is used within the text, in the list of contents (p. xxv), the heading to the section (p. 172), and the index, the name of the earlier rector, Johann *Heinrich* Ernesti (who had died in 1729), is given. See also Robert Stevenson, "Bach's Quarrel with the Rector of St. Thomas' School," *Patterns of Protestant Church Music* (Durham, NC: Duke University Press, 1953), 67–77.

72. See *NBR* 172 (*BD* 3, no. 820, p. 314).

73. Leonard Hutter, *Compendium locorum theologicorum*, ed. Wolfgang Trillhaus (Berlin: De Gruyter, 1961), 1–4: "Locus primus. De Scriptura sacra."

74. These views were first published in Ernesti's *Institutio interpretis Novi Testamenti* (Leipzig, 1761), two years after he was appointed professor of theology in Leipzig, at a time when the theological faculty was less strictly Orthodox.

75. See Robin A. Leaver, *J. S. Bach and Scripture: Glosses from the Calov Bible Commentary* (St. Louis: Concordia 1985).

76. See further Paul S. Minear, "J. S. Bach and J. A. Ernesti: A Case Study in Exegetical and Theological Conflict," *Our Common History as Christians: Essays in Honor of Albert C. Outler*, ed. John Deschnew, Leroy T. Howe, and Klaus Penzel (New York: Oxford University Press, 1975), 131–55; a revised version appeared as "The Musician Versus the Grammarian: An Early Storm Warning," in Minear, *The Bible and the Historian: Breaking the Silence About God in Biblical Studies* (Nashville: Abingdon, 2002), 25–36. But perhaps too much has been made of Ernesti's "rationalism," since our understanding of it may reflect more the overt rationalism of Christoph Friedrich von Ammon, who copiously annotated his edition of Ernesti's seminal study, widely circulated during the nineteenth century: Johann August Ernesti, *Institutio interpretis Novi Testamenti. Editionem quintam suis observantionibus auctam curavit Christop. Frider. Ammon* (Leipzig: Weidmann, 1792; English translation: *Principles of Biblical Interpretation*, trans. Charles Hughes Terrot (Edinburgh: Clark, 1832–33; rpt., Eugene: Wipf & Stock, 2006). While he asserted that the books of the Bible should be investigated in the same way one would approach the writings of classic Latin and Greek authors, Ernesti nevertheless abandoned neither the essential grammatical approach to Scripture of the older Lutheran theologians, nor their basic understanding of Scripture as being the direct inspiration of the Spirit of God.

77. See Hans-Joachim Schulze, "Über den Endzweck der Kirchenmusik in Leipzig nach 1750," *BJ* 81 (1995): 37–58.

78. This particular debate was begun with the controversial lecture by Friedrich Blume: "Umrisse eines neuen Bach-Bildes: Vortrag das Bachfest der Internationalen Bach-Gesellschaft in Mainz," *Musica* 16 (1962): 169–76; translated as "Outlines of a New Picture of Bach," *Music and Letters* 44 (1963): 214–27. A flood of literature, both critical and supportive, ensued, the debate centering on the "new image of Bach," whether or not the composer was now to be regarded as a non-religious composer. Although Blume has his loyal supporters, the consensus is that his case that Bach lost his personal faith, as well as his commitment to writing music for the church, is overstated, and subsequent research has undermined the basic tenability of this position.

79. Michael Marissen, *The Social and Religious Designs of J. S. Bach's Brandenburg Concertos* (Princeton: Princeton University Press, 1995); Michael Marissen, "The Theological Character of J. S. Bach's 'Musical Offering,'" *Bach Studies 2*, ed. Daniel R. Melamed (Cambridge: Cambridge University Press, 1995), 85–106.

CHAPTER 3

Architectural Settings

Christian F. Otto

St. Thomas's Church in Leipzig, adjacent to St. Thomas's School where Bach worked as cantor for almost half a century, retains him inside and out.[1] He is buried beneath a prominent slab within, and outside a realistic statue stands near a main entrance (fig. 3.1). Yet the association between Bach and architecture is less close than these commemorations suggest. His remains were moved only in 1949 from their original location across town in St. John's Church (the cemetery church destroyed in World War II) in anticipation of the two-hundredth anniversary of his death.[2] The photographic likeness of the statue is the result of an anatomical investigation of what was presumed to be Bach's skull undertaken in the 1890s; the completed full statue was placed where it now stands in 1907–8.[3] The conflation of Bach and architecture that we presently experience at St. Thomas's Church is a reality of our time, not Bach's. In the *longue durée* of his death, Bach has taken possession of the architecture that embraced him in life.

If we wish to consider the built domain within which Bach lived and worked, we confront a double dilemma. His architectural world is mostly gone, replaced and rebuilt, extensively altered or entirely destroyed, especially during World War II. Nor did Bach leave a record of his responses to the buildings and cities of his life. Yet in limited fashion, we are able to reconstruct visually from graphic and documentary sources significant aspects of the architecture that Bach experienced during his daily comings and goings. And in this process, it is possible to gain some sense of those physical settings within which his music was performed. This awareness may in turn deepen our understanding of his place in the culture of which he and his music were a part.

The area that we now refer to as Central Europe was in Bach's time the territory of the Holy Roman Empire, as it existed from the end of the Thirty Years' War until it was dissolved in 1806.[4] Within the Empire, general policies of defense, foreign affairs, and legalities were directed from Vienna by Habsburg emperors. Yet power was diffused

Figure 3.1. When Bach was buried (fig. 9.11, p. 288), no monument to the deceased cantor was erected. However, Felix Mendelssohn, who in 1829 had helped his generation rediscover the greatness of Bach as a choral composer by reviving the St. Matthew Passion a century after its first performance, proposed a monument to Bach in 1840; this was dedicated in 1843 in the presence of Bach's last surviving grandchild and placed behind St. Thomas's School. The much grander monument (1908) by Carl Seffner, positioned near the then-new west entrance to St. Thomas's Church (1886–88), where Bach's remains now rest, reflected the composer's newly won, universally recognized stature.

throughout the territory by means of well over twelve hundred independent principalities, counties, ecclesiastical states, imperial towns, lordships, and knights. Princes and town councillors acted individually, while offering nominal allegiance to the emperor. Urban structure was determined by smaller cities such as Munich, Würzburg, and Dresden, which evolved with an eye to Habsburg Vienna. In these cities, building was driven by interdependent social groups for whom boundaries of authority were blurred and variable, resulting in complex transactions among church, court, and burghers.

Layered over this political and jurisdictional complex was a religious one, with particular implications for architecture and music. The Protestant revolt occurred within imperial borders and Martin Luther had been active in the immediate areas where Bach later lived. And while most countries in Europe became predominantly Protestant or Catholic, the Empire remained divided between the denominations. An opposition is commonly noted in the literature between Protestant music in the north and Catholic art and architecture to the south. Sir Kenneth Clark writes pointedly on this issue: "Although the Lutheran reform prohibited many of the arts that civilize our impulses, it encouraged church music. . . . the choir and organ became the only means through which society could enter the world of spiritualized emotion." Clark concludes by equating Bach's northern, Protestant music with southern, Catholic architecture: "We find that we can illustrate Bach's music by a contemporary building. The Bavarian pilgrimage church of the Vierzehnheiligen ("fourteen saints") was built by an architect who was only two years younger than Bach. He was called Balthasar Neumann, and . . . I think he was certainly one of the greatest architects of the eighteenth century."[5] These assertions about religion, music, and architecture, more facile than informative, can in fact be made specific and telling, the task to which we must now turn.

City, Church, Court

The cities where Bach was born and lived, from Eisenach to Leipzig, were medieval foundations (e.g., see fig. 7.5 [Eisenach], p. 239; fig. 0.2 [Lüneburg], p. 3; fig. 1.8 [Weimar], p. 88; fig. 1.12 [Cöthen], p. 92; plates 5 [Arnstadt] and 14 [Leipzig]). In them,

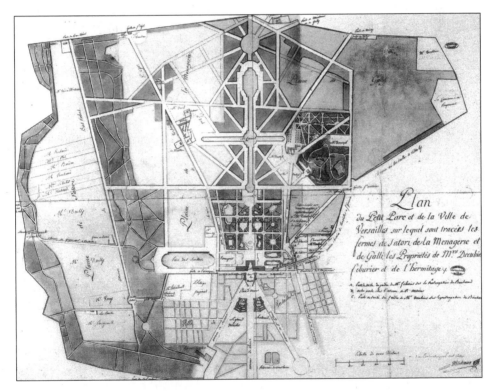

Figure 3.2. This site plan of Versailles, ca. 1807, shows the larger setting of the Versailles area, which is dominated by a monumental central axis that consists (from top to bottom) of the Grand Canal, formal gardens, palace, town, and triad of wide streets. This axis, which organizes city, buildings, and nature into a vigorous axial geometry, extends for more than two and a half miles. Growing from modest hunting lodge to the grandest architectural symbol of absolute monarchy embodied in the person of its builder, King Louis XIV (r. 1661–1715), Versailles was imitated by rulers all over Europe. Begun in the 1660s, it became the primary residence of the king in 1668. Louis was a direct inspiration to August the Strong, who sought (less successfully than his model) to reign in the nobility and centralize political, economic, and cultural power in Saxony and Poland; the architectural transformation of Dresden can be attributed to his desire to put his realm on a footing comparable to that of Louis XIV's France.

Figure 3.3. Lüneburg's brick hall church of St. Michael's—depicted here in a painting (ca. 1700) by Joachim Burmeister, a drawing instructor at the Ritterschule (fig. 0.4a, p. 5)—was dedicated in 1418 after sixty years of construction and remained essentially unchanged until the eighteenth century. It had in Bach's time an iron rood screen over six feet high separating the choir area from the congregation as well as a famous but recently desecrated altarpiece (fig. 0.3a, p. 4). Despite the excellent choral library that included German and Italian Catholic music to Latin texts, Bach likely sang only music in German here, as ordained in a regulation following the dissolution of St. Michael's monastery in 1655. The cantor was August Braun, teacher of the Ohrdruf cantor Elias Herda, who apparently had left Lüneburg under less than ideal auspices, so his traditionally assumed role in Bach's coming to Lüneburg is uncertain.

fortification walls and gates were tightly wrapped around densely packed buildings, irregular streets meandered through town, limited open space served markets.[6] The shape of these cities, determined during the eleventh into the fifteenth centuries, was fundamentally different from the urban design associated with the absolutist society of the later seventeenth and eighteenth centuries, which proposed grand schemes superimposed over the fabrics of existing cities and the landscape, such as the vast planning for palace, gardens, and adjoining town at Versailles (fig. 3.2), the arrangement of imposing squares and broad avenues that replaced large parts of Turin, and the expansive extension of city and fortifications realized at Nancy.[7] Even the cities that Bach visited, with the partial exceptions of Dresden and Berlin, were similar to the medieval town settings within which he lived.

From 1695, when he joined his brother Johann Christoph in Ohrdruf, until 1708, when he settled in Weimar, Bach's musical life played out within a distinctive architecture, that of the medieval hall church.[8] In this building type, narrower side aisles are as high or almost as high as the wider nave, creating a large, hall-like space (fig. 3.3). The hall church may have been derived from monastic refectories and the impact of de-ritualized layouts constructed by religious orders such as the Cistercians, for whom the church was a place of prayer, an *oratorium*, rather than a model of the heavenly Jerusalem. For these orders, the sermon was more important than liturgical pageantry;

what mattered was gathering around the pulpit to hear the preacher—a condition that would be reinvigorated by Lutheran practice. The hall churches that Bach experienced consisted of stone walls and vaults; they were essentially masonry containers, amply lit by large windows, that functioned as ideal boxes for music.

In Ohrdruf, Johann Christoph Bach served as organist at the Church of St. Michael, where he also gave Johann Sebastian organ lessons.[9] The church burned in 1753 and was rebuilt, but was destroyed in World War II. We know the exterior of the original structure from an eighteenth-century oil painting, which depicts a medieval hall church with tall, narrow windows combined with simple, seventeenth-century architectural forms (fig. 0.12a, p. 16).[10] After five years in Ohrdruf, Bach matriculated at St. Michael's School in Lüneburg, a Latin school for commoners. During this first of several short stays outside Thuringian-Saxon territory, he sang in the Matin's Choir of St. Michael's Church. The interior of this hall church, which contained slender piers that supported ribbed vaults, was well lit by tall arched windows.[11] From Lüneburg, Bach could travel to nearby Hamburg to listen to organist Johann Adam Reinken at the Church of St. Catherine (fig. 3.4). Built 1320–1426,[12] its interior was a version of the hall church, a so-called pseudo-basilica. Though the nave was higher than the aisles, it did not support a clerestory, and the entire interior, nave and aisles both, ended in a seven-sided choir.

In 1703, after a six-month stay in Weimar (to which we return below), Bach was appointed organist in the New Church (formerly St. Boniface's, later the "Bach Church") at Arnstadt, where he served three years. Centrally located in a prosperous town of about four thousand inhabitants, the church was built in the fourteenth century, extensively

Figure 3.4. The thirteenth-century church of St. Catherine in Hamburg, built originally on two marshy islands, had just sprouted its distinctive steeple with two lanterns when Jan Adam Reinken began his long reign as organist (1658–1722). It was Reinken's famous artistry and the church's fabulous four-manual organ that motivated the teenage Bach, then living in Lüneburg, to visit Hamburg. St. Catherine's also had a strong position in Lutheranism, being the first Hamburg parish to accept the Reformation and boasting as one of its pastors Philipp Nicolai, whose chorales "Wachet auf, ruft uns die Stimme" and "Wie schön leucht' uns der Morgenstern" were the basis for Bach's eponymous cantatas (BWV 140 and 1). (Drawing by Jess Bundsen, 1812.)

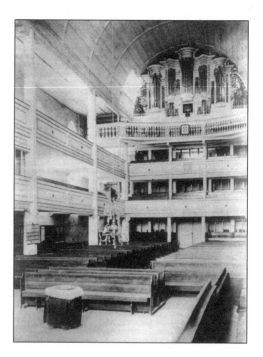

Figure 3.5. Arnstadt, New Church, view from altar to entrance. Like many churches of the time, the New Church had separate organ and choir lofts: the choir, directed by the cantor and accompanied by a small portative organ, was under the organ loft, whereas modern, soloistic music for small ensemble could be led by the organist in the organ loft. It was impossible to have any sort of visual contact between the two lofts, requiring the organist to move to the choir loft to accompany the choir. However, Bach's contract did not specify accompanying or conducting the apparently not-very-good choir, so he refused to have anything to do with it unless the student prefect was replaced by a professional choir director. (The organ in this picture is a nineteenth-century instrument dismantled in 1911.)

damaged in the urban conflagration of 1581, and rebuilt from 1676 to 1683.[13] The new, hall-like interior consisted of a large rectangular space flanked by wooden balconies and was covered by a wooden barrel vault (fig. 3.5). Part of the organ that Bach tested and approved in July 1703 is preserved in a local museum (fig. 0.14, p. 19); initially it was located high up in the church, just beneath the vault. It was from Arnstadt that Bach undertook his long visit to Lübeck in October 1705, where he listened to Buxtehude's "Abendmusik" in the medieval church of St. Mary's (fig. 3.6).[14] Unlike the hall church, this was an imposing Latin cross basilica, with a two-towered facade and flying buttresses outside, and inside a nave with clerestory and ribbed vaults, lower vaulted aisles, and a fully developed choir with apsidal chapels. At no other point in his life would Bach enter a medieval space developed on such a grand scale and with such sophisticated differentiation.

Yet two years later, the Lübeck experience may have found a modest resonance. Following his time in Arnstadt, Bach spent a year as organist at the Church of St. Blaise in Mühlhausen, begun about 1240 as a Latin cross basilica (hence the two-towered facade, transept, and deep choir) but completed in the 1270s as a hall church with nave and aisles equal in height, bundled piers, ribbed vaults, and tall, wide windows with tracery and stained glass[15] (fig. 3.7). These design elements, in contrast to the other hall churches within which Bach worked, produced an interior with the diffused light and continuous space of a High Gothic ecclesiastical structure such as Lübeck. Bach

Figure 3.6. (*Left*) A port located between the North Sea and the Baltic, the imperial free city of Lübeck became head of the Hanseatic League in the fourteenth century and today still preserves substantial vestiges of its late medieval aspect, among them St. Mary's Church, founded ca. 1200 as the parish church of the town's patricians. Built with the red brick that characterizes much of the old city, the church is dominated by two western towers and a system of flying buttresses. Although its once-elaborate decoration does not survive, Bach would have seen Thomas Quellinus's high altar (1696–7), of which some marble figures have been preserved. Bach's over-long visit to Lübeck in 1705–6 gave him the inspiring experience of hearing the great organist, composer, and musical entrepreneur Dietrich Buxtehude, but at the cost of incurring the displeasure of the authorities in Arnstadt, since he was neglecting his duties there.

Figure 3.7. (*Right*) With a history going back to the first millennium, Mühlhausen became an imperial free city in 1180 and was a member of the Hanseatic League from 1418. By the thirteenth century, the economic resources of Mühlhausen enabled the building of the city's two main churches, St. Mary's and St. Blaise's (Divi Blasi), whose interior is here depicted and where Bach was organist 1707–8. Unsatisfied with local musical standards, Bach left for Weimar, but not before submitting a plan for the rebuilding of the organ. Not only was his plan carried out, but Bach was also commissioned after his departure to write (now lost) cantatas celebrating the town council elections, normally the responsibility of the organist of St. Blaise's, although such works were actually performed at St. Mary's. Other Bach family members later worked in Mühlhausen, including Bach's errant son Johann Gottfried Bernhard at St. Mary's.

promoted rebuilding the organ at St. Blaise's, located on a balcony above the main entrance, the one proposal for reconstituting an organ that we have in his hand.[16]

These hall churches are very different from the new ecclesiastic architecture that had been evolving since 1700 in Bohemia, Austria, and Bavaria,[17] and with which Bach's music has been compared, specifically with churches by Balthasar Neumann, as Clark asserted. To specify the difference, we may consider an extraordinary eighteenth-century building, Neumann's project for the Benedictine monastery church at Neresheim.[18] Although Neumann only began the design in 1747 and the building was not completed until the 1790s, long after Bach's time and indeed Neumann's death in 1753, it brilliantly develops new approaches to ecclesiastic architecture that revolutionize traditional design. The Neresheim plan may be read as an amalgam of transformed hall-church and basilica, with nave and choir balanced to either side of crossing and transept (fig. 3.8). The rectangular outer walls contain five monumental free-standing circular forms. Two cross ovals in the nave are balanced by two similar circular forms in the choir, all centered by domical vaults perched on frighteningly thin supports. The longitudinal oval of the crossing is defined by four pairs of columns that support a dome; smaller longitudinal ovals to the sides establish a transept. The circular units of nave, crossing, and choir are maintained as complete wholes by means of spatial fragments inserted between them, and all are separated from the outer wall by a spatial layer. Both the curved forms and straight walls are porcelain white. In contrast to the stereometric shell of the crossing dome, the lower vault shells in nave and choir are extensively carved away by tall, wide lunettes. Together with the slender supports, they open to a blaze of light that floods the interior through large windows. The overwhelming experience of the interior is a brilliant, trans-

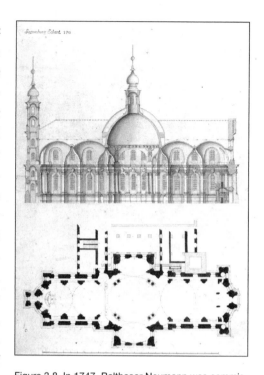

Figure 3.8. In 1747, Balthasar Neumann was commissioned to design the Benedictine monastery church at Neresheim because the abbot was impressed by Münsterschwarzach, a Benedictine monastery church that Neumann had designed twenty years earlier. But Neumann insisted that the two buildings should not be alike. And indeed, his new creation was so unusual that the abbot, though schooled in architecture, found it difficult to understand the project based on plans and sections, such as those shown. Nonetheless, recognizing it as exceptional, he pushed forward with construction according to Neumann's plans, even after the architect's death in 1753. Within the church, monumental, freestanding curvilinear openwork forms and huge windows create a transparent, dynamic, light-saturated space of extraordinary power.

parent space that contains monumental, curved architectural forms. The color-saturated vault frescoes, the dazzling liturgical furniture, the imposing organ arranged over the western wall are all subsumed by the movement, transparency, and spectacle of space.

Bach never experienced a contemporary architecture like this, nor was his music performed in such ecclesiastical spaces. Neumann's architecture and Bach's music were coetaneous achievements in different media, located near one another, but not experienced together.

The years 1708 to 1723 saw a change in status for Bach from the municipal positions that he had held to princely appointments—and a change in venue for his music from parish churches to princely chapels and palace chambers. Travels during this decade and a half also took him to Weissenfels, Halle, Hamburg, Dresden, Carlsbad, and Berlin, introducing a more complex range of built environments in relation to his music.

Bach's move to Weimar as court organist and chamber musician for Duke Wilhelm Ernst of Saxony-Weimar, 1708–17, meant that the main locus of his activity was the Wilhelmsburg castle (fig. 3.9). Destroyed by fire in 1618, the structure was rebuilt beginning the next year. But it was only in 1662, under the direction of Johann Moritz Richter, who began to oversee the reconstruction in 1651, that the castle was completed. As part of this campaign, the chapel known as "der Weg zur Himmelsburg" or simply the "Himmelsburg" was realized in 1658.[19] The castle burned again in 1774, and was rebuilt from 1789 to 1803 in very different form under the direction of Johann Wolfgang Goethe. Paintings provide us with views of the castle in Bach's time, and a gouache painting of about 1660 depicts the chapel interior. The castle consisted of three new wings of unequal size, older buildings and a tower, and a fortified wall arranged around a large interior court, a compromised and modest princely ensemble by the standards of the early eighteenth century. The chapel interior contained three tiers of niches and balconies that were treated in a colorful if stiff manner (fig. 3.10). Its dramatic moment was the ceiling, which opened into a rectangular space that contained the organ located unexpectedly above the altar rather than above the entrance.

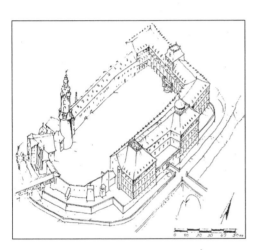

Figure 3.9. The Thuringian city of Weimar on the River Ilm was the residence of the Ernestine dukes of Saxony-Weimar until 1918. A castle is documented in 975 and the city was founded in the mid-thirteenth century, by which time both belonged to the Wettin family. The chapel is located within the central section (with the raised roof) of the wing at the top of the picture. The elder and senior of Weimar's corulers during Bach's time there was the stern Wilhelm Ernst, who lived in the Wilhelmsburg; the younger and junior duke (with whom Bach got along especially well) was Ernst August, whose "Red Palace" was reached via the covered bridge, shown in the lower left. Apparently, Bach utilized that bridge more than Wilhelm Ernst approved, for the latter tried to prevent Bach's visiting the younger duke. A fire in 1774 destroyed all but the fortified tower area of the Wilhelmsburg.

The castle Neu-Augustusburg at Weissenfels (fig. 3.11a and plate 8), which Bach visited for several days in February 1713, built by Johann Moritz Richter and his son from 1660 to 1693, showed what the Weimar castle might have been had it been designed anew: an imposing,

Figure 3.10. The chapel (called "Weg zur Himmels-burg," translatable as "the path to the heavenly cit-adel") in the Wilhelmsburg palace is where much of Bach's greatest organ music, including reworkings of earlier works, first sounded. During his short term of service here in 1703 as violinist, Bach may have also acted as substitute organist, because the court organist Johann Effler (d. 1711), who had close connections to the Bach family, was unwell. In this way Duke Johann Ernst's son Wilhelm Ernst, who succeeded his father shortly thereafter as co-regent of the duchy, became aware of Bach's extraordinary gifts, leading to Bach's appointment in Weimar in 1708 as organist and chamber musi-cian. Bach, however, aspired to higher status and was in 1712 promoted to concertmaster with the duty of composing monthly cantatas, which he conducted from the musicians' gallery above the ceiling of the chapel; the music thus floated down into the chapel as if from heaven itself, the musi-cians themselves being unseen.

unified exterior employing a consistent architectural vocabulary[20] (fig. 3.11a–b). Three multistory wings arranged in a C-shaped plan contain a broad interior court and em-phasize the central axis leading to the main entrance. Architecturally, the chapel of 1663–82 was similar to the Arnstadt New Church and Weimar Himmelsburg: a tall, deep hall with two tiers of balconies along the side walls, covered by a barrel vault. The original Protestant combination of altar and pulpit, 1678–83, was replaced by the pres-ent altar in 1746, when the duchy became Catholic. A restoration of 1951–54 returned the interior to its original whites and grays.

Bach visited Halle in 1713 and 1716, first to compete for the position of organist at the parish church of Our Lady, later to test the new Christoph Cuncius organ in the church.[21] Here he would have experienced an imposing version of a familiar eccle-siastic interior (fig. 3.12). The sixteenth-century hall church extended for almost fifty meters from entrance to choir, divided into ten bays. The broad nave and narrow aisles were separated by elegant piers, an intricate net ribbed vault rose above them, and sub-stantial windows opened the outer walls. The result was the most monumental, well-lit, and uniform hall church that Bach experienced.

After a decade at the Weimar court, Bach changed positions to the court at Cöthen, where he remained until 1723, with return visits in 1724, 1725, and 1729. Though the principality of Anhalt-Cöthen was small and possessed little political authority, it was flourishing economically and culturally. The castle of 1597–1608 was a modestly scaled, irregular structure surrounded by a moat, medieval in appearance with several towers and drawbridge (fig. 3.13).[22] Extensive gardens arranged in square and rectangular patterns surrounded the castle outside the moat. Bach served as music director for the prince's capella, which performed under his direction in the throne room, rebuilt in 1822 as a neoclassical mirror hall.[23] The palace chapel, its austerity reflecting the simplicity of Calvinist workmanship, was a modest space with flat groin vaults, squarish

Figure 3.11. Located in the north wing of Neu-Augustusburg palace at Weissenfels and oriented to the north, the chapel has been called "a Baroque *Gesamtkunstwerk*" in its integrated architectural, sculptural and painterly elements that seem "almost Catholic" in their richness. Contributing to this effect were the architects Johann Moritz Richter and son, the Italian stuccoists Giovanni Caroveri and Bartolomeo Quadri, and the painter Johann Oswald Harms (fig. 8.2, p. 246; plate 16). Nonetheless, the chapel, which was dedicated unfinished in 1682, is in the tradition of a Saxon Protestant court chapel, although the chapel was converted to the Catholic usage of the Dresden electoral court after the Weissenfels ruling family died out in 1746. Musicians performing in religious services under court music director Johann Philipp Krieger from 1680 to 1725 included instrumentalists and singers of the ducal capella, choirboys, and town musicians.

piers, and small windows, a simplified, seventeenth-century version of the hall church (fig. 3.14).[24]

In his documented visits to Erfurt, in July 1716, and to Carlsbad (Karlovy Vary since 1918) in May 1718 and 1720, Bach experienced small, medieval settings. Erfurt was a city in which newer, more elaborate fortifications contained older walls in an expanded city (fig. 3.15).[25] But from the 1660s into the 1690s, the population fell from over fifteen thousand to barely eleven thousand. During the course of the 1670s, the elector of Mainz, who numbered Erfurt among his possessions, reduced the municipal autonomy previously enjoyed by the city and asserted his absolutist authority. The citadel on the northwestern edge of town was massively built up from 1701 to 1727 by the military architect Maximilian von Welsch. Welsch was also responsible for a few new, if modest, buildings— the customs house (*Packhof*), the city hall (*Rathaus*) extension, the Governor's buildings (*Statthaltereigebäude*), a church facade—all begun before Bach's visit. Both the change in governance from the later seventeenth century, and the new building in the early eighteenth, were associated with the Schönborn, the politically powerful family of extraordinary patrons of art and architecture. They promoted some of the greatest buildings in eighteenth-century Europe, such as the Würzburg Residenz, discussed below, but they brought little patronage to Erfurt.

Carlsbad remained a diminutive spa town into the nineteenth century (fig. 3.16).[26] Following the discovery of hot mineral springs, Emperor Charles IV instigated its establishment in the 1340s, based on his experience of Italian health resorts. Construction

Figure 3.12. In early 1714 Bach was offered, without applying, the post of organist at Our Lady's Church in Halle. The city, located on the Saale river a short distance from Leipzig, had been annexed by Brandenburg-Prussia in 1680. He accepted the position, yet tried to negotiate better terms in a way that casts doubt on his intentions. Was his interest motivated by thoughts of bettering his Weimar situation, by discontent in Weimar, or by the planned new organ (no longer extant), much grander than that in Weimar? And did he finally turn down the job because of dissatisfaction with the salary and duties involved; because of doubts about settling in the capital of Pietism, home of Johann August Francke and Christian Thomasius (fig. 2.15, p. 131) and of a university known for its revolutionary curriculum and unorthodox theology; or because he had just been promoted to concertmaster in Weimar? In any event, in 1716 Bach was invited back to Halle to test the completed new organ, and later his music was performed there under the direction of his son Wilhelm Friedemann, who served as organist from 1746 to 1764.

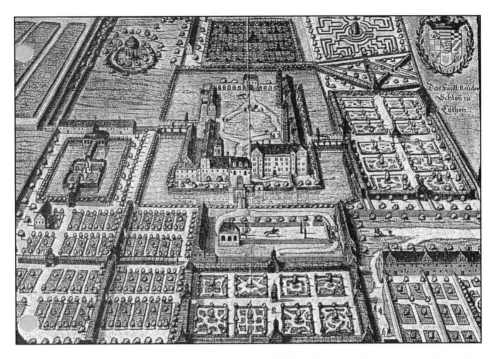

Figure 3.13. Unpretentious Cöthen had been one of the residence sites of the princes of Anhalt since 1606, others being Dessau, Bernburg, and Zerbst. Located north of the old town, the castle eventually consisted of four wings. The south wing (on the right), or "Ludwigsbau," is of special interest because here on the third floor was located the throne room, where music was performed for Prince Leopold under Bach's direction. Further to the right, a bridge leads to the formal gardens; at the upper right is a labyrinth, a type of garden especially popular in Anhalt. Such gardens had counterparts in musical labyrinths that groped their way through a confusing array of keys (such as one attributed to Bach, BWV 591); both types could be interpreted as metaphors for the confusion encountered and choices to be made on one's spiritual journey through life in search of salvation (see fig. 2.11, p. 124).

of the first baths followed, but a more demanding architecture began to emerge only in the 1730s with the church of St. Mary Magdalene by K. I. Dientzenhofer, more than a decade after Bach's last visit there.

In these city visits from the first years of the eighteenth century until 1720, Bach experienced a medieval architecture similar to that which surrounded him from Eisenach to Cöthen. None of these sites offered the kind of contemporary building found in nearby territories or the outskirts of Vienna, driven by the political necessity of representation and prestige, ultimately derived from Louis XIV's megalomania at Versailles, and exemplified by a grand Neumann project realized for the Schönborn in Würzburg.

Although many members of the Schönborn family deliberated on the Residenz project and several architects worked on it at various times, Neumann made most of the decisions about the project from its inception in 1719 until its virtual completion in the late 1740s.[27] The vast building stood between an expansive plaza on one

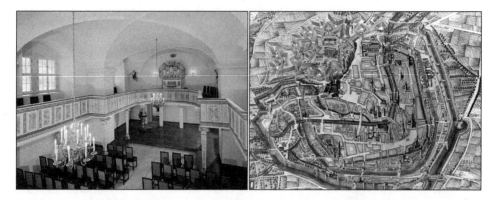

Figure 3.14. (*Left*) Cöthen, chapel interior, view to altar. Although the principality of Anhalt accepted Calvinism as its official religion in 1596, only Anhalt-Cöthen was required to maintain this status after Anhalt was divided in 1606. Members of the ruling family were not buried in the palace chapel, depicted here, but rather in the town church of St. James, which has been the church of the reformed community in Cöthen since the sixteenth century. Bach would have had no professional duties in the court chapel, since Prince Leopold's Reformed Protestantism rejected elaborate church music, but Bach was obliged to have his son Leopold August baptized here to satisfy regulations imposed by Leopold to the disadvantage of orthodox Lutherans in Cöthen, whose parish church was St. Agnes's, built by the estranged mother of the prince, Gisela Agnes.

Figure 3.15. (*Right*) Erfurt, bird's-eye view of city, ca. 1730. The city with the greatest claim to be *the* Bach city is Erfurt, where the wider Bach family exercised a particularly important role in musical life (fig. 0.9, p. 13). But Erfurt is also interesting as a Lutheran city ruled in principle by the Catholic archbishop-elector of Mainz, usually a member of the Schönborn family, members of which were prince-bishops in Würzburg (fig. 3.17, plate 19). In 1244 Erfurt wrested itself from the grip of Mainz, although it never attained the status of an imperial free city or a residence city after the former authority was restored in the later seventeenth century, the city was instead governed loosely through an administrator. The Catholic sovereignty over Erfurt—a hotbed of the Reformation and where Martin Luther studied and taught—meant that both Catholic and Protestant churches existed there during the Bach period.

side, and gardens and fortifications on the other (fig. 3.17). Six internal courts helped illuminate the multistoried complex of spaces and corridors, which contained administrative and storage facilities, apartments, a church, and an imposing ceremonial sequence of spaces. The compositions of the elevations, marked by pavilions, multiple entrances, and banks of ornate windows, were augmented by sculpture and color, and topped off by broad slate roofs. The ceremonial center of the building opened from a cour d'honneur into a vestibule scaled to accommodate the turning radius of a coach and horses. It was extended by the elongated octagon of the sala terrena that in turn opened through large windows and doors to the garden. The stair occupied its own hall north of the vestibule (plate 19). One broad flight led to a landing from which two parallel flights continued to the main floor, permitting the space to unfold in stages rather than putting the entire ensemble on display at a single glance. Supported on columns and slender piers, the stair rose from a ground floor with

Figure 3.16. Carlsbad, view of city. The still popular Bohemian spa city of Carlsbad (Karlovy Vary), named for Holy Roman Emperor Charles IV and now in the Czech Republic, twice drew the physically infirm Prince Leopold of Anhalt-Cöthen to its therapeutic waters and elegant facilities. On these trips (1718, 1720), he took musicians with him, and therefore Bach was not in Cöthen when his first wife, Maria Barbara, died; he learned that he was a widower with four children, ages five to eleven, only upon his arrival back in Cöthen. Carlsbad may have also provided the venue for Bach's contact with Bohemian nobles such as Count Franz Anton Sporck, to whom Bach lent autograph parts to some of the future Mass in B Minor. Systematic investigation of the "Bohemian connection" currently under way could lead to significant discoveries concerning Bach and the Catholic Habsburg realm.

partial light to the brilliantly lit upper level. Here the grand open space rose above broad landings and large windows to the imposing vault, its surface transformed by Giambattista Tiepolo's fresco depicting the four continents. The stair led to the White Hall (*Weisser Saal*), a rectangular room located above the vestibule, transformed by luxuriant, sculptural stucco by Antonio Bossi. This in turn opened to the Emperor's Hall (*Kaisersaal*), an elaborate, elongated octagon like the sala terrena below, but far taller and more elaborate: colossal engaged columns, a voluminous vault lightened by tall lunettes, and windows rising from floor to cornice. Red scagliola columns, mirrors, gilding, and crystal chandeliers gave the room brilliance and shimmer. The vault fresco by Tiepolo presented a resplendent, partially mythologized vision of Würzburg history.

The Würzburg Residenz, although especially brilliant, was one among scores of similar structures built by members of larger and smaller courts throughout the imperial territories.[28] Yet none of Bach's court appointments, including his Dresden and Berlin experiences, offered an architectural setting with the urban presence, grand scale, monumental symmetry, complexity of form and space, and richness of detail that inform the Residenz. As in the ecclesiastical realm, the stations of Bach's life at court only tangentially touched the new architecture.

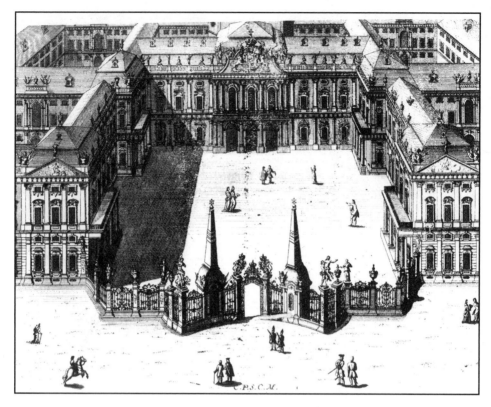

Figure 3.17. Under the patronage of the Schönborn family, two of whom were prince-bishops of Würzburg, architect Balthazar Neumann (see also fig. 3.8) served as architectural and city planning advisor for Würzburg. His major project there was an awe-inspiring new residence for the ecclesiastical ruler that included administrative offices, storage, and stables. The focal point of the Würzburg Residenz is seen in this detail of an etching (1757) by J. B. Gutwein after a drawing by M. A. Müller: the grand entrance and the cour d'honneur. However, the view does not indicate the extensive gardens and all the other associated buildings. The grand ceremonial staircase (plate 19), for which the Residenz is especially famous, is in the center wing.

Leipzig

At midday on Saturday, May 22, 1723, four wagons of Bach's household goods arrived in Leipzig; he and his family followed two hours later in two coaches and moved into an apartment (that would be renovated and enlarged in 1731–32) in St. Thomas's School. Leipzig (fig. 0.8, p. 11; fig. 3.18; fig. 9.1a–d, pp. 268–69) was the second largest city in Saxony after Dresden, its population growing from over twenty thousand in 1700 to more than thirty-two thousand by 1750[29] (fig. 3.18). Three yearly trade fairs, manufacturing, and book publishing generated enormous wealth in the city. A lively cultural and intellectual life was created by the university, and by the existence of private and semipublic libraries—the municipal library (*Ratsbibliothek*), the *Bibliotheca Paulina*, and the university library, open to the public twice weekly. Private art collections included work by

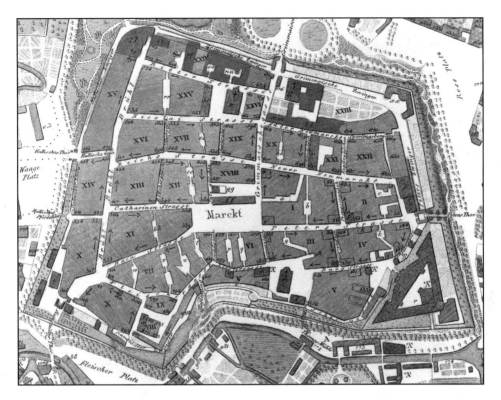

Figure 3.18. In this eighteenth-century plan of Leipzig, the compact size of the bustling commercial city and the relative location of various landmarks is easily grasped. In the center is the large marketplace with the long, rectangular town hall (fig. 3.20), where Bach took his oath of office as cantor of St. Thomas and city music director. Directly behind (above) it is the Naschmarkt (fig. 3.21), at the left (north) end of which is the stock exchange (*Börse*). The official municipal church, St. Nicholas's (fig. 3.24), is a few blocks directly east (above), and St. Thomas's is close to the city wall southwest of the marketplace, both churches being in plazas of their own. Immediately southwest of the latter church is St. Thomas's School (fig. 9.2, p. 271), where Bach lived and taught. North of the market on the southwest corner of Katharinenstraße, in which Zimmermann's coffee house (fig. 3.19) was located, and the Brühl stands the Romanus family house (fig. 9.1c, p. 269). At the eastern end of the Grimmaischegasse on the right and just inside the city wall stood the university church of St. Paul, where Bach conducted his *Trauermusik* (BWV 198) for Electress Christiane Eberhardine (fig. 0.19, p. 27); the beloved church was torn down by East German authorities in 1968 to make room for new university buildings. At the southwest corner of the walled city was the Pleissenburg, the Saxon Electoral fort, where Roman Catholic services were held.

Dürer, da Vinci, Rembrandt, Rubens, Titian, and Veronese. The sense of well-being and security felt in Leipzig is revealed by the gardens, orangeries, and garden houses that proliferated outside the fortifications; these battlements would be pulled down in the 1760s and the area they had occupied developed into a promenade.[30]

The dense fabric of the city was contained within fortified walls built in the thirteenth century and renewed in the fifteenth and sixteenth.[31] A large market opened the center of town, flanked along its eastern edge by the imposing city hall (*Rathaus*). The tower and tall, steep roof of St. Thomas's Church dominated the west edge of the city, while opposite it the towers of St. Nicholas's Church marked the eastern side of town. The massive tower and fortifications of the Pleissenburg fortress jutted out from the south-western corner, university buildings were strung along the eastern flank of town, spires of parish churches rose here and there above the dense collection of steep house roofs.

The general impression of Leipzig as a medieval city contrasted with transformations occurring along its streets. From the end of the seventeenth century into the 1760s, one third of the housing stock was replaced or rebuilt. The appearance of entire streets changed. A contemporary report noted that "bad or gabled [i.e., old fashioned] houses, plentiful elsewhere, are not present here." It continued: "Many houses have beautiful bay windows, gilt ornaments, galleries and statuary above, they are decorated with carvings from top to bottom."[32] The character of this rich domestic architecture can be seen in the formidable row of houses at Katharinenstraße 12, 14, 16, with shops at street level, elaborate two-story roofs, facades enriched by columns and statuary, substantial windows, and a filigree of decoration spun over the central bays (fig. 3.19). Bach's musical life intersected with the middle house of this group, which contained Zimmermann's Coffeehouse, where his Collegium Musicum regularly met. And the Bachs maintained neighborly relations with the Bose family, settled next door to St. Thomas's School in a palatial structure of about 1580 that the gold and silverware manufacturer Georg Heinrich Bose rebuilt in 1711 (now the Leipzig Bach Archive); on an upper floor of the house, a special *Festsaal* was used for playing music.

Figure 3.19. In Bach's day, drinking coffee was very much an adult and *galant* activity (fig. 9.6, p. 278–79), associated with reading newspapers, lively conversation, and listening to music. In 1723 the Collegium Musicum (essentially a student music club) connected to the New Church began performing under Georg Balthasar Schott in Zimmermann's Coffeehouse in the Katharinenstraße, shown here, with summer performances in Zimmermann's Coffee Garden outside the city's Grimma Gate. Bach took over the group in 1729 and continued to lead it at least until Zimmermann's death in 1741 (except 1737–9, when he handed it over to his student Carl Gotthelf Gerlach, organist at the New Church). There was also at least one other, similar group performing at a different coffeehouse, but Bach's concerts—which involved not only the Collegium, but his family and other students, town musicians, and visiting artists (some of them of star quality)—had the best reputation. Although performances were given throughout the year, extra ones were scheduled during the fairs.

In contrast to this lively construction of private residences, the important civic buildings in Leipzig had been realized in earlier eras. The impressive City Hall, for example, begun in the 1550s and renovated in 1672, dominated the large market that opened the center of the city (fig. 3.20).[33] Its long masonry walls of three stories were topped by an

Figure 3.20. After his succession as elector of Saxony and election as king of Poland, August III went to Leipzig to receive the homage of its inhabitants on April 20–21, 1733, an event captured in an engraving by Johann Georg Schreiber. According to an eyewitness, on the first day the people wore white-gray clothing with white buttons and got into formation in the market square at eight o'clock in the morning to await the royal party, which arrived about four o'clock through the Grimma Gate. After the king had settled into his apartment in Apel's House across from the City Hall, the crowd gave a threefold *Salve!* and then a threefold *Vivat!*, then exited in orderly fashion waving their hats. The next day they returned to the marketplace at eight o'clock, dressed now in black coats and facing the City Hall (left side of picture, with tower), whereupon they repeated the oath of fealty read out to them, the king listening with his hat off. Upon conclusion of the oath, the king raised his hand and shouted, "*Vivat!*" which the crowd repeated with such enthusiasm that the king smiled. August III was then transported to Apel's House, where he held a sumptuous banquet for the nobility and other notables.

Figure 3.21. Presumably taking its name from the good tidbits to eat that were sold there, such as in the *Garküche* or eating-house (the long building on the right), the Naschmarkt (*naschen*, to savor or eat with pleasure, especially sweets) was also the site of Leipzig's stock market, shown here at the end of the plaza with the back of the Town Hall at left. During the years 1727–49, the theatrical troupe of Caroline Neuber (fig. 5.1, p. 192) sometimes appeared on an open-air stage in the Naschmarkt. Engraving by G. Bodenehr, ca.1700.

imposing cornice, with a massive roof above enlivened by six multistory dormers. A tower and balcony marked the central cross-axis of the market, and an arcade created a sheltered walkway at ground level. The freestanding stock exchange (*Börse*) located on one end of the Naschmarkt was more recent, 1678–87, built by Christian Richter after a design of the important Dresden architect Johann Georg Starcke (fig. 3.21).[34] The building cube on a one-story base was articulated by decorated pilasters and spandrels, quoins, a rich frame around the entrance, and a balustrade with statuary. An impressive, freestanding double stair led to the front entrance. Prominent buildings such as these from the seventeenth century, established the presence of bourgeois political and economic authority in the urban life of the city.

Both of these domains were distinct from the medieval architectural setting that shaped Bach's musical life. The centerpiece of this activity was St. Thomas's Church and its associated school, in which Bach and his family lived together with the boarder pupils (fig. 9.2, p. 271). The Leipzig city councilor responsible for overseeing St. Thomas's Church was Gottfried Lange (fig. 9.3, p. 272), who supported Bach's desire to carry out his office in the style of a capellmeister (music director) rather than as a cantor, the latter office implying strong academic interests as well as teaching responsibilities.[35] Moreover, Bach wanted to maintain a freelance, subsidiary career as an organist, since he had no organist obligations in Leipzig and yet was famous as a performer on the organ and as an expert in organ design.

St. Thomas's Church was built and rebuilt into Bach's time (fig. 3.22).[36] A new church had been consecrated in 1218, its rebuilt (and present) choir in 1355. The nave, constructed anew in 1482–96, was changed inside in 1570 with the addition of galleries. An octagonal tower added in 1537 was crowned with a new lantern in 1702, providing a prominent urban marker. The consequence of this building history was, for all practical purposes, two interiors: the older choir—deep, narrow, and low–separated by gate and altar from the later nave—a six-bay

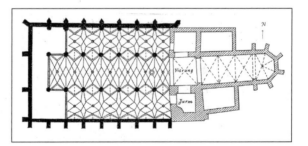

Figure 3.22. The history of Leipzig begins in 1160, when Margrave Otto the Rich of Meissen granted a city charter to the Castle of Libzi and surrounding area; foundations of a church dating from that period exist below the present choir and crossing of St. Thomas's Church. Silver mining in the hills south of the city (Erzgebirge) gave the city the means to improve its ecclesiastical architecture; by 1496 the Romanesque nave had been replaced by a hall church, an expansion that required moving the city wall—an indication of how highly the church was regarded. Although there have been additions to the church since then, these have mostly been removed so that the present building, shown in this plan, suggests the form it had around 1500.

Figure 3.23. St. Thomas's was ranked second among Leipzig's churches, but has become Leipzig's most beloved and famous one, no doubt because Bach held the title of cantor of St. Thomas's School (where he also lived) and is buried in the church. In the thirteenth century it was part of an Augustinian monastery, and the students at the associated school began the tradition, still followed, of contributing to the music at other city churches. The interior decor of the church, where twelve of Bach's twenty children were baptized, has changed greatly since Bach's time. For one thing, the splendid baroque altar, the initial money for which had been willed by the mayor Jacob Born and which is visible in this painting of 1885 by Hubert Kratz, was removed in 1887, being considered "too Catholic."

hall church, almost square in plan, with nave and aisles of similar heights and widths (fig. 3.23). The slender, polygonal nave piers supported billowing vaults spun over with a set of interwoven ribs, creating an open, spacious interior reminiscent of the hall churches that Bach experienced from Ohrdruf to Mühlhausen. Distinctive here were the substantial wooden galleries, which filled the aisles, and a large gallery located over the crossing arch. The organ was located over the western entrance to the nave. The pews were not arranged toward the choir, but instead faced one another across the length of the interior, emphasizing the width of the hall and its separation from the choir. The resulting tension between east-west and north-south directions within the cubic interior, and the several levels created by galleries and organ balcony, enhanced the potential of a spatially arranged music.

Bach was also responsible for music in St. Nicholas's Church, where, however, the tone for activities was set by Councilor Abraham Platz, Bach's nemesis on the city council and for a time one of the three rotating mayors of Leipzig.[37] St. Nicholas's church was the official municipal church. The Superintendent performed his official functions here, here municipal celebrations occurred, and it was here on May 30, 1723, that the new director of the city music presented his inaugural cantata, *Die Elenden sollen essen* (BWV 75). The interior of the church today, in contrast to its rough and awkward exterior, is a spectacle of white fluted columns topped by feathery plumes for capitals, from which elegant palm leaves arch into a ribbed vault. All of this derives, however,

from a late-eighteenth-century remod-
eling, which transformed the interior
that Bach would have experienced. Indeed, St. Nicholas's Church predated St.
Thomas's, even if only the foundations
of the two facade towers remain from
the late twelfth century. The choir and
attached north chapel are fourteenth-
century; the balancing south chapel
dates from 1467. A squarish hall church
was built between facade and choir,
begun in 1513 and consecrated in 1526,
its nave and aisles of equal height and
width, covered by ribbed net vaulting
supported by polygonal piers (fig. 3.24).
Galleries set within the aisles faced the
nave, large windows opened the walls,
and two modest apsidal chapels located
to the north and south opposite one another established a minor cross axis. This
interior from Bach's time, in short, was
similar to that of St. Thomas's Church as
a space for music.

A collegium musicum was tradition-

Figure 3.24. Although a twelfth-century church provided the basic ground plan of the present Church of
St. Nicholas in Leipzig, the latter's history really dates
from a sixteenth-century rebuilding, represented here,
that introduced net vaults with their patterns of inter-
locking, six-section stars. In 1555 the octagonal central tower was added, then further raised and crowned
with cupola and lantern (1730–34) during Bach's
period of service. The present Corinthian capitals on
columns and pilasters supporting the galleries and the
palm-frond decoration that sprouts from the top of the
columns in the nave were added in a major late-eighteenth-century renovation. St. Nicholas's Church was
the highest ranked of Leipzig's churches, since it was
the official municipal church. Thus, Bach's works celebrating the installation of a new town council (BWV
29, 69, 119, 120, and 193) were performed here, as
were his audition cantatas BWV 22 and 23.

ally connected with the organist and music director of the New Church, which represents
the third church of importance to Bach in Leipzig.[38] The New Church was a rectangular
space organized in unexpected ways, the result of its odd building history (fig. 3.25). Originally the medieval church for the Franciscan monastery (*Barfusskirche*), it was rebuilt
from 1488 to 1504 as a two-aisled hall. With the removal of the choir in the sixteenth century, the church was secularized, then re-sanctified in 1698 as the Protestant New Church.
Rebuilt during the later nineteenth century as St. Matthew's Church in Neo-Gothic form,
it was destroyed in 1943, the debris removed in 1949. An engraving of the interior as Bach
would have known it shows five massive piers down the middle that support ribbed vaults
and divide the interior in two equal halves along the entrance-altar axis. Two tiers of
galleries are wrapped asymmetrically around three sides of the interior (entrance, north
wall, altar), with organ and galleries centered on the south wall. Above the galleries, rows
of large windows opened the interior to ample light. The result was a bright, two-part hall,
in which sight lines and perhaps sound quality were interrupted by the heavy piers.[39]

Dresden and the New Architecture

In Leipzig, the lively construction of imposing houses offered a contemporary architecture very different from the overall setting of the medieval city with its older civic and religious structures. But from there, Bach could and did travel to places where a new architecture flourished, and we must also consider this work in thinking about his music.

Bach's most extensive exposure to current architectural practice was Dresden, which he had visited in 1717, and to which he would travel many times during his Leipzig years, including 1725, 1731, 1733, 1736, 1738, and 1741 (plate 18). During these decades, Dresden was being rapidly transformed into a resplendent Residence city, from the beginning of August the Strong's reign in 1694 (Friedrich August I, elector of Saxony, and from 1697 August II, king of Poland (fig. 1.2a, p. 77), through the death of his son and successor Elector Friedrich August II (King August III of Poland) in 1763 (plates 15 and 17).[40] August's key architect was Matthäus Daniel Pöppelmann, who had trained within the office of works from 1680 on.[41] August sent Pöppelmann to Vienna and Rome, "to examine the current manner of constructing both palaces and gardens, but in particular to consult with the outstanding architects and artists about the designs . . . of the [Dresden] palace." August's interest in architecture, often consuming, concerned building not only in itself but also as a form of political activity. "Princes win immortality," he wrote to his son, "through great buildings as well as with great victories." He intended to completely rebuild his Dresden palace in grand

Figure 3.25. Located in the northwestern part of the city, the New Church, built on the site of the former Franciscan Church, was consecrated in 1699. It was the third-ranked of the four churches for which the cantor of St. Thomas had musical oversight, and hence a student prefect, not the cantor, directed the third choir of St. Thomas in motets and chorales performed on Sundays there. However, in 1701 the enterprising organist and law student Georg Philipp Telemann (fig. 8.1, p. 245) had founded an organization of music-loving students, the Collegium Musicum, which augmented these meager musical resources with much more sophisticated repertory on special occasions. In 1729 Bach's student Carl Gotthelf Gerlach was appointed organist at the New Church; that year Bach took over the Collegium Musicum from its director G. B. Schott.

Figure 3.26. Dresden, Zwinger, view by Bellotto (1754). The greatest architectural monument to the ambitions of August the Strong is the Zwinger, seen in this view (ca. 1752) by Bernardo Bellotto (also known as "Canaletto"). The Zwinger was built 1711–28 to designs of Matthäus Daniel Pöppelmann, who, after study trips to Italy and elsewhere, spent his professional life entirely in the service of the Dresden court, where he became senior state architect in 1718. This view shows the spacious courtyard that served as a parade ground and for other purposes. Spectators could view events from several levels (as depicted in the painting). The Kronentor (Crown Gate), seen at right, was shaped using both architectural and sculptural elements—an example of how eighteenth-century architecture and sculpture were often integrated one with the other.

Figure 3.27. Not a residence, the Zwinger provided both outdoor and indoor venues for colorful court entertainments. This pen and ink drawing by A. M. Wernerin depicts the Carousel of the Elements, a production that was part of the marriage celebration of the electoral Crown Prince Friedrich August II (later King August III) to the Habsburg princess Maria Josepha in 1719. Other kinds of spectacle, such as military exercises, equestrian ballets, medieval-style tournaments and jousts, enclosed hunts, and even naval exercises (with the courtyard flooded) also took place here.

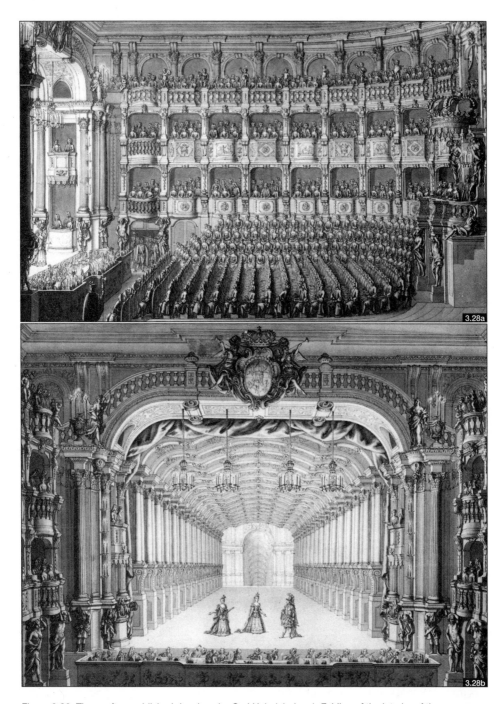

Figure 3.28. These often-published drawings by Carl Heinrich Jacob Fehling of the interior of the new opera house in the Zwinger were long thought to represent a performance of the opera *Teofane* by the Venetian composer Antonio Lotti for the wedding of the electoral Crown Prince Friedrich August II to the Habsburg princess Maria Josepha in 1719. However, Michael Walter (2000) has cast doubt on both the work depicted and the occasion. What can be said is that the drawings were included in a 1729 collection of images intended to memorialize the 1719 wedding, for which the opera house was built, although the drawings themselves probably date from years after the event. See also fig. 8.16 (p. 259).

form after a devastating fire of 1701, a project that would never be completed. One spectacular part of it was realized, however: the so-called Zwinger, which must have attracted Bach's attention.

Zwinger refers to a fortification bastion, out of which the building was developed as a monumental stadium for races and festive celebrations (fig. 3.26).[42] By 1718, the Zwinger was being accepted as a building in its own right, to serve as the setting for the marriage ceremonies of the crown prince to the emperor's daughter the following year (fig. 3.27). It was a remarkable structure, a large rectangle expanded on the longitudinal axis by smaller rectangles and sweeping crescents, arranged around a broad open space. Richly designed oval pavilions enlivened with a spirited sculptural program marked the apex of the crescents; rectangular halls anchored the corners. On one side, a long wing established the flank of the rectangle with a monumental entrance in the form of a crown at its center.[43] The drama of the architecture and the space it commands is driven home by a particular aspect of the Zwinger: its function as a set of viewing platforms. A broad masonry strip at its base, terraces, balconies, exterior stairs, interiors that face out through large openings,

Figure 3.29. Georg Bähr, designer of Dresden's beloved signature Church of Our Lady (*Frauenkirche*), trained as a carpenter, but his expertise grew to include mechanics, architectural drawing, and many other arts. This led to his appointment as Dresden's master carpenter and then cleric of works (*Bauvoigt*) as well as to architectural commissions. Fond of Greek-cross plans, Bähr modified his original design of Our Lady's Church to an octagon with choir and altar extended outward. A controversial feature was the huge, steep dome, the stability of which is a tribute to his ability as a structural engineer. Each side of the exterior is decorated with a projecting frontispiece consisting of pilasters and triangular pediment, and each corner is a stair-tower. In a Lutheran city ruled by a Catholic, the church was a municipal project viewed as a Protestant antipode to the grand buildings arising under August the Strong (who nonetheless gave support to it).

even the flat roof of the Kronentor wing, all provide areas at different levels that offer multiple views of the court and the architecture. This highly ornate viewing platform, a complex amalgam of building and sculpture, a grandstand as much on display as for display, extroverted but focused into the space it contained, was the liveliest and most complex performance of the new architecture that Bach would have experienced.

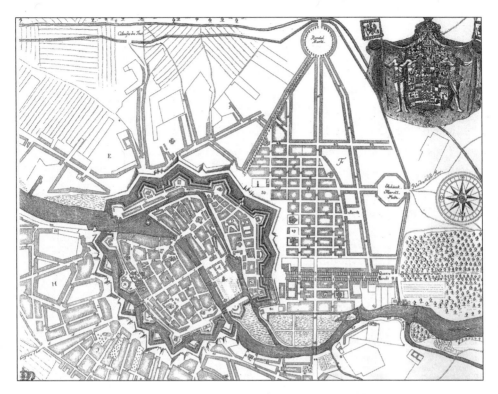

Figure 3.30. This detail of a plan of Berlin by G. Dusableau (1737), oriented with south at the top, shows the historic core of the city surrounded by massive fortifications. The Spree River flows through the center of the city from left to right. The royal palace is marked by "A". The straight, wide street that extends across the river to the northeast (lower right) would be developed as Unter den Linden. To the southwest of the fortified city is the planned, formal extension of the city, built in the 1680s and 1720s. A triad of streets branch out from the circular market (Rondel Markt, top right). The central north-south street is the Friedrichstraße, which runs through a grid of blocks; along the western edge of this are the octagonal and square markets. Also outside the defensive walls, but to the northeast, are the unplanned extensions of the city, marked by "H," "J," and "K."

An opera house (fig. 3.28a–b) was nestled into the southeast corner of the Zwinger, a pendant to the Redoutenhaus in the northeast corner. Within a masonry building shell begun in 1718 by Pöppelmann, the wooden interior was designed by the Venetian theater architect Alessandro Mauro, who also produced the scenes, machines, and gilding of the interior.[44] The typically deep stage occupied half the interior, proscenium and audience the other half. Orchestra seating and three tiers of boxes, arranged on a horseshoe plan, could accommodate an impressive two thousand viewers. Rapidly constructed, the interior was rebuilt in 1738 and again in 1749–50.

If Bach's involvements with events at the Zwinger and opera remain unclear, we do know that he gave concerts on the Silbermann organ in Our Lady's Church, one of Dresden's most dramatic new buildings, commissioned not by the court but by the city council (fig. 3.29). Perhaps the most imposing Protestant church to be built in the century following the end of the Thirty Years' War, Our Lady's Church dominated the Dresden sky-line.[45] Designed by Georg Bähr, the church was begun in 1726, consecrated in 1734, and completed in all its detail by 1743. The circular, vertical interior was capped by a pierced dome, which opened to the volumi-nous, double-shelled masonry dome of the exterior. Several stories of balconies with steep seating were arranged along the walls to focus the congrega-tion visually and aurally on the

Figure 3.31. The golden age of Potsdam, located near Berlin in the electorate of Brandenburg, was the reign of the enlightened but absolute Hohenzollern monarch Frederick II ("the Great"; r. 1740–86). Aggressively bellicose yet philosophical, artistic, and refined, he made Prussia a great European power while simulta-neously causing his court to become a center of French culture and ideas. There being already a royal residence in Potsdam (fig. 8.9, p. 252), the king created "Sanssouci" (1745–8), with its re-fined interiors and terraced gardens to designs by his architect Georg Wenzeslaus von Knobelsdorff, as a pleasure palace. It is seen here from the gardens in an engraving by G. B. Probst (ca.1750).

pulpit, indicating the importance of sermons (plate 20). Bach's organ recitals in the dramatically vertical church exposed him to a unique religious setting, a multilevel spatiality more concentrated than the Zwinger.

When Bach visited Berlin in 1719 to purchase a harpsichord (fig. 8.8, p. 251), he would have experienced a city different from any other he had known, even on visits to Dresden and Leipzig. The medieval core of the double city Berlin/Cölln, familiar in kind but newly defined by fortifications completed in 1683, had been expanded to the west and south with a large-scale grid and generous, rectangular markets[46] (fig. 3.30). Dorotheen Stadt, begun 1674, was anchored by the broad Linden-Allee (laid out already in 1647), and Friedrichstadt, several times its size, was begun in 1688. The imposing scale and rigorous order of these efforts, which easily doubled the physical size of the older city, presented a distinctively new attitude toward urban construc-tion, as would be seen later in Turin and Nancy.

Bach's return visits to Berlin, following the succession of Frederick II ("The Great") (plate 13) as King of Prussia in 1740, introduced him to a new architecture consonant with this urbanism: for example, in Potsdam there was the summer palace of Sanssouci (fig. 3.31); in Berlin, the new opera house (fig. 3.32).

Sanssouci and the opera were projects by Georg Wenceslaus von Knobelsdorff, ap-pointed superintendent of the royal palaces and gardens upon Frederick's ascension to

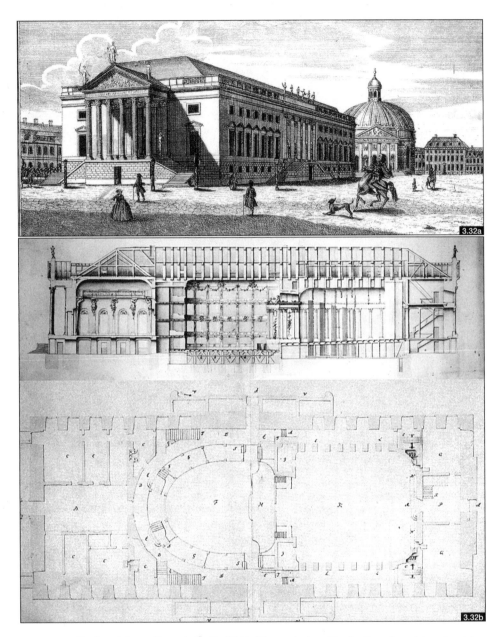

Figure 3.32. The Royal Opera House in Berlin (1741–43) was designed by the Prussian aristocrat, painter-architect, and trusted royal advisor Knobelsdorff, who renounced a military career for art and architecture. It was the only realized component of a grand plan that was to have included a royal palace and the Academy of Science and Letters—collectively, a "Forum Fridericianum"—at the head of Unter den Linden. This represented the vision of the young King Frederick II ("the Great"), who immediately after succeeding to the throne in 1740 made the opera house, which opened in 1742, his first project—he was determined to demonstrate priorities different from those of his brutal, militaristic father. Having been denied the grand tour that was a normal part of a nobleman's education, Frederick sent Knobelsdorff to Italy, Paris, and Dresden to study contemporary architecture before entrusting the opera house to his care. The undecorated facade (a), then unique in Germany, reflects an austere and monumental architectural taste. Engraving by David Schleuen, ca. 1770.

the throne.[47] To support the king's taste for French art, Knobelsdorff traveled to Paris by way of Dresden in the fall of 1740 for intense immersion in its new architecture. This experience and his close association with Frederick resulted in distinctive designs of sparse elegance, distinguished by simple, unornamented, carefully proportioned building masses outside, and restrained, graceful, refined rocaille decoration inside.[48] These characteristics informed Knobelsdorff's opera house of 1741–43 (later altered, enlarged, and reconstructed), the first freestanding building of this type. It was in this opera house, as later reported by C. P. E. Bach in 1774, that Bach demonstrated his acute awareness of acoustics. If one whispered into a corner of the rectangular hall, the sound could be clearly heard in the opposite corner but nowhere else.[49] Perhaps this perceptiveness of aural architectural performance also informed Bach's visual and spatial sensibilities toward buildings that provided settings for his music as well as the cities in which he lived.

Notes

This essay has profited greatly from the close readings and detailed suggestions of William Cowdery and Raymond Erickson. I thank them both for their assistance and contributions.

1. Werner Felix, *Johann Sebastian Bach* (Leipzig: Deutscher Verlag für Musik, 1984), 184.
2. Werner Neumann, *Auf den Lebenswegen Johann Sebastian Bachs*, 4th rev. ed. (Berlin: Verlag der Nation, 1962), 307–9.
3. For background on the Holy Roman Empire, see the literature cited in Chapter 1.
4. Kenneth Clark, *Civilization, A Personal View* (New York: Harper & Row, 1970), 226.
5. Walled medieval cities were not determined by any standard set of urban forms and spaces. Their arrangements were unique according to topography, economic activity, political position, cultural beliefs, and the circumstances of their building. Their plans included an extensive range of radial, linear, market-based, and modified grid configurations. The notion of the medieval town as a cone-shaped buildup of structures, from low, outer ring to soaring cathedral spire at the center of town is romanticized fiction. See A. E. J. Morris, *History of Urban Form Before the Industrial Revolutions*, 2nd. ed. (New York: John Wiley and Sons, 1979), 66–120; Howard Saalman, *Medieval Cities* (New York: Braziller, 1968).
6. A succinct reprise of the state of knowledge about Versailles, the subject of a vast literature, is Jean-Marie Pérouse de Montclos, *Versailles* (Paris: Editions Mengès, 1991; English translation New York: Abbeville Press, 1991). On Turin, see Martha D. Pollock, *Turin 1564–1680, Urban Design, Military Culture, and the Creation of the Absolutist Capital* (Chicago: University of Chicago Press, 1991). On Nancy, see Paulette Choné, *Le grand Nancy, histoire d'un espace urbain* (Nancy: Presses universitaires de Nancy, 1993).
7. Spiro Kostof, *A History of Architecture, Settings and Rituals*, 2nd ed. (New York: Oxford University Press, 1995), 343f.
8. *Editor's Note*: To assist the reader unfamiliar with architectural terminology, there follow brief definitions of a number of standard terms used in the ensuing discussion.

basilica: a church with three aisles separated by two rows of columns or piers; the middle aisle (nave) is higher than the roof over the side aisles and has a clerestory.

bay: the compartments into which a nave is divided by vertical elements such as piers or columns; also, a recess or opening in a wall.

clerestory: the upper part of the nave that rises above the roof of the aisles and is opened by windows to light the interior.

cour d'honneur: the area, often used for ceremonial activities, delimited on three sides by the central and parallel side wings of a palace.

crossing: the intersection of nave and transept.

dormer: a window set vertically in a roof; also, the gable holding it.

Latin cross: a cross with the vertical member longer than the horizontal one.

lunette: a space, usually over a door or window, that may contain a sculpture, another window, a mural, etc.

pier: a masonry support, often rectangular in plan, and distinct from a column.

quoin: the dressed stones on building corners, arranged alternately large and small.

sala terrena: ground-level interior space or room.

scagliola: plaster (gypsum and glue mixed with colored marble or stone dust) made to look like marble, mostly used on interior columns, pilasters, and moldings.

spandrel: the triangular space between the curve of an arch, the horizontal line at its apex, and the vertical line at its springing; also used for the space between two contiguous arches.

transept: the structure that crosses the long side of the church at right angles between nave and altar area, forming the "arms" of the cruciform.

vault: the curved ceiling structure, usually masonry, on the inside of a building such as a church. In a *barrel* or *tunnel vault*, the curve is semicircular for the length of the vault; a *groin vault* results when two barrel vaults of same size are built at right angles to each other, resulting in elliptically curved edges (groins); the medieval *ribbed vault* involved ribs that served as a structural skeleton, crossing diagonally at the midpoint of each bay of the ceiling, with the rest of the area of the vault filled in with lighter material. The ribs had a decorative as well as structural function.

9. The most detailed compendium of Bach sites is Martin Petzoldt, *Bachstätten aufsuchen* (Leipzig: Kunst und Touristik, 1992; rev. ed. Frankfurt a. M.: Insel, 2000), to which references in this essay are made. Four additional texts are useful as illustrated collections that include buildings and cities: Werner Felix, *Johann Sebastian Bach*; Hans Conrad Fischer, *Johann Sebastian Bach, Sein Leben in Bildern und Documenten* (Neuhausen-Stuttgart: Hänssler, 1985) [Hänssler-Musikbücher 11]; Winfried Hoffmann, *Reisen zu Bach, Erinnerungsstätten an Johann Sebastian Bach* (Berlin/Leipzig: VEB Tourist Verlag, 1985); and Werner Neumann, *Auf den Lebenswegen Johann Sebastian Bachs*.

10. Fischer, *Bach*, ill.12. Petzoldt, *Bachstätten*, 159–61, notes that the location of a new organ, under construction from the 1670s to 1713, was changed several times. It eventually was located above the west entrance, with the musicians' balcony stacked above it.

11. Neumann, *Lebenswegen*, 37–40.

12. The church tower was topped off in 1657–59, the tower of the western facade completed 1732–37. Hermann Hipp, *Freie und Hansestadt Hamburg, Geschichte, Kultur und Stadtbaukunst an Elbe und Alster* (Cologne: DuMont Buchverlag, 1989), 162–64.

13. Neumann, *Lebenswegen*, 45–49.

14. Brunhilde Windoffer, *Bachsteinbauten zwischen Lübeck und Stralsund* (Berlin: Nicolaische Verlagsbuchhandlung Beuermann, 1990), 68, 73–75, 77.

15. Ernst Badstübner and Wolfgang Hanke, *Die Blasiuskirche zu Mühlhausen*, 3rd rev. ed. (Berlin: Union Verlag, 1984) [Das christliche Denkmal, Heft 56].

16. *NBR*, 40, from Werner David, *Johann Sebastian Bachs Orgeln* (Berlin: aus Anlass der Wiederöffnung der Berliner Musikinstrumenten-Sammlung, 1951), 83. Quoted and discussed in Konrad Küster, *Der junge Bach* (Stuttgart: Deutsche Verlags-Anstalt, 1996), 156–59.

17. Introductions to this new architecture are: Thomas DaCosta Kaufmann, *Court, Cloister, and City: The Art and Culture of Central Europe, 1450–1800* (Chicago: University of Chicago Press, 1995); Alastair Laing, "Central and Eastern Europe," in *Baroque & Rococo, Architecture and Decoration*, ed. Anthony Blunt (New York: Harper & Row, 1978), 165–296; Rolf Toman, ed., *Baroque. Architecture, Sculpture, Painting* (Cologne, Könemann, 1998).

18. Jörg Gamer, "Die Benediktinerabteikirche Neresheim," in *Balthasar Neumann in Baden-Württemberg: Bruchsal-Karlsruhe-Stuttgart-Neresheim* [exhibition catalog] (Staatsgalerie Stuttgart, 1975), 93–119.

19. Neumann, *Lebensweg*, 83–87; Fischer, *Bach*, ill. 35, 37, 42; Petzoldt, *Bachstätten*, 176–80. [The drawing that is fig. 3.9 was done by Prof. Herman Wirth and appears in his "Von der Wasserburg an der Ilm zum Weimarer Residenzschloß," *Burgen und Schloßer* 1 (Braubach am Rhein, 1992), 31. On new research concerning the Himmelsburg, see Helen Geyer, *Bach in Weimar* (1708–17) (Göttingen: Hainholz, 2008) and the forthcoming work by Weimar architechtural historian Alexander Grychtolik. —Ed.]

20. Neumann, *Lebensweg* 97; Rose-Marie and Reiner Frenzel, *Kunst- und Kulturführer Leipzig, Halle und Umgebung* (Leipzig: Edition Leipzig, 1993), 139f.

21. Frenzl, *Leipzig*, 56f. Caspar Kraft designed the building and supervised construction from 1530 until his death in 1540. Nickel Hoffmann completed the church, 1545–49.

22. Neumann, *Lebensweg*, 108, 111; Petzoldt, *Bachstätten*, 68f.

23. It was here that Bach's patron, Prince Leopold, held his morning *levée* or ceremonial awakening and dressing. The prince's bed, moved in and out each day, was called the "Himmelbett," because its baldacchino depicted the heavens. Information from Inga Streuber of the Bach-Museum und -Gedenkstätte, Cöthen. Moreover, according to Ms. Streuber, Leopold preferred to do his actual sleeping elsewhere and only held the ceremonial *levée* in the throne room. (This reminds one of how Louis XV of France likewise preferred less formal surroundings for sleep, and so had to move each morning to the royal bedroom for his *grande levée*.) —Ed.

24. Hoffmann, *Reisen zu Bach*, 89. Left to deteriorate over the years, the chapel has been restored to baroque form.

25. *Geschichte der Stadt Erfurt*, ed. Willibald Gutsche (Weimar: Hermann Böhlaus Nachfolger, 1986), 145–57.

26. Neumann, *Lebenswegen*, 117.

27. Erich Hubala and Otto Mayer, *Die Residenz zu Würzburg* (Würzburg: Edition Popp, 1984).

28. Ekhart Berckenhagen, *Barock in Deutschland, Residenzen* [exhibition catalogue], Museumsgebäude Berlin-Charlottenburg, September 1 to November 6, 1966 (Berlin: Verlag Bruno Hessling, 1966).

29. An older but excellent introduction to the urbanism and architecture of Leipzig is *Leipziger Bautradition* (Leipzig: VEB Bibliographisches Institut, 1955) (Leipziger Stadtgeschichtliche Forschungen, Heinz Füßler, ed., Heft 4.) Also see Hoffmann, *Reisen*, 91–145 and Petzoldt, *Bachstätten*, 74–109. On the seventeenth- and eighteenth-century architecture of Leipzig, the classic text is Nikolaus Pevsner, *Leipziger Barock, Die Bau-*

kunst der Barockzeit in Leipzig (Dresden: Verlag von Wolfgang Jess, 1928; rpt. Leipzig, VEB E.A. Seemann Verlag, 1990).

30. A 1740 oil painting by Alexander Thiele depicts the western outskirts of Leipzig (Stadtgeschichtliches Museum, Leipzig).

31. Engraved bird's-eye view of Leipzig, dated 1614, in *Leipziger Bautradition*, fig. 63.

32. Pevsner, *Leipziger Barock*, 1–9.

33. Bird's-eye view of the market and Rathaus, engraving by J. G. Schreiber, 1712 (Leipzig, Stadtgeschichtliches Museum); market elevation of Rathaus dated 1672, showing stone arcade, see *Leipziger Bautradition*, fig. 12.

34. *Leipziger Bautradition*, fig. 79.

35. Ulrich Siegele, "Bach and the domestic politics of Electoral Saxony," *The Cambridge Companion to Bach*, John Butt, ed. (Cambridge: Cambridge University Press, 1997), 17–34.

36. *Leipziger Bautradition*, 40–46. A gouache painting by Hubert Kratz, dated 1885, shows the "Bach interior" before the renovation that was begun in 1886. The church was restored again in 1961–64.

37. Siegele, "Bach and domestic politics," *Leipziger Bautradition*, 32–34.

38. Siegele, "Bach and domestic politics," Felix, *Bach*, fig. 55.

39. Of minor importance was the Universitätskirche St. Pauli, which saw the performance of Bach's *Trauer-Ode* and perhaps Cantata 191; Neumann, *Lebenswegen*, 199, and Butt, *Cambridge Companion*, 116.

40. A vivid impression of the city is given in an oil painting of 1748 by Bernardo Bellotto, called Canaletto (plate 18).

41. Hermann Heckmann, *Matthäus Daniel Pöppelmann, Leben und Werk* (Munich/Berlin: Deutscher Kunstverlag, 1972); *Matthäus Daniel Pöppelmann, 1662–1736, Ein Architekt des Barocks in Dresden*, exhibition catalogue, Staatliche Kunstsammlungen Dresden, March 13, 1987–May 13, 1987.

42. For the Zwinger, see in addition in note 44, Eberhard Hempel, *Der Zwinger zu Dresden, Grundzüge und Schicksale seiner künstlerischen Gestaltung* (Berlin: Deutscher Verein für Kunstwissenschaft, 1961).

43. The counterpart to this wing remained a temporary structure, to be eventually completed in the nineteenth century as the Gemälde Galerie, designed by Gottfried Semper.

44. Martin Hammitzsch, *Der moderne Theaterbau. Der höfische Theaterbau, der Anfang der modernen Theaterbaukunst, ihre Entwicklung und Betätigung zur Zeit der Renaissance, des Barock, und des Rokoko* (Berlin: E. Wasmuth, 1906) (Beiträge zur Bauwissenschaft 8); Günther Meinert, "Das große Opernhaus am Zwinger" in *Pöppelmann*, exhibition catalogue, 74.

45. Matthias Gretzschel, *Die Dresdner Frauenkirche* (Hamburg: Ellert und Richter, 1995). On design theory of the time regarding Protestant church architecture, see Leonhard Christoph Sturm, *Architektonische Bedenken von Protestantischen kleinen Kirchen Figur und Einrichtung* (Hamburg, 1712). Destroyed in World War II, Our Lady's Church has been rebuilt from the surviving rubble.

46. Uwe Kieling, *Berlin, Baumeister und Bauten, Von der Gotik bis zum Historismus* (Berlin/Leipzig: VEB Tourist Verlag, 1987), 55–57; Petzoldt, *Bachstätten*, 32–37.

47. Tilo Eggeling, *Studien zum friederizianischen Rokoko: Georg Wenceslaus von Knobelsdorff als Entwerfer von Innendekorationen* (Berlin: Mann, 1980); Hans-Joachim Kadatz, *Georg Wenzeslaus von Knobelsdorff, Baumeister Friedrichs II* (Munich: Verlag C.H. Beck, 1983).

48. *Sanssouci, Schlösser, Gärten, Kunstwerke*, bearbeitet von einem Autorenkollektiv der Abteilungen Schlösser und Garten unter Leitung von Hans-Joachim Giersberg (3rd rev. ed., Potsdam: Generaldirektion der Staatlichen Schlösser und Gärten, 1974).

49. Hoffmann, *Reisen*, 180.

CHAPTER 4

Musician-Novels of
the German Baroque

Stephen Rose

One of the biggest unknowns of the German Baroque is the mind-set of its musicians. Take Johann Sebastian Bach as an example. Whereas his compositions have been scrutinized by generations of scholars, there is little direct evidence of his opinions or his social environment. Bach rarely aired his views in letters, seemingly preferring to express himself in music rather than in words. As Carl Philipp Emanuel Bach said, "with his many activities he scarcely had time for the most necessary correspondence, and accordingly did not indulge in lengthy written exchanges."[1] Even less evidence survives about the outlook of Bach's poorer, obscurer contemporaries, such as the town pipers who played fanfares from the city walls, the military musicians who went on long campaigns, or the fiddlers and hurdy-gurdy players who offered entertainment in taverns and on the street.

One group of sources, however, offers insights into the mind-set of musicians at all levels of society. These sources are the novels by and about musicians:

Johann Beer, *Der simplicianische Welt-Kucker oder abentheuerliche Jan Rebhu* (The Simplician telescope on the world, or the adventurous Jan Rebhu) (n.p., 1677–79)

Daniel Speer, *Ungarischer oder Dacianischer Simplicissimus* (The Magyar Simplex) (n.p., 1683)

————, *Türckische-Vagant* (The Turkish vagrant) (n.p., 1683)

————, *Haspel-Hannß* (Bibbin-Hans) (n.p., 1684)

Wolfgang Caspar Printz, *Musicus vexatus oder Cotala* (Cotala, the harassed musician) (Freiberg, 1690)

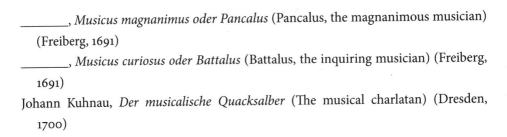

_____, *Musicus magnanimus oder Pancalus* (Pancalus, the magnanimous musician)
(Freiberg, 1691)

_____, *Musicus curiosus oder Battalus* (Battalus, the inquiring musician) (Freiberg,
1691)

Johann Kuhnau, *Der musicalische Quacksalber* (The musical charlatan) (Dresden,
1700)

The authors of these books came from the generation of musicians immediately
before Johann Sebastian Bach. Three of them (Johann Beer, Johann Kuhnau, and Wolfgang Caspar Printz) worked in the same area of central Germany as Bach. Beer was
concertmaster at the Weissenfels court, where Bach later had the title of honorary music director (*Capellmeister von Haus aus*), and Kuhnau was Bach's predecessor as cantor
of St. Thomas's in Leipzig. Daniel Speer inhabited a more distant region: although born
in Breslau (present-day Wrocław), he traveled widely in Hungarian and Romanian
lands, and later settled near Stuttgart. Nonetheless, the musician-novels are sufficiently
close together—both chronologically and geographically—to offer a composite picture
of the German musical environment around 1700.

The musician-novels are indebted to German popular literature of the seventeenth
century. Their scatological and obscene humor is similar to that found in chapbooks,
cheap printed booklets of jokes and comic anecdotes. Indeed, in the 1660s and 1670s
several chapbooks were published with attributions to stereotyped figures of street musicians, such as *Jan Tambour* (the drummer), *Leyermatz* (hurdy-gurdy man), or *Pol-
nische Sackpfeiffer* (the Polish bagpiper). There is no evidence that these books were
actually written by such musicians; rather, the itinerant minstrels may have been included as sales ploys, perhaps because of their general reputation as entertainers. The
same stereotyped musicians also make cameo appearances in Printz's writings, usually
as targets of his contempt.

The picaresque writings of Johann Jakob Grimmelshausen constitute another important influence on musician-novels. Grimmelshausen's novels portray the lives of
rogues, delinquents, and other members of the underworld. *Der abentheurliche Simplicissimus* (1669) features an orphan who is exposed to the worst of the brutality of
the Thirty Years' War (fig. 4.1); *Die Landstörtzerin Courasche* (1670) depicts a military
prostitute who ends up among the gypsies that follow armies. Particularly relevant for
our purposes is Grimmelshausen's *Der seltzame Springinsfeld* (1670), where the principal character is the offspring of a dishonorable union between a runaway Greek noblewoman and an Albanian tightrope walker. In the novel Springinsfeld recounts his life as
a traveling entertainer, as a military musician, and then as a demobilized soldier (with
a wooden leg) who earns his keep by playing the fiddle on the street and in taverns. To

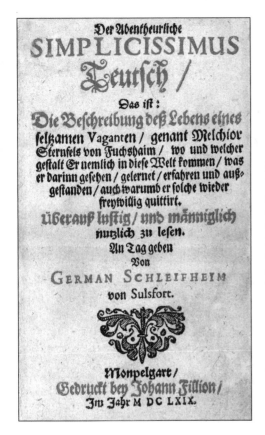

Figure 4.1. *Der abendtheurliche Simplicissimus Teutsch* (The adventurous very simple person, plainly told) is a landmark in German literature, one that has inspired new literary and musical works even into the present age. Although it lacks a rigorous plot design, the work continually engages readers, possibly because of the comic antihero that is its author-narrator, and because of the actual life experiences underlying it. In a wryly modest and often satirical tone, it recounts a series of fascinating and harrowing adventures, both realistic and purely imaginary, yet there is also a deeply religious undercurrent. The popularity and impact of the book can be inferred from the fact that Grimmelshausen followed it with nine others on the Simplicissimus or Simplicius theme. Several authors discussed in this chapter followed the trend with their own Simplicius books.

judge by the popularity of Grimmelshausen's novels, the middle-class reading public was fascinated by such social outcasts as Springinsfeld. The novels of Beer and Speer exploit this fascination, depicting musicians as similarly disreputable figures. Printz and Kuhnau, on the other hand, try to reverse the stereotype and show that musicians can be respectable members of society.

As lowly and comic genres, novels in the seventeenth century were usually published under pseudonyms or anonymously. A major task in studying the musician-novels is to unravel the chain of pen-names, puns, and cross-references that link the books to their authors.[2] Another consideration is that the term "novel" was applied to these writings only retrospectively. The title-pages of Speer's and Printz's books use the term "Lebens-lauff" (life story); indeed, all the novels save Kuhnau's *Musicalische Quacksalber* are written in the first person, as fictional autobiographies. Hence the term "novel" may obscure the contexts of oral storytelling from which these books stem, but for convenience it will be retained here, as convenient shorthand for the genre.

The following essay will introduce the reader to the characteristics of the novels and will suggest how they might shed light on Baroque musicians. In particular, this essay explains how the novels amplify our knowledge of Bach's environment, showing the full significance of short remarks that survive in the few primary documents about Bach.

Johann Beer and the Novelist's Fantasy

Johann Beer (1655–1700) was a court musician at Weissenfels from 1676 until his death (fig. 4.2). When he was in his twenties he wrote prolifically: between 1677 and 1683 at least seventeen of his novels were published. This abundant output may have been stimulated by economic necessity: Beer had briefly been a student at Leipzig, where he probably met publishers who catered to the rising demand for popular literature. In addition, Beer said that several of his novels stemmed from the stories he had told to his school friends in Regensburg, a clue to the links between oral storytelling and printed narratives.[3] He also implied that his desire to write was compulsive, like an itch: "I sit at my writing-table not to fill the world with fancy oratory. Instead I write for pleasure, for I am always itching between the ears with jolly caprices, and I must deal incessantly with this irritation."[4]

Many of Beer's novels include musical scenes or short tales told by passing musicians. In *Das Narrenspital* (1681), for instance, the protagonists visit a lunatic asylum, where one wing houses musical fools who "have driven themselves insane by studying and meditating upon composition, solmization, and the numbering of the tones."[5] Musicians also appear as itinerant entertainers, particularly in *Teutsche Winternächte* (1682) and its sequel, *Die kurtzweiligen Sommer-Täge* (1683). Both novels are set at the castles of minor Austrian nobility, where such vagrants as traveling musicians, demobilized soldiers, and penniless students offer welcome relief from the tedium of everyday life. In *Sommer-Täge* the protagonist Willenhag is mourning the deaths of his father and son, but "whenever I saw a beggar or other vagrant

Figure 4.2. One of the most interesting cultural personages of the German baroque is Johann Beer, opera singer, violinist, keyboardist, and composer on the one hand, and writer of both music-theoretical works and novels on the other. Born in Austria, he spent most of his career serving the Dukes of Saxony-Weissenfels in Halle before it became Prussian territory in 1680 and then in Weissenfels, where Bach would later be honorary music director.

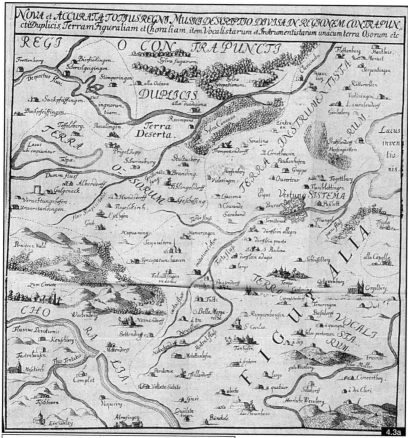

Figure 4.3. Beer's wit and feistiness is evident in his satirical *Bellum musicum* (Musical war) of 1701, in which the outcome is a treaty that, among other things, forbids country organists to realize figured bass (explained in fig. 4.6) because they are so bad at it. The book's highly amusing illustrations include a map (a) of the imaginary Cymbalic Empire with political units, geographical features, and towns all having names that pun on musical terms. Thus there are the rivers Choralia, Fortefluss, Pianofluss, and Fluss Simplicitatis (note the allusion to Grimmelshausen, fig. 4.1), and towns like Sackpfeiffingen (*Sackpfeife* = bagpipe), Triangel, Ciaccona, Sonatina, Rittornellen, and Syncopationsshausen.

Another delightful illustration is the musical soldier (b), who is a composite of various instruments: among the "armaments" depicted are some sort of wind instruments for legs (note the finger holes), cornetto-like protrusions emanating from the waist, a drum for a hat, a bow being held by a violin-arm, and a lute-like fingerboard and sackbut (the early form of the trombone).

loitering on the road or outside the castle I gave him some beer-money if he would tell me the tale of his life. Thus I dispelled my sadness, and I made a note of the best stories."[6]

Another feature of Beer's writing is the way that his characters use fanciful metaphors, often involving music. In *Der politische Feuermäuer-Kehrer* (1682), a monk preaches a sermon that refers to the fate of John the Baptist, who criticized Herod's adultery and consequently was beheaded. The monk uses a musical analogy to warn of the pitfalls of John's honesty: "If you play the truth, you'll hit someone on the head with your bow. If you whistle repentance, they'll smash your teeth with a shawm."[7] Beer's musical metaphors reach a pinnacle in *Bellum musicum* (1700), an account of the battle between Princess Harmonia and the musical bunglers of Germany (fig. 4.3a–b). Harmonia's armies consist of white and black notes, arranged in five lines like a stave. There is also a group of Greek commanders (named after the church modes) and the lieutenant Fuga (who rushes between the four members of his chief staff, named Cantus, Altus, Tenor and Bass). But some of Harmonia's forces are unreliable: Corporal Trillo takes fright and starts shaking, while the semitones aim the cannon-fire either slightly too high or too low. Later, musical scales are used as ladders to assault the walls of a fortress. When hostilities eventually cease, the musical notes that turned traitor are hung, drawn and quartered, until the quarter-notes have become sixty-fourth-notes. These elaborate metaphors would delight any trained musician; indeed, *Bellum musicum* was derived from a 1683 pamphlet that Beer devised to amuse the musicians invited to the wedding of the Weissenfels court music director, Johann Philipp Krieger.

Only in one of Beer's novels, *Der simplicianische Welt-Kucker oder abentheuerliche Jan Rebhu* (1677–79), is the main character a musician, and then merely for the first installment of this four-part book. *Welt-Kucker* is a picaresque novel, modeled on Grimmelshausen's *Simplicissimus* (as is evident from the catchpenny tag *simplicianische* in Beer's title). Like Simplicissimus, Jan Rebhu is orphaned as a child and must therefore proceed in the world without parental guidance; he goes through a series of adventures, alternating between fortune and poverty like a ball tossed up and down by fate. "Now we rejoice, now the shawm plays another tune. Today we are happy, tomorrow sad . . . today we are healthy, tomorrow we are ill."[8]

Initially Rebhu is taken to a court to serve as a soprano. The court, like that at Dresden, is dominated by Italian musicians; Rebhu is taught by a castrato and there are long conversations between the foreign musicians about the merits of various performers. Soon Rebhu is thrown into a series of erotic adventures, as an Italian countess and later a noblewoman, "Squalora," try to seduce him. He is threatened with execution but escapes to Venice with the Italian countess, where they lead a life of hedonism, avoiding churches as if these were hospitals. Rebhu's adultery with the countess leads him to the brink of execution but at the last minute he is again reprieved. The execution scenes and eroticism were staple ingredients of popular literature, presumably included to attract as many readers as possible. Later installments of the story contain other popular motifs such as a shipwreck, a desert island, and Turkish battles.

In its embrace of the secular world, a picaresque novel such as *Der simplicianische Welt-Kucker* offers a corrective to the emphasis on Lutheran piety in many studies of the German Baroque.[9] Beer's characters behave roguishly and amorally, without regard for their status or reputation. Such antics were probably intended to titillate his readers and let them experience an outcast's life vicariously. But Beer may have also had a serious point in mind. In 1697, during a dispute with Gottfried Vockerodt about the morality of music, he argued that musicians should not be judged on their behavior or religious beliefs, but on their musical achievements alone.[10] Furthermore, elements of the picaresque can be detected in the lives of some Baroque musicians. Perhaps the best example is the audacious behavior shown by the young Bach, who brawled with a bassoonist in Arnstadt and got into trouble with the church authorities there.[11] The young Bach had a taste for obscenities and double entendres, as evidenced in his insulting of the bassoonist and in the Quodlibet (BWV 524) for a Bach family reunion;[12] here is a parallel with the coarse language and racy behavior of *Der simplicianische Welt-Kucker*. The earthy exuberance of the picaresque may thus be a significant strand in German Baroque life, as much as the Lutheran piety or the personal diligence that are emphasized in many biographies of Bach.

Daniel Speer: the Musician as Traveller

Daniel Speer (1636–1707) also drew on the picaresque model of the adventurer in his novels. *Dacianische Simplicissimus* (1683) recounts the life of an orphan (Simplex), who is forced by religious persecution to leave his Silesian homeland and to travel through Hungary, Transylvania, and Romania. Simplex trains as a drummer and then as a trumpeter, serving numerous noblemen in the wars against the Turks during the late 1650s and early 1660s.[13] The novel lacks the irony and satire of the writings of Beer, Printz, and Kuhnau; instead it reads like a travelogue, with many descriptive passages (some taken verbatim from contemporary topographies). At the time of publication its description of Hungarian lands was highly relevant, for there was great public appetite for information about these territories that had again been invaded by the Turks (culminating in the Siege of Vienna, 1683). It is unclear how far *Dacianische Simplicissimus* is autobiographical, although some details of the narrative do coincide with the few known facts of Speer's early life (for instance, the childhood in Breslau; being orphaned at the age of seven; and traveling to avoid religious persecution). Further evidence that Speer journeyed to Hungarian lands is arguably found in his later publication, *Musicalisch-Türckischer Eulen-Spiegel* (1688); this contains transcriptions of eastern European dances, which Speer claimed to have witnessed firsthand on his travels.

Türckische Vagant (1683) is the sequel to *Dacianische Simplicissimus* and describes the continuation of Simplex's travels, from Constantinople to the Middle East (including Lebanon, Babylon, and Baghdad). This sequel has few references to music and hence is of limited interest to musicologists. Moreover, it is not autobiographical, instead being based on the travel accounts of two sixteenth-century Germans, the preacher Salomon Schweigger and the botanist Leonhard Rauwolf.[14] Heavy borrowings were typical of travel literature of the time, because any literate traveler would read and be influenced by existing guidebooks. Here, though, the extent of the borrowings suggests that Speer never went to the Middle East and was merely trying to satisfy the public curiosity about that region.

By contrast, Speer's *Haspel-Hannß* (1684) moves away from travel writing and back to the genre of the picaresque. It tells the story of Hans, a deformed orphan who embarks on apprenticeships first in spindle-making and later in music, but runs away from his master halfway through each apprenticeship. Thus equipped with two half-learned trades, he travels to fifteen university towns in central Europe (among them Greifswald, Prague, Tübingen, Altdorf, and Leipzig). These towns are not described with the close detail of Speer's first novel; they instead form the backdrop for Hans's pranks and thieving.

Speer's novels perpetuate the image of the musician as a social outsider; in *Dacianische Simplicissimus* and *Türckische Vagant*, Simplex's status as a stranger is intensified by his observation of foreign lands and cultures. Although Speer's novels are unusual in their focus upon Eastern Europe, his descriptions of long and hazardous journeys would have been recognized by many musicians. Johann Joachim Quantz traveled as a journeyman instrumentalist and also when music was silenced locally during mourning periods; Franz Benda roamed between Prague, Dresden, and Warsaw; many composers, including Printz, Johann David Heinichen, and Daniel Gottlob Treu, went to study in Italy. Indeed, such travels were a major reason why the reading public was attracted to the life stories of musicians. This is already evident in the chapbooks named after stereotyped street musicians. *Der überaus lustige und kurtzweilige Scheer-Geiger* (1673) claims to include "five hundred humorous and pleasant anecdotes, which the merry fiddler heard during his prolonged journeys around Germany, France, Spain, and Italy, and which have been noted down by him diligently, word for word." The preface to *Der pohlnische Sackpfeiffer* (1663) mentions the bagpiper's military adventures with the Cossacks and Tartars, even though such escapades do not feature at all in the contents of the chapbook. Travel continued to be a theme of the many autobiographies of German musicians that were published in the mid-eighteenth century.

Wolfgang Caspar Printz and the Embattled Musician

The three novels by Wolfgang Caspar Printz (1641–1717) have a more serious intent, aiming to uphold the status of instrumental musicians and integrate them within urban society. His novels are set in the world of municipal musicians—the salaried instrumentalists who undertook watchman duty, played from the towers, and supplied instrumental music in church. Such instrumentalists had a variety of titles (such as *Stadtpfeifer, Kunstpfeifer,* or *Hausmann*), and could be found in almost every German town. Many of Bach's ancestors had held such jobs, including his father, Johann Ambrosius Bach, who served as town musician in Eisenach from 1671 to 1695. Printz himself belonged to a higher level of musician—he was cantor and court composer in Sorau—but he still had experienced the world of the municipal musicians. As a teenager he learned the trombone and cornetto from the town piper in Weiden and "assisted him by playing hundreds of times from the tower."[15] Later, as a theology student at the University of Altdorf, he shared meals with the local town piper and again took on some of the duties of playing from the tower.

Printz's first novel, *Cotala* (1690), is cast as the fictional autobiography of a young instrumentalist from birth, through his apprenticeship and journeyman years, until he finally gains mastery, gets a permanent job, and marries. The novel contains many colorful tales of pranks from Cotala's years as an apprentice. Its main focus, however, is on how Cotala must defend his profession against detractors who see music as dishonorable. In the seventeenth century a wide range of professions (including shepherds, bailiffs, hangmen, skinners, and linen-weavers) were regarded as dishonorable by urban artisans, and instrumentalists were sometimes grouped with these social outcasts.[16] Cotala is the son of a wheelwright—an honorable trade—and his father opposes his musical interests as disreputable and unlikely to lead to a secure income: "If you don't want to learn the wheelwright's craft, learn what you want, but don't become a minstrel."[17] Such parental opposition to a child's interest in music was a common theme in musicians' lives of the period, occurring in John Mainwaring's *Memoirs of the Life of Handel* (London, 1760) and in Telemann's autobiography. (When Telemann wrote a school opera, his mother and other "enemies of music" prophesied that "I would become a juggler, tightrope walker, itinerant musician or monkey-trainer, unless music was taken away from me."[18]) Later Cotala defends music against insults from intellectuals and ignorant artisans. In such disputes, Cotala asserts that his trade is honest because, like those craftsmen regulated by guilds, he has learned music via an apprenticeship.

Printz's second novel includes the life story of Pancalus, another instrumental musician. Here there is less emphasis on Pancalus's training and more on his travels in Italy, in particular his time at the court of the Marquis of Pomponio. The musicians at this court find their place in the court hierarchy jeopardized by other court servants: first the tailor, then the wine steward, cooks, barbers, and gardeners all claim precedence over musicians. The musicians defend their status by asserting the importance of music, pointing to its emotional, religious, and political power, and noting that it requires both manual and intellectual skill in its practitioners.

The episode allows Printz not only to rehearse arguments for the worth of musicians, but also to stress the pitfalls of court employment. Although Printz himself worked at the Sorau court, in *Pancalus* he criticized the hypocrisy of courtiers—"the greatest art of a court-flatterer is to act and appear entirely different from how he is"[19]—and he even claimed that courtly service is inimical to the honesty of an "upright German." Printz was not alone in his misgivings about courtly service: Telemann in his autobiographies of 1718 and 1740 was wary about the volatility of courtly employment. But other musicians, such as Johann Beer, preferred courtly life over the mediocrity of urban culture. As one of the characters in Beer's novels says:

> It's much more pleasant if you're at court at a well-set table with beautiful and lovely music, than to be invited to a wedding in town, first by a furrier, then by a tanner. At the town wedding you must settle for roasted sparrows and blackbirds rather than pheasants; you get red-and-yellow children's sweets rather than sweetmeats; and instead of delightful music you get an earful from the minstrels, imperiling you with grave illness or deafness unless you're bled soon afterwards.[20]

In the case of Printz's *Pancalus*, though, the rejection of courtly service was a sentiment also held by many urban artisans; it supports Printz's wish that musicians be properly integrated within urban society.

In Printz's third novel the eponymous protagonist, Battalus, is another municipal musician and he also travels to Italy, but as a military shawm player. The focus of the novel, though, is a dispute between Battalus and the so-called beer-fiddlers (freelance instrumentalists) about the right to play at weddings. Similar clashes between municipal musicians and freelancers are documented in many German towns of the seventeenth century; for instance in Eisenach, Bach's father Johann Ambrosius repeatedly complained how the beer-fiddlers were encroaching on his income.[21] In Printz's novel, the dispute is dramatized as a comedy, with the municipal musicians and the beer-fiddlers stating their claims to superiority before a judge (Musophilus). Printz created a binary division between the two groups of musicians, a division clearly biased in favor of the municipal instrumentalists:[22]

Beer-fiddlers	*Municipal musicians*
Cannot read music	Play from notation
Happy to be paid with beer	Charge fees
Play for peasants	Play for burghers
Lower the honor of their audience	Play in church to enhance devotion
Music full of consecutive fifths and octaves	Music has correct voice-leading

As might be expected, Musophilus rules in favor of the municipal musicians, instructing that the beer-fiddlers be confined to playing at taverns, village fairs, dances, and peasant weddings. Printz satirized the beer-fiddlers mercilessly; a similarly unflattering portrayal was offered by Johann Beer in his *Bellum musicum*, where Harmonia's adversaries—the musical bunglers—are identified as beer-fiddlers and small-town organists.

Yet Printz's depiction of the beer-fiddlers was a caricature, distorted for rhetorical effect. The historical evidence is that there were many overlaps between beer-fiddlers and more prestigious instrumentalists. Franz Benda said that he learned many new ideas about how to play the violin from a Jewish tavern musician in Prague. Telemann is well known for his fascination with the "true barbaric beauty" of Polish and Moravian fiddlers that he heard in Pless and Cracow.[23] In some towns, too, the unlicensed instrumentalists were far more accomplished than the pejorative title of "beer-fiddler" would suggest. In Leipzig during the 1700s these freelance musicians were performing fashionable church music at the New Church.[24]

Printz's three novels give the impression that professional musicians faced prejudice from all levels of society—whether from uncomprehending artisans, jealous court servants, or aggressive beer-fiddlers. In part this was a device of epideictic rhetoric: Printz aimed to elevate the municipal musicians by pouring scorn (*vituperatio*) on their enemies. He took a similar approach in his compositional manual *Phrynis Mitilenæus oder Satyrischer Componist* (1666–67; revised 1696); this treatise is presented as a travel narrative, in which the stereotypes from the chapbooks (including *Leyermatz* and *Schergeiger*) act as foils to the qualities of a competent composer (fig. 4.4).

Yet the disputes over the worth of music also intruded into the lives of musicians. According to Printz's autobiography, he was the "target of constant arrows of persecution" from his employers and colleagues.[25] At one point he was accused of being a drunk and a lowlife; on another occasion an attempt was made to poison him. Printz's prickly personality might have encouraged such animosity, but Bach was also embroiled in the disputes surrounding musicians. As a child he would have been aware of his father's economic rivalry with the beer-fiddlers in Eisenach. Later, as an organist at Mühlhausen, he used very similar language to Printz when complaining about the "vexation" and "hindrance" he experienced from the town's inhabitants.[26] Bach's most wounding dispute, though, occurred during the late 1730s with Johann August Ernesti, headmaster of the Thomasschule. Ernesti was inspired by Enlightenment ideals to reform the curriculum, substantially reducing the time spent on music. When Ernesti found a boy practicing music, he would scold, "What? You want to be a beer-fiddler too?"[27] For Bach, such an insult would have stung deeply, not only because it put all musicians in the same category as tavern players, but also because it invoked the competitors who ate into his father's income. Printz's novels thus participate in a long-running debate over the worth of musicians in German society.

Figure 4.4. Originally appearing in three parts (1676, 1677, and 1679) and then in 1696 as the complete edition shown here, the *Phrynis Mitilenaeus oder Satyrischer Componist* (Phrynis of Mitilene [a city on the island of Lesbos] or satirical composer) of Wolfgang Caspar Printz sets out, as the title page explains, both to tell a satirical story by politely pointing out the mistakes of unlearned and ignorant composers and also to teach how to compose without errors. In so doing, Printz treats meter, variation, basso continuo, modes, temperament, rhythm, and counterpoint, and also describes a musical labyrinth (see fig. 3.13, p. 153). Although Printz's attacks on the beer-fiddlers and town trumpeters are hardly "polite"—terms such as "horse-fifths," "cow-octaves," and "sow-fourths" sarcastically denigrate the uneducated players' improper use of intervals—his book is an encyclopedia of musical knowledge into which is folded the story of the travels of Phrynis, who seeks to improve his skills in composition by going to Latium (Italy). The travelogue takes up but a seventh of the text, so that the book really is the first truly comprehensive treatment of music theory in baroque Germany.

Johann Kuhnau and the Didactic Novel

Johann Kuhnau's *Musicalische Quacksalber* (1700) is the most carefully structured of the musician-novels and also the most didactic, being modeled on the "political novels" of Christian Weise. Weise had briefly taught Kuhnau at the Zittau Gymnasium and was a highly influential writer and teacher of the period (figs. 4.5, 4.6). His novels sought to teach prudent and politic behavior to the upwardly mobile,

Figure 4.5. (*Top left*) Christian Weise was one of eighteenth-century Germany's most important educators and literary figures. After university studies in Leipzig, he spent most of his career as rector of the gymnasium in Zittau (1678–1708). His prodigious output of dramas, novels, poetry, practical books, and orations had great influence in the Bach period and beyond. He used oratory and theater to prepare his students for the social challenges of life, as is exemplified in the plays he wrote for the annual theater festivals in Zittau, performed by the gymnasium students; each festival consisted of one play based on a biblical story, one based on a political-historical event, and one of un-predetermined content with a comic epilogue. This is demonstrated by the titles of the three plays given on the title page of their publication 1684: the first deals with an Old Testament figure, *The persecuted David*; the second, *The Sicilian Argenis*, a historical one; and the third, *The world upside-down*, promises amusing situations.

Figure 4.6. (*Bottom left*) Weise commissioned music for his plays. Reproduced here is a song by Johann Krieger (younger brother of Johann Philipp Krieger) for the character Kemuel in Weise's 1682 biblical play *Jacobs doppelte Heyrath* (Jacob's double marriage). The role was taken by the student Johann Kuhnau, later Bach's immediate predecessor in Leipzig, one of whose "biblical sonatas" for keyboard would be entitled "Jacobs Heyrath." (Worth noting also is that the aria "Ach, mein Sinn" in Bach's St. John Passion [BWV 245] is based on the first stanza of "Der weinende Petrus," in Weise's *Der grünenden Jugend nothwendigen Gedancken* [1675].) In the part marked "continuo," numbers and accidentals constitute the "figures" of the "figured bass;" that is, the harpsichordist or organist would play the bass melody in the left hand while improvising ("realizing") with the right harmonies indicated by the figures (see also fig. 0.10, p. 14). This is the most fundamental and universal aspect of baroque keyboard performance practice.

usually by providing negative and humorous examples of clumsy self-seekers. Kuhnau applied much the same tactic to music, using the ignorance and clumsiness of the "musical charlatan" as a foil to the qualities of the true virtuoso. As Kuhnau wrote,

> we often watch a slovenly tooth-puller instead of a skilled doctor, or listen to a
> bagpipe instead of an agreeable, quiet lute in order to learn how great a gulf exists

between art and ignorance and how much something splendid and delicate is to be preferred over that which is rustically wild and clumsy.[28]

Kuhnau's tactic thus echoes Printz's use of bungling beer-fiddlers in *Battalus* and *Phrynis Mitilenæus* as a foil to the competence of municipal musicians.

Kuhnau's charlatan, Caraffa, is a German musician who conceals his incompetence by pretending to be that most desirable of commodities, a visiting Italian virtuoso.[29] The first half of the book recounts how Caraffa is received by a collegium musicum in a German town. Initially Caraffa hoodwinks the local musicians with his boasts about his virtuosity. Through various crafty ruses (such as claiming that his hand was injured by a mugger) he avoids having to perform anything complex before them. But the collegium's suspicion is aroused, and they request him to set first a psalm and then a madrigalian verse to music; Caraffa can only complete these tasks by plagiarizing existing pieces of music. Later Caraffa flees from the collegium and embarks on a picaresque series of adventures, conning a series of patrons, pupils, and village musicians. He receives his comeuppance, however, in a university town where the students mock his boastfulness and reduce him to a pathetic, self-pitying figure. Eventually he repents of his former ways and embarks on a new life.

The novel ends with the sixty-four precepts of "the true virtuoso and happy musician," a statement of Kuhnau's ideal conduct for a professional musician. Kuhnau outlines the skills in improvisation and composition necessary in a true virtuoso, and prescribes behavior that is modest and pious. This didactic ending is again modeled on Weise, who often closed his novels with lists of idealized qualities. Kuhnau's precepts are a rare moment in the musician-novels where a Lutheran outlook prevails over the otherwise secular viewpoint. The precepts emphasize that music is a divine gift, to be shared freely. Musicians should not boast of their skills because these are merely loaned to them by God. With such advice, Kuhnau taps into a Lutheran tradition about sharing one's talents that dates back to Martin Agricola's *Musica instrumentalia deudsch* (1529), if not earlier.[30] Yet even here there are secular elements: the notion of a "true virtuoso" draws on Aristotelian notions of virtue, and the premise underlying a political novel such as *Quacksalber* is that individuals can learn the skills with which to control their destiny.

Kuhnau's novel was highly influential: his precepts were quoted (in whole or in part) by several writers, including Andreas Werckmeister in *Cribrum musicum* (1700); Johann Georg Ahle in his *Musikalisches Winter-Gespräche* (1701); Friedrich Erhardt Niedt in the second book of his *Musicalische Handleitung* (1706); and by Johann Mattheson in *Exemplarische Organisten-Probe* (1719), *Das forschende Orchestre* (1721), and *Grosse General-Bass-Schule* (1731). Central to the success of Kuhnau's novel was his technique of cloaking its didacticism with amusing tales. Several compositional treatises of the period use a similar tactic, mingling instruction with entertainment. It has already been mentioned how Printz's *Phrynis Mitilenæus* (1676–67; revised 1696) is presented as a travel narrative, with characters representing both skilled and incompetent musicians. Friedrich Erhardt Niedt began his *Musicalische Handleitung* (1700), a book that Bach used in his own teaching, with a fictional autobiography aiming to show the advantages of studying figured bass rather than organ tablature. Johann Georg Ahle (whom Bach succeeded as organist in Mühlhausen's Church of St. Blaise) wrote a series of treatises where musical matters are discussed via convivial conversations (see, for instance, his "seasonal conversations": *Musikalisches Frühlings-Gespräche* (1695), *Musikalisches Sommer-Gespräche* (1697), *Musikalisches Herbst-Gespräche* (1699), and *Musikalisches Winter-Gespräche* (1701)).

Thus the musician-novels are interesting not only in themselves but also for their wider significance. The narrative techniques and humorous tone of the novels infiltrate many compositional treatises of the eighteenth century. In addition, the novels illuminate the mind-set of German Baroque musicians. Clearly the relationship between literature and life is complex, and care must be taken when relating the novels to the historical situation of musicians such as Bach. It is likely that the chapbooks and Beer's *Simplicianische Welt-Kucker* largely perpetuate crude stereotypes of musicians, whereas the satirical narratives of Printz and Kuhnau hold a distorting mirror up to the musical life of their time. This satire cannot be understood without a good grasp of the social situation of musicians. Printz's novels, with their detailed discussion of the honor of instrumental musicians, can only be fully comprehended when one considers the many documented conflicts over the status and worth of musicians. For a musician such as Bach, whose outlook is so poorly documented, the novels help us to envisage his world in its earthy, harsh, and often comic immediacy.

Notes

1. *NBR*, 400. (*BD* 3, no. 803, pp. 289f.)
2. The author's forthcoming monograph, *Musician-Narratives of the German Baroque*, will discuss questions of attribution, as well as the literary and cultural context of the musician-novels, their representation of the social status of musicians, and the rising interest in musicians' autobiographies in the early eighteenth century.
3. Johann Beer, *Des abentheurlichen Jan Rebhu Ritter Spiridon aus Perusina* (n.p., 1679), dedication. References in this essay are to the original editions of the novels; modern editions (where available) usually indicate the original pagination.
4. Beer, *Der simplicianische welt-Kucker oder abentheuerliche Jan Rebhu* (n.p., 1677–79), book 2, sig.)(2^r.
5. Beer, *Das Narrenspital* (n.p., 1681), 140. Solmization, the pedagogical system whereby musical notes are sung to different syllables, was the subject of theoretical controversy in seventeenth-century Germany.

6. Beer, *Die kurtzweiligen Sommer-Tägen* (n.p., 1683), 365f.

7. Beer, *Der politische Feuermäuer-Kehrer* (Leipzig, 1682), 60. The shawm was a double-reed instrument, in some ways the ancestor of the oboe but louder, coarser, and better suited to the outdoors.

8. Beer, *Der simplicianische Welt-Kucker*, book 1, 1.

9. On the prevalence of Lutheran piety, see Günther Stille, *J. S. Bach and Liturgical Life in Leipzig*, trans. J. A. Bouman, Daniel F. Poellot, and Hilton C. Oswald (St. Louis: Concordia, 1984).

10. Beer, *Ursus vulpinatur* (Weissenfels, 1697), 28.

11. *NBR*, 43–46 (*BD* 2, no. 14, pp. 15–18).

12. Robert. L. Marshall, "Towards a Twenty-first-Century Bach Biography," *The Musical Quarterly* 84 (2000): 497–525, esp. 501. I am grateful to Laurence Dreyfus for these suggestions about the picaresque.

13. For details of the depiction of trumpeters, see Henry Howey, "The Lives of *Hoftrompeter* and *Stadtpfeifer* as portrayed in three novels of Daniel Speer," *Historic Brass Society Journal* 3 (1991): 65–78.

14. Konrad Gajek, *Daniel Speers romanhafte und publizistische Schriften* (Wrocław: Wydawnictwo Uniwersytetu Wrocławskiego, 1988), 60–80.

15. Johann Mattheson, *Grundlage einer Ehrenpforte* (Hamburg, 1740), 261. The cornetto was the leading virtuoso wind instrument in seventeenth-century Germany. Like a brass instrument, it is sounded by lip vibration against a mouthpiece, but it has finger holes like a recorder, allowing melodic versatility and virtuosity.

16. Kathy Stuart, *Defiled Trades and Social Outcasts: Honor and Ritual Pollution in Early Modern Germany* (Cambridge: Cambridge University Press, 1999).

17. Wolfgang Caspar Printz, *Musicus vexatus oder Cotala* (Freiberg, 1690), 15.

18. Mattheson, *Grundlage einer Ehrenpforte*, 356.

19. Printz, *Musicus magnanimus oder Pancalus* (Freiberg, 1691), 199.

20. Beer, *Die kurtzweiligen Sommer-Tage*, 421.

21. Fritz Rollberg, "Johann Ambrosius Bach. Stadtpfeifer zu Eisenach von 1671–1695," *BJ* 24 (1927): 133–52.

22. Printz, *Musicus curiosus oder Battalus* (Freiberg, 1691), 204–11.

23. Douglas Lee, *A Musician at Court: An Autobiography of Franz Benda* (Warren, MI: Harmonie Park Press, 1998), 15; Mattheson, *Grundlage einer Ehrenpforte*, 360. See also John Spitzer and Neal Zaslaw, "Improvised Ornamentation in Eighteenth-Century Orchestras," *Journal of the American Musicological Society* 39 (1986): 524–77, esp. 545–48.

24. Arnold Schering, *Musikgeschichte Leipzigs 2: von 1650 bis 1723* (Leipzig: Kistner & Siegel, 1926), 290f.

25. Mattheson, *Grundlage einer Ehrenpforte*, 272.

26. *NBR*, 57. (*BD* 1, no. 1, pp. 19f.)

27. *NBR*, 172. (*BD* 3, no. 820, p. 314.)

28. Johann Kuhnau, *Der musicalische Quacksalber* (Dresden, 1700), 6f.

29. *Der musicalische Quacksalber* has been translated into English by John R. Russell as *The Musical Charlatan* (Columbia, SC: Camden House, 1997), but, as George J. Buelow notes in his review (*Music and Letters* 79 [1998]: 427f.), Russell renders many musical terms inaccurately.

30. Stephen Rose, "The Mechanisms of the Music Trade in Central Germany 1600–40," *Journal of the Royal Musical Association* 130 (2005): 1–37, esp. 30f.

CHAPTER 5

Leipzig: The Cradle of German Acting

Simon Williams

Because of Bach, Leipzig has always been a crucial city in the development of German music, and for a few years during Bach's lifetime it appeared that Leipzig might also have a similar impact upon the development of theater. But ultimately no theater artist of the stature of Bach emerged in Leipzig. This was due in part to the straitened circumstances of theater in Germany for much of the eighteenth century, because German actors and playwrights lacked the regular patronage—royal, ecclesiastical, or municipal—that would allow them to practice and develop their art. This was in contrast to musicians, who generally had steady and reliable institutional support during the Bach period.

It was not until the last quarter of the eighteenth century that cities in German-speaking lands developed a network of regular theaters that encouraged the growth of a vigorous and diverse theatrical culture in the way that London, Paris, and Madrid had done from the mid-sixteenth century on. Prior to that the only German theaters that could afford to mount productions with any degree of technical sophistication were in the courts of the larger and more prosperous of the German principalities; such theaters were of course isolated from popular audiences. The repertoire on these court stages was composed almost exclusively of Italian opera and French tragedy, and it was performed solely for the benefit of the monarch and his courtiers in the original language. The rest of the German population, if it desired professional theatrical entertainment at all, would find it only in the offerings of troupes of actors who toured the country, playing in large communities and small, in any space they could rent, indoors or outdoors, that provided a basic space for theatrical performance (fig. 5.1a). Most German actors were constantly on the road, living in poverty, and, because they were vagrants, suffering the suspicion and contempt of those who lived in the communities through which they passed. Their repertoire was composed primarily of *Haupt- und Staatsaktionen* (literally "political and principal plays"), a hybrid theatrical genre that had arisen from the debased versions of Elizabethan and Jacobean plays performed by the English Comedians during the seventeenth century, the scenarios of the commedia dell'arte, folk drama, and other popular sources. Acting was probably coarse and exaggerated, improvisation was as much the rule as the exception, and scenes of extreme and shrill pathos would coexist, sometimes simultaneously, with gross, farcical comedy.

Theater is essentially an urban art, as it depends upon a population large enough to fill the auditorium on a regular basis and a culture in which it is assumed that matters of communal interest are properly subjects for public representation, debate, and discussion. While no German cities in the early eighteenth century, with the exception of

Figure 5.1. (*Above and facing page*) Friederike Caroline Weissenborn, the "Neuberin," was the real, if not nominal, head of the acting company she formed with her husband Johann Neuber that was active 1727–43, and again 1744–50. The Neuber troupe performed all over Germany, both in the open air (*a*) and in regular theaters, and acquired status and patents as official court theater company to the courts of Saxony, Brunswick-Lüneburg-Wolfenbüttel, and Schleswig-Holstein. It performed the notable premieres of Gottsched's *Der sterbende Cato* (1731) and Lessing's *Der junge Gelehrte* (1748), both in Leipzig. Caroline's repertoire ranged from low comedy to neoclassical tragedy, including the title role of Corneille's *Medée* (in German) (*b*); she also wrote sharp-edged prologues, such as *Ein deutsches Vorspiel* (A German prologue, 1734) (*c*), allegorically depicting the Neuberin's feud with Joseph Ferdinand Müller (who had now acquired the Saxon patent); *Der alte und neue Geschmack* (The old and new taste; 1737), in which Hanswurst, played by the Neuberin, was "banned" from the stage; and *Der allerkostbarste Schatz* (The most valuable treasure, 1741), in which she made fun of her former mentor Gottsched, leading to a permanent break between them. Johann Adolf Scheibe, known best today for his critique of Bach's complex compositional style, composed theater music for her in Hamburg (1738).

Vienna, could provide a suitable urban environment, Leipzig was among the few that showed promise. It did not have an unusually large population, but as the site of three great annual trade fairs, it enjoyed seasonal influxes of visitors, all of whom were eager for entertainment. Furthermore, Leipzig was surrounded by a number of large to medium-sized cities—Halle, Merseburg, Gera, Zwickau, Chemnitz, and Dresden—that offered troupes the prospect of additional audiences without them having to travel too far.[1] Leipzig was also the seat of a great university, noted for the study of law, and during the Bach period it was a center in which attempts were made to regularize the German language, in order to allow it to be developed as a literary medium. Leipzig was also the center of the German publishing industry. Size-wise and culturally, it offered a potentially excellent site for the growth of theater. It had, however, one disadvantage: not being the capital of its electorate (which honor went to Dresden), Leipzig possessed no resident court that would sponsor the performance of opera and French drama on a well-equipped stage.

Like most European cities, Leipzig had a tradition of sporadic theater performance going back to the late Middle Ages. Records indicate that mystery cycles were performed during the sixteenth century, and there had been a regular tradition of school and university plays since the seventeenth.[2] From 1685 on, however, Leipzig acquired a more individual theatrical profile as it became the headquarters for the first troupe of German players, under the leadership of the actor Johannes Velten, that attempted to introduce some discipline in acting and to raise the quality of the repertoire by bringing "regular" French drama—that is, drama that was constructed according to the three neoclassical unities of time, place, and action—onto the popular stage in the hope that it might displace *Haupt- und Staatsaktionen*. Velten's reputation rested on his hopes to reform the theater, but his preeminence arose primarily from his holding the *Privilegium* from the elector of Saxony, a document similar to the patent issued to certain theater companies by the English royalty, which gave the company permission to perform in the name of the monarch. In England, only patentees were allowed to perform plays in public, but in the disunified political world of Germany, public order was less rigorously imposed and it was impossible to limit performance solely to those who were officially sanctioned. *Privilegia*, which were granted by several royal rulers in Germany to troupes of actors, therefore indicated that whichever troupe held them enjoyed royal favor. Through them the monarch requested that, within his territories at least, the actors receive privileged treatment. *Privilegia* helped troupes find places to perform and persuaded local tradespeople to give them some aid in mounting their productions; they might also have helped attract audiences into the rather constricted spaces where the actors normally had to erect their temporary stages. Given Leipzig's geographical position and its three great fairs each year, the patent for Saxony was especially prized, and when theatrical troupes multiplied in the course of the eighteenth century, competition for it became quite ruthless.

The first attempt to establish a permanent theater in Leipzig was in connection with opera rather than spoken and improvised drama. As Leipzig, in contrast to Dresden, had no opera, in 1692, Nicolaus Adam Strungk, the vice-capellmeister at the Dresden Court, was granted a patent by Johann Georg IV to build an opera house in Leipzig and to sponsor performances there for the next ten years during fair time. The theater, designed by the Italian architect Girolamo Sartorio, was constructed entirely of wood and was erected on the Brühl. It was not an especially remarkable building, though it was sizable. The auditorium comprised fifty boxes in five tiers, and the stage was well equipped with the latest machinery to change the scenes. Some found this opera house possessed "charm," but in contrast to court theaters or to the opera house that had been built by the merchants in Hamburg (fig. 8.4, p. 247), it was considered to be "poverty stricken."[3] The Brühl was also marshy (see fig. 3.18, p. 157), so the theater had poor foundations, a circumstance that turned out to be symbolic for the entire enterprise of bringing opera to Leipzig. When Strungk died in 1700, the *Privilegium* was taken over by his widow, and after her death it passed to a son-in-law, Samuel Ernst Döbricht. None of these successors could rid the theater of the considerable debt accumulated during its construction, Strungk having depended entirely on his own resources to build it, with no subvention from the court in Dresden and no support from the city of Leipzig. The opportunities to recoup his debt were extremely limited: because the *Privilegium* only permitted the house to be open during the fairs, all it could mount was a mere fifteen performances a year. The entire operation had eventually to be wound up in 1720—three years before Bach's arrival. Nevertheless, the enterprise had been far from negligible. Despite the narrow window of opportunity for performance, the first Leipzig opera staged the premieres of a hundred works during the twenty-seven years of its existence, and, between 1701 and 1704, Georg Philipp Telemann (then studying at the University of Leipzig) served as its director (fig. 8.1, p. 245). In fact, Telemann claimed to have written "several and twenty" operas for this theater both during and after his directorate, but only one of these, *Die Satyren in Arcadien* (1719), has survived.[4] After the theater was forced to close its doors, it was visited by the odd troupe of actors or singers, but in 1729 it was deemed to be unsafe and was pulled down. Opera in Leipzig did not thereby die, but now had to be performed elsewhere in the city in spaces not specifically devoted to musical performance and mostly by troupes for whom opera was not a priority.

It was therefore upon the spoken drama, not opera, that Leipzig built its reputation as a theater city, which has led to its being widely acknowledged as "the cradle of German acting." This reputation was based primarily on the artistic and scholarly collaboration of the actress Caroline Neuber with Johann Christoph Gottsched. On the surface, these are an unlikely pair to have entered into artistic partnership. Caroline, who was born in 1692, grew up in Zwickau in a household dominated by an abusive father and did not escape until she was twenty-six, when she threw herself out the window of her home into the arms of a friendly bush and soon after that into those of a student, Johann Neuber. After their marriage, the two joined Karl Ludwig Hoffmann's company of Polish-Saxon players, which was at that time the holder of the Saxon *Privilegium*. Neither of the Neubers were especially talented actors, but between them they had a great head for business and organization, and in August 1727, some months after the death of Hoffmann, they received the patent for Saxony and took over the direction of the company. Gottsched, like Neuber, had found his way to Leipzig as a refugee, though from military service, not a broken home. Born in Königsberg in Prussia in 1700, he had left his native town because he was so tall and strong that he would almost certainly have been drafted into the Prussian army.[5] After arriving in Leipzig, he soon became president of the "German Society," which was devoted to the fostering and "reform" of German literature; rose through the ranks of the faculty of the University of Leipzig; and was appointed, at the age of thirty-four, professor of logic and metaphysics (fig. 0.18, p. 25).

Neuber and Gottsched had contrasting personalities that rarely complemented each other. Gottsched, who perhaps unfairly has become the butt of much laughter in German literary history, wished to create a German culture equal to that of other western European countries and in so doing advocated, possibly too unquestioningly, the wholesale adoption by the Germans of French literary forms. For Gottsched, the function of theater and literature was to arouse respect for order and authority in audiences and readers rather than to appeal to the imagination of the individual. His unattractive literary style, his literal conception of the arts, and his heavy pedantry did not greatly recommend him to his contemporaries and have won him few friends since. Nevertheless, the German language in the early eighteenth century was undeveloped as a literary medium, and even though Gottsched's own writings did little to improve German literature, he raised awareness as to how backward it was. Indeed, he is one of the earliest figures of the German Enlightenment, which, by the end of the eighteenth century, had transformed German literature and the stage. Neuber, a distinctly more impulsive character than Gottsched, had ambitions that were centered mainly on the theater. She too appreciated the capacity of theater to mete out moral instruction to its audiences, but with a greater understanding as to how the play of the imagination can aid in this goal. Like Gottsched, she wished to see the quality of theater raised in Germany.

Gottsched had no particular liking for theater, but he had seen the Hoffmann troupe perform in Leipzig soon after his arrival and recognized that through reforming the theater it might be possible to bring about the greater reforms he envisaged for German culture. He did not find a sympathetic ear among members of the Hoffmann troupe, which was content mainly with *Haupt- und Staatsaktionen* and improvised comedy. But this was prior to the arrival of the Neubers. Once they took over, he found willing partners. Caroline Neuber focused her energies primarily on improving the art and technique of acting and the professional and social status of the actor. In place of the unpredictable and often crude characterization practiced by the majority of actors, she encouraged the troupe to cultivate a style based on the performance of French tragedy. Elegance rather than the articulation of raw emotion should be the basic aim of the actor in both tragedy and comedy. Verse should be delivered with full attention to "noble and poetic expression,"[6] and the actors should control their movements so that their deportment on stage was closer to dance (see chapter 6) than to the frequently gross and exaggerated gestures that were common on the spoken stage. The "Leipzig School," as this mode of acting came to be called, was entirely subject to the values and measures of French court culture, in "declamation, gesture, positioning, ordering, grouping."[7] Not only was Neuber concerned about artistic matters, she became deeply involved in the moral life and professional reputations of her actors. She fed and housed unmarried actresses under her own roof and strongly discouraged actors from spending time in

Figure 5.2. Johann Christoph Gottsched's *Versuch einer critischen Dichtkunst vor die Deutschen* (Proposal for a serious German poetic style) (1730; revised editions in 1737, 1742, and 1751) was an epoch-making work of literary theory. Adopting the ideals of the French classical theater, Gottsched advocated controlled formal principles and the "imitation of nature" (which precluded the conjuring up of imaginary worlds such as occurred in opera) to produce a less bombastic and more rational and purposeful German drama than then existed. He explained how to write a tragedy as follows: The poet chooses a moral principle he wants to impress on his audience in a sensory way. Then he recalls a common story that illuminates the truth of this principle. Next, in order to give credibility to his story, he looks to history to find famous personages who experienced something similar, and he thereby obtains the names of the characters in his story. He then devises all the circumstances of the subplots or episodes ... so that the main plot will be genuinely believable. He divides the material into five parts [acts] of approximately equal length, arranging it so that the ending flows naturally out of what precedes. (See also fig. 0.18, p. 25.)

their traditional place of resort, the tavern. The entire company was expected to help in maintaining its physical plant: women sewed costumes, men painted and restored the scenery and props. Accordingly a corporate life developed in the company that would in turn lead to an increasingly consistent and seamless ensemble on stage.

Gottsched's primary concern was the regularization of the repertory by introducing plays imitative of French tragedy, with classical or heroic settings, with "regular" plots that observed the neoclassical unities of place, time, and action, and given in performances that were stylistically disciplined and avoided the crude mix of genres that was characteristic of *Haupt- und Staatsaktionen* (fig. 5.2). The model for this reformed drama was Gottsched's own tragedy, *Der sterbende Cato* (The dying Cato, 1732), which was based upon Joseph Addison's *Cato* and a version of the story by the French tragedian Deschamps. Although Gottsched's work is slavishly imitative of French neoclassical tragedy and written in alexandrines[8] that fall on the ear with leaden beat, the sheer novelty of the work made it popular, and it stayed in the Neuber repertoire for several seasons. But Gottsched's tragedy was only one of a large number of new German plays that were added to the repertoire by Neuber's company. Performance statistics are impressive. Of the more than two hundred works performed by the Neuber troupe over a twenty-year period,[9] the vast majority were either new plays in the neoclassical

mode or adaptions or direct translations from the French. *Haupt- und Staatsaktionen*
did not disappear entirely, but they lost their dominant place in the repertory, and
their passing was formally marked in 1737 when the Neuber company staged a ritual in
which Hanswurst, the clown who was symbolic for the genre as a whole, was expelled
from the stage (though, as Lessing slyly observed, he soon crept back to the theater in
other guises).[10] However, it is no exaggeration to claim that Leipzig during the Neuber-
Gottsched era became the center for the writing of German tragedy, which led to the
city becoming effectively the intellectual center of Germany until the 1770s.[11]

The reforms achieved by Gottsched and Neuber were neither complete nor pain-
less. It was difficult to apply them systematically as the troupe was constantly on the
move. Although Leipzig remained their headquarters and provided them with their
largest audiences, they could not survive here alone; over the years they traveled as
far afield as Hamburg, Augsburg, and, in 1740–41, to St. Petersburg, where they were
guests of the Russian court. Theater in Leipzig was also becoming a cutthroat business
and other troupes were constantly looking for the chance to enhance their position.
When August the Strong died in 1733, his successor-son Elector Friedrich August II
removed the Saxon patent from the Neubers and granted it to Joseph Ferdinand Müller, who had been Hanswurst in the Neuber company until 1729. Müller had left as his
importance in the company dwindled due to the gradual disappearance of *Haupt- und
Staatsaktionen*, so the elector's decision, which Neuber appealed in vain, was especially galling, because it signified a setback to the reforms she had undertaken. It also
deprived her of the best theatrical quarters in Leipzig. Until this point she had devoted
tremendous energy and resources to equipping and appointing the Fleischhaus theater above the meat market, but when she lost the patent she was forced to vacate the
premises. For two years, the Neubers did not visit Leipzig, but the city was essential
to their livelihood. When they returned, it was to perform in less desirable places
often far from the city center; even the celebrated expulsion of Hanswurst took place
in the obscurity of a temporary stage close to the Grimma Gate. In fact the last ten
years of Caroline Neuber's career, from the return from Russia in 1741 to her effective
retirement in 1750, are a sad record of increasing hardship, audience indifference, and
isolation.

The relationship with Gottsched never ran smoothly. Relations between the Neubers
and the professor were cordial enough in the early years of their cooperation, and letters demonstrate that they had a unity of purpose. But popular audiences were often
resistant to moral instruction from the stage, and few relished a constant diet of heroic
neoclassical tragedy. Neuber discovered to her cost that the reformed repertoire did not
guarantee a healthy box office. She did not therefore stick to the reforms as resolutely as
Gottsched might have wished. Soon after she returned to Leipzig from her Russian trip,

Figure 5.3. Around 1760, Gotthold Ephraim Lessing famously denounced J. C. Gottsched, denying that the latter's neo-classicizing reforms actually improved German drama. But throughout his life as playwright and critic he also followed Gottsched's Enlightenment-driven principle that drama should be used to teach moral lessons. Lessing's protago-nists were not heroic historical figures from the distant past, but ordinary people, which is why his plays are classified as middle-class or bourgeois drama. His early play *Die Juden* (The Jews), finished in Berlin in 1749 just after Lessing fin-ished his studies in Leipzig, shows how prejudices result from misconceptions, and argues that blanket judgments of peoples lead to false generalizations. Lessing's championing of universal tolerance is best illustrated by his later master-piece *Nathan der Weise* (Nathan the wise) (see also figs. 0.20 and 0.21, pp. 29 and 31).

she staged an act of *Der sterbende Cato* in which Gottsched's advocacy for historically accurate costumes was openly mocked, leading to a total break between them.

But a more substantial underlying cause for their estrangement may have resided in Neuber's espousal of new dramatic forms and idioms. Throughout the twenty-two years (1728–50) in which the Neubers toured, classical tragedy in the French style was never absent from the repertoire; Racine's tragedies were always popular, as were the German-themed but classically oriented tragedies of the most accomplished of the Leipzig tragedians, Johann Elias Schlegel, in the troupe's later years. But audience taste was shifting from the heroic ambience of the Baroque age toward plays set in a do-mestic environment, which provided an opportunity for the display of sentimental-ist emotions, a fashion already current in the theaters of London and Paris. In fact, sentimentalism—a highly refined and effusive mode of displaying the tenderness of one's feelings for one's fellow beings and for those less fortunate than oneself—found its way into the Neuber repertoire as early as the 1730s, in translations and adaptations of the comedies of Marivaux, Destouches, and Regnard, which took an increasingly large share of the repertoire. During the 1740s, German writers in turn responded to sentimentalism. The Neubers were among the first to stage the mild comedies of man-ners by the fabulist and poet Christian Furchtegott Gellert, also a professor at Leipzig University; in 1748, they premiered the first dramatic work by Gotthold Ephraim Less-ing, *Der junge Gelehrte* (The young scholar) (fig. 5.3); and they put on some of the early comedies of the prolific Leipzig writer Christian Felix Weisse, who would go on to write

Figure 5.4. Born into an educated family, Christian Felix Weisse came to Leipzig in 1745 as a student of philology and theology. There he became a close friend of Lessing because of their common literary and theater interests, and they both translated and wrote original plays for the Neuber troupe in exchange for theater passes. However, their friendship did not survive Lessing's departure from Leipzig in 1748. Weisse remained in Leipzig, active in a variety of pursuits ranging from writing plays for Heinrich Gottfried Koch to editing a learned journal and becoming the city's collector of taxes. He developed a lively interest in the English ballad opera and French comic opera (which he got to know in Paris, 1759–60). His poetry was later set by composers ranging from Bach's critic J. A. Scheibe to the giants of the Viennese Classical School: Haydn, Mozart, Beethoven.

highly successful *Singspiel*—operatic works with spoken dialogue—and two popular plays suggested by Shakespearean themes: *Richard III* (1759) and a bourgeois tragedy in the style of contemporary domestic drama, *Romeo und Julia* (1767) (fig. 5.4).[12] This latter drama required a more realistic approach to acting than the Leipzig style offered, and unfortunately it was beyond the powers of the Neubers to adapt to it. In fact, their troupe's decline in the late 1740s must be attributed in part to the incompatibility of their formal style with the more idiomatic prose dialogue and finely nuanced comedy of a drama set in the everyday environs of contemporary Germany rather than one taken from classical mythology or the heroic periods of history.

While Leipzig may have given birth to acting as a systematic discipline in Germany, the infancy of the art only lasted a brief decade or so. The Neubers spent the final years of their careers performing exclusively in Dresden and Leipzig, where they drew smaller and smaller audiences and were abandoned by almost all their actors, especially those whose skills were more suited to the new repertoire, now being better performed by other troupes, which provided the Neubers with ever stiffer competition. The most notable of these was the celebrated troupe led by Johann Friedrich Schönemann, which regularly visited Leipzig and included among its actors (from 1739) the great Konrad Ekhof, who would provide the model for performing the realistic dramas of Lessing and his contemporaries, and whom Lessing himself saw as the ideal actor of his works. Schönemann's troupe became an increasingly powerful draw for ambitious actors throughout the 1740s (fig. 5.5). The Neubers suffered the greatest of all their losses in 1748 when Gottfried Heinrich Koch, the mainstay of their troupe for a good twenty years, left them to join Schönemann.

ól. Joh. Friedr. Schönemann

Figure 5.5. Despite his education (he studied medicine), the actor-impresario Johann Friedrich Schönemann chose around age twenty to join a wandering troupe that offered low comedy with humans and marionettes; then he joined the Neuber troupe in 1730, continuing his Harlequin and other comic roles but soon getting involved in Gottsched's and the Neubers' reform theater, even playing in Gottsched's *Der sterbende Cato*. After breaking with the Neuberin, he offered her troupe stiff competition in Leipzig, but, failing to get the Saxon royal patent, then set his sights on Prussia, where in 1745 he received the Prussian Royal Privilege to present "regular" plays, although he later returned to comedy again.

Koch had joined the Neubers in 1728, a twenty-five-year-old student who could no longer afford to continue studying law at Leipzig University. An unusually versatile man, he could lend his hand to any task the theater required—he was an adept writer, a skilled designer and painter of scenes, and an admired actor both in heroic tragedy and Molièresque comedy—and had been indispensable in the creation of the corporate spirit that was so distinguishing a mark of the Neuber troupe. The move to Schönemann was not, however, particularly successful. Koch was a multifaceted performer, but not an especially profound one. He was probably quite slick on stage, so he quickly found himself at loggerheads with the severe and serious Ekhof, whose ideal for acting was the realization of whatever was unique and hidden within the characters he played (fig. 5.6). Koch soon left the troupe to set up on his own, and during the St. Michael's fair—the great autumn trade fair—found himself competing for audiences with both Schönemann and the Neubers, who occupied the only two indoor spaces available for theater at this time. He had to perform then in the open air. Soon after this (1748) the Neubers retired, and in 1751 Koch took over their theater in Quandt's Hof in the Nikolaistraße (fig. 5.7). Although he staged some of the new drama here—among which were translations of Moore's *The Gamester* and George Lillo's *The London Merchant*[13]—Koch never entirely freed himself of the *Haupt- und Staatsaktionen* and the harlequinades that went with it; in fact, he probably did not want to, since in the theater old tastes die hard, and the archaic genre still had many followers. But by the 1750s, his repertoire was beginning to look dated and he attracted audiences less by balancing the old with

Figure 5.6. Hans Konrad Dietrich Ekhof was judged by Lessing, to whom he is often compared, as "the person who has done more for the entire German theater than anyone else in its history." This extraordinary judgment was based on Ekhof's activity as an actor, teacher, translator of French comedies, author of theater pieces and poetry, advocate for the socially marginalized theater community, and leader of several theatrical companies, most of this, however, occurring after the Bach period. Ekhof apprenticed with Johann Friedrich Schönemann, living the life of an itinerant actor while also functioning as a director. Later, in 1753, Ekhof established in Schwerin an academy for the training of actors. Throughout his life he sought to raise the status of the acting profession and to show by example that actors could behave with as much probity and propriety as others. He died in 1778.

the new than by resorting to the *Singspiel*, which, mainly as a result of Koch's intervention, soon became the generic designation for a light play with songs, in which the spoken text was usually pleasant but unremarkable and the appeal of the performance depended as much upon the versatility of the actors as it did on the attractiveness of the music. Koch's success hung mainly on his revival of one of the most successful English ballad operas of the century, *The Devil to Pay* (1731), by Charles Coffey. (Ballad operas had spoken dialogue along with songs.) It had failed when it was first staged by Schönemann, but Koch commissioned a new translation from Weisse, *Der Teufel ist los*, which was instantly successful at its premiere in Leipzig in 1752 and spawned a multitude of imitations, including Weisse's own *Der lustige Schuster* (The merry cobbler) (1766) and *Die Jagd* (The hunt) (1770), which still receives the occasional production in Germany today. From the *Singspiel* grew the popular German opera, which would find its fullest articulation in the stage works of Mozart (*Die Entführung aus dem Serail*, *Die Zauberflöte*), Beethoven (*Fidelio*), and Weber (*Der Freischütz*).

But this glorious future could not be anticipated in 1752; in fact, in terms of acting, *Der Teufel ist los* may even have been retrogressive. The work required "grace and poetic coloring" from the actors and encouraged them to develop their talents at dancing and singing. But by this time, as we have seen, German playwrights were coming increasingly under the influence of the middle-class drama of England and France, so the spoken theater was developing in a direction that would require even more realistic characterization from the actor than the sentimental drama did. Nevertheless, Koch

Figure 5.7. Born in the Saxon city of Gera, Heinrich Gottfried Koch's career revolved mostly around Leipzig not far to the north. Although he was active all over the German-speaking world—Hamburg, Prague, Vienna, Göttingen, Zittau, Zerbst, Lübeck, and, in his last years, Berlin (1771–75), where he enjoyed great success—it was to Leipzig, where he had studied, that he constantly returned, first as an actor with the Neuber and Schönemann troupes, then as the head of his own troupe, founded in Leipzig (1748) and awarded the Saxon privilege the next year. As an actor Koch specialized in comic roles, and had a special affinity for Molière, developed by watching French actors. As a director he got involved with producing comic opera, and his 1752 production of *Der Teufel ist los*, which drew Gottsched's ire, launched a vigorous pamphlet war.

did not eschew the new repertoire and when, in 1756, he staged the first performance in Leipzig of Lessing's bourgeois tragedy, *Miss Sara Sampson*, the playwright himself was in attendance and approved of what he saw. But any further theatrical activities were curtailed by the outbreak of the Seven Years' War. Koch left Leipzig for northern Germany, where in 1758, Schönemann having retired from the stage for a career in horse trading, he took over the leadership of the troupe. Ekhof had already left Schönemann to act in the Hamburg Nationaltheater, but when this fell through, he rejoined the old troupe. He failed, however, to achieve any rapport with Koch, and the two men finally parted company in 1764. By then, the war being over, Koch was able to return to Saxony, where he signed a three-year contract to perform plays in German in the Dresden Court Theater—a significant step forward for the cause of German theater—and he turned his attention once more to Leipzig, which was on the verge of an important stage in its cultural development, the building of a permanent theater.

With the exception of the opera house on the Brühl, no building had been constructed in Leipzig specifically for the performance of theater throughout the first part of the eighteenth century. Over the years, a variety of sites, both indoor and outdoor, had been used for performances, which in addition to Neuber's Fleischhaus, the opera house, and the theater in Quandt's courtyard, included a booth in Bose's Gardens (fig. 9.1a, p. 268), another in Enoch Richter's garden on the Hintergasse, a temporary stage by the Peterstor and in the Naschmarkt (fig. 3.21, p. 159), and the Great Blumenberg theater in a dyer's factory,[14] not to mention a tavern, *The Three Swans*, where performances had been given early in the century.[15] In 1766, however, permission was acquired and funds advanced by the merchant Zemisch to build a permanent theater on the ruins of Ranstadt Bastei, in the northwest on the old city walls (fig. 5.8). Built on the same design as the Royal Theater in Dresden (fig 3.28, p. 165), this was a classical construction with an elegant auditorium surrounded by three rows of boxes and a perspective stage with a depth of four wings and sufficient machinery to effect smooth scene changes. It was a gracious building, distinguished, according to a contemporary account, by its "regularity, orderly correct perspective, splendor, but not at the expense of simplicity, taste and novelty in décor, imagination and invention in the planning, and with strength in the execution of the allegorical painting."[16] This painting was the celebrated Renaissance-style curtain painted by Adam Friedrich Oeser, which depicted the courtyard of a classical temple, in which the statues of Sophocles and Aristophanes are worshipped by a variety of figures from the classical theater while Shakespeare is seen, rather mysteriously, only from the back, hurrying away, according to the program, toward "the temple of truth."[17] According to Goethe this indicated that "Shakespeare . . . without predecessors or followers, without concerning himself about models, went to meet immortality in his own way."[18]

Whether the theater itself showed an ambition for a similar immortality is to be doubted. The opening night on October 10, 1766, under the direction of Koch, looked toward the past rather than striking out on its own path. It opened with a performance of Johann Elias Schlegel's *Hermann*, a dramatization of the battle between the Germans

Figure 5.8. Despite the large amount of dramatic activity in Leipzig, there was no first-rate performing space for theatrical productions during Bach's lifetime. Therefore, a great deal of performing by the most important troupes, including Neuber and G. H. Koch companies, was done in the open air. Therefore, the inauguration of the new theater on the Ranstadt Bastei was greatly welcome. Originally entrusted to Koch and his troupe (1666–68), the theater was the venue for a wide range of dramatic productions. In particular, Leipzig and the new theater became the center of the German Singspiel, while also maintaining French classics and the bourgeois dramas of Lessing and others in its repertory.

and the Romans in the Teutoburger Forest, one of the founding myths of German nationalism, but cast in a rigorously unified form that was entirely characteristic of French
neoclassicism. This was followed by a ballet, and the evening finished with a comedy
translated from an original by the French playwright Regnard, dating from 1700, *Die
unvermuthete Wiederkunst* (The unexpected return). Despite this conventional beginning, the opening of the Ranstadt Bastei was an auspicious occasion, mainly because
the theater remained open. While it frequently changed directors—Koch only stayed
for about two years—and was used by several different troupes, it provided Leipzig
with the first regular theatrical entertainment. Although few of the great works of
the German classical period received their first performance in Leipzig, all the major
stage works of Lessing, Goethe, and Schiller, as well as the first German translations
of Shakespeare, were staged here soon after their first performance elsewhere. When,
toward the end of the century, the theater acquired a permanent company, it would offer regular entertainment to the merchants, students, and literati of Leipzig during the
summer and move to Dresden for the winter to entertain the court.

Leipzig did not fulfill its early promise as the "cradle of German acting" mainly because it reached its theatrical peak prior to the great flowering of theater in the last
decades of the eighteenth century. It could have maintained its salient position because the German theater turned out to be a "regional" theater in which the small cities
made as great a contribution to the development of theatrical culture as provincial
and national capitals did. But in the last three decades of the century, the plays and
acting styles that would transform the theater were born elsewhere: at the Mannheim
National Theater under the directorship of Heribert von Dalberg; at the Hamburg town
theater under the direction of the great realistic actor Friedrich Ludwig Schröder; at
the Vienna Burgtheater, reconstituted in 1776 into a national theater by Joseph II; and,
most importantly, at the Weimar Court Theater under the direction of Goethe and
Schiller at the turn of the century. These were the institutions that would determine
the future course of the German theater. Leipzig responded to them, often through
productions at the Ranstadt Bastei, very effectively, but already by the end of Bach's life,
in 1750, there were signs that its position as the leading city in German theater was only
a passing one.

Notes

1. W. H. Bruford, *Theatre, Drama, and Audience in Goethe's Germany* (London: Routledge &
   Kegan Paul, 1950), 14.
2. Heinrich Blümner, *Geschichte des Theaters in Leipzig* (Leipzig: Brockhaus, 1818), 9–20.

3. Fritz Hennenberg, *300 Jahre Leipziger Oper. Geschichte und Gegenwart* (Munich: Langen Müller, 1993), 11f.

4. *The New Grove Opera*, ed. Stanley Sadie, 4 vols. (London: Macmillan, 1992 and 1994) 4: 677.

5. See chapter 1, note 3. —Ed.

6. Friedrich Johann Reden-Esbeck, *Caroline Neuber und ihre Zeitgenossen* (Leipzig: Barth, 1881), 72.

7. Eduard Devrient, *Geschichte der deutschen Schauspielkunst*, ed. Rolf Kabel & Christoph Tilse, 2 vols. (Munich and Vienna: Langen Müller, 1967), 1: 294.

8. The alexandrine is a verse type consisting of twelve syllables (or thirteen if the ending is feminine) with a caesura after the sixth syllable. The "German alexandrine," established by Martin Opitz, *Buch von der deutschen Poeterey* (1624), lacked the rhythmic variability of the quantitative French alexandrine, being accentual iambic hexameter with the caesura after the third foot. M. L. Gasparov, *A History of European Versification*, trans. G. S. Smith and Marina Tarlinskaja, ed. G. S. Smith with L. Holford-Strevens (Oxford: Clarendon Press, 1996), 130–32, 192–97. —Ed.

9. Tabulated by Richard Daunicht in *Die Neuberin: Materialien zur Theatergeschichte des 18. Jahrhunderts* (Heidenau: Ministerium für Kultur, 1956), 99–131.

10. Bruford, 61.

11. Bruford, 85.

12. In fact, neither work has very much to do with Shakespeare. See Simon Williams, *Shakespeare on the German Stage 1587–1914* (Cambridge: Cambridge University Press, 1990), 58–62.

13. Eduard Devrient 1: 334.

14. Blümner, 51.

15. Gustav Wustmann, *Leipzig's Theater vor 100 Jahren* (Leipzig: Rweusche, 1879), 6. Wustmann lists twelve different performance sites used during the eighteenth century.

16. Quoted in Gertrud Rudloff-Hille, *Das Theater auf der Ranstästei: Leipzig 1766* (Leipzig: Museum für Geschichte der Stadt Leipzig, 1969), 14.

17. Rudloff-Hille, 21.

18. J. W. Goethe, *Truth and Fiction: Relating to My Life*, tr. John Exenford, 2 vols. (London: Robertson, Ashford and Bentley, 1902) 1: 337.

CHAPTER 6

Courtly, Social, and Theatrical Dance

Meredith Little

Dance permeated the culture of Bach's world, in the ballroom and on the stage, at court and in middle-class life (fig. 6.1). Surprisingly, the dominant dance form during Bach's lifetime was not German or Italian, but French. French court dancing was easily recognized by its graceful, nonchalant affect, and by its noble carriage of the body, its precise and disciplined step technique, its modest turnout of the legs from the hips, and its balanced yet dynamic floor patterns. It dominated the theatrical and social dance scene, and influenced body language and deportment in Saxony as in most other European courts and cities. It was not only elegant to watch; it actually taught nobility to all who had the opportunity and discipline to practice, and it survives to this day as ballet.

Dance, as movement of the body in space, is much harder to notate than music, which explains our sparse, speculative understanding of most of dance history before the twentieth century. It is our good fortune, however, that the dance of Bach's age is an exception: over 330 choreographies from the French court dance repertoire have been preserved in a special dance notation

Figure 6.1. The importance and popularity of dance in Bach's world is reflected in the fact that Bach launched his most ambitious publication project, the four-part *Clavierübung* (1726–41) with six suites (which he called "partitas") of stylized dances. At first published serially, as this title page of the first edition of the first partita reflects (1726), they were then collectively published as Opus I (1731). The title page reads: "Keyboard Practice, consisting of Preludes, Allemandes, Courantes, Sarabandes, Gigues, Menuets, and other Galanteries, composed . . . by Johann Sebastian Bach, High-princely Capellmeister of Anhalt-Cöthen and Director of Music in Leipzig. Partita I, published by the Composer, 1726."

known as *chorégraphie*, and numerous dance instruction manuals exist, published by French, English, Spanish, and German authors. This essay first describes the technique of French court dancing as performed in German-speaking regions; then it takes up courtly social dancing and its etiquette, using as an example the menuet as danced in Bach's Saxony. It then discusses theatrical dancing in the French serious style as well as the comic or "grotesque" style. It concludes with an assessment of the creative role of French court dance in Bach's time and culture and in his music.

French Court Dancing in Germany

French court dance was the origin of ballet as we know it today. It arose and developed through the work of dancing masters at the court of Louis XIV from about 1660 on, thus shortly before Bach was born.[1] French court dance was an original, distinctive improvement over all previous forms in Europe because of its inherent and disciplined elegance. *Chorégraphie*, the notation system developed by the same dancing masters, made possible the dissemination of whole dances throughout European courts and cities, and by the early eighteenth century French court dancing was internationally accepted not only in German courts and cities but in England, Scotland, Spain, Portugal, areas of what is now the Czech Republic, the Low Countries, and Sweden. In later years, it also spread to Russia and to the European colonies in North and South America, Australia, and New Zealand.

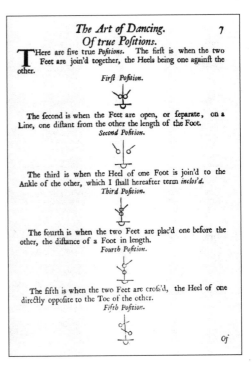

Figure 6.2. The five positions of the feet that are still fundamental to modern ballet were established already in the seventeenth century by the royal dancing master and choreographer Pierre Beauchamps, head of the Royal Academy of Dance founded by Louis XIV. The basic positions and steps, as well as the choreographies to dances that used them, were preserved and transmitted internationally though a notation first published in Raoul-Auger Feuillet's landmark *Chorégraphie* (Paris, 1700; fig. 6.3), which was translated into English by John Weaver, "the Father of English Ballet," as *Orchesography* (London, 1706), illustrated here. Turnout of the legs from the hips is required to form the five positions, as shown also in other dance illustrations in this essay.

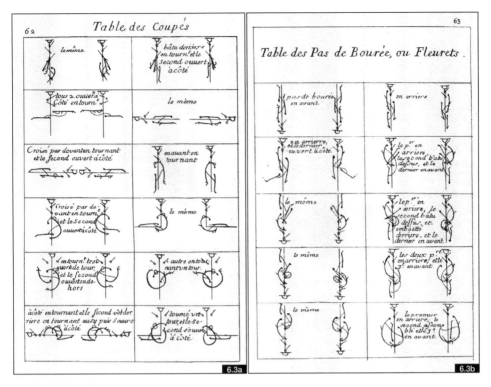

Figure 6.3. These two pages from Feuillet's *Chorégraphie* show *coupés* and *pas de bourées*, which are common step-units used in French court dancing. Illustrated are step-units beginning on the left and right foot, forwards and backwards. The *coupé* consists of two steps and the *pas de bourée* has three. The tables continue (not shown) with dozens of subtle variations for each type of step-unit. Although Feuillet's claim that he invented the dance notation publicized through his *Chorégraphie* has been viewed with some skepticism by dance historians (who believe that it owes something to a system invented by the royal dancing master Pierre Beauchamps), there is no doubt about the efficacy of Feuillet's notation in propagating throughout Europe the style of dance cultivated at the French court and in French ballet and theater.

The steps were organized by the five positions for the feet (fig. 6.2). The legs were turned slightly outward from the hips, allowing the dancer to look graceful even when moving sideways.[2] The five positions for the feet are the same ones still used in ballet, but the degree of turnout in the early eighteenth century was less severe than it is today.

Individual steps were formed into recognizable step-units, such as the *pas de bourée* and *pas coupé* (fig. 6.3), which were then set into phrases according to the imagination and taste of the choreographer. The arms moved in a calculated opposition to the legs, so as to create a graceful picture. In figure 6.6b, a dancer steps forward on his right foot with his left arm and hand gracefully in opposition. The floor patterns, or figures traced by the dancers, incorporated balance and symmetry (figs. 6.4, 6.9). A dancing couple would generally do the same or similar steps but on opposite feet, moving alternately

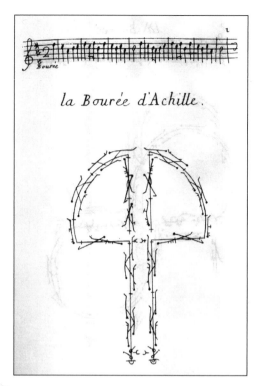

Figure 6.4. "La Bourée Achille" from *Reçueil de Dances Composées par M. Pecour* (Paris, 1700). The first page of a social dance for one couple, with the gentleman on the left and the lady on the right. The steps are written along a track, which shows the floor pattern of the dancers. Tiny horizontal lines mark off measures along this track, corresponding to bars in the music above. The dancers begin at the bottom of the room, proceeding forward for two measures, then sideways away from each other and around to face again, in a balanced fashion. Each one has approximately the same steps to do but on opposite feet. Guillaume-Louis Pecour succeeded Pierre Beauchamps as royal choreographer to Louis XIV. His choreographies represent the largest body of work by a single person (more than one hundred dances) preserved in Feuillet notation.

in opposite directions and in parallel directions, around each other, toward and away, keeping the overall figure in balance but with ever-changing relationships.

A defining feature of French court dancing was the strongly centered carriage of the body (figs. 6.5, 6.6b). Nobility was expressed in an erect posture that was neither stiff nor slack, with the head set squarely on the shoulders, neither tilted upward in disdain nor bent downward in humility. The arms and legs moved in graceful ways from a controlled and tranquil center, but the dancer never abandoned the nonchalance that a modern writer has termed "an eighteenth-century cool."[3] "Nonchalance" in dance is the effort of extreme discipline and expert training over many years, completely disguised in an appearance of simplicity.

To achieve this centeredness required long hours of practice. By Bach's time, dancing lessons began in childhood and continued for many years or even decades. In 1700, when he was fifteen years old, Bach came as a scholarship student to St. Michael's School in Lüneburg. Here he became acquainted with French court dance practices because they were taught at the nearly Lüneburg Ritterschule, a school for young aristocrats. The daily schedule there around 1700 provided students with dancing lessons after lunch as well as free time on the dance floor after supper. Even though Bach did not attend the Ritterschule himself, he might have studied dance

Figure 6.5. A gentleman and a lady ready to make the first reverence before dancing as depicted in Pierre Rameau's *Le mâitre à danser* (Paris, 1725). The dancers are beautifully poised, yet alert, dignified and graceful. The gentleman holds his three-cornered hat in his left hand, while the lady delicately holds her skirt.

or at least played the violin for dancing lessons and classes;[4] thus, even if he had not been trained in French court dancing as a child, he would have encountered it there, at least as a teenager.

Daily schedule at the Knight's School in Lüneburg about 1700[5]

A.M.	5:30	Wake-up
	6:00	Morning prayers
	6:30	Classes
	10:00	Fencing
	11:00	Lunch
P.M.	12:30	Dancing lessons or French lessons
	3:00	Riding lessons or private tutoring
	6:00	Supper
	6:00–8:00	Free time on the dance floor
	8:00	Evening prayers
	9:00	Lights out

Equally important as a noble carriage of the body was an expertise in performing reverences. Two of these were done at the beginning and ending of every dance, once to the king (or presiding presence) and once to one's partner (figs. 6.5, 6.8a–b). Both dancers performed dance reverences with the back straight, the gentleman bowing from the waist and the lady lowering the eyes and bending the legs to lower the body but remaining upright. Proper footwork was required for each type of reverence. A variety of formal reverences were essential for any appearance at court, whether dancing was involved or not (see also fig. 0.8, p. 11).

It was the French dancing masters who taught not only the latest French dances, but the noble carriage of the body, the reverences, and other formalities necessary

Figure 6.6. When Louis Bonin published his *Zur Galanten und theatralischen Tantz-Kunst* (Frankfurt and Leipzig, 1711) (*a*), his days as a theatrical dancer were behind him and he was teaching at the University of Jena. French by birth, he choreographed and danced in operatic productions in France and Germany, and was court dancing master in Eisenach from 1704 to 1707, where he taught the duchess and her daughters as well as organized and choreographed extravagant costume balls for the ruling family and courtiers. His book is less a technical manual (there are no choreographies or illustrations), than a treatment of behavior, etiquette, dance character, and the practical value of dancing by someone who regards dance as something essential for a good life.

 The frontispiece to Bonin's dance treatise (*b*) shows a scene that typified the central role of dance in the life of the upper and aspiring middle classes: the regular private instruction by a dancing master, who played the dance tunes of the moment on his violin as he coached his students, although not here. Although the illustration shows a regular violin in use, it was quite common for dancing masters to employ a miniature violin, called a *pochette* because of its pocket-sized dimensions, that was sufficient for teaching in small quarters.

for a court appearance. Dancing masters were much in demand in Bach's Germany and dancing classes were available on a regular basis, not only for the aristocrats who learned from the court dancing masters, but for middle-class people who paid a dancing master for weekly or biweekly lessons (fig. 6.6b). Some dancing masters were French, such as Louis Bonin, author of *Die neueste Art zur galanten und theatralischen Tanz-Kunst*[6] (fig. 6.6a–b). Others were native-born Germans such as Gottfried Taubert, whose 1,176-page treatise on French court dancing, though often verbose and academic, contains valuable, detailed explanations of social dance technique and style (fig. 6.7). Taubert taught French court dancing during his eleven years at the University of Leipzig, then moved in 1702 to Danzig, where he continued his career as a dancing master, returning in 1714 to Leipzig, where he completed and published his treatise in 1717, six years before Bach's arrival there. He or his treatise may have been consulted by Pierre Rameau, who authored the definitive French treatise on French dancing, *Le maître à danser* (fig. 6.9); Rameau stated specifically that he traveled to Germany before publishing his own work in 1725.[7] It is interesting to note that more treatises on French court dancing were published in German-speaking lands in the early eighteenth century than in France.

Dancing masters grew in number in Saxony during Bach's lifetime. The Leipzig city directory of 1701, for example, listed three French dancing masters, but by 1736 there were twelve, out of a total listing of about twenty thousand persons.[8] Undoubtedly there were many more whose names did not appear in the directory. In Dresden, where the elector had one of the most elaborate, splendid, and expensively maintained courts in Europe outside of Paris, a continuous interest in French dancing can be traced from as early as 1620, when Gabriel Mölich was sent to Paris for training. By the early eighteenth century, numerous French dancing masters worked at the court, teaching dancing and putting on the balls and ballets that were so in demand (fig. 6.8a–b).

Some of these dancing masters are better known from their other activities. Pantaleon Hebenstreit, a dancing master at Dresden, was also a virtuoso performer on many instruments at court. He had supported himself during his student years in Leipzig by teaching French dancing, and later did the same at the courts of Weissenfels and Eisenach, before coming to the Dresden court in 1714. Jean-Baptiste Volumier had been a ballet composer, conductor, and dancing master at the court in Berlin before assuming leadership of the court orchestra and ballet at Dresden (1709–28). Bach was probably personally acquainted with both of these men.

Figure 6.7. The Saxon-born Gottfried Taubert studied at the University of Leipzig and was married at St. Thomas's Church (1698). Whether or not his encyclopedic three-volume treatise on dance, the title of which translates as *The Thorough Dancing Master, or Systematic Explanation of the Art of French Dance* (Leipzig, 1717), was approved, as he claims, by the philosophy faculty of the university, the work treats dance in broad historical perspective, with a focus on French court dance as the embodiment of proper ideals of behavior, especially useful for the middle class. As a consequence, he has no use for the kinds of popular, comic, and grotesque dance such as described by Lambranzi (fig. 6.12) and his treatment of French theatrical dance is sketchy (he frowned on the idea of women dancing on the stage). Taubert's influence, while difficult to measure, nonetheless extended to his being cited in Johannes Mattheson's *Der vollkommene Kapellmeister* of 1739.

Social Dancing

Social dancing was a formal affair, with everyone arrayed in their finest apparel while conforming to a great variety of rules and protocols. A ball was usually held in a large, well-lighted and heavily decorated room. Hierarchy and order

Figure 6.8. The depiction (a) and accompanying
description of a formal ball at Versailles was published in Jacques Bonnet's *Histoire générale de la
danse* (Paris, 1723). The ball celebrated the marriage of the Duc de Bourgogne in 1695. Essentially
the same protocols (the presence, couples dancing alone with everyone else watching, etc.) were
followed elsewhere, such as in the formal court
ball in the Riesensaal (literally, gigantic hall) of the
Dresden electoral palace during festivities in 1719,
as recalled in a drawing by C. H. J. Fehling (b). In
this case the cause for celebration was the marriage of the Saxon prince-elector Friedrich August
II to the Habsburg princess Maria Josepha (daughter of the Holy Roman Emperor).

Ball paré dans la Sale, nomée : le Riesen-Saal .

were strictly observed. Only one couple danced at a time, while the others watched and
admired their performance. Spectators were also present, enjoying and evaluating the
expertise of the dancing couple. The ruler, or other important personage, dominated
the scene from his seat at the head of the room facing the dancers, with the musicians
at the foot of the room or in a special area set aside for them. The rest of the people
were arranged in order of rank around the sides of the dancing area, with spectators in
back. One writer glowingly described a formal ball he witnessed at Versailles in 1695
(fig. 6.8a).

> The King [Louis XIV] had the Galerie de Versailles divided into three parts, by two
> balustrades each four feet high. The part in the center was for the ball. There was

a raised platform with two steps. Covered with the most elegant Gobelin rugs, on which were ranged in the back armchairs of crimson velvet with great golden decorations, for the kings of France and of England, with the Queen, Mme. de Bourgogne, and all the princes and princesses of the blood. The three other sides were lined, in the first row, with very elegant armchairs for the ambassadors, the princes and princesses of foreign countries, dukes, duchesses, and the other high officers of the kingdom. Other rows of chairs behind these armchairs were for the persons of distinction of the Court and City. To the right and left of the center of the ball were the amphitheaters for spectators. To avoid confusion they had to enter through a turnstile, one after the other. There was also a small, separate amphitheater for the twenty-four violins of the King, with six oboes and six soft flutes.

The whole Galerie was lighted by great crystal chandeliers enhanced by a number of candelabra with large candles. The King had invited by ticket the most distinguished people of both sexes from the Court and the City, asking them to appear at the ball only in decent clothing, their finest and most appropriate, in order to have the assemblage be the most brilliant possible. As a result the least of the clothes cost about three or four hundred pistoles. Some were of velvet covered with gold and silver brocade and a golden shield, which cost up to fifty *écus l'aulne*. Others were dressed in cloth of gold or silver. The ladies were no less garmented; the luster of their jewels in the lights made an admirable effect.

As I was seated on a banister opposite the platform where the King was placed, I estimated that this magnificent assemblage was composed of seven or eight hundred people, whose different adornments made a spectacle worthy of admiration. M. and Mme. de Bourgogne opened the ball with a courante. Then Mme. de Bourgogne took the King of England [the deposed James II] to dance; he took the Queen of England; she, the King, who took M. le Duc de Berri. Thus successively all the princes and princesses of blood danced, each one according to his rank. M. le Duc de Chartres, today the Regent, danced there a menuet and a sarabande of such exquisite grace, with Mme. la Princesse de Conti, that they attracted the admiration of all the Court.[9]

Formal ceremonial balls such as the one just mentioned also occurred in German courts, produced by the ruler to celebrate significant events of the realm (fig. 6.8b). They served the political purpose of emphasizing the grandeur of the electorate or other political entity, keeping would-be troublemakers busy with healthful exercise while building confidence, loyalty, and respect. Less elaborate balls frequently took place in lesser courts and in private homes, and in the studios of dancing masters, who usually held formal balls for their students at least weekly. But even on these occasions, the same hierarchy and order prevailed, with one person designated as "king" at the head of the room, and one couple at a time dancing in order of rank or importance.

Dancers' attire in Germany varied as fashion styles changed over the years, according to Taubert.[10] Generally, gentlemen wore hats with wigs, long hair bound neatly in back and gathered with a ribbon. They also wore a long jacket made of wool or silk, which covered short, tight pants that met hosiery at the knee. Gloves covered the hands. Shoes for dancing were light and flexible, with pointed toes, a single sole, low heels, and flaps.

Ladies were given more latitude. Taubert mentions a lace *Frontage*, a flounced dress, and a wide *Contusch*, which was a dress resembling a coat with sleeves.[11] A "hoop skirt" might be made of colorful linen stretched out by hoops made of whalebone, extending from the hips to the lower end of the calves. According to Taubert, some ladies also carried fans and wore false taffeta birthmarks or patches in the shape of the sun, moon, and stars. A lady with bad posture was advised to wear a long busk forcibly holding in her protruding stomach, and stays to raise the breasts while forcing the shoulders back and downward. Worst of all, she might have to wear a covered neck iron, which would forcibly pull back her neck and head.

Formal balls continued to be popular over the years, despite attire that today intrigues more than it charms. Masquerade balls were also much loved, dancing in costume with a mysterious, masked person being enjoyed then as now. On the other hand, there were *Wirthschaften*. As one writer describes them, *Wirthschaften* were balls at court imitating the courtiers' impression of festivities at old rural inns and weddings. Courtiers intentionally dressed as rustics and performed old-fashioned peasant dances instead of the French court dances, a practice that was part of an eighteenth-century craze for the simplicity of country life.[12] One may assume that actual peasants continued to dance their own traditional dances in their villages, even as the courtiers sought to imitate them in the German courts and cities that were then under the sway of French styles.

The Menuet

No better example of the elegance, order, variety, and nonchalance of French social dancing exists than in the menuet, which more than any other dance characterizes the entire eighteenth century in Europe. Taubert devotes 118 pages of his treatise to it. In its basic form, the dancing couple made reverences to the king and to each other, then danced to diagonally opposite ends of a rectangle. Facing each other, they danced along a figure "Z," first sideways, then passing each other in the center of the long segment of the "Z," and then each proceeded to the place in which the other one had begun (fig. 6.9).

Figure 6.9. These two illustrations from Pierre Rameau's *Le maître à danser* show the path of the dancers in a "Z" figure as well as the presentation of right hands.

The dance itself consisted of several "Z" figures, a presentation of right hands, circling around and then back to the opposite ends of the "Z," more "Zs," a presentation of left hands, more circling around, maybe more "Zs," and the climax that was the presentation of both hands, followed by more circling around and a return to the foot of the room and the final two reverences.

The steps of the menuet, as the dancers traced their figures, could be simple but were at times complex and varied. The simplest menuet step-unit consisted of four tiny steps set to two measures of music. Dancers learned to perform menuet step-units forward, backward, and to both sides, on a diagonal, and in circles while turning the body. Several varieties of this simple step-unit existed, some incorporating a modest hop or tiny leap, others varying the way the four tiny steps fit with the two measures of music. Taubert describes a host of other step variations in his treatise, such as *balancés* (balancing on one foot while leaning slightly to that side, then repeating on the other foot to the other side), and *jettés* (small, low hops or leaps), and, in fact, most of the other step-units common in French court dancing. Taubert even includes the difficult steps usually associated with theatrical dancing, such as *pirouettes* (turning the whole body around), *entrechâts* (beating the legs together in the air while doing a high jump), double-time step-units, and even steps used mostly in the comic dance repertoire such as the *pas tortillé* (the foot tracing a wavy line instead of straight line while stepping).

It is not yet clear whether Taubert's often athletic menuet step variations were limited to Germany or were also practiced in France and other countries. What is important is that the menuet, at least in Germany, permitted and even encouraged improvisation.

The simple "Z" floor pattern, and the general format consisting of the presentation of hands, were the constants that underlay endless variations as to the types of step-units used and number of "Zs" and circles undertaken. Sometimes, no one knew until the performance what surprising step-units would be inserted into the basic pattern. Decorum must prevail, however, and Taubert even gives a rule for this: "In short: a well-prepared dancer must not tie himself down in the Menuet. Instead, he should mingle these steps here and there and another time other steps, but always attractively and fitting correctly into the cadence."[13]

Figure 6.10. "La Barberina" (Barbara Campanini) was a brilliant Italian dancer, painted here by Antoine Pesne, who established her reputation at the Paris Opera, Europe's ballet capital. Jean-Philippe Rameau composed special music for her in his opéra-ballet *Les Fêtes d'Hébé* (1739). Dubbed "The flying goddess," she sought to escape a contractual commitment to perform at the Berlin Opera in 1744, but Frederick the Great had her brought to Berlin from Venice under military guard; in the Prussian capital she was the reigning star at a huge salary—nearly twenty times what the court harpsichordist C. P. E. Bach received. However, as with all his prime donne and ballerinas, the king offered these terms on the condition she not marry, so Campanini was dismissed when she became engaged in 1748. European theatrical dance at this time utilized the vocabulary of French court dance but with additional elements of choreographic embellishment and virtuosity beyond the capabilities of amateurs. It was not until the nineteenth century that ballerinas adopted toe shoes and the technique of dancing *en pointe*.

One cannot discuss the flexibility permitted the dancers without mentioning the extemporizing required of the musicians. Menuet accompaniment required a long piece of music, much longer than the short bipartite (AABB) or rondeau (ABACA) menuet pieces that have been preserved. The musicians had to keep playing until the dancers performed their final reverences, and it seems likely there were occasions in which they did not know in advance how many measures of music were needed because they did not know how many circles the dancing couple would make between each presentation of hands, or how many "Zs" they would do. The way to achieve length in a menuet was not by an inner expansion of the musical material, as in a concerto or sonata, but by an "additive" structure—adding together and repeating the various sections of several bipartite or rondeau pieces. Several different menuets might be used, with all sections repeated at least once, undoubtedly the origin of the "menuet and trio" type of piece (for example, AABB CCDD AABB EEFF AABB, a bipartite menuet with two bipartite trios). Thus, the two hundred measures of music, counting repeats, in the menuet and trio of Bach's E Major Partita for solo violin (BWV 1006) is not unusual for a danced menuet. It is even possible that the musicians might have inserted a different type of dance music as part of the dance accompaniment. This is suggested by the long, festive menuet that closes Bach's First Brandenburg Concerto (BWV 1046), a menuet in rondeau form with numerous couplets, one of which is a polonaise! However, with Saxony being so closely aligned with Poland in Bach's time, it is not hard to imagine that polonaises could be incorporated within menuet music, especially since both are in triple meter.

The menuet was only one of the French social dances. Other popular types included gavottes, bourées, courantes, sarabandes, loures, specially choreographed menuets, rigaudons, passepieds and gigues, as well as numerous others with fanciful or personalized titles.[14] Each of these was minutely choreographed and at least several minutes in length; each required attentive, skillful practice in order to render the subtle details accurately and with nonchalance. Over two hundred social dance choreographies survive in notation, with their music. They were usually performed "as is" in the notation, rather than with the freedoms Taubert describes for the menuet.

Theatrical Dancing

Ballets, often with moralistic overtones, were a frequently enjoyed diversion during Bach's lifetime, especially at court (fig. 6.10), in larger cities and at universities. A theater equipped with a stage was the most elegant venue, but any large area could be transformed into a theater by using a portable stage. Thus one also encountered ballets in decorated sports halls, palace courtyards or gardens (fig. 6.11), in the gathering places of university students, in large private homes, and in dancing masters' studios at the beginning or ending of the *assemblées* or weekly balls.

A ballet in early-eighteenth-century Germany can be thought of as roughly analogous to a Bach cantata in length and scope. Ballets might be about 20–30 minutes long, though some were longer; they worked out a single theme or subject by using several contrasting dance entries with musical accompaniment and stimulating costumes and scenery. Samuel Rudolph Behr's 1713 dance treatise describes thirty-four ballets or ballet-like presentations, which he terms *Inventiones*. Here is one of them:

> 19. *A ballet, wherein the four elements are presented*
>
> The first *Entrée*, called Fire, is performed by a lady with a nice figure who has a dress of expensive dark-red purple. Her hair is interwoven with several colored bands. Her cheeks are like red roses, and in her alabaster hands (which the snow frequently harmed) she carries the famous Phoenix bird.

The second *Entrée*, the Air, is performed by another lady, dressed in a sky-blue garment. Her golden locks fall freely, and her coat is striped in many colors like a rainbow. She has full cheeks and a bird-like face.

The third *Entrée* is Water, also danced by a lady, who has a dress of flowing taffeta. She wears a fine coral necklace, is bedecked with sea-green ribbons, and wears a ship's cap.

The fourth *Entrée*, the Earth, is likewise danced by a lady, who has a dress of floral-patterned brocade, and a small dog on her arm. In her hand she carries an aromatic bouquet.[15]

This is only one example, chosen for its clearly contrasting personages who carry in their hands a symbol of their character. All of Behr's ballets are different from each other. Some have all male dancers, some have many more than four *entrées*, some describe certain steps or patterns to be used, some have characters

Figure 6.11. The opéra-ballet *The Four Seasons* was performed in the outdoor theater erected in the Great Garden of the Dresden palace as part of the wedding festivities of the prince-elector and Maria Josepha of Austria in 1719. The illustration reflects a long tradition of the court ballet: the noble courtiers, both men and women, would perform as well as witness the spectacle. In fact, in this particular production there were no professional singers or dancers employed. Although such practice goes back at least to Italian Renaissance courts, it was developed further in France, where in his younger days Louis XIV himself would take leading roles in the court ballets. The participation of the court was made feasible by the fact that intensive dance instruction and practice was part of the noble lifestyle. Pen and ink drawing by C. H. J. Fehling, Dresden, after 1726.

from Greek mythology, and one even incorporates a menuet within its *entrées*. Behr states that ballets are usually preceded by an overture and ended with a Grand Ballet for a group of dancers performing more difficult steps and figures than before. He also indicates that steps from the French court dance repertoire were used in these ballets.

At least two styles of ballet have been identified. Behr's *Inventione* No. 19 probably reflects those in the serious French noble style, or derived from that style, in which the characters performed specially choreographed dances using many of the more difficult step-units of French court dancing. From France, over a hundred ballet *entrées* performed at the French court are preserved in notation, many with the names of the dancers and the work in which they were performed.[16] These *entrées* are similar to the social dance choreographies in their elegance and grace, but more difficult to perform because of the technique required as well as the characterization and theatrical

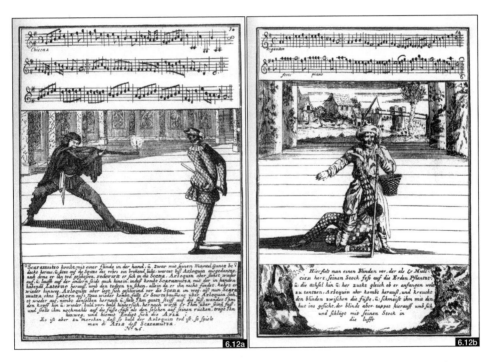

Figure 6.12. Almost a third of the fifty scenes illustrated in Part 1 of Gregorio Lambranzi's *Neue und Curieuse Theatralische Tantz-Schule* (Nuremberg, 1716) involve characters of the commedia dell'arte. They did not recite fixed texts but rather improvised scenarios (such as given in the captions to the illustrations here). As in Feuillet's *Chorégraphie*, each dance is given a corresponding melody—many of them identifiable, despite Lambranzi's claim that he composed them. Although Italian by birth, Lambranzi apparently spent much time in Germany. It is thought that this book might have been intended for or used in educational institutions where theatrical performance played an important role, but many of his dances could also have served in popular theater to characterize or parody the lower classes. Bach's "Peasant" Cantata *Mer hahn en neue oberkeet* (BWV 212) provides a musico-dramatic parallel of such characterization.

costumes not seen in social dancing. From German sources, however, no similar theatrical dances have survived in notation.

The other style of dancing was termed comic or "grotesque." It is a part of the long commedia dell'arte tradition, in which the characters entertained the audience with improvised, pantomimic dancing that, in a broadly farcical manner, criticized, ridiculed, or satirized society. Some of the stock commedia dell'arte characters were Harlequin, Scaramouche, the Doctor, Scapino, and several others easily identified by their clothing, the items they carried, and their steps. In Bach's time, French court dance step-units were a basic component of the style; even though the steps were usually done in a distorted form, the dancers had to know the authentic style in order thus to make fun of it.

Harlequin (figs. 6.12a–b) dresses in a multicolored costume made of a patched, triangular, or diamond-shaped design, in a garment that covers him from neck to feet and is usually belted.[17] He carries a wooden baton that he uses for various purposes, such as hitting people. From his belt hangs a small pouch from which he may pull various props during his antics. His face is half-covered with a black mask.

In the scene or vignette depicted in figure 6.12a, Harlequin dances, then assumes his characteristic multidirectional posture in which he seems to be facing several directions at once. Scaramouche enters on the left, muffled in a cloak and bearing a musket in his hand. He lights a candle at the end of his musket to see better, then shoots Harlequin dead and retreats. Harlequin falls, then gets up and runs off. Scaramouche reenters with a lantern to look for the dead body. Harlequin enters, lies down, and Scaramouche trips and falls over him but is still able to carry away a stiff "dead" body.

In figure 6.12b a blind man enters, hears the music and sets his staff firmly on the ground while vainly trying to dance by jerking his shoulders. Harlequin enters, crawls between the blind man's feet, and throws his hat in the blind man's face. The blind man gropes about and strikes the air with his staff. In the following picture, not shown here, Harlequin taunts and teases the blind man, then laughs loudly at him.

It is clear from these short scenes that the commedia dell'arte practices often stepped over the line of decorum and good taste. In France, the enormously popular Italian troupe that had been in residence at court since 1660 and shared the Palais Royale with Molière, was summarily dismissed by the king in 1697 because they put on a satirical piece making fun of the king's mistress, Madame de Maintenon.[18] In Saxony, the Leipzig professor Johann Christoph Gottsched led a reform of the German stage in 1737, probably for even worse conduct than making fun of the blind. Gottsched's reform included the formal expulsion of Harlequin, who was officially "executed" on stage by the actress Caroline Neuber and her troupe (see chapter 5).[19]

Ballet in Germany often took place during occasions when other, larger works were being performed. Dancing occurred as a part of those works, but also as a relief from them between the acts. Ballet *entrées* constituted an integral part of longer theatrical pieces such as operas, pastorals, and comedies, in which characters often entered the stage dancing. Scholars are unsure today just when the serious or comic styles were used. Presumably, an *entrée* executed by a noble personage within an opera was danced in the serious style, whereas an *entrée* by groups of less than noble character, such as farmers or shepherds, would have been done in caricature.

On the other hand, separate ballet *entrées*, or even whole ballets, were frequently danced between the acts or at the conclusion of Italian operas, serious plays, and other theatrical works such as Latin School plays. These ballets were necessary to allow for costume and scene changes, but they also provided the audience with refreshment and contrast. Ballet as a nonverbal art was the perfect foil to art forms depending on words, and comic ballet in the commedia dell'arte style was an even greater contrast, bizarre and eccentric rather than rational.

Bach and His Dancing World

One easily concludes that the elegance, nobility, and nonchalance of French court dancing was the lifeblood of society in German courts and cities. The court at Eisenach, Bach's birthplace, employed Pantaleon Hebenstreit as a dancing master before the turn of the century; other dance masters, such as Jean-Baptiste Volumier, were likely acquainted with Bach. As noted above, Bach definitely encountered French dancing as a teenager in Lüneburg, where he may have accompanied dance lessons and formal balls as a violinist. Certainly he knew the reverences, for he was presented at many courts, many times. Dancing masters were numerous in Leipzig, where he lived, teaching the disciplined practices and noble carriage that facilitated most human interactions.

A large French dance troupe often performed at the Dresden Court. Bach undoubtedly saw French ballets during performances of Italian operas and other theatrical works; for example, Johann Adolf Hasse's *Cleofide* (fig. 8.11, p. 254), which he likely attended in September 1731, would have had ballets between the acts during scene changes. Far from being the purview of a small elite, French court dancing prevailed, not only in German courts but also in the cities, by the early eighteenth century. Its training in the noble style had intrigued and engaged the middle class, to which the numerous dancing masters practicing in Leipzig, and their treatises, attest. Even the whimsical but popular Italian commedia dell'arte performances used French steps, though irreverently. How fortuitous that the birth of J. S. Bach in the later seventeenth century coincided with the birth of classical ballet in France.

Notes

Editor's Note. Bach wrote many pieces that bear titles of dance types. These were usually grouped together to form suites, i.e., a sequence of dances such as the so-called "French Suites" (BWV 812–17) for keyboard. Sometimes suites were preceded by an opening non-dance movement, as in the so-called "English Suites" (BWV 806–11) and the six "Partitas" (BWV 825–30) that constitute Part I of the *Clavierübung* (fig. 6.1). If this movement was in the form of a "French overture," which consists of a regal section in duple meter followed by a lively fugue-like section, with a possible return of the opening section, the complete work—overture plus dances—might be designated by the French term *Ouverture*. This synecdochal naming of a dance suite from the opening, non-dance movement that precedes it derives from the usage of French composers of the later seventeenth century who wrote for the ballets and balls at the court of Louis XIV. Examples of this in Bach are his four Ouvertures for Orchestra (BWV 1066–69) and the "Overture in the French Style" (BWV 831) in Part II of the *Clavierübung*. However, few if any of Bach's works with dance titles were actually intended for dancing.

The influence of dance on Bach is not limited to pieces with dance titles, however. In fact, many works of his *without* dance titles show the characteristics of specific dance types. Thus one can recognize the bourée character of the first movement of Brandenburg Concerto No. 2 (BWV 1047), the gavotte rhythm of "Quia fecit mihi magna" of the *Magnificat* in D Major (BWV 243), and the sarabande structure and style of the final chorus from the St. Matthew Passion, "Wir setzen uns" (BWV 244/78). The Goldberg Variations (BWV 988) contain several examples of dance-inspired music, from the sarabande-like melody of the "Aria" to the gigue-like Variation 7 and the passepied- or *giga*-like Variation 19. Over one hundred arias in both secular and sacred cantatas show similar influences. See note 20, below.

1. For further information, see Wendy Hilton, *Dance of Court and Theater: The French Noble Style, 1690–1725* (Princeton: Princeton Book Co., 1981; rpt. 1997; Meredith Little and Natalie Jenne, *Dance and the Music of J. S. Bach*, expanded edition (Bloomington, IN: Indiana University Press, 2001), chapter 1; Meredith Little and Carol Marsh, *La Danse Noble: An Inventory of Dances and Sources* (Williamstown, NY: Nabburg, 1992); Francine Lancelot, *La Belle Dance: Catalogue raisonné fait en l'an 1955* (Paris: Van Dieren, 1996. For a video (videotape and DVD) introduction to the individual French baroque dances, see Paige Whitley-Bauguess, *Introduction to Baroque Dance Types* (1999), 2 vols., and *Dance of the French Baroque Theater* (2005), both distributed by Baroquedance.com.

2. Turnout persists in ballet to this day, though to a greater extent than in the early eighteenth century. Turnout of the legs from the hips may be seen in illustrations in this essay.

3. Shirley Wynne, "Complaisance: An Eighteenth-Century Cool," *Dance Scope* 5/1 (1970): 22–35.

4. According to Eckhard Michael (personal communication), director of the Museum of the Principality of Lüneburg, the academic curriculum of St. Michael's School was the same as that of the associated Ritterschule. —Ed.

5. Based on research by James Robert Morgan (Mason City, IA). Source: Michaelisschule Archiv.

6. Frankfurt and Leipzig/zu finden bey Joh. Christoph Lochner/Buchhandler. Anno 1711.

7. Paris, 1725; Eng. tr. C. W. Beaumont as *The Dancing Master* (London: C. W. Beaumont, 1931; rpt. New York: Dance Horizons, 1970), 74, chapter 15.

8. Kurt Petermann, ed., *Nachwort* in facs. rpt. of Taubert's *Rechtschaffener Tanzmeister* (Leipzig, 1717), in *Documenta Choreologica* 22 (Leipzig: Zentralantiquariat der DDR, 1976).

9. Jacques Bonnet, *Histoire générale de la danse* (Paris, 1723; rpt. Geneva: Slatkine Reprints, 1969), 129–32); trans. Meredith Little, formerly published in an article entitled "Dance Under Louis XIV and XV: Some Implications for the Musician," *Early Music* 3 (October 1975): 332.

10. Information concerning costume is from Angelika Gerbes, "Gottfried Taubert on Social and Theatrical Dance of the Early Eighteenth Century" (Ph.D. diss., The Ohio State University, 1972), 73–77.

11. Gerbes, 76.

12. Böhme, *Geschichte des Tanzes in Deutschland* (Wiesbaden: Breitkopf & Härtel, 1967) 1:144–45, as quoted in Gerbes.

13. Taubert, 732; Engl. trans. by Gerbes, 319.

14. For a bibliographically correct listing of the extant dances, with cross-references and indexes, see Meredith Little and Carol Marsh, *La Danse Noble: An Inventory of Dances and Sources* (Williamstown, NY: Nabburg, 1992).

15. Samuel Rudolph Behr, *L'Art de Bien Danser, Die Kunst wohl zu Tantzen* (Leipzig, 1713), 72f. (Engl. trans. by Meredith Little); rpt. in *Documenta Choreologica* 2, with *Nachwort* and index by Kurt Petermann (Leipzig: Zentralantiquariat der DDR, 1977).

16. For references, see Meredith Little and Carol Marsh, *La Danse Noble*.

17. Information on Harlequin is from Susan Bindig, "Dancing in Harlequin's World" (Ph.D. diss., New York University, 1998), chapter 3. The specific examples of burlesque dancing here described are found in Gregorio Lambranzi, *Nuova e curiosa scuola de'balli theatrail*, Nuremburg, 1716, reproduced in facsimile by Dance Horizons, New York, 1972.

18. James Anthony, *French Baroque Music from Beaujoyeulx to Rameau*, revised and expanded ed. (Portland, OR: Amadeus Press, 1997), 191.

19. Susan Bindig, "Dancing in Harlequin's World," 113f.

20. Listings of Bach's music with dance titles and of non-dance music influenced by dance idioms are found in the appendices of Meredith Little and Natalie Jenne, *Dance and the Music of J. S. Bach.*

PART II

Bach in Context

CHAPTER 7

Bach and Luther

Robert L. Marshall

I

In the year 1708, that is, at the age of twenty-three, young Johann Sebastian Bach re-signed his respected post as organist of St. Blaise's Church in the imperial free city of Mühlhausen. He announced, among other things, that he intended to devote himself to creating what he described as "a well-regulated church music."[1] Apparently his first systematic effort at fulfilling this self-proclaimed goal was the composition of what he called an *Orgelbüchlein*—a little organ book—actually an extensive series of miniature, but highly sophisticated and expressive organ chorales, whose contents were to include chorale preludes for the principal feasts of the church year, a series of chorales on the articles of the catechism, and, finally, a collection of miscellaneous hymns for a large variety of occasions and circumstances (fig. 2.9, p. 119).

It is now thought that work on the *Orgelbüchlein* had commenced much earlier than had hitherto been assumed—virtually as soon as Bach had taken up his new duties as court organist at Weimar.[2] But even though Bach continued to work on it over the course of the next five or six years, the ambitious project was left unfinished. Of the 164 chorales originally planned only forty-six were ever completed. But it is worth noting that of these forty-six no fewer than twenty-eight—well over half—are Reformation-era cho-rales, twelve of them by Martin Luther himself. Had the *Orgelbüchlein* been completed, it would have contained thirty of the thirty-six chorales ascribed to the Reformer.

Indeed, it is hardly possible to overstate the importance of the Lutheran congre-gational chorale in the music of J. S. Bach. Of the approximately 1,130 compositions attributed to Bach, 450 (or more than one in three) are chorale settings, ranging from simple four-part harmonizations (fig. 7.1) to chorale preludes, variations, partitas, and fantasias for the organ to chorale motets and cantatas for voices and instrumental

Figure 7.1. Between 1784 and 1787 there appeared in four serial parts, then together as one volume, the 371 four-part chorale settings (that is, for soprano, alto, tenor, and bass) of J. S. Bach. Collected and edited by Johann Philipp Kirnberger and Carl Philipp Emanuel Bach (although Kirnberger did not live to see the publication), this collection can be regarded as the oldest musical textbook still in use for the teaching of harmony and counterpoint. Its value was clearly indicated by C. P. E. Bach in his preface: "There is perhaps in the whole science of writing nothing more difficult than this: not only to give each of the four voices its own flowing melody, but also to keep a uniform character in all, so that out of their union a single and perfect whole may arise." In this particular case, the chorale is "In dich habe ich gehoffet, Herr" (I have hoped in You, Lord), as used as the closing movement of the cantata "Falsche Welt, dir trau'ich nicht" (False world, I do not trust you) (BWV 52), but Bach also used the melody in his Orgelbüchlein (BWV 640) as well as in another organ version for manuals only (BWV 712).

ensemble. Moreover, a disproportionately large number of these compositions are not only based on Lutheran chorales but literally on the chorales of Martin Luther himself and other poets of his generation. The dominant position occupied by the chorales of Martin Luther and his contemporaries—in comparison to those composed later in the sixteenth century, or those from the Baroque and Pietist periods—is dramatically evident in every category of Bach's oeuvre.

While the chorale preludes of the *Orgelbüchlein* were to be miniature in scale—each one only a page or two in length—in Bach's other collections of organ chorales the individual compositions frequently assumed breathtaking dimensions. The seventeen so-called "great" (i.e., large-scale) organ chorales (BWV 651–67) were also begun in Weimar, very likely at about the same time as the *Orgelbüchlein*, but these were revised (though again never quite completed) late in Bach's life. They may well have been deliberately conceived as providing a contrasting counterpart to the miniature format of the *Orgelbüchlein* chorales, representing, as it were, the epic as opposed to the lyric modes

Figure 7.2. Bach's intimate connection to Luther received its most public acknowledgment in the publication of the third part (1739) of the composer's ambitious serious of keyboard publications to which he gave the overall title *Clavierübung*. The title page specifically states that it contains "various preludes on the catechism and other hymns for the organ," a clear reference to Luther's catechisms (figs. 2.4–6, pp. 110–12). The *Clavierübung III* appeared not long after Bach had been criticized for his "turgid" style, but C. F. Mizler (fig. 9.8b, p. 281) came to his defense, noting that in the new publication Bach "has here given new proof that in this field of composition . . . no one will surpass him . . . and few will be able to imitate him."

of chorale composition—or perhaps they were regarded as an analogue to the smaller and larger catechisms of Martin Luther (fig. 2.4, p. 110, and fig. 2.5a–b, p. 111).

Although the rationale of the design of the collection of seventeen great chorales, taken as a whole, is not altogether clear, it is clear that the chorales of Martin Luther quite literally occupy pride of place. The group is framed by Luther's *Komm, Heiliger Geist, Herre Gott* (Come, Holy Spirit, Lord God) (BWV 651) at the beginning and, at the end, by his *Komm Gott Schöpfer, Heiliger Geist* (Come, God, Creator, Holy Spirit) (BWV 667). The midpoint is marked by an elaborate setting of yet another of Luther's invitatory chorales, addressed this time to the second person of the Trinity: *Nun komm, der Heiden Heiland* (Now come, Savior of the heathens) (BWV 659). The opening measures of the opening composition, *Komm, Heiliger Geist* (BWV 651), evoke at once the sense of monumentality and grandeur that Bach was striving for in this collection.

Monumentality is also the hallmark of Bach's mammoth collection of keyboard music, the *Clavierübung* (Keyboard practice), the four volumes, or Parts, of which were published over a period of fifteen years during Bach's Leipzig period. The first installment of the first Part (BWV 825–30), a book of keyboard partitas (i.e., suites), appeared in 1726; the final volume, the Goldberg Variations (BWV 988), appeared in 1741. Only the third Part of the *Clavierübung* (BWV 669–89) is devoted to sacred keyboard music (fig. 7.2). It consists of twenty-one organ chorales: nine chorales constituting the Lutheran *Missa brevis* (Kyrie and Gloria), and twelve settings of catechism chorales. This time the reference to Luther's Large and Small Catechisms is overt: There are two settings, one large and one small, for each of the six catechism chorales. It may be more than mere coincidence that Part III of the *Clavierübung*, with its collection of liturgical chorales for the organ, was published in the year 1739, the year of the bicentennial celebration of the adoption of the Augsburg Confession in Leipzig.

Bach's last great contribution to the literature of the organ chorale, the Canonic Variations on *Vom Himmel hoch da komm ich her* (From heaven on high I come here)

(BWV 769), published in 1747 or 1748, has as its substance what the author of the text, Martin Luther, described as a "children's song for Christmas Eve." Bach's treatment of the venerable and beloved children's song, however, is not child's play. As its title suggests, the Canonic Variations are a compositional tour de force, a display of the most rigorous techniques of strict canon. It is known that the Canonic Variations were composed, and published, as part of Bach's initiation into C. F. Mizler's honorary Society of Musical Sciences. Nonetheless, the work could have been conceived as a companion work to the other magnum opus of contrapuntal craft with which the composer was occupied at just this time in the final years of his life: *Die Kunst der Fuge* (The art of fugue) (BWV 1080). The two publications, taken together, reflect not only the two general spheres, into one or the other of which all music necessarily belongs—either the sacred or secular—they also represent the two fundamental principles of musical invention as they were inherited and described by musical theorists and commentators from time immemorial: *The Art of Fugue* manifesting the principle, or the genre, of "free" composition, that is, works making use of original, freely invented thematic material; the Canonic Variations on *Vom Himmel hoch*, on the other hand, belonging to the age-old tradition of the "bound" composition: works based on a pre-existent melody.

In turning to Bach's vocal music, we encounter, once again, the dominating presence of the Great Reformer. First of all, two of Martin Luther's most revered chorale texts serve—once again—as a frame: this time for Bach's life work as a church cantata composer. Bach's earliest chorale-based cantata is the Easter composition *Christ lag in Todesbanden* (Christ lay in the bonds of death) (BWV 4), presumably composed during Bach's year at Mühlhausen, 1707/8. At the other end of the composer's life the cantata on *Ein feste Burg ist unser Gott* (A mighty fortress is our God) (BWV 80) was put into its final form (after numerous revisions) sometime between 1744 and 1747 and was very possibly Bach's last German church cantata altogether.

But the period of Bach's most concentrated involvement with the chorale in the context of cantata composition falls almost exactly in the middle of his career. The beginning of that involvement, in fact, can be dated precisely: to the first Sunday after Trinity, June 11, 1724, when the composer began his second full year as cantor of St. Thomas and director of church music for the city of Leipzig. On that day Bach launched a series of weekly cantatas, all of which were to be based on a congregational chorale appropriate for the particular Sunday or feast of the church year. It is tempting to think that the decision to inaugurate such an ambitious cycle of chorale cantatas specifically during the year 1724–25 was informed by a desire to commemorate the two-hundredth anniversary of the first Lutheran hymnbook publications: the so-called *Achtliederbuch* (Book of eight hymns, the very first Lutheran hymnbook), the two Erfurt *Enchiridia*, and the *Geistliche Gesangk Buchleyn* (Little spiritual songbook), all of which appeared in the year 1524.

Over the course of the next nine months, Bach composed or performed at least forty-four such chorale or chorale-paraphrase cantatas, concluding the series on Easter Sunday, 1725, with a performance of a revised version of his early masterpiece *Christ lag in Todesbanden*. Virtually all of the cantatas, however, were newly composed—and composed at the astonishing rate of at least one per week. Not surprisingly, in this repertoire, too, the hymns of the Reformation generation occupy the same pre-eminent position as they do in Bach's organ works. Over a third of the cantatas of the 1724/25 cycle are set to texts of Luther and his contemporaries.

And, once again, Martin Luther's own hymns stand out not only numerically but also by virtue of their placement in the cantata cycle. Almost all the auspicious and high feasts of Bach's chorale cantata cycle were celebrated with compositions based on the hymns of Martin Luther: for the first Sunday of Advent, the official beginning of the church year, Bach composed a new cantata on Luther's *Nun komm, der Heiden Heiland* (BWV 62), traditionally the principal hymn for that day. (Bach had already composed a cantata on *Nun komm* [BWV 61] ten years earlier, during his Weimar period.) Luther's chorales were also chosen for the first two days of Christmas.

Bach also turned to Luther for the cantata intended for performance on the twenty-first Sunday after Trinity. In the year 1724 that Sunday fell on October 29, thus making it the last Sunday before Reformation Day. The chorale Bach chose to set on this occasion (as BWV 38) was *Aus tiefer Not schrei ich zu dir* (In deep need I cry to Thee). That hymn had long been associated with the twenty-first Sunday after Trinity, perhaps because the reassuring response to this earnest plea for comfort—Luther's poetic rendering of the 130th Psalm—was about to be offered a few days hence, namely, on Reformation Day. For Reformation Day itself Bach evidently performed a setting of *Ein feste Burg*, but in an early version that no longer survives. Before the chorale cantata cycle was completed, Bach would compose three further Luther chorale cantatas and would add yet another to the repertoire in later years.

II

The reasons for Johann Sebastian Bach's attraction to the chorales of Martin Luther are manifold (fig. 7.3). Luther was not only the founder and guiding spirit of the Protestant Reformation, he was a poet of genius and, as a composer (or at least a melodist), remarkably imaginative, versatile, and effective. Apart from all liturgical and theological considerations, Bach, as a musician, was particularly fascinated by two types of melody writing cultivated and indeed mastered by Luther. The first category consisted of melodies in the major mode. These tunes proceed to clear tonal goals, creating a sense of tonal direction and conveying an almost palpable sense of purposefulness. In conjunction with their texts, they project an aura of sublimity or majesty. Bach was understandably attracted to the solid, sturdy, sharply profiled, "honest" tunes of such melodies as those of *Ein feste Burg* and *Vom Himmel hoch*. He was able to capture the "healthy," affirmative attributes of these tunes in simple harmonizations. But they also inspired him to displays of contrapuntal artifice that clothe the folklike tunes in something like the musical equivalent of the mantle of royalty, while they also represent a devoted and devout musician's labor of homage. Perhaps, too, such grandiose designs were conceived as a reflection, or symbol, of the miraculous intricacy and order of God's universe.

But Martin Luther was also gifted at creating melodies that occupied the opposite end of the stylistic and expressive

Figure 7.3. This painting of Luther in his Augustinian monk's garb from the workshop of Lukas Cranach the Elder, an artist especially close to the people and events of the Reformation, was done ca. 1523, a time when Luther had already been excommunicated, although he occasionally still dressed as a monk. He joined the strict Augustinian order in 1505, to the chagrin of his father, was ordained in 1507, and then went to the brand-new, progressive University of Wittenberg for his doctorate, which he received in 1512. In 1510, however, he went to Rome on matters concerning his order, but was appalled at the laxity of the clergy there. The resulting disillusionment coupled with the burden of his own scruples helped pave the way for his ultimate revolt from the established Church.

spectrum from that represented by *Ein feste Burg* and *Vom Himmel hoch*—and Bach was just as attracted to them. I am referring to melodies such as *Aus tiefer Not schrei ich zu dir* or *Ach Gott vom Himmel sieh darein* (Ah, God look down from heaven). Quite unlike the readily accessible, modern-sounding, major-mode melodies of the former, those of *Aus tiefer Not* and *Ach Gott vom Himmel* sound archaic, indeed exotic, even alien. They belong to the church modes obsolete even in Bach's time, in particular the Phrygian mode, in which the second scale degree is only a half-step above the tonic pitch. When such melodies, like Luther's, are well crafted—with sharply delineated contours and sensitive placement of the characteristic steps and intervals of the mode—they can be both memorable and deeply expressive.

The archaic idiom of hymn melodies of this sort frequently inspired Bach to adopt a self-consciously retrospective compositional style when setting them as cantata movements or even as organ chorales.

III

Bach's stature as the greatest composer of the Lutheran church has long since been beyond debate. Indeed, it is not infrequently suggested that, next to Luther himself, Bach may well be the most important Lutheran in history. Even so, it is quite possible that we might, if anything, actually be underestimating the importance of Martin Luther in the life and artistic development of Johann Sebastian Bach.

Some years ago the eminent literary critic Harold Bloom developed a provocative theory of poetic influence, which he published under the title *The Anxiety of Influence*. Bloom's central thesis, enunciated at the outset of his book, is this: "Strong poets make . . . history by misreading one another, so as to clear imaginative space for themselves." He continues: "[Strong poets] . . . wrestle with their strong precursors, even to the death. Weaker talents idealize; figures of capable imagination appropriate for themselves."[3]

Although Bloom speaks only of lyric poets, his thesis clearly applies to great (or, in Bloom's preferred term, "strong") creative artists of any medium. For example, in the sphere of music, we are all aware of the giant shadow, and the attendant Anxiety of Influence, that Beethoven cast on virtually all the composers of the nineteenth century that followed him, and the similar, quite suffocating, influence that Richard Wagner exerted on his contemporaries and followers. Beethoven himself admitted to having to struggle with the overwhelming influence of both Mozart and Haydn. As for Mozart: he demonstrably did not reach full artistic maturity until he had seriously studied and absorbed the music of J. S. Bach.

Bloom calls attention to a notable exception to his theory of influence. He writes: "The greatest poet in our language is excluded from the argument. . . . Shakespeare belongs to the giant age before the flood, before the anxiety of influence became central to poetic consciousness."[4] In an important sense J. S. Bach, like Shakespeare, belonged to "the giant age before the flood" in the history of music. In the same sense that one could assert, admittedly with some hyperbole, that there were "no great poets" before Shakespeare, it is possible to argue that there were "no great composers" before Bach. It is true that Bach has the reputation of being the "culmination of an era." In the famous words of Albert

Schweitzer: "Bach is a . . . terminal point. Nothing comes from him, everything merely leads up to him." In a far more profound sense, however, Bach was in fact the *beginning* of an era. He was, upon reflection, the *first great composer*—at least in modern times: that is, the era that continues still—and is, in fact, ours. In the beginning was Bach, the ultimate source of all modern Anxiety of Influence in the art of music. This means that, unlike all his great and famous successors, Bach had no great musical precursor with whom to wrestle. Whoever was there—Buxtehude, Vivaldi—he merely "swallowed up."

In this connection Harold Bloom cites an example of what he calls "Goethe's . . . appalling self confidence." The immortal poet once wrote: "Do not all the achievements of a poet's predecessors and contemporaries rightfully belong to him? Why should he shrink from picking flowers where he finds them? Only by making the riches of the others our own do we bring anything great into being."[5] Bach, it seems, did not suffer from the Anxiety of Influence any more than did Goethe. He, too, felt free to "pick the flowers where he [found] them." In the list of composers whom Bach (as reported by his son Carl Philipp Emanuel) had "heard and studied" in his youth, we find the names of Froberger, Kerl, Pachelbel, Fischer, Struck, "some old and good Frenchmen," Buxtehude, Reinken, Bruhns, and Böhm.[6] A respectable list, but there are clearly no giants among them: no Beethovens, Mozarts, Wagners—or J. S. Bachs—again, because, for all intents and purposes, at least in Bach's world, none had existed. (Of course, there were brilliant musicians, even musicians of genius, before Bach: Josquin des Pres, Claudio Monteverdi, to mention just two. But it is doubtful that Bach knew their music, or perhaps even their names. It is not even certain whether he was aware of the music, or the name, of his greatest German predecessor, Heinrich Schütz.) What is even more striking, however, is that the name of the composer who surely had the greatest influence of all on the formation of Bach's mature style, the one to whom he was clearly most indebted, is missing entirely from his son's list of acknowledgments: Antonio Vivaldi.

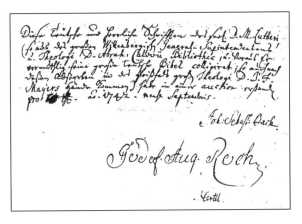

Figure 7.4. In 1742 Bach bought at an estate auction a (second) complete copy of Luther's works. The set had been part of the eighteen-thousand-volume library of Johann Friedrich Mayer coming into the hands of the Leipzig theologian Andreas Winckler, from whose estate Bach purchased the books.

As far as his art was concerned, Bach did not so much have formidable individual precursors to confront as prevailing idioms, conventions, and traditions to study, assimilate, and transcend. But any serious artist, especially an artist of genius, must have a worthy model against whom he can measure, and challenge, himself. Surely the only mortal who could be described as having served, in the deepest sense, as a model and inspiration for Johann Sebastian Bach—someone worthy of his emulation, stimulating his creative imagination, and serving indeed as an inspiration (exciting both admiration and awe)—was Martin Luther.

There can be little doubt that Bach revered Martin Luther, strongly identified with him, recognized him as a supremely towering figure, as a truly "great man," and venerated him almost to the point of obsession. One telling symptom of this reverence is to be found in Bach's personal library. Dominating this library were writings of Luther, which Bach possessed several times over, including at least two extensive, and expensive, collected editions. As one authority reports:

> There were twenty-one fat folio volumes devoted to the writings of Martin Luther
> in Bach's library. If one then adds the quarto volume of Luther's *Hauß Postilla* and
> the octavo volume of Johannes Müller's *Lutherus Defensus*, which were also in his
> library, then something of the high regard Bach had for the great German Reformer
> and his writings can be clearly seen.[7]

Particularly intriguing is the seven-volume edition of Luther's *Schriften*, which Bach purchased from a dealer at a book auction in 1742. Bach seems to have paid the considerable price of ten thalers for the deluxe edition of Luther's works. (Bach's annual income at Leipzig was around seven hundred thalers, or some sixty thalers per month.) But Bach actually paid more than ten thalers. The price on the receipt has been changed, no doubt from something considerably higher: perhaps double or even triple the putative price (fig. 7.4).

One can only agree with the explanation proposed for the alteration of the price of the volumes, namely, that Bach may have been "reluctant to reveal to his wife how much he paid for them."[8] The document reads:[9]

> These German and magnificent Writings of the late D.[octor] M.[artin] Luther (that
> came from the library of the great Wittenberg theologian D.[octor] Abrah:[am]
> Calovius, which he probably used to compile his great *Teütsche Bibel*; and also, after
> his death, passed into the hands of the equally great theologian D.[octor] J.[ohann]
> F.[riedrich] Mayer) [I] have acquired for 10 thl. Anno 1742. Mense Septembris.
>
> Joh. Sebast. Bach

IV

Bach's profound veneration for Luther is not difficult to understand. First of all, it obviously built upon the respect and reverence naturally flowing to the founder of the composer's religious confession. But there were other sources nurturing Bach's personal identification with the Reformer; for example, the almost familial bond deriving from their common national—indeed, regional—heritage. Like Luther, Bach was a native Thuringian. Moreover, Bach was born and spent the first ten years of his life in Eisenach, that is, in the shadow of the Wartburg, where Luther, after his defiant stand at the Diet of Worms, had taken refuge and translated the New Testament into German and therewith had determined the precise form in which the Holy Word that was at the core of the new dispensation would be proclaimed to the German-speaking world (fig. 7.5).

There is another element as well coloring the nature of Bach's personal relationship with Luther, one having to do, once again, with the extraordinarily gifted creative individual's need for a credible model, a "great man" worthy of, and capable of inspiring, emulation. In his classic essay *Moses and Monotheism*, Sigmund Freud allows himself a lengthy digression in order to speculate on what, exactly, is a "great man."[10] After discounting such attributes as beauty, physical strength, military heroism, and worldly success in general, he adds:

> We should certainly not apply the term to a master of chess or to a virtuoso on a musical instrument, and not necessarily to a distinguished artist or a man of science. In such a case we should be content to say he is a great writer, painter, mathematician, or physicist, a pioneer in this field or that, but we should pause before pronouncing him a great man. When we declare, for instance, Goethe, Leonardo da Vinci, and Beethoven to be great men, then something else must move us to do so beyond the admiration of their grandiose creations.[11]

After further such teasing Freud finally concludes:

> It is the *longing for the father* [emphasis added] that lives in each of us from his childhood days, for the same father whom the hero of legend boasts of having overcome. And now it begins to dawn on us that all the features with which we furnish the great man are the traits of the father. . . . The decisiveness of thought, the strength of will, the forcefulness of his deeds, belong to the picture of the father; above all other things, however, the self-reliance and independence of the great man, his divine

[*sic*] conviction of doing the right thing, which may pass into ruthlessness. He must be admired, he may be trusted, but one cannot help also being afraid of him.[12]

One need not be a doctrinaire Freudian to find that this insight rings true. And it is hardly necessary to argue that these attributes of the great man, which Freud, of course, proceeds to apply to Moses, apply just as well to Martin Luther. As far as the present discussion is concerned, it is important to remember that Bach had no father. He was an orphan: his mother died when he was just nine years old, his father three months thereafter—a month short of Bach's tenth birthday. Bach, then, experienced the catastrophic deprivation of his parents; and this calamity understandably put the boy on his guard, engendering in him, we may be sure, an attitude of "basic distrust" against an unreliable, even treacherous world. Under such circumstances, it is readily apparent why Bach would have been drawn to religion, especially to the Lutheran religion with its message of personal faith and salvation, one, moreover, that would have provided him with the ideal image of the admirable, inspiring, awe-inspiring, longed-for father.

There was yet a further, perhaps decisive reason, why Bach would have been drawn to the person and doctrine of Martin Luther, and that is the uniquely important place Luther accorded to music. Luther put it most succinctly in his *Table Talks* (at least one copy of which Bach owned) when he said: "Music is an outstanding gift of God and next to theology. I would not want to give up my slight knowledge of music for a great consideration. And youth should be taught this art; for it makes fine skillful people"[13] (fig. 7.6).

It is important to recognize that Luther's enthusiasm for music embraced both its least pretentious and most sophisticated manifestations: from the simple folklike tunes to be sung by the congregation to the most

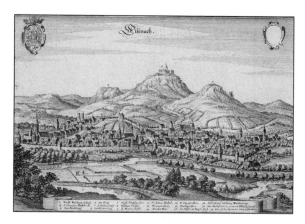

Figure 7.5. Both Bach and Luther had deep, formative connections to Eisenach, for both were pupils at the Latin School associated with St. George's Church and participated in the tradition of *Kurrende*—whereby poor choirboys would wander around the town singing for donations. Luther's lifelong devotion to and skill in music is well known, but he also returned to Eisenach following the Diet of Worms in 1521, when he was outlawed by Emperor Charles V. On his way back to Wittenberg from Worms, Luther preached to enthusiastic crowds in Eisenach, but a few days later he was "kidnapped" by agents of his supporter Elector Frederick the Wise and brought to the Wartburg castle overlooking the town, where Luther disguised himself as the squire Junker Jörg. He left the castle on March 1, 1522, after completing his translation of the New Testament (fig. 2.7, p. 113).

Figure 7.6. Martin Luther's *Tischreden* (Table-talk) was a posthumous publication drawing together over sixty-five hundred of Luther's sayings, aphorisms, and opinions on a host of topics ranging from the theological to the mundane. These were recorded by his friends and disciplines in various, especially informal, circumstances, such as when sitting around the dinner table, from which the collection derives its name. As a result, there is an unguarded frankness to some of the utterances, affording readers a path to understanding Luther the man in a way that his formal prose does not. First published twenty years after Luther's death in 1566, with John Aurifaber as editor, the *Tischreden* was reprinted twice the following year and yet again in 1568, and in 1569 a new edition appeared with new material. The *Tischreden* was not included in the early editions of Luther's complete writings, but it is known that Bach owned a copy in addition to his two sets of Luther's works.

elaborate polyphonic settings. Nowhere, perhaps, is Luther's admiration for the highest musical art expressed more eloquently and lyrically than in this passage recorded in the *Table Talks*:

> How strange and wonderful it is that one voice sings a simple unpretentious tune . . . while three, four, or five other voices are also sung; these voices play and sway in joyful exuberance around the tune and with ever-varying art and tuneful sound wondrously adorn and beautify it, and in a celestial roundelay meet in friendly caress and lovely embrace; so that anyone, having a little understanding, must be moved and greatly wonder, and come to the conclusion that there is nothing rarer in the whole world than a song adorned by so many voices.[14]

For all its enthusiasm and poetic exuberance this passage could serve as a technically precise description of a typical polyphonic chorale setting such as one encounters in a church cantata by J. S. Bach.

The implications of such statements for Bach's self understanding—and Bach almost certainly knew them—are abundantly clear: Martin Luther, quite literally, has done nothing less than justify (even glorify) Bach's existence as a musician and indeed defined his earthly mission.

This is a slightly revised version of the Kessler Reformation Lecture, originally entitled "Luther, Bach, and the Early Reformation Chorale," given in 1995 at the Pitts Theology Library at Emory University in Atlanta.

Notes

1. An English translation of the complete text of Bach's letter of resignation (actually a request for dismissal) is printed in *NBR*, 57 (*BD* 1, no. 1, p. 19).
2. Christoph Wolff, "Chronology and Style in the Early Works: A Background for the Orgel-Büchlein," in *Bach: Essays on His Life and Music* (Cambridge, MA: Harvard University Press, 1991), 299.
3. Harold Bloom, *The Anxiety of Influence: A Theory of Poetry* (New York: Oxford University Press, 1973), 5.
4. *Ibid.*, 11.
5. *Ibid.*, 52.
6. For C. P. E. Bach's comment, made in reply to an inquiry from the early Bach biographer Johann Nicolaus Forkel, see *NBR*, 398 (*BD* 3, no. 803, p. 289).
7. Robin A. Leaver, "Bach and Luther," *Bach: The Quarterly Journal of the Riemenschneider Bach Institute* 9/3 (July 1978): 11f.
8. Leaver, *Bachs theologische Bibliothek, eine kritische Bibliographie. Bach's Theological Library: A Critical Bibliography* (Neuhausen-Stuttgart: Hännsler-Verlag, 1983), 14 (Beiträge zur theologischen Bachforschung 1).
9. *Ibid.*, 42. Incidentally, this document evidently contains the only surviving written reference to Martin Luther in Bach's hand.
10. Sigmund Freud, *Moses and Monotheism*, trans. Katherine Jones (New York: Random House, 1939), 136–40.
11. *Ibid.*, 138.
12. *Ibid.*, 140.
13. Carl F. Schalk, *Luther on Music: Paradigms of Praise* (St. Louis: Concordia House, 1988), 34.
14. *Ibid.*, 21.

CHAPTER 8

Bach and the Lure of the Big City

George B. Stauffer

Although Bach faced many different kinds of responsibilities in his positions as organist, orchestral player, concertmaster, court music director, and finally cantor of St. Thomas and city music director, one can nevertheless trace several continuous threads running through the fabric of his forty-seven-year career. These include his methodical rise from one position to another (with steady increases in salary), his constant sensitivity to slights and criticisms, and his repeated demands for improved musical forces. There is another strand that deserves more attention than it has received, however, and that is Bach's constant attraction to life in the big city, traceable from Lüneburg through to Weimar, Cöthen, and Leipzig.

For Bach, the lure of the big city remained constant. Put more specifically, he kept his eyes focused on three big cities: Hamburg, the most important of the *Hansestädte*, or free industrial towns; Berlin, the political capital of Prussia; and Dresden, the political capital of Saxony.

Indeed, our earliest biographical account of Bach the musician presents the picture of a young chorister and budding keyboard player threading his way from Lüneburg, the small salt-mining town on the heath, to the commercial metropolis of Hamburg, to hear the venerable Johann Adam Reinken play on the organ of St. Catherine's Church.[1] The most detailed primary descriptions of Bach from the eighteenth century—the Obituary of 1754 (written jointly by Carl Philipp Emanuel Bach and Johann Friedrich Agricola) and Carl Philipp Emanuel's letters to the early biographer Johann Nikolaus Forkel—stress the four unmitigated triumphs of Johann Sebastian Bach's life, all conquests that took place in the big city: the vanquishing of French organist Louis Marchand in Dresden in 1714, the bestowal of approval from Johann Adam Reinken in Hamburg in 1720, the brilliant organ concert before the Russian ambassador and "many persons of rank" in Dresden in 1736, and the visit with Frederick the Great in

Berlin in 1747 that ultimately produced *The Musical Offering* (BWV 1079).[2] But they also underline the big-city orientation of Bach's interests during the Leipzig period.

Or, to take another piece of evidence, after listing the composers his father esteemed highly during his last years, Carl Philipp Emanuel Bach added in his report to Forkel that Johann Sebastian followed "everything that was worthy of esteem in Dresden and Berlin."[3] Indeed, the list of composers itself stressed this fact. It began with

> Johann Joseph Fux (Viennese composer and theorist)
>
> Antonio Caldara (Viennese composer)
>
> George Frideric Handel (London composer)

but then continued with

> Reinhard Keiser (Hamburg opera composer)
>
> Johann Adolph Hasse (Dresden opera composer)
>
> Carl Heinrich Graun (Berlin music director and opera composer)
>
> Johann Gottlieb Graun (Berlin concertmaster)
>
> Georg Philipp Telemann (Hamburg city cantor)
>
> Jan Dismas Zelenka (Dresden court music director)
>
> Franz Benda (Berlin court first violinist)

This is a veritable big city *Who's Who in Music*. And Carl Philipp Emanuel pointed out that his father was personally acquainted with all but the first four. Thus Bach's personal connections with big-city musicians were remarkably strong. Although information on Bach's trips to the big city is sketchier than one would wish, it is nevertheless possible to reconstruct in outline, at least, his journeys.

Hamburg

Bach's visits to Hamburg took place at two distinct periods of his life: first, between 1700 and 1703, his school years in Lüneburg, when he made "several trips," and second, during the fall of 1720, when he competed for the organist post of the St. Jacobi Church (see Table 1). Carl Philipp Emanuel's remark that his father saw a good bit of Telemann "in his youthful years" suggests that Bach's 1720 trip to Hamburg may well have been his last, since it was there that Telemann was posted from 1721 to the end of his life in 1767[4] (fig. 8.1). Telemann and Bach seem to have become acquainted between 1709 and 1712, when the former was working in Eisenach (Bach's birthplace and a Bach family center).

Figure 8.1. Georg Philipp Telemann was about four years older than his friend Bach, yet outlived him by seventeen years. Although he visited Paris, Telemann worked primarily in Protestant Germany, notably Hamburg, where from 1721 he was cantor of the Johanneum Latin School and music director for the city's five main churches as well as, from 1722 to 1738, director of the Hamburg Opera. Bach may have been encouraged by Telemann, godfather to Carl Philipp Emanuel, to apply for the cantor position in Leipzig in 1723 after Telemann, the leading and most prolific German composer of his time, had turned it down. Telemann wrote a poem on the death of Bach, hailing him as "the Great" for his organ playing, characterizing his compositions as "the highest art," and noting his continuing legacy through his students. The two also shared membership in Mizler's Corresponding Society of Musical Sciences. Engraving by Daniel Preisler after Ludwig Michael Schneider, 1750.

In 1712 Telemann began his tenure as music director at St. Catherine's Church and the Church of the Barefooted Friars in Frankfurt, where he remained until 1721. It was during the Frankfurt years, in 1714, that he stood as godfather for Carl Philipp Emanuel.[5]

Table 1: Bach's Documented Visits to Hamburg

1700 to 1703	Several visits to hear the organist of St. Catherine's Church, Johann Adam Reinken[6]
1720—between November 11 and 23	Visit to audition for the organist position of St. Jacobi Church[7]

Bach's connection with Hamburg has normally been viewed in terms of organ music: Bach, the aspiring organist, travels to Hamburg in the early 1700s to hear the dean of North German players, Reinken (fig. 8.2). Many years later, in 1720, Bach returns to Hamburg as a mature virtuoso, to exhibit his skills as an organist in connection with the job opening at St. Jacobi's Church. At the request of those present, he improvises, for almost half an hour, on the chorale *An Wasserflüssen Babylon*, as Hamburg organists had done in years past for the Saturday Vespers service. He is consequently praised by Reinken, who remarks, "I thought this art was dead, but I see that in you it still lives."[8] Although Bach withdraws from the competition, which is won, in the words of the Hamburg music theorist and Bach-watcher Johann Mattheson, "by an untalented

journeyman, the son of a well-to-do artisan, who could prelude better with his
thalers than his fingers," the trip represents Bach's apotheosis as the last great
representative of the North German
school of organ playing.[9]

Certainly Reinken's presence and the
large, impressive organs in Hamburg's
principal churches were important
motivations for Bach's visits (fig. 8.3).
Bach clearly admired Reinken's instrument in St. Catherine's Church and later
singled out its reeds and thirty-two-foot
pedal stops for praise to his pupil Johann
Friedrich Agricola.[10] In recent years,
however, other aspects of Hamburg music-making have entered into the picture
of Bach's stays as well. Not only Reinken's
organ music but his chamber works, too,
appear to have played a critical role in
the young Bach's development.[11] Evi-

Figure 8.2. Despite the freely sketched quality of this
pen and ink drawing by J. O. Harms, who worked as
a stage designer for the Hamburg opera from 1695 to
1705 (plate 16), one recognizes the distinctive steeples
of the Hamburg churches Bach saw on his visits there.
In particular, the two lanterns of the steeple of St. Catherine's Church (center right) are clearly rendered, as is
the square tower of the Jacobi Church (second from
right) from which the steeple rises. On the other hand,
the image does not capture the intensive water traffic
on the Elbe River as it flows through this commercial
city in the Hanseatic league, nor does it make very evident the fortifications along the far shore, which were
not tested during the devastating Thirty Years' War because of Hamburg's shrewdly calculated neutrality.

dence of this are three early keyboard works: two multi-movement sonatas and a fugue
(BWV 965, 966, and 954); all are based on trio sonatas from Reinken's *Hortus Musicus*
of 1687. In these works, Bach does not merely reorganize Reinken's chamber music to
fit well on a keyboard, but often reworks and "recomposes" the material. The result is a
series of compositional studies rather than straightforward arrangements of Reinken's
sonatas. Thus they do not belong chronologically with the transcriptions of concertos
by Vivaldi and Duke Johann Ernst in the Weimar years (1708–17) (BWV 591–96 and
972–87), but rather with the Corelli (BWV 579), Legrenzi (BWV 574), and Albinoni
(BWV 946, 950, and 951) fugues of a decade earlier. Hamburg, therefore, may also have
been the source of Bach's initial exposure to chamber music, as presented in the town's
civic concerts, weekly Collegium Musicum programs, and printed editions.

It is not insignificant, either, that Bach's early visits to Hamburg took place during
the golden period of the Oper am Gänsemarkt, or Goose-Market Opera, an establishment cofounded by Reinken (fig. 8.4). The opera productions, heavily influenced first by
French and then by Italian traditions, attracted talented young composers such as Handel
and Mattheson, and it seems unlikely that the equally eager-to-learn Bach would not
have taken advantage of the opportunity to view the nationally known spectacle (fig. 8.5).

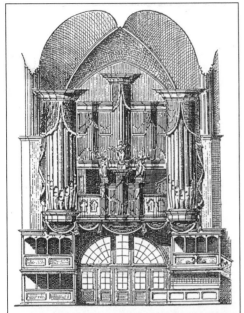

Figure 8.3. In 1990–92, this organ at Hamburg's St. Jacobi Church, one of the few surviving instruments on which Bach himself played, was restored to look much as it had when Bach auditioned for the organist's post on it in 1720. At that time the organ, originally built in the sixteenth century, had just undergone a thorough rebuilding and expansion by the famous Hamburg organ-builder Arp Schnitker, who had also rebuilt Hamburg's largest organ—the four-manual, sixty-seven-stop organ in St. Nicholas's. Schnitker expanded the keyboards to four octaves, reusing old and supplying new stops (a total of sixty), and adding—despite the protest of (a jealous?) J. A. Reinken of St. Catherine's—a thirty-two-foot pedal stop sounding two octaves below the written note. Although all the pipes were melted down in World War I, they have been remade to original specifications, whereas some parts of the present organ, including the wood carvings of Christian Precht, date back to the late seventeenth century.

Figure 8.4. Hamburg, Oper am Gänsemarkt. This unpretentious building of 1677 in fact enveloped a real opera theater, designed by the Italian architect Girolamo Sartorio and equipped with all kinds of modern stage machinery. Existing from 1678 to 1738, the Hamburg Opera was the first permanent German opera company not sponsored by a court. Cofounded by J. A. Reinken and J. Theile, among others, it ran into opposition at the start from Hamburg's clergy and in the end lost out to less elevated and sophisticated types of musical entertainment—but not before mounting 270 new productions, among them Handel's first opera, *Almira* (1705), under Reinhard Keiser's direction. The opera was still thriving, under Telemann, when Bach, who may have experienced it during his Lüneburg period, returned in 1720. Anon. watercolor.

Although that thought is speculation, we can point to one possible concrete link between Bach and the Hamburg opera. Passed down in the so-called Möller Manuscript and the Andreas Bach Book—two important Bach-family manuscripts containing predominantly North German music, the type of repertory that would have been known to the young Johann Sebastian—are transcriptions from three operas: Lully's *Phaeton* of 1683, Marais' *Alcide* of 1693, and Steffani's *La Briseide* of 1696.[12] This suggests a connection with Hamburg, for all these operas were revived in the eighteenth century, and operas by Steffani and Lully, at least, were regular fare in the North German city.[13]

Finally, there is the matter of church music (fig. 8.6). It seems likely that Bach chose to perform his early Cantata 21, *Ich hatte viel Bekümmernis*, as part of his

Figure 8.5. In this stage design by Oswald Harms for a forest with a kind of inverted single vanishing point perspective, one can make out vertical lines that mark the outside edges of each pair of flats; these were set in tracks in the floor so they could be whisked offstage while being simultaneously replaced by another set of flats—enabling the scene to be transformed in an instant. The fact that the pairs of flats were spaced at a distance from each other from the front to the back of the stage meant that an illusion of a third dimension of continuous, rather than stepped, depth could be created, as the example clearly shows. Oswald was considered one of the premiere scene designers and painters of his age, and he worked in many places associated with Bach: Dresden, Weissenfels, and Hamburg (plate 16) among them.

audition in 1720 for the position of organist at St. Jacobi's Church in Hamburg.[14] But why did he choose to present such a relatively old-fashioned composition, one based heavily on psalm-texted choruses that were some fifteen years behind the times? Perhaps because Bach judged the text of *Ich hatte viel Bekümmernis* to be in the North German tradition. If he had been composing in the year 1700, that would have been true. But time had passed him by. The publication of Erdmann Neumeister's *Geistliche Cantaten statt einer Kirchenmusik* ("Spiritual Cantatas Instead of Church Anthems") in 1704 or so marked the arrival of a new era of cantata texts, texts of a very dramatic, personal nature that were full of vivid imagery and contrasts (fig 2.12, p. 126). By 1720, Neumeister's texts were being used and mimicked throughout North Germany. With them, Mattheson and others were advocating a newer, lighter church style derived from opera. Indeed, Cantata 21 drew fire from Mattheson for its antiquated, repetitive treatment of text:

> In order that good old Zachow[15] may have company, and not be quite so alone, let us set beside him an otherwise excellent practicing musician of today, who for a long time does nothing but repeat:
>
> "I, I, I, I had much grief, I had much grief, in my heart, in my heart. I had much grief, etc., in my heart, etc., etc., I had much grief, etc., in my heart, etc., I had much grief, etc., in my heart, etc., etc., etc., etc., etc. I had much grief, etc., in my heart, etc., etc." Then again: "sighs, tears, sorrow, anguish (rest), sighs, tears, anxious

longing, fear and death (rest) gnaw at my oppressed heart, etc." Also: "Come, my
Jesus, and refresh (rest) and rejoice with Thy glance (rest), come, my Jesus (rest),
come, my Jesus, and refresh and rejoice . . . with Thy glance this soul, etc."[16]

Thus Bach may have been out of step with the Hamburg church music scene, which
was looking to more progressive styles.

Berlin

Turning to Berlin (fig. 8.7), we can trace at least four visits by Bach to the Prussian
center: an early visit from Cöthen in 1719 to pick up "das zu Berlin gefertigte Claves-
sin" ("the harpsichord manufactured in Berlin") and three stays during the last decade
of the Leipzig years. It is also likely that
he attended the wedding of his son Carl
Philipp Emanuel in Berlin in 1744 as well
(see Table 2).[17] The trip from Cöthen has
given rise recently to much speculation
over the influence of the new Berlin
harpsichord on Bach's writing. We know
that the instrument was a large, fine,
"big city" harpsichord—to be precise, a
two-manual harpsichord made by Michael Mietke, the well-known builder
to the Berlin court.[18] In the bass range,
at least, the instrument most certainly
went beyond the normal C–c' compass
of the more prosaic Middle German
harpsichords[19] (fig. 8.8). In recent studies, a number of Cöthen works have been
linked with the new instrument: the
revised (and familiar) version of Brandenburg Concerto No. 5, several English
Suites, the early version of the Chromatic Fantasia and Fugue in D Minor (BWV
903a).[20] Whether or not these specific
works are tied to the Berlin instrument,
there is no doubt that Bach's interest in
harpsichord music blossomed between

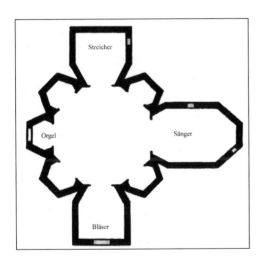

Figure 8.6. Hamburg's St. Gertrude's Chapel, built in
the 1390s and destroyed by the great Hamburg fire
of 1842, was originally built as a court chapel but in
1580 became a subsidiary of St. Jacobi's Church. Its
octagonal shape with three annexes was utilized from
the early seventeenth century for Venetian-style polychoral music, so that the congregation seated in the
middle would hear music coming from as many as four
directions. Not surprisingly, the chapel became widely
known for its large-scale musical performances, in
particular Passion music; in 1644 a new style of Passion was introduced, in which texts of commentary and
reflection supplemented the canonical Gospel text. J.
S. Bach's passions are later examples of this type. To
pay for the sacred concerts—for they were not liturgical services—seat reservations and libretti were sold, a
practice later adopted by the Hamburg Opera.

Figure 8.7. Berlin, since the fifteenth century the capital of the Mark and Electorate of Brandenburg and from 1701 the capital of the Kingdom of Prussia, is documented since the mid-thirteenth century. Situated in the valley of the Spree River, which flows through it (fig. 3.30, p. 167), Berlin acquired, especially in the seventeenth century, an extensive system of canals that still meander through the city. In Bach's time, the city experienced tremendous growth, not a little because of the religious tolerance that existed there; this attracted thousands of Huguenots fleeing Louis XIV's France (the Prussian rulers viewing themselves as protectors of Reformed, i.e., Calvinistic, Protestantism), who brought with them business savvy and an ethic of hard work. Even Catholics were more or less welcome in Protestant Berlin: St. Hedwig's Cathedral, the first Catholic church built in Berlin since the Reformation, rose in 1747, the year of Bach's famous visit to Frederick the Great. Engraved view of about 1760.

1720 and 1723: witness the composition of the Inventions and Sinfonias (BWV 772–86 and 787–801), the first volume of the *Well-Tempered Clavier* (BWV 846–69), and a large series of keyboard suites, to say nothing of Brandenburg Concerto No. 5 (BWV 1050) and the Chromatic Fantasia and Fugue (BWV 903). The Berlin influence, via the new harpsichord, was surely a critical factor in this development.

Table 2: Bach's Documented Visits to Berlin

1719—after March 1	Trip to purchase a new harpsichord for Prince Leopold of Anhalt-Cöthen[21]
1741—from before August 5 to no later than August 25	Extended visit, staying with Georg Ernst Stahl[22]
1744—early in the year	Possible visit, to attend the wedding of C. P. E. Bach and Johanna Maria Dannemann[23]
1745—December 10	Visit to attend the baptism of grandson Johann August Bach[24]
1747—May 7 to 8	Visit to the court of Frederick the Great at the City Palace in Potsdam and organ recital at the Church of the Holy Spirit[25]

Figure 8.8. German harpsichord making in the baroque period was concentrated in the central and northern regions, where Bach lived. One center was Berlin, where Michael Mietke became harpsichord maker to the court in 1707, although he lost his position, along with all the musicians, when Friedrich Wilhelm became King of Prussia in 1713 and dissolved the musical establishment. Since some of those musicians were hired by Prince Leopold, Bach may have learned of Mietke's work from them and thus come to order a harpsichord for Cöthen that he picked up in Berlin in 1719. Only a few Mietke instruments survive (such as this one in Berlin), but they, like other German harpsichords, have an "S"-shaped bent-side (unlike French harpsichords). German makers, no doubt influenced by organs, also sometimes, if rarely, made harpsichords with three manuals and a sixteen-foot register that sounded an octave below the note played. German harpsichords had a crisp attack that served polyphony well, while lacking the luxuriously resonant sound of French instruments.

In 1740, Bach's son Carl Philipp Emanuel was formally appointed harpsichordist to the court of Frederick the Great. From then until his death in 1750, Sebastian visited Berlin several times. Of the trips, the visit with Frederick the Great is the best known, thanks to newspaper reports and the authoritative account in the 1754 Obituary (fig. 8.9):

> In the year 1747 [Bach] made a journey to Berlin and on this occasion had the opportunity of being heard at Potsdam by His Majesty the King in Prussia. His Majesty himself played him a theme for a fugue which he at once developed, to the particular pleasure of the Monarch, on the pianoforte. Hereupon His Majesty demanded to hear a fugue with six obbligato voices, which command he also fulfilled, to the astonishment of the King and the musicians there present, using a theme of his own. After his return to Leipzig, he set down on paper a three-voiced and a six-voiced so-called *ricercar* together with several other intricate little pieces, all on the very theme that had been given him by His Majesty, and this he dedicated, engraved on copper, to the King.[26]

But more interesting with regard to the lure of the big city is the correspondence between Bach and his cousin Johann Elias Bach over the stay of August 1741. Sometime before August 5, Bach traveled to Berlin, staying with the physician Georg Ernst Stahl, privy councilor at the court and a family friend. Stahl lived in a house on Unter den Linden, the main thoroughfare in the center of Berlin, and he may have had a hand in arranging Bach's visit[27] (fig. 8.10). During Bach's absence, Johann Elias, who served for a time as the Bach family amanuensis, wrote from Leipzig to say that Anna Magdalena had been ailing for a week, and perhaps it would be best if Bach returned home. In his letter, Elias then continued:

> [to this predicament should be] added the fact that St. Bartholomew's Day and the Council Election here will occur in a few weeks, and we should not know how we should conduct ourselves with respect to the same in Your Honor's absence. It is indeed painful to us to have to disturb Your Honor somewhat by such news in your present peace and contentment, but since unavoidable necessity required it, we have good confidence that our most worthy Papa and Cousin respectively will not take the same amiss.[28]

Anna Magdalena recovered, and Bach returned to Leipzig in time to compose *Wünschet Jerusalem Glück* (BWV Anh. 4) for the change of Town Council.[29] But the message of Elias's letter is clear: Bach was eager to remain in Berlin, the big city, and was even willing, it seems, to neglect his obligations as cantor of St. Thomas's and town music director of Leipzig to prolong his stay. This recalls an earlier incident—Bach's chastisement by the Arnstadt Church Council in 1706, when he extended his sojourn in

Figure 8.9. When Bach came to Potsdam to visit Frederick the Great in 1747, the pleasure palace of Sanssouci ("Without care") (fig. 3.31, p. 168) had just been inaugurated. However, it was not there that Bach performed on the Silbermann fortepianos, improvising on the theme that Frederick gave him. Rather, Bach, accompanied by his eldest son Wilhelm Friedemann, attended Frederick at the City Palace (Stadtpalais), which was destroyed in World War II.

Figure 8.10. In addition to his institutional patrons, both individual and collective, Bach also profited from the patronage of aristocrats and middle-class personages, especially in Leipzig, Dresden, and Berlin. One such person was the Prussian royal counselor and physician Georg Ernst Stahl, who developed a close relationship with Bach's sons Wilhelm Friedemann and Carl Phillip Emanuel, but also was acquainted with their father. Stahl's music library reflected his deep interest in music of Bach and his sons; it included Bach's six partitas, the *Musical Offering*, and the inventions. In addition, there was a version of Cantata 210, likely performed for Stahl's wedding in 1741, which Bach probably would have attended but for concerns over his wife's health.

Lübeck beyond the agreed time. In both cases, Bach's state of "peace and contentment" centered on the big city.

For the remaining Berlin visits Frederick the Great's newly established opera company comes into question (fig. 8.11). Set up in 1742, the troupe gave performances twice a week in Knobelsdorff's new theater (fig. 3.32a–b, p. 169). Forkel connected Bach's favorable assessment of the hall (Bach judged the acoustics to be most satisfactory) with the visit of 1747.[30] But Forkel's apparent source of the anecdote, Carl Philipp Emanuel's letter of 1774, does not specify which year the test took place, so the incident could have occurred during the trips of 1744 (if Bach was indeed in Berlin at the time) or 1745. The visit of December 10, 1745, in particular, occurred during the heart of the opera season, which ran from November to March.

Even if Bach missed the performances themselves, he surely would not have failed to discuss the latest developments in opera with his friend Carl Heinrich Graun, Frederick's resident opera composer. Bach's 1745 visit, for instance, took place less than four weeks before the first performance of Graun's *Adriano in Siria*, which premiered on January 7, 1746. Can we doubt that Bach observed the preparations? Graun's contribution to the court was chiefly in the realm of opera seria. But in 1747 an entire Italian troupe was summoned to perform opera buffa, so that lighter works, including Pergolesi's comic intermezzo[31] *La Serva Padrona* (1748), also formed part of the operatic fare at Frederick's court. Berlin, then, stood not only as a center of *galant* chamber music—to which Bach paid homage in the trio of *The Musical Offering*—but also as a hub of progressive opera, whose light, airy style Bach emulated in his own

Figure 8.11. In addition to being a passionate amateur flutist, Frederick the Great was a talented composer and connoisseur of music who knew what he liked. One thing he did not like was *improvised* embellishments, so common in Italian practice, so he ordered his performers not to deviate from the written notes. However, he did not eschew written-out embellishments for an existing composition, especially when he himself composed them, as the illustrations demonstrate. On the left is a Berlin copy of an unornamented aria from J. A. Hasse's *Cleofide*—an opera likely seen by Bach in its Dresden premiere in 1731; on the right is Frederick's own embellished version of the same (beginning in the fourth system). The elaborate ornamentation was for one of his star singers, the castrato Porporino (1717–83), who had performed in the opening performance in the new opera house (fig. 3.32, p. 169) in 1742.

late vocal works. During the Potsdam visit of 1747 Bach also may have presented the Flute Sonata in E Major, BWV 1035, to Frederick's flute-playing chamberlain, Michael Gabriel Fredersdorf.[32] The *galant* style of the work may reflect Bach's interest in composing in a fashionable way for the transverse flute, a favored instrument at the Berlin court.

Frederick's musical priorities are underscored in the salaries he awarded to his players. During the 1744–45 season, Graun, as an opera composer, received two thousand thalers; Carl Philipp Emanuel Bach, as court harpsichordist, earned three hundred.[33] Johann Sebastian's salary in Leipzig was seven hundred thalers. Bach was quick to quibble over money: one needs only think of his remark to Georg Erdmann that the fresh air in Leipzig deprived him of funeral fees.[34] The disparity between his income and Graun's must have been irksome (and one can add that in Dresden the salary gap was even greater: there, Court Music Director Johann Adolf Hasse was paid six thousand thalers his first year—more than eight times Bach's salary in Leipzig!).[35]

Dresden

From the surviving documents we can trace seven trips to Dresden (fig. 8.12): one from Weimar in 1717, and six from Leipzig between 1725 and 1741 (see Table 3). With a host of composers of international stature such as Jan Dismas Zelenka, Giovanni

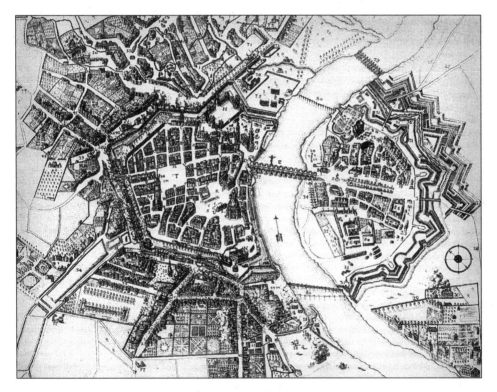

Figure 8.12. Dresden, its architectural transformation under the Polish Saxon kings more or less completed, had a population of about thirty-five thousand when this plan of ca. 1758 was made. About a day's journey from Leipzig, Dresden began as two distinct settlements, first a Slavic one on the north (here, right) bank of the Elbe River, then, by 1216, a German town across the river. Paradoxically, the former is known as the *Neustadt* (New City), whereas the latter, which became and still is the main part of Dresden, is called the *Altstadt* (Old City). A visitor entering the Old City from the Augustus Bridge (E) would see on the right the new Catholic court church (G); to the left of the church is the electoral palace (F), above which is clearly seen the Zwinger (H), with its large, enclosed parade ground. The Church of Our Lady is to the left of the bridge and near the river, about midway between the bridge and the fortifications below.

Figure 8.13. (*Left*) The German-born Johann Adolf Hasse spent most of his early career in Italy, becoming (with Handel) the most important composer of Italian opera of his time. From 1731 to 1763 he lived mostly in Dresden as court music director and also director of the court opera. Bach likely came to Dresden to hear Hasse's *Cleofide*, starring his diva wife Faustina Bordoni, in 1731 (Bach played a recital in the Sophienkirche the next day, allegedly with Hasse and Faustina present). Although there is no absolute proof of Bach being personally acquainted with the Hasses, it is hard to believe that they were not: the couple visited Leipzig on several occasions and admired Bach's artistry, according to Bach's first biographer Forkel, who got much of his information from Bach's sons and students. A few pieces by Hasse are also in the second Clavierbüchlein for Anna Magdalena Bach.

Figure 8.14. (*Right*) The Polish-born Sylvius Weiss, the leading lutenist of his time, travelled to Rome in the entourage of Prince Alexander of Poland before he first performed in Dresden (1717), after which he was hired as a member of the royal-electoral Saxon orchestra, where he remained until his death in 1750; in 1744 he was the highest-paid musician at the court. One of the greatest of all lutenists, his skill as musician was compared with that of Bach, whom he knew well: for example, in 1739 he spent a month in Leipzig, often visiting the Bachs. Bach's trio for violin and harpsichord in A (BWV 1025) is an arrangement of a lute suite by Weiss; it is also possible that Bach's lute music was either commissioned by or written for Weiss. In all, Weiss composed nearly six hundred works, the largest body of lute music by any composer.

Alberto Ristori, Antonio Lotti, Johann David Heinichen, Johann Georg Schürer, and Hasse (fig. 8.13); a battery of singers trained in the latest operatic style, such as soprano Faustina Bordoni and castrato Giovanni Bindi; and an orchestra of virtuosi including the flautist Pierre Gabriel Buffardin and lutenist Sylvius Weiss (fig. 8.14), Dresden possessed a professional glitter quite unmatched in Leipzig. As it is well known, in his 1730 complaint to the Leipzig town council about performance conditions at the Thomasschule, the "Short but Necessary Draft for a Well-Appointed Church Music," Bach cited the Dresden orchestra as a model musical establishment, one in which the musicians, "paid by his Royal Majesty . . . are relieved of all concern for their living, free from chagrin, and obliged each to master but a single instrument."[36] Here was Bach's ideal, as far as an orchestra was concerned. Others, as far away as France, shared his high estimation. Jean-Jacques Rousseau, for instance, printed Hasse's seating arrangement of the Dresden orchestra in his *Dictionnaire de musique* of 1768, holding it up as an exemplary model for France as well as other countries (figs. 8.15, 8.16).

Table 3: Bach's Documented Trips to Dresden

1717—fall	Visit, at the invitation of concertmaster Jean-Baptiste Volumier, to compete with French organist Louis Marchand at the electoral court[37] (fig. 8.17)
1725—September 19 to 20	Two organ recitals at St. Sophia's Church[38]
1731—September 14 to 21	Organ recital at St. Sophia's Church and a concert at the Dresden Court; probably attends the premiere of Johann Adolf Hasse's opera *Cleofide*[39]
1733—July 27	In Dresden for several days; submission of the *Missa* of the B Minor Mass to Friedrich August II[40]
1736—December 1	Organ recital at the Church of Our Lady[41]
1738—before May 22	In Dresden for several days[42]
1741—before November	Extended trip to Dresden; visit with Count Keyserlingk[43]

Fortunately, we have one example of Bach's writing for the Dresden court: the *Missa* (that is, the Kyrie and Gloria, BWV 232[1]) of the B Minor Mass. The autograph parts, which survive in the Saxon State Library,[44] point unambiguously to a Dresden performance. The Dresden watermark of the paper, the hurried but calligraphic copying by Bach family members, the unusually large format and oversized rastral, and the abundance of performance indications added unevenly to individual movements all suggest that Bach prepared the parts with an imminent performance in mind.[45] Bach's systematic use of the solo singers and solo players—the musicians "obligated to master but a single instrument"—in the arias of the *Missa* demonstrates his desire to take full opportunity of the rich resources of the Dresden Court *capella* and to exhibit the individual performers to best advantage. In the arias of the Gloria, for instance, Bach exploits each solo voice and each section of the instrumental band:

Movement	*Setting*
"Gloria in excelsis"	Chorus
"Laudamus te"	Soprano 2, Violin solo

"Gratias agimus tibi"	Chorus
"Domine Deus"	Soprano 1 and Tenor, Flauto traverso solo
"Qui tollis"	Chorus
"Qui sedes"	Alto, Oboe d'amore solo
"Quoniam tu solus"	Bass, Corno da caccia, Bassoon 1 and 2 solos
"Cum Sancto Spiritu"	Chorus

In no other *Missa* setting does Bach work through the solo voices and solo instruments so methodically. The B Minor *Missa* of 1733 is a type of display piece, for a virtuoso ensemble. And the Lombardic rhythm in the "Domine Deus," notated in the

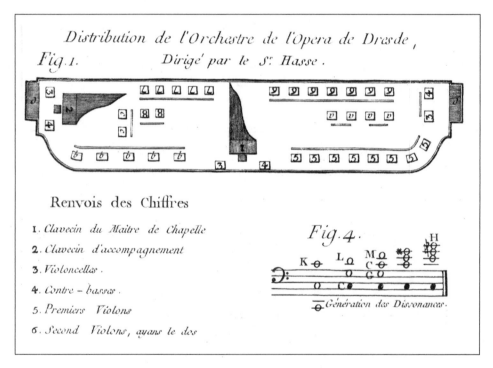

Figure 8.15. The fame of the Dresden orchestra was such that Jean-Jacques Rousseau, in his *Dictionary of Music* (Paris, 1768), printed a plan of its seating arrangement ca.1745. (Orchestral seating did not become standardized until the late-nineteenth century.) Indicated are 1. the music director, leading from the first harpsichord, which would have accompanied recitatives; 2. the second harpsichord, which played with the full orchestra; 3. cellos and 4. double basses, important for rhythmic coherence and hence distributed in three pairs around the orchestra pit; 5. first violins (with backs to the audience) and 6. second violins (facing first violins), distributed to the right of the conductor along with a. four violas. The winds and horns are on the left, including 7. "oboes," although "flutes and oboes" is undoubtedly meant, and b. bassoons (facing the oboes). Filling in the middle range are c. horns and 8. two more violas. Finally, d. trumpets and drums are at the far left and right. This orchestra of more than forty players who specialized in single instruments was cited by Bach as an ideal.

Figure 8.16. A detail from figure 3.28b (p. 165) shows that the seating plan of the Saxon royal court orchestra illustrated in figure 8.15 had already been established before 1730. Despite the uncertainly of the date of the scene depicted (between 1719 and 1729), it is possible to determine some of those depicted: on the right first flutist Pierre-Gabriel Buffardin (possibly assisted by Johann Joachim Quantz, of the Royal-Polish Capella, who had just switched from oboe to flute) and first lute Sylvius Weiss (fig. 8.14). Leading the strings until 1728 was concertmaster Jean-Baptiste Volumier; who was immediately succeeded by the Vivaldi student Johann Georg Pisendel.

Dresden parts but not in Bach's score, shows his concern for capturing the essence of the French performing style then in vogue at the Dresden court.[46]

There seems to be little doubt that Bach attended the premiere of Hasse's *Cleofide* on September 13, 1731, in Pöppelmann's opera house in the Zwinger complex in Dresden. Bach presented an organ recital at St. Sophia's Church the next day, and he most certainly took advantage of the opportunity to hear the first performance of Hasse's work, an event widely publicized at the time. There can no longer be any question that the virtuoso Italian operatic style and the polished French instrumental playing of the Dresden court musicians had a tangible effect on the works Bach wrote back in Leipzig for the Collegium Musicum, works such as the Orchestral Overture in B Minor (BWV 1067), the B Minor Flute Sonata (BWV 1030), the G Minor Gamba Sonata (BWV 1029), and many of the late secular cantatas.[47]

But this brings us back to Leipzig and Bach's life there. By way of conclusion, let us consider two provocative points in light of our brief survey of Bach's visits to the big city.

Figure 8.17. Louis Marchand was a renowned French organist and harpsichordist who, according to Bach himself (there is no other independent account of it), was invited by the Dresden concertmaster J. B. Volumier to a musical "duel" with Bach. In the end, however, Bach won by default, Marchand having left the city without announcing his departure, presumably to avoid embarrassment at the hands of the German master. Nonetheless, Bach is known to have admired Marchand and knew his harpsichord music, which, according to a contemporary account, Bach played "in his own manner, i.e., very lightly and with much art."

Opera and the "Big City Ditties"

In his seminal Bach biography of 1802, based on materials provided by Wilhelm Friedemann and Carl Philipp Emanuel Bach, Forkel reported that Johann Sebastian "was always received in an exceedingly honorable manner in Dresden, and often went there to hear the opera. He generally took his eldest son with him. He used to say, in joke, some days before his departure: "Friedemann, shan't we go again to hear the lovely Dresden ditties?"[48]

In the past, this has been viewed as no more than friendly banter, a symbol of Bach's muted disdain for the *galant* airs of the big city. In recent times, however, the remark has been taken more seriously. These "ditties" have been shown to have influenced works such as the "Peasant Cantata" (*Mer hahn en neue Oberkeet*, BWV 212), the "Coffee Cantata" (*Schweigt stille, plaudert nicht*, BWV 211), and *The Contest Between Phoebus and Pan* (*Geschwinde, ihr wirbelnden Winde*, BWV 201).[49] One of the more famous controversies in Bach's lifetime is the dispute over his seemingly old-fashioned style, which critic Johann Adolph Scheibe decried in 1737 as "turgid and confused" and having "an excess of art" (i.e., complexity).[50] Even before then, however, Bach seems to have made an effort to adjust his style–in secular works at least–to the latest *galant* trends. The adjustment coincides with the beginning of his regular journeys to the big city.

Moreover, in the past twenty-five years it has been discovered that, in a number of instances, Bach literally took the Dresden ditties home: the famous G major-G minor pair of menuets in Anna Magdalena's Notebook of 1725 (BWV Anh. 114–15) (fig. 9.9, p. 283), studied and loved by generations of young pianists, is now known to be the work of Carl Friedrich Petzold, Dresden court organist.[51] And the Polonaise in G Major (BWV Anh. 130), from the same volume, can now be assigned to Hasse.[52] When added to the "Pièce pour le Clavecin" (piece for harpsichord) by J. C. Richter—either Dresden court organist Johann Christoph Richter or, less likely, the Dresden court oboist Johann Christian Richter—found in the Clavier Book for Wilhelm Friedemann Bach of 1720 (fig. 0.7, p. 9), the big city connection becomes all the more tangible. One should note that the Richter piece was added to Friedemann's album in 1725 or later—that is, after Bach commenced his periodic Dresden trips.[53] One can also wonder how many more of the remaining anonymous pieces in Anna Magdalena's Notebook of 1725 may turn out to be urban tunes.

Bach in the Final Two Decades of His Life

Although it might seem audacious to accuse Bach of having ego problems during the final two decades of his life, there *are* indications of a certain defensiveness. For example, even though he sought another position after losing the showdown with the Leipzig town council in 1730, he did not succeed in finding another job. Moreover, he did not submit a résumé to Mattheson for a biographical entry in the 1740 *Grundlage einer Ehren-Porte*, the "Foundation of an honor gate" of Germany's most illustrious musicians.

With regard to the job search, one cannot question that Bach attempted to land a big city position. The Hamburg audition of 1720 was highly successful—only the required bribe to the church treasury was lacking. In 1733 Bach wasted no time submitting the B Minor *Missa* to Friedrich August II: the *Landestrauer*, or period of mourning, for Friedrich August I, during which no elaborate music could be performed, was lifted on July 2, 1733. Just three weeks later Bach was in Dresden, presenting the parts of the *Missa* and presumably performing the piece as well as part of his application for a court composer position. And the composition of *The Musical Offering* and its presentation to Frederick the Great may be viewed as another fishing expedition by Bach, hoping to land a lucrative job in Berlin.

But what of the well-known letter of 1730 to his school companion Georg Erdmann? Here Bach voices to his old chum his dissatisfaction with Leipzig and his desire to find a new position. However, why write to Erdmann in Danzig? Erdmann, as the Imperial Russian Resident Agent in Danzig, does not seem to have been a man with great pull. And Danzig would have been a step down, even from the conservative Lutheran center of Leipzig. One wonders if Bach feared not being able to land a position in a more progressive center, a fear that may have been borne out in part when he had to wait three years for action on his application in Dresden, only to receive the title of court composer without compensation. Even here he had to reapply for reconsideration in 1736. Bach, it seems, was well connected to big city musicians, but not with big city aristocrats.

That the work written for the initial Dresden application—the *Missa* of what would become the B Minor Mass—is a masterpiece goes without saying. The "Gloria in excelsis" chorus, for instance, is an ingenious amalgamation of dance, concerto, and imitative counterpoint. The instruments, then the voices, enter in well-defined sections of imitation. The words "Gloria in excelsis Deo"—"Glory be to God on high"—are set in the idiom of a sprightly, triple-beat dance. Or consider the extraordinary musical imagery of the aria "Quoniam tu solus sanctus." Bach paints the text "And Thou alone art most high" by writing an aria in which Christ—represented iconographically by the horn, the traditional sign of nobility—is indeed the only high voice. All other participants—the narrator (a bass) and his instrumental accompanists (two bassoons and continuo)—are below Christ, musically. This is a wonderfully ingenious conceit, a musical exegesis of the highest order. But in the process of creating a theologically meaningful work, Bach sacrifices clarity of texture. To emphasize the "lowness" of the non-Christ figures, Bach employs four independent bass parts, whose lines often cross one another. The "Gloria in excelsis" and the "Quoniam tu solus sanctus" are each compositional *tours de force*. Yet one wonders what sort of impression they made on Elector Friedrich August II.

Bach may have overshot the mark. If we compare his music with that of a resident Dresden court composer such as Zelenka, we find that Bach's writing is too multilayered, too contrapuntally unified, and too serious for Dresden audiences. In Zelenka's *Magnificat* in D Major (Z.108), for instance, written in Dresden in 1725, the choruses and arias are more *galant*. The textures are more transparent, the phrase structures are more symmetrical, the harmonic and dynamic contrasts are more exaggerated. Zelenka's music points ahead to Mozart, and it may have been this highly palatable style that appealed to the elector and his court.[54] Bach's *Missa* appears to have been performed once, and then sent to the archives of the court library rather than retained in the chapel collection of active repertory, where more practical works such as Zelenka's *Magnificat* were kept on hand, ready for use.[55] And finally, on the matter of Bach's autobiography: As early as 1717, in *Das beschützte Orchestre*, Mattheson asked Bach to clarify a point of genealogy. Later, in the *Exemplarische Organisten-Probe* of 1719 and the *Grosse General-Bass-Schule* of 1731, Mattheson appealed to Bach for a full résumé, to be used in the forthcoming *Grundlage einer Ehren-Pforte*, which contained biographical sketches of the most prominent musicians of the day. When the *Ehren-Pforte* finally appeared in 1740, it did not contain an entry for Bach, despite his fame as an organist, his numerous publications, and his position as Leipzig Thomaskantor, one of the most important musical posts in Germany.

Several factors may explain Bach's failure to respond to Mattheson.

First, Mattheson was an imposing literary figure. He was secretary to the British Ambassador in Hamburg and wrote in German, English, and French. He was author of eighteen books. Bach, by contrast, was a reluctant correspondent. If the poems "Erbauliche Gedanken eines Tobackrauchers" (Edifying thoughts of a tobacco smoker) or "Durchlauchtigst zarter Prinz den zwar die Windeln decken" (Serene and gracious Prince, though cradle coverings deck thee) are any indication of Bach's literary tastes, it is understandable that he might have felt intimidated by Mattheson's polished style.[56] Mattheson had the urbanity of a big-city sophisticate; Bach had the limitations of a provincial Thuringian church organist. When Mattheson needed intellectual sustenance, he read Voltaire and Lessing; when Bach turned to literature, he opened his Calov Bible.[57]

Second, there is the matter of Bach's modest education. Handel, Telemann, Heinichen, and many other big city composers had university training. Bach's formal education went no further than St. Michael's Choir School in Lüneburg. This deficiency would have become painfully evident in a published biography. For these reasons, perhaps, Bach appears to have declined Mattheson's request for a vita, thus depriving posterity of a reliable autobiographical sketch.

Finally, there is the area of public debate. When Bach was criticized by Johann Adolph Scheibe for composing in an old-fashioned manner, he overreacted by means of a long polemic written on his behalf by the Leipzig professor of rhetoric Johann Abraham Birnbaum. In fact, Scheibe's criticisms were neither unreasonable nor unfounded.[58] Bach's responses—there was rebuttal and surrebuttal of increasing length— seem defensive and out of proportion to the issue at hand.[59]

And in the very last year of his life, Bach took up the attack against Johann Gottlieb Biedermann, a minister in Freiburg who advocated Latin studies over musical training in the school curriculum. Bach claimed that the "rector" had a "*Dreckohr.*" The term *Dreckohr*, or filthy ear, was so scandalous that Mattheson, who reported the incident in 1751 in *Sieben Gespräche der Weisheit und Musik*, explained it to his readers in French as "a base and disgusting expression, unworthy of a Capellmeister [music director], a poor allusion to the word 'rector.'"[60] Slander aside, we must consider the topic. While Mattheson in Hamburg and Marpurg in Berlin were discussing the weighty issues of German national style and Enlightenment aesthetics, Bach was squabbling with a church minister over local choir-school training.

Bach's frustrations over being "marooned" in Leipzig may well account for his gradual withdrawal from public duties and his increasing interest in private projects during the last decade of his life. Fulfillment and acceptance in the big city were left to his sons and students: to Carl Philipp Emanuel Bach in Berlin and Hamburg; to Johann

Friedrich Agricola and Johann Philipp Kirnberger in Berlin; to Wilhelm Friedemann Bach, for a time, and Gottfried August Homilius and Christoph Transchel for a longer period, in Dresden; and to Johann Christian Bach in London.

For Johann Sebastian Bach, the big city remained a strong stylistic stimulus. But at the same time, it stood as a haunting reminder of unattained luster. Bach did not make it into the urban "network," so to speak, until the nineteenth century. By that time, his mortal remains had long since turned to dust. But the championing of his works by Carl Friedrich Zelter, Johann Nepomuk Schelble, Gaspare Spontini, Felix Mendelssohn, Johannes Brahms, and other urban sophisticates insured that Bach would enjoy a long, happy *after*life in the big city.

Notes

1. Johann Nicolaus Forkel, *Über Johann Sebastian Bachs Leben, Kunst und Kunstwerke* (Leipzig, 1803; repr. Berlin: Henschelverlag, 1982), 22.
2. See, respectively, *NBR*, 301–3 (*BD* 3, no. 666, pp. 82–5); *NBR*, 396f. (*BD* 3, no. 801, p. 285); and *NBR*, 399 (*BD* 3, no. 803, p. 289).
3. *NBR*, 398–400 (*BD* 3, no. 803, pp. 288–90).
4. *Ibid.*
5. *BD* 2, no. 67, p. 54 and *NBR*, 400 (*BD* 3, no. 803, p. 289).
6. *NBR*, 300 (*BD* 3, no. 666, p. 82).
7. *NBR*, 89–91 (*BD* 2, no. 102, pp. 77–79).
8. This was reported in the 1754 Obituary. See *NBR*, 302 (*BD* 3, no. 666, p. 84).
9. Johann Mattheson, *Der musicalische Patriot* (Hamburg, 1728), 316; *NBR*, 91.
10. As can be seen from Agricola's comments in Jacob Adlung's *Musica Mechanica Organoedi* of 1768. See *NBR*, 364 (*BD* 3, no. 739, p. 191).
11. Christoph Wolff, "Johann Adam Reinken und Johann Sebastian Bach: Zum Kontext des Bachschen Frühwerkes," *BJ* 71 (1985): 99–118; rev. English version, "Bach and Johann Adam Reinken: A Context for the Early Works," in Wolff, *Bach: Essays on his Life and Music* (Cambridge, MA: Harvard University Press, 1991), 56–71.
12. Berlin, Staatsbibliothek zu Berlin–Preussischer Kulturbesitz, *Mus.ms. 40644* and Leipzig, Leipziger Städtische Bibliotheken, *Musikbibliothek, III.8.4*, respectively. *La Briseide* has also been credited to Pietro Torri.
13. Helmuth Christian Wolff, *Die Barockoper in Hamburg* (1678–1738) (Wolfenbüttel: Möseler, 1957), passim.
14. Paul Brainard, "Cantata 21 Revisited," in *Studies in Renaissance and Baroque Music in Honor of Arthur Mendel*, Robert L. Marshall, ed. (Kassel: Bärenreiter and Hackensack, NJ: Boonin, 1974), 237, and *NBA* I/16, Kritische Bericht, 137.
15. Friedrich Wilhelm Zachow, organist of Our Lady's Church in Halle and Handel's early teacher.
16. Johann Mattheson, *Critica musica* (Hamburg, 1725), 368. Translation from *NBR*, 325 (*BD* 2, no. 200, p. 153).
17. *NBR*, 87 (*BD* 2, no. 95, p. 73).

18. See Sheridan Germann, "The Mietkes, the Margrave and Bach," in *Bach, Handel, Scarlatti: Tercentenary Essays*, Peter Williams, ed. (Cambridge: Cambridge University Press, 1985), 119–48; and George B. Stauffer, "J. S. Bach's Harpsichords," in *Festa Musicologica: Essays in Honor of George J. Buelow*, Thomas J. Mathiesen and Benito V. Rivera, eds. (Stuyvesant, NY: Pendragon Press, 1995), 289–318.

19. Alfred Dürr, "Tastenumfang und Chronologie in Bachs Klavierwerken," in *Festschrift Georg von Dadelsen zum 60. Geburtstag*, Thomas Kohlhase and Volker Scherliess, eds. (Stuttgart: Hänssler, 1978), 73–88.

20. Alfred Dürr, "Zur Entstehungsgeschichte des 5. Brandenburgischen Konzerts" and "Tastenumfang und Chronologie," *BJ* 61 (1975): 63–69 and 73–88, respectively; and George B. Stauffer, "J. S. Bach as Revisor of His Own Keyboard Works," *Early Music* 13 (1985): 85–98.

21. *NBR*, 87 (*BD* 2, no. 95, pp. 93f.).

22. *NBR* 212f. (*BD* 2, nos. 489f., 490, pp. 391f; Michael Maul, "'Dein Ruhm wird wie ein Demantstein, ja wie ein fest Stahl beständig sein.' Neues über die Beziehungen zwischen den Familien Stahl und Bach," *BJ* 87 (2001), 10.).

23. *BD* 1, no. 49, pp. 118f. (commentary).

24. *BD* 2, no. 540, p. 422.

25. *NBR*, 224 (*BD* 2, no. 554, pp. 434f.).

26. *NBR*, 302f. (*BD* 3, no. 666, p. 85). The encounter between Bach and Frederick the Great is the topic of James R. Gaines's book *Evening in the Palace of Reason* (New York: HarperCollins, 2005).

27. Maul, Michael, *op. cit.*, 7–22.

28. *NBR*, 212f (*BD* 2, no. 489, p. 391).

29. Only the text for the work survives.

30. Forkel, *Über Johann Sebastian Bachs Leben*, 45.

31. Comic intermezzi were short, humorous operas, first performed during the intermissions of the more weighty opera seria. *La Serva Padrona*, with just two singing roles, soprano and bass, and light chamber scoring, set the stage for the rise of comic opera in the eighteenth century.

32. An early manuscript copy of the sonata bears the inscription "after the composer's autograph, which was written anno 17, when he was at Potsdam, for privy chamberlain Fredersdorff." See *BD* 3, p. 623 (Anh. I, no.3).

33. Eugene Helm, "Carl Philipp Emanuel Bach," in *The New Grove Bach Family*, Christoph Wolff, ed. (New York: W. W. Norton, 1983), 257.

34. Letter of October 28, 1730 to Erdmann, then Imperial Russian agent in Danzig, *NBR*, 152 (*BD* 1, no. 23, pp. 67f.).

35. Wolfgang Horn, *Die Dresdener Hofkirchenmusik 1720–1745* (Kassel: Bärenreiter, 1987), 60.

36. *NBR*, 145–151 (*BD* 1, no. 22, pp. 60–64).

37. *NBR* 79f., 301f., 408, 427f. (*BD* 1, no. 6, pp. 26f. and *BD* 2, no. 441, p. 348).

38. *NBR*, 117f. (*BD* 2, no. 193, p. 150).

39. *NBR*, 311 (*BD* 2, no. 294a, p. 214).

40. *NBR*, 158 (*BD* 1, no. 27, pp. 74f.).

41. *NBR* 188 (*BD* 2, no. 389, pp. 279f.).

42. *NBR*, 200f. (*BD* 1, no. 42, 107.).

43. *BD* 2, no. 498, p. 397.

44. Under the call number Mus. 2405-D-21.

45. For a more extended discussion of these points see George B. Stauffer, *Bach: The Mass in B Minor* (New Haven: Yale University Press, 2003), 32–38.

46. One should note that when Bach later returned to the "Domine Deus" music for the *Gloria in excelsis Deo* (BWV 191), a Latin work that was most probably performed in Leipzig in 1745, he dropped the use of Lombardic rhythm.

47. See George B. Stauffer, "Music for 'Cavaliers et Dames': Bach and the Repertoire of his Collegium Musicum," in *About Bach*, Gregory G. Butler, George B. Stauffer, and Mary Dalton Greer, eds. (Urbana, IL: University of Illinois Press, 2008), 135–156.

48. Forkel, *Über Johann Sebastian Bachs Leben*, 86. Translation from *NBR*, 461. Bach's phrase for "Dresden ditties" was "Dresdener Liederchen."

49. Marshall, "Bach the Progressive"; Alfred Dürr, *Die Kantaten von Johann Sebastian Bach* (2nd ed., Kassel: Bärenreiter, 1985), 959–66 and 984–98; and Hans-Joachim Schulze, "Melodiezitate und Mehrtextigkeit in der Bauernkantate und in den Goldbergvariationen," in *BJ* 62 (1976): 8–72.

50. The controversy is described and the pertinent texts are translated in *NBR*, 337–53 (*BD* 2, no. 400, pp. 286f.; no. 409, pp. 296–305; no. 413, p. 309; no. 420, p. 322; no. 436, p. 336; no. 442, pp. 360–62; no. 552, pp. 432f.).

51. Hans-Joachim Schulze, "Ein 'Dresdner Menuett' im zweiten Klavierbüchlein der Anna Magdalena Bach," *BJ* 65 (1979): 45–64.

52. Karl-Heinz Viertel, "Zur Herkunft der Polonaise BWV Anhang 130," in *Muzikoloski Zbornik* 13 (1977): 36–43.

53. Wolfgang Plath, *NBA* V/5, *KB*, 62, 93f.

54. It is also clear that in certain sections of the Credo of the B Minor Mass, written in the last two years of his life, Bach made an effort to write Latin church music with a *galant* slant. This is especially apparent in the "Et incarnatus est," which was inserted into the Credo after the other movements were completed. See Christoph Wolff, "'Et incarnatus' and 'Crucifixus': the Earliest and Latest Settings of Bach's B Minor Mass," in *Eighteenth Century Music in Theory and Practice: Essays in Honor of Alfred Mann*, Mary Ann Parker, ed. (Stuyvesant, NY: Pendragon Press, 1994), 12f., and Stauffer, *Bach: The Mass in B Minor*, 116–20.

55. Janice B. Stockigt, "Consideration of Bach's *Kyrie e Gloria* BWV 232¹ within the Context of Dresden Catholic Mass Settings, 1727–33," in *International Symposium: Understanding Bach's B Minor Mass*, Discussion Book (Belfast: Queens University, 2007) 1: 56–58.

56. "Erbauliche Gedanken" appears in Anna Magdalena's Notebook of 1725; it is reproduced in *NBA* V/4, 98, and *The Bach Reader* (2nd ed., New York: W. W. Norton, 1966), 97f. "Durchlauchtigst zarter Prinz," for the newborn Emanuel Ludwig, appears in the dedication copy of Partita I from *Clavierübung I* sent to Prince Leopold in 1726; it is reproduced in *BD* 1, no. 155, p. 223 and *NBR*, 129f.

57. That is, his three-volume edition of Luther's German Bible, with commentary by Abraham Calov. Bach studied the text intensely, underlining many passages and making comments in the margins of his personal copy (fig 0.24, p. 36). See *The Calov Bible of J. S. Bach*, Howard H. Cox, ed. (Ann Arbor: UMI Research Press, 1985).

58. George J. Buelow, "In Defence of Johann Adolph Scheibe against Johann Sebastian Bach," *Proceedings of the Royal Musical Association* 101 (1977): 5–100.

59. Reproduced in *BD* 2, no. 400, pp. 286f; no. 409, pp. 296–305; no. 413, p. 309; no. 420, p. 322; no. 442, p. 324; and no. 552, pp. 432f. and in English in *NBR*, 338–53.

60. Johann Mattheson, *Sieben Gespräche der Weisheit und Musik* (Hamburg, 1751). Reproduced in *NBR*, 241–43 (*BD* 2, no. 592, pp. 461–64).

CHAPTER 9

Bach in Leipzig

Christoph Wolff

Johann Sebastian Bach the composer is a thoroughly familiar figure today, much more familiar to us than to any previous generation—and this despite an ever-growing historical distance. Never before has Bach's immense musical output been so present as we experience it today, more than 250 years after his death: vocal and instrumental works, large- and small-scale pieces, single compositions as well as groups of works—all are available worldwide in numerous editions, in an abundance of live performances, private and public, and in an immense and ever-growing number of recordings. No matter whether presented by so-called historically informed experts or by musicians who prefer more conventional performing styles, whether jazzed up or electronically synthesized, the sound, character, and quality of Bach's music appear to be well-known and easily recognizable. Professional musicians, connoisseurs, even amateur listeners manage to distinguish Bach's highly individualized musical language from that of a Handel, Vivaldi, or Rameau—to mention only three of his major contemporaries.

Johann Sebastian Bach the *man*, the human being, is quite another matter. Bach's life, at least as compared with his music, is not only much less known, but a deeper interest in his biography seems to be missing. Perhaps related to a lack of exciting details, a very modest frame of reference generally seems to suffice in order to understand the basic premises of Bach's musical development: his roots in a Thuringian family of professional musicians and his life stations in various Central German places—organist in Arnstadt and Mühlhausen, court organist and concertmaster in Weimar, music director at the court of Anhalt-Cöthen, finally cantor at St. Thomas's in Leipzig. Bach's physiognomy is known from the Leipzig painter Haussmann's official portrait, the only authentic portrait of Bach, showing the learned composer at age sixty (plate 1b); there he offers the viewer a friendly yet rather neutral look. Moreover, he challenges the onlooker by holding—in a somewhat provocative gesture—an

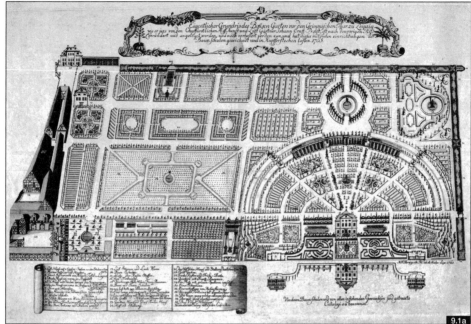

Figure 9.1. (*This page and opposite*) In Bach's day, Leipzig in electoral Saxony was a bustling, economically and intellectually vibrant city of about thirty thousand people. Neither a Residenzstadt with resident ruler nor a "free" city like Mühlhausen, it was allowed a high degree of self-government by the electors through a city council that had approximately thirty-three members, mainly businessmen and lawyers, who were elected for life. The council was divided into three groups, each with a mayor, who rotated into power for one year; this precluded a single person or family from gaining too much power. (The entire council voted only on the most important issues.) Leipzig had for centuries hosted international trade fairs three times a year, so it was a city in which the merchant and professional classes served as local aristocracy, as reflected in the new private buildings, gardens, and amenities that were transforming the city.

For example, the Grossbosischer Garden (Great Bose Garden) (*a*) near the Grimma Gate was designed by the architect Leonhard Christoph Sturm (see also plate 20) in the French representational style for Leipzig businessman and city council member Caspar Bose. It was the first large private garden built just outside the city wall. By the 1730s about 130 such garden-parks existed, both public and private. The gardens of the new Weissenfels palace Neu-Augustusburg (fig. 3.11a, plate 8) were probably influenced by Bose's garden, which was adorned with sculptures and fountains, and even had an orangerie, theater, and concert hall.

The merchant and manufacturer Andreas Dietrich Apel hosted the royal family when they came to Leipzig in his imposing home (dubbed "The King's House") (*b*) on the south side of the Marketplace (fig. 3.20, p. 159). Between 1728 and 1741 Bach occasionally led performances in front of Apel's House to a royal audience listening from a balcony. Such music, performed by students and other participants in his Collegium Musicum, did not fall within Bach's responsibilities as cantor or director of the city music, so more likely were prompted by Bach's desire to be noticed and patronized by the court. Engraving by Ernst Scheffler, 1749.

A few years after his election as mayor of Leipzig (1701), Conrad Romanus (who appointed Telemann director of music in the New Church) built an imposing new residence (c) at the corner of Katharinenstraße and the Brühl, depicted here completed, save for a statue by the principal sculptor of the Dresden Zwinger, Balthasar Permoser, soon to occupy the corner niche. The popular Romanus was not able to enjoy his elegant home for long: in 1705 he was arrested and imprisoned for life, allegedly for embezzlement, although (suspiciously) he was never tried. But his family, including his daughter (a future Bach librettist; fig. 9.4a), continued to live in the house and enjoy the respect of the community.

In the early eighteenth century, Leipzig residents began to benefit from municipal efforts to make the city more attractive to live in and to visit. In 1700 an underground sewage system, beginning in the Thomasgasse, was begun, and the following year street lighting (d) was introduced. The new development was celebrated by a medal with the text "LEIPZIG STREET LIGHTS ON, SO ONE CAN SEE WELL," and in 1714 the chronicler Johann Jacob Vogel reported that not only did the seven hundred municipal street lights replace private lanterns, "but also many sins, especially against the fifth, sixth, and seventh commandments, were remarkably checked and strongly hindered."

enigmatic canon, knowing full well that the canon's musical contents will remain totally obscure to the uninitiated. Was Bach an inaccessible, unapproachable human being?

Because the evidence concerning Bach the person is far less imposing than his musical legacy, Bach's biographers have, from the very beginning, cared rather little about the everyday life of this man, about the personality of this musician who is identified so completely with his work and whose character image is often defined by a mere stereotype: unyielding stubbornness. For the music historian, there has seemed to be insufficient information pertaining to Bach's personality and everyday life that might suit a scholarly discussion, whereas his music has offered fascinating and unlimited material for examination and exploration, ranging widely from analysis and interpretation to studies of musical sources, performance practice, theoretical aspects, reception history, and aesthetics.

Bach's everyday life, for example, has been understood in a rather schematic fashion, generally reduced to regular activities and routine operations during his Leipzig years, such as musical exercises at school on weekdays and the performance of church pieces on Sundays and feast days. This, however, barely sketches out the framework within which he had to live and work as cantor, let alone the various aspects of his manifold professional engagements and the broad spectrum of his private activities. It is certainly difficult to gain more detailed insight into Bach's everyday life and the external conditions under which he conducted his work, and to develop a deeper and more accurate understanding of Bach the human being. The reasons for this situation are obvious, most notably the paucity of personal writings and correspondence. In this regard, Mozart, Beethoven, Wagner, Mahler, and many other composers have much more to offer biographical studies with a particular focus on personality. The plentiful and rich correspondence of the Mozart family, for example, opens up very many aspects of the composer's life, his thoughts and feelings—a distinct contrast to the meager material provided by the few Bach letters that rarely touch on human elements, not to mention expressions of feelings.

However, it is worth noting here that the correspondence of Bach's second son, Carl Philipp Emanuel, is among the most important of eighteenth-century musicians, and, in terms of both quantity and contents, it actually resembles the Mozart family correspondence.[1] This makes us wonder: Did Johann Sebastian Bach limit his writings to organ reports, recommendations for students, business letters, and financial receipts? Could he really have refrained from regular and personal correspondence? Of course, he did not, for we know that from 1738 to 1742 he had a private secretary, his nephew and student Johann Elias Bach; Johann Elias's draft correspondence and copy books on behalf of his uncle survive and inform us about Bach's travels, publication plans, rental of music, and other matters during that time.[2] This clearly suggests that Bach—considering his busy life—most probably needed secretarial assistance prior to 1738 and after 1742 as well, and that he also maintained records of his correspondence in the form of drafts and copybooks. There is a clear indication for the latter in a well-known letter written in 1730 to his childhood friend and school classmate, Georg Erdmann of Danzig, wherein Bach refers to specific points made in a letter written four years earlier. That very letter came to light only in 1984 (in a Moscow archive) and demonstrates that Bach must have had a copy of it when he wrote that later piece of correspondence.[3] Therefore, we can safely assume that the Bach correspondence originally amounted to much more than what has come down to us, that he actually kept copybooks of his correspondence, and that the extant material sadly represents a mere fragment of what once existed.

Figure 9.2. The School of St. Thomas, which was adjacent to St. Thomas's Church, was already about five hundred years old when Bach came to Leipzig. Originally founded within an Augustinian monastery, after the Reformation it was converted to a Latin School with resident (*alumni*) and non-resident (*externi*) pupils. In Bach's time, the alumni, who had to earn their tuition and room and board by singing at various Leipzig churches on Sundays and special occasions, numbered approximately fifty, the externi about one hundred. The school had the reputation of academic excellence, not surprising considering the close personal connections that existed between it and many faculty members of the University of Leipzig. The building that housed the school was renovated in the sixteenth century and again in 1731–2, after which the school was rededicated, for which Bach provided a now lost cantata.

Yet, even if we had more material than we now possess, a psychobiography of Bach would be entirely out of the question, for the style of written communication in the early eighteenth century, even on a personal level, does not reveal the kind of insight needed for a psychobiography in the modern sense. At the same time, a biography that would focus primarily on external dates and events would quickly become entangled in trivialities. Therefore, if we want to take a closer look at the everyday life of Bach, or at least at some aspects of it, we must look for an image of the composer that is less abstract and hence provides a basis for a better understanding of the immediate context and conditions of Bach's creative work. For present purposes, the focus will be on the composer's Leipzig years, which represent the longest and most significant of his creative periods.

I

In 1723, at age thirty-eight, Bach accepted an appointment as cantor at St. Thomas's and music director of the four main churches in Leipzig, the most distinguished musical office in Protestant Germany (fig. 9.2). We normally think of the official obligations of the cantor of St. Thomas primarily in terms of providing music for the regular and special worship services throughout the ecclesiastical year. This stood indeed at the center of Bach's professional activities for twenty-seven years, clearly documented by the multitude of works he wrote for this purpose. But what is the framework in which these compositions originated?

When Bach took over the cantorate at the St. Thomas's School, he moved from court service to municipal employment. We can be sure that Bach expected here and there to run into difficulties with church, school, and town administrations, but he certainly would have realized that even a slow, inflexible, and frugal civic bureaucracy provided a more stable and reliable support structure than any absolutist government that invariably depended on the unpredictable caprices of princes (fig. 9.3). Yet Bach, who had been Cöthen capellmeister, the second-highest paid court official, now had to adjust to a collegial system with a strict rank order where the cantor was only "number three," after the school's rector and conrector. This also meant for Bach, as one of the top four school officers, regular administrative duties in addition to teaching specific subjects. Bach's administrative obligations included admissions (for the cantor had to test the musical proficiency of the applicants, a prerequisite for admission) and the regular service, one week every month, as inspector of the school dormitories.

Figure 9.3. A student of philosophy and law in Leipzig and Erfurt, Gottfried Lange lectured in Halle, developing close connections with Thomasius (fig. 2.15, p. 131), and at the Dresden court rose to the highest level possible for a non-nobleman: state secretary of the Office of the Privy Cabinet. In 1710, through the intervention of the military governor of Leipzig Count Joachim Friedrich Flemming (whom Bach honored with cantatas), he was elected to the Leipzig city council, where for three decades he represented the interests of the Dresden court against more provincial councillors such as Abraham Platz and Jacob Born; in 1717 August the Strong secretly ordered that Lange be given the next available mayoral position, which he held from 1719 to 48. Lange supported Bach's candidacy in Leipzig, may have been the librettist for Bach's earliest Leipzig cantatas, and was present at the baptism of Bach's first Leipzig child, who was named for him. He and his wife are buried in St. Thomas's Church, not far from Bach.

The inspector's duties were clearly outlined in the school's handbook, published in a new edition just a few weeks after Bach took office.[4] The inspector had to make sure that students kept their books and personal belongings in order and that no more than one student was in one bed. He was to prevent students from playing cards and other games, from drinking and smoking, from emptying chamber pots out of the window. He kept the key to the infirmary, conducted the morning and evening prayers, and enforced the daily schedule:

A.M.	5:00	Wake-up call (6:00 in winter)
	7:00	Academic lectures
	10:00	Study period
	11:00	Lunch
P.M.	12:00	Singing exercises
	1:00	Academic lectures
	3:00	Study period (3:00–4:00 often singing at funerals)
	6:00	Dinner
	6:30	Study period
	9:00	Bedtime

All that was certainly no easy task, let alone a pleasant one. But there was no way out of the regular inspection service, hardly an activity inspiring anyone's musical creativity!

Bach had managed to receive dispensation from teaching Latin, generally one of the cantor's responsibilities. Here Bach benefited from Georg Philipp Telemann's negotiations before he turned down the job offer made to him in 1722 (before Bach was asked to apply). Like Telemann, Bach agreed to a salary reduction so that a substitute could be hired for the Latin classes. This permitted him to concentrate on the teaching of music, which included daily choral exercises and instrumental lessons and resulted in a rather tight schedule of the kind he surely had not been used to in his previous court positions at Weimar and Cöthen. But the unfamiliar discipline clearly had anything but a paralyzing effect, for it accompanied Bach's ambitious project of putting together a new and large repertoire of church music that would serve for the decades to come.

The decision to establish a repertory of church cantatas of his own composition had been Bach's very own. He was under no obligation to write his own music; many of his predecessors had limited their activities in this respect by making use of works by other composers—something Bach made the exception rather than the norm. Moreover, he was certainly not expected to employ an instrumental apparatus that in size, variety, and playing requirements greatly exceeded previous practices. For instance, he introduced transverse flutes, oboi d'amore and da caccia, violoncello piccolo, and concertato organ; these had not previously been featured in Leipzig church music. Even more strikingly, never before had the vocal ensemble and the solo singers been so challenged in terms of technical demands.

This becomes immediately apparent if one compares the music presented during the previous decades by Johann Kuhnau, Bach's distinguished predecessor, with that of the new cantor. Even a superficial comparison between Kuhnau's *Magnificat* in C

Figure 9.4. Born into the wealthy Romanus family but not spared by tragedy—she lost two husbands and all her
children before turning to poetry and literature—Christiane Mariane von Ziegler
(a) for many years enjoyed the support
and active advocacy of the feminist-
leaning J. C. Gottsched (fig. 0.18, p.
25), becoming a member of Gottsched's
Deutsche Gesellschaft (German Society) in Leipzig—which awarded her its
poetry prize in 1732 and 1734—and in

the intervening year being honored with the title of
imperial poet laureate by the philosophy faculty at
the University of Wittenberg. The extent to which
she and Bach collaborated is uncertain, although
in 1725 Bach wrote nine cantatas (BWV 68, 74, 87,
103, 108, 128, 175, 176, and 183) on texts that,
in somewhat different form, were published by
Ziegler in her Versuch in gebundener Schreibart
(An attempt at poetry) (1728).

Although she did not upstage her mentor-hus-
band J. C. Gottsched, Louise Adelgunda Victoria
Gottsched (the Gottschedin) (b) was a gifted writer;
translator of literary, scholarly, and scientific works;
musician (and possible participant in Bach's Collegium Musicum); and composer who studied with
J. S. Bach's student J. L. Krebs. She was a full,
willing partner in her husband's literary reform program (some say she had the finer intellect and wit).
Her play Pietisterey im Fischbein-Rocke (1736)
was based on a French model and, because of
its attacks on religious groups of the time, caused
a huge furor, leading to new censorship and libel
laws. The fact that the work was published anonymously, gave false publication information, and

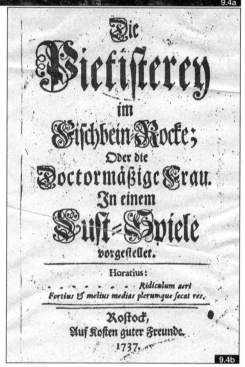

implied in the prefatory material that the author was a man points to the limits of freedom of religion and
expression then as well as challenges faced by women who wanted a public voice.

Major (with Christmas *laudes*) and Bach's first large-scale work written for Leipzig, the
Magnificat in E-flat Major (BWV 243a) of Christmas 1723 (also with inserted *laudes*
movements), immediately reveals not only the conceptual and stylistic differences, but
particularly the greater technical challenges of Bach's music for both voices and instruments. For this reason, Bach had to put the vocal and instrumental instruction at the
school on an entirely new and unprecedented level. What assisted him in maintaining
a consistently high level of vocal expertise were pieces such as the motet "Singet dem
Herrn ein neues Lied," BWV 225, which addressed all necessary skills required of his
singers.

The musical program for the 1723 Christmas season demonstrates impressively what Bach wanted to present. In roughly two weeks, from December 25 to January 9, we find no fewer than seven feast days: the three Christmas days, the Sunday after Christmas, New Year's Day, the Sunday after New Year's Day, Epiphany, and the First Sunday after Epiphany, after which the weekly schedule resumed. Bach performed at least one major piece of concerted music on each feast day (on Christmas Day actually two), eight of which were newly composed.[5] Only one re-performance of an earlier work occurred.[6] Such a steady and inexorable schedule affected all participants in the enterprise: composer, copyists, singers, and instrumentalists alike.

Let us briefly consider the weekly working rhythm for the composition and performance of a multi-movement cantata, the principal piece of music for the Sundays and feast days of the ecclesiastical year. Some sixty cantatas were needed for an annual cycle, and Bach wrote altogether five such cycles for Leipzig. The process from the beginning of the preparatory work to the performance of the completed piece shows the following pattern:

1. Selection of text (also arranging of texts—approximately six per cantata booklet—and preparing ca. twelve such booklets per year for publication);
2. Composition of choruses, arias, recitatives, and chorales—generally in that order (beginning on Monday, if not before; preparing music paper and score; order of movements determined by need to have more elaborate pieces ready first);
3. Organization and supervision of copying effort to make performing parts (assembling copyists around tables in the cantor's office and the library);
4. Review of performing materials (proofreading, correcting, entering articulation and other performing marks);
5. Rehearsal (generally no more than one read-through performance on Saturday);
6. Sale of booklets (libretti) to obtain extra funds for additional performing forces.

We must also consider the fact that the weekly cantata and regular daily teaching schedule at the St. Thomas School were not Bach's only responsibilities. There were also weddings, funerals, and special events, particularly those related to the university (fig. 9.5), for, like his predecessor Kuhnau, Bach was in charge of major musical performances that took place under the auspices of the university. He did not discharge these duties with reduced efforts. On the contrary, a work such as the Funeral Ode (BWV 198) for the electress of Saxony and queen of Poland, presented at an academic memorial service in October 1727, shows how deliberately Bach competed with the poet of the ode, philosophy professor Johann Christoph Gottsched of the university, in designing a French-style musical tombeau, one of Bach's most remarkable and delicately orchestrated compositions (including two transverse flutes, two gambas, two lutes)—designed for the sophisticated (academic) listener.

II

A major advantage of municipal service as opposed to court service consisted in the opportunity to engage in professional activities on a private level. Bach knew how to make the best of that situation. Most important among his additional occupations was the directorship of the Collegium Musicum, an early bourgeois concert association founded by Telemann in 1704 (when he was organist at the New Church in Leipzig). In 1729, after some earlier irregular engagements with that organization, Bach took over the directorship of the Collegium Musicum, which brought together professional musicians, competent amateurs, and general music lovers once a week, and twice weekly to meet the demands during the Leipzig trade fair in the spring and fall of each year. One can imagine the impact this regular activity must have had on Bach's schedule for the entire decade of the 1730s until he passed on the directorship to one of his students in the early 1740s.

Figure 9.5. Shortly before Bach moved to Leipzig, one of the most celebrated criminal trials and executions took place, as recounted in the *Historical Account of the Life and Crimes of the Unrepentant Thief and Church-robber Johann David Wagner, Otherwise Known as "Mouse David," Who on November 21, 1721 in Leipzig Was Condemned to Death by Beheading on Account of His Crimes and Whose Body, After the Execution, Was Bound to the Wheel . . .* (Leipzig, 1722). The ritual of execution is described in detail, including how all the city gates were closed, save the Grimma Gate, through which the execution procession (here depicted), having begun at the City Hall, passed on the way to the place of execution outside the walls. Among the marchers was a group of choirboys (top left) from St. Thomas's School, whose new master the next year would be J. S. Bach (see also fig. 0.3b, p. 4).

The so-called *ordinaire concerten* (ordinary concerts) provided the opportunity for innovative programming that included the newest kind of instrumental repertories of various origins (e.g., Telemann's *Musique de Table* and concertos by Locatelli), vocal works (including Italian solo cantatas by Porpora and Pergolesi),[7] or guest appearances by out-of-town virtuosos (such as Dresden's Hasse and wife Faustina). Carl Philipp Emanuel Bach reported later that "no master of music was apt to pass through this place [Leipzig] without making my father's acquaintance and letting himself be heard by him."[8] First and foremost, however, the Collegium Musicum provided Bach with the opportunity to present new pieces of his own, as for example his large-scale "drammi per musica" (secular cantatas). Works such as *The Contest Between Phoebus and Pan* (BWV 201) and the "Coffee Cantata" (BWV 214) (see fig. 9.6) represented dramatic scenes as a substitute for opera. The Leipzig opera house had gone bankrupt in 1720, and the Leipzig public seems to have appreciated the kind of revival of dramatic music offered by the Collegium. For real opera, however, they had to travel to Dresden (half a day's trip). But they could stay home if they wanted to experience something that could not be heard anywhere else, such as concertos for one and more harpsichords performed by Bach and his sons, an entirely new genre of composition that stands at the very beginning of the later tradition of the piano concerto.

Bach's motivation to expand his activities significantly beyond the duties of the St. Thomas cantorate was not primarily driven by economic considerations. His decent if modest salary and free residence was regularly supplemented by income from funerals and weddings, memorial services and the like. Hence there was no need to generate additional income, although—we can be sure—Bach appreciated such opportunities. What clearly mattered more, though, was the broadening of the scope of his Leipzig activities, i.e., he practically redefined the office of cantor by giving it a capellmeister's stamp. Of course, he thereby also created problems, which becomes clear from a statement made by the mayor of Leipzig in conjunction with the search for a successor to Bach in 1750: "The school needs a cantor and not a capellmeister."[9]

At any rate, Bach's expansive approach included frequent appearances inside and outside of Leipzig as keyboard virtuoso. His travels generally did not take him very far, but they included several trips to Berlin and frequent visits to Dresden, then the cultural capital of Germany. Such concerts definitely contributed to Bach's growing reputation as "the greatest organist and clavier player that we have ever had" (so stated in Bach's obituary of 1750/54).[10]

Related to Bach's activities as keyboard virtuoso were his services as a consultant and organ expert, an area in which he virtually had no peers. But he did not only design and test organs, he also played a significant role in the development of new keyboard instruments, most notably the lute clavier (a gut-strung variant of the harpsichord) and

9.6a

9.6b

Figure 9.6. (*This page and facing*) **COFFEE AND LEIPZIG**   Coffee became part of Leipzig life in 1694, when Johann Lohmann began to serve it in an establishment on the ground floor of Apel's House (fig. 9.1b) on the Market. It was immediately controversial, having associations with the exotic and sensuously satisfying lifestyle of the Turk—a sculptured Turk, mounted in 1720, graces the entrance to the still-functioning coffeehouse "Zum Kaffeebaum" (*a*)—and an (unproven) reputation as an aphrodisiac (fig. 1.4c, p. 81). Subsequently, it became a regulated substance and a subject of polemical tracts. The frontispiece of one publication (1707, from a French original), the title of which translates as *On the Misuse of Hot and Stimulating Foods* (*d*), indicates that women, at first excluded from the public coffeehouses, formed "coffee circles" at home to ensure their own enjoyment of the beverage. Both the alleged dangers and the modishness of coffee are indicated in the caption: "Even if we all now drink ourselves to death, it will nonetheless be the fashionable thing to do."

In the same way, Bach's humorous "Coffee Cantata" (BWV 214), undoubtedly performed by his Collegium Musicum in Zimmermann's coffeehouse (fig. 3.19, p. 158) and/or garden, plays on the dangers coffee was thought to present to young women: the father Schlendrian finally persuades his coffee-addicted daughter to give up her habit by threatening not to allow her to get married. However, Bach's cantata includes a final recitative, not in the published text (1732) by Bach's important Leipzig librettist Christian Friedrich Henrici (pen-name Picander), in which the daughter then informs the audience in an aside that she will only marry someone who allows her to drink her coffee.

Bach's little family drama was not the only musical treatment of the coffee topos: there are several others known, including an earlier French cantata by Nicolas Bernier and other settings of Picander's text. One of the later is depicted in (*b*), a setting of Picander's second aria "Ei! Wie schmeckt der Coffee süsse" (Oh, how sweet coffee tastes!), for soprano, two violins, and "cembalo" (harpsichord). Interestingly, the keyboard part has "*f*" and "*p*" markings but no figured-bass symbols. Moreover, numerous poems and songs contributed to the coffee debate; in the popular song collection *Singende Muse an der Pleise* by Sperontes, for example, both sides of the issue are represented. The text to the song illustrated (*c*), from the 1741 edition, begins: "Dearest sisters, come here! / The time has come! / Cease your work / and enjoy a mouthful / of this marvelously rich drink / from the strength of noble beans / the distant Moors here and there / select for drinking."

the fortepiano (here he is known to have suggested to Silbermann how to improve the mechanical action of the early prototype of the modern piano). Bach's critique of Silbermann's early fortepiano caused the maker to withdraw the model, only to reintroduce an improved version in the mid-1740s. Contemporary reports also link Bach to the design of the viola pomposa and violoncello piccolo, both of which he made use of in his cantatas. In general, Bach's scores document well his interest in new instrumental sonorities. Apparently, Bach also had a hand in the construction of the oboe da caccia, a hybrid oboe consisting of a wooden shaft and a brass bell. Bach used this instrument very effectively, most prominently in the Christmas Oratorio, Part II (BWV 248); its pastoral sinfonia features a rare quartet of double-reed instruments: two oboi d'amore and two oboi da caccia.

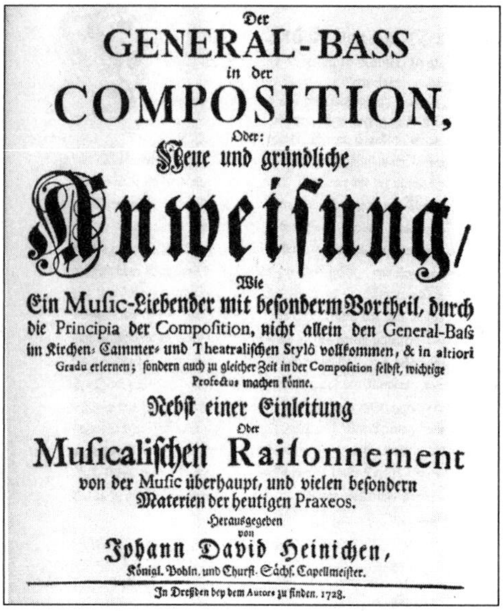
Der
GENERAL-BASS
in der
COMPOSITION,
Oder:
Neue und gründliche
Anweisung,
Wie
Ein Music-Liebender mit besonderm Vortheil, durch die Principia der Composition, nicht allein den General-Baß im Kirchen- Cammer- und Theatralischen Stylô vollkommen, & in altiori Gradu erlernen; sondern auch zu gleicher Zeit in der Composition selbst, wichtige Profectus machen könne.
Nebst einer Einleitung
Oder
Musicalischen Raisonnement
von der Music überhaupt, und vielen besondern Materien der heutigen Praxeos.
Herausgegeben
von
Johann David Heinichen,
Königl. Pohln. und Churfl. Sächs. Capellmeister.
In Dreßden bey dem Autore zu finden. 1728.

Figure 9.7. *Der General-Bass in der Composition* (Dresden, 1728) by Johann David Heinichen, a landmark publication of a thousand pages, is theoretical and practical, not only treating the principles of musical composition in the widest sense but also instructing keyboardists in improvising accompaniments from figured bass. Bach had it in his library and even was a distributor for it. Heinichen, who showed musical gifts early on, studied in Leipzig at St. Thomas's School and the University, then went to Weissenfels in 1706 to practice law, but soon was drawn into the court's musical life as composer. Back in Leipzig in 1709, he wrote operas for the company there (which dissolved in 1720) and led a collegium musicum. The next year he went to Italy, writing operas for Venice and, in 1712, teaching composition to Prince Leopold, Bach's later Cöthen patron (plate 11). In 1717, the Saxon electoral prince Friedrich August II engaged him as music director in Dresden, a post he held until his death in 1729.

Bach himself kept a rather extensive collection of instruments at his house. His estate catalog lists no fewer than five harpsichords, two lute claviers, one spinet, two violins, one piccolo violin, three violas, one viola pomposa, two violoncellos, one gamba, and one lute.[11] He certainly needed some of these instruments for instruction, studio performances, the Collegium Musicum, and to supplement church instruments. It is documented, however, that he also lent instruments to others for a fee. This instrument rental service was supplemented by a small shop for books and music. Available were not only his own publications (i.e., the *Clavierübung*), but also the works of his sons, some of his students, and colleagues (fig. 9.7). Newspaper ads indicate that major treatises such as J. D. Heinichen's *Art of the Thorough Bass* or J. G. Walther's *Musical Dictionary* (1732) were available from the cantor of St. Thomas's in Leipzig,[12] whose image can clearly not be reduced to that of an ordinary Lutheran cantor—Bach was an

Figure 9.8. Throughout his career, Bach was a dedicated and demanding teacher who produced some notable musical protégés. Among those in Leipzig were Johann Philipp Kirnberger, who, in his *Die Kunst des reinen Satzes in der Musik* (The art of strict musical composition, 1771)—a two-volume treatise that deals not only with harmony and counterpoint but also with matters like the tempo implications of meter signatures and the character of dances—sought to codify Bach's style and approach to musical composition (a). In the 1780s he joined forces with C. P. E. Bach to collect and publish all of Bach's four-part chorales (fig. 7.1, p. 230), although he did not live to see them in print. Finally, while in the service of Princess Anna Amalia of Prussia (Frederick the Great's sister), he helped create a music library that would play a major role in the transmission of Bach's music to the later eighteenth century and beyond.

Although he once referred to Bach as friend and patron, some scholars believe that Lorenz Christoph Mizler von Kolof, editor of the learned music journal *Neu-Eröffnete Musikalische Bibliothek* (1736–54) (b), was also a student of Bach. Mizler enrolled at the University of Leipzig in 1731; his former teacher Johann Matthias Gesner, whom Bach had known in Weimar, had just become head of St. Thomas's School (to 1734). Mizler was much influenced by the modern thinking of the philosopher Christian Wolff, the scholar-poet Gottsched, and the composer-theorist Johannes Mattheson, while still convinced of the mathematical basis of music. In 1738 he formed an elite learned correspondence society, the Society of Musical Sciences; among the members were Telemann, Handel, and, from 1747, Bach.

eminently practical, versatile, and entrepreneurial man, the "compleate musician" par excellence. It hardly seems a coincidence that this universalist, all-comprehensive attitude is reflected in Bach's creative output, which shows practically no limits with respect to genre, compositional technique, performing demands, styles and sonorities.

From a historical perspective, one of the most influential side-activities Bach engaged in consisted in his private teaching, an area in which he had little if any competition from among his fellow composers anywhere in Europe. The significance of Bach the teacher does not rest on his giving instruction to well-paying university students of noble origin, who came to Leipzig (then the preeminent German university) primarily for the study of law, but they included after all several young aristocrats (like Count Franz Ludwig von Dietrichstein), the father of Mozart's and Beethoven's later patrons in Vienna. More important and of lasting influence, however, was the fact that Bach attracted professional musicians from afar, among them most notably students like Johann Philipp Kirnberger, Christoph Nichelmann, Johann Friedrich Agricola, and Lorenz Christoph Mizler, who later figured among the leading music theorists of the eighteenth century (fig. 9.8a–b). Their publications in fact codified Bach's teaching, not in sets of rules but in the broader parameters of contrapuntal and harmonic structures that constituted a new framework for the art of composition. In fact, it was Bach's students who put German music theory in the later eighteenth century back on the map.

Probably no other experience impacted Bach's everyday life as significantly as his being constantly surrounded by highly gifted and motivated students. The students in this category were generally not those who took paid lessons. Instead, they were apprentices and assistants who, in exchange for services (for example, copying and performing), received the benefit of Bach's instruction. An interesting document reveals details of a musical habitat in Bach's household, which could not have been much different from that of his father and grandfather. Johann Philipp Kräuter, in a letter to the Augsburg town council that sponsored his studies with Bach, describes a situation that basically amounts to instruction twenty-four hours a day, seven days a week: living with Bach, having free access to his library, working with him and for him—in other words, a situation of mutual dependency (he also mentioned that Bach reduced his regular annual fee of one hundred florins for him).[13] When Heinrich Nicolaus Gerber (father of the lexicographer Ernst Ludwig Gerber) reported that during his years of study in Leipzig Bach on more than one occasion played for him, and just for him, the entire *Well-Tempered Clavier*[14] (fig. 10.4, p. 302), it sheds light on the conditions under which compositions such as the "Forty-eight," *Clavierübung* (fig. 6.1, p. 207, and fig. 7.2, p. 231), and *The Art of Fugue* could originate—works that were specifically designed for the connoisseur, not the dilettante.

III

Professional activities, whether related to official duties or to commitments of another kind, are invariably bound up with the structures of private life. We have little information about Bach's private life in general and his family life in particular. Still, the picture

Figure 9.9. Anna Magdalena Wilcke married Johann Sebastian Bach in Cöthen in December 1721. Some months earlier, she had joined Prince Leopold's musical establishment as a well-paid singer (half of Bach's salary as court music director). However, by marrying Bach, she entered a household with four children from Bach's first marriage plus his late wife's unmarried sister; perhaps not surprisingly, then, when the family moved to Leipzig in 1723, her singing career was sharply curtailed, although as late as 1790 a biographical dictionary of musicians mentions her as "a splendid soprano." Within a few years of their marriage, Bach had presented his wife with two little keyboard books, one in 1722 and one in 1725. In the second is a little aria, shown here, that might be said to musically symbolize their loving union, since the melody and text were written out by Anna Magdalena and the bass line by Bach. With the text beginning "Every time I fill my pipe with fine tobacco . . ." (Bach apparently liked to smoke), the song takes on a family intimacy that is only deepened with the knowledge that on the opposite page their little son Heinrich had earlier written out the music in his child's script.

that emerges from both direct and indirect evidence unmistakably points to the fact that life with and for his family was of great importance to Bach. Having grown up in a family of musicians himself, he remarked about his children in a letter written in 1730 to an old friend, not without pride, "They are all born musicians, and I can assure you that I can form an ensemble both vocaliter and instrumentaliter within my family particularly since my wife sings a good, clear soprano, and my eldest daughter, too, joins in not badly"—one notices that Bach mentions here only the women in his family.[15]

Bach's relationship with Anna Magdalena, his second wife—sixteen years his junior—was manifold from the beginning. When Maria Barbara, his first wife, died in 1720 while he was away on a trip with Prince Leopold of Cöthen, he needed someone who would be a good mother for his small children; Friedelena (Maria Barbara Bach's older sister), who had lived in Bach's household since 1708, apparently was unable to take over their care. At the same time, for Bach, offspring of a musicians' family, a wife with the orientation of a professional musician seemed to have been a near prerequisite. Hence, we are not surprised to find Anna Magdalena's hand among the major copies of Bach's works such as the solo cello suites (BWV 1007–12), the solo violin sonatas and partitas (BWV 1001–6), the organ trio sonatas (BWV 525–30), or the performing parts of the B Minor Mass (BWV 232). Anna Magdalena, formerly a court singer who frequently joined her husband in concert engagements outside of Leipzig, apparently also had an interest in keyboard performance (fig. 9.9). Therefore, Bach prepared two albums for her (clavier books of 1721 and 1725) in which he entered some of his best pieces (partitas [BWV 827 and 830] and early versions of the French Suites (BWV 812–17), but also some compositional exercises; moreover, little Wilhelm Friedemann and Carl Philipp Emanuel dedicated to their stepmother their earliest attempts at composition.

Mrs. Bach was, of course, much more than an assistant, student, colleague, and critic. She was the mother of a steadily increasing family. The affection between Bach and his wife is well documented, not only in an aria from the 1725 album, "Willst du dein Herz mir schenken, so fang es heimlich an" (If you want to offer me your heart, then you must begin in secret), but also in some of the letters drafted by Johann Elias Bach, Bach's nephew, tutor for his children, and private secretary. Here we read that Bach planned to surprise Anna Magdalena with rare yellow carnation plants; she was a great fan of gardening. Similarly, Bach tried to get for his wife a rare singing bird from a friend in Halle, again because Anna Magdalena had an interest in such birds.[16] "She values this unmerited gift more highly than children do their Christmas present, and tends them with such care as is usually given to children. . . ."[17]

Bach also shared grief and worries with his wife. Not only did they mourn the death of several children who died for the most part shortly after birth, they also showed concern for two of their adolescent sons. Anna Magdalena's oldest son, Gottfried Heinrich, born in 1724, was mentally retarded, although in C. P. E. Bach's words he was "a great genius who didn't fully develop."[18] Johann Gottfried Bernhard, born in 1715, apparently was a real troublemaker. A letter in 1738 by Bach to a friend provides vivid testimony:

> With what pain and sorrow . . . I frame this reply. Your Honor can judge for yourself as the loving and well-meaning father of Your Honor's most beloved offspring. Upon my (alas! misguided) son I have not laid eyes since last year, when I had the honor to enjoy many courtesies at Your Honor's hands. Your Honor is also not unaware that at that time I duly paid not only his board but also the Mühlhausen draft which presumably brought about his departure at that time), but also left a few ducats behind to settle a few bills, in the hope that he would now embark upon

a new mode of life. But now I must learn again, with greatest consternation, that he once more borrowed here and there and did not change his way of living in the slightest, but on the contrary has even absented himself and not given me to date any inkling as to his whereabouts. What shall I say or do further? Since no admonition or even any loving care and assistance will suffice any more, I must bear my cross in patience and leave my unruly son to God's Mercy alone, doubting not that He will hear my sorrowful pleading and in the end will so work upon him, according to His Holy Will, that he will learn to acknowledge that the lesson is owing wholly and alone to Divine Goodness.[19]

A year later, Johann Gottfried Bernhard Bach died in Jena.

The professional development of his musical sons became a major interest; Bach often took initiatives on their behalf because of his fatherly ambitions. For instance, he himself composed and wrote the letter of application for the post as organist of St. Sophia's Church in Dresden that Wilhelm Friedemann Bach submitted in 1733. Moreover, he copied out the audition piece (BWV 541) for his son.[20] While these actions could certainly be seen as overprotective, Bach undoubtedly devoted much time and effort to laying a crucial musical foundation for his sons. It is also significant that he encouraged both Wilhelm Friedemann and Carl Philipp Emanuel to take up university study in order to broaden the scope of their education (fig. 9.10a–c). He seems to have paid a great deal of attention to their developing individual qualities—none of his sons were trained to imitate the father's musical orientation, and all the brothers turned out to be very different from one another, thereby confirming their father's ideals of individuality.

What the Bach sons developed in the 1730s and '40s in terms of independence and originality, their father had achieved in his very own way, in a remarkable departure from old-established patterns. He always pursued his professional goals in an uncompromising way, even at the expense of going to jail for a month in order to force the issue of leaving his post in Weimar that had become unbearable. Bach had no trouble putting up a fight with his superiors if he thought it was worth it and if it would serve his artistic and professional goals.

This independence, after all, gave him the freedom to conduct his Leipzig office unlike any of his predecessors, with a multiplicity of engagements on the side. There were, of course, immediate repercussions of this situation in his creative output, in the form of works that deliberately transcended his official obligations. A piece of church music such as the St. Matthew Passion (BWV 244) was, in terms of scale and scope, not necessary—Bach went beyond the needs of the office. The same is true, in a different way, of *The Art of Fugue* (BWV 1080) as well.

There is another aspect that seems to have mattered to Bach in later years, also as an element of everyday life, and that is a growing sense of history, or rather a sense of his own place in history. We observe that, at the moment when his older sons left their parental home, Bach started to prepare a family genealogy: his first draft dates from ca. 1735 (around his fiftieth birthday). Later, he added to this annotated family tree a collection of music that has come down to us via C. P. E. Bach as the so-called "Alt-Bachische Archiv" (old Bach archive, fig. 0.10, p. 14).[21] What a broad historical spectrum opens here, looking at both the musical past and the musical future of the family; ancestors on the one side, his own children on the other. Bach now makes provisions for his musical legacy, for he understands like nobody else that the unique features in the works of some of his ancestors serve not only as backdrop but also as foundation of his own music, as much as he hoped his own would be backdrop and foundation for the music of the younger generation.

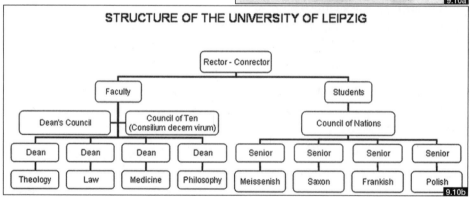

Figure 9.10. **THE UNIVERSITY OF LEIPZIG**   The University of Leipzig, founded in 1409, was one of two in electoral Saxony, its traditional rival being in Wittenberg. (However, the real competition came from the brand-new, innovative, and much more liberal university in nearby Prussia-controlled Halle.) Following medieval tradition, the three to four hundred students were divided into "nations" that originally reflected territories of the duchy of Saxony (b), and those holding the master's degree could vote for the rector and also on teaching appointments, although senior professorial appointments were always approved by the elector. In fact, August the Strong took a lively interest in university matters, and actually worked to infuse it with the new ideas of the Enlightenment.

The university buildings were mostly around the university church of St. Paul, although their run-down condition caused much complaint in the early eighteenth century. The teaching staff consisted of salaried and tenured "Ordinary Professors" and part-time "Extraordinary Professors," who had to scrape together an income from student fees, private teaching, and the like. The methods of instruction were gradually modernized in the eighteenth century, with the use of German increasing at the expense of Latin. Teaching was mainly in the form of lectures, the professor pontificating from his "Chair" (a), and only gradually were new

Ein Student zu Leipzig
im 17ten Jahrhundert .

9.10c

pedagogical approaches like Socratic dialogue, study groups, and the like introduced.

Contemporary accounts indicate that the more privileged students were often there more to enjoy student life than to study: dancing and fencing masters (fig. 6.7, p. 213), and riding instructors were associated with the university as well, and students sometimes got out of hand. Moreover, there was a fairly rigid social division after the foundational studies under the philosophy faculty ("philosophy" here implies all the liberal arts from physics to poetry): the "haves" (c) tended to study law, the proper training for a court bureaucrat, whereas the "have nots" took up theology in the hope of becoming a village pastor or schoolteacher.

Although burdened by traditions that slowed it down, the university was not without people and activities that looked forward. The theology faculty showed itself on occasion remarkably modern in its attitudes (fig. 0.21, p. 31), and J. C. Gottsched (fig. 0.18, p. 25) made Leipzig Germany's literary capital. Bach had contact with many university faculty and students, provided the music for four university religious services each year, and composed and performed his *Trauermusik* for Electress Christiane Eberhardine (fig. 0.19, p. 27) in 1727 for a solemn university occasion.

When Bach later made "archival" fair copies of his principal works, most of which had not been published, when he devised a workable method for distributing his musical estate so that the repertory would be parceled optimally, he must have realized the unparalleled qualities of the St. Matthew Passion, the B Minor Mass, the *Well-Tempered Clavier*, the works for solo cello and violin, etc. Bach the composer and Bach the human being must have derived self-confidence and assurance from the awareness that music would carry on in his family, among his pupils, and that his own work would eventually have a future well beyond the realm of the family.

In sum, the life of Bach the cantor of St. Thomas was not filled with an abundance of excitement, let alone earth-shaking events (fig. 9.11). Nevertheless, the many little pieces of information form a mosaic that shows a profile in which Bach appears much less abstract and much more human, a real person emerging out of incredibly complex structures of professional and private life. This does not, however, make the unique phenomenon of Bach the composer more plausible or explainable. On the contrary, considering the multiplicity of challenges, burdens, and trivialities of Bach's everyday life, his creative achievements appear to be even greater, more miraculous.

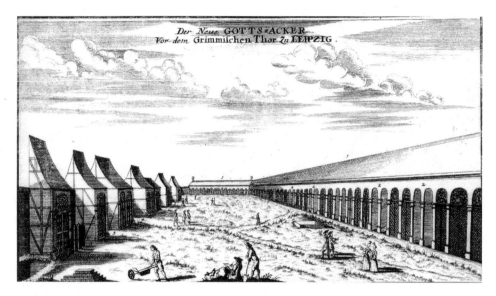

Figure 9.11. Bach, who died on July 28, 1750, was buried here on July 31, his remains being accompanied to the new St. John's Cemetery by the Grimma Gate by the entire faculty and student body of St. Thomas's School, which he had served twenty-seven years. The legend on the engraving explains some of the cemetery's features: 1. the encircling arc of chapels for the deceased; 2. empty chapels; 3. unfinished chapels; 4. between the two middle unfinished chapels, the entrance from the old cemetery into the new one. Bach's position in Leipzig meant that some of the funeral costs were covered by the city, but there was no monument erected. In 1894, his remains were moved to under the altar of nearby St. John's Church, and in 1950 relocated again to the choir of St. Thomas's.

Notes

1. *The Letters of C. P. E Bach*, trans. and ed. Stephen L. Clark (Oxford: Oxford University Press, 1997).

2. The complete edition of the German texts *Die Briefentwürfe des Johann Elias Bach*, ed. Evelin Odrich and Peter Wollny, *Leipziger Beiträge zur Bach-Forschung*, vol. 3 (Hildesheim: Georg Olms Verlag, 2000). See excerpts in *NBR*, 199 (*BD* 2, no. 423, p. 325), 204 (*BD* 2, no. 448, p. 366), 204f. (*BD* 2, no. 455, pp. 369f.), 205 (*BD* 2, no. 458, p. 371), 205f. (*BD* 2, no. 462, p. 373), 206 (*BD* 2, no.462, p. 373), 217f. (*BD* 2, no. 477, p. 384), 218 (Odrich and Wollny, no. 44), 212f. (*BD* 2, no. 489, p. 391), 213 (*BD* 2, no. 490, p. 392), 213f. (*BD* 2, no. 493, p. 394), 216 (*BD* 2, no. 511, p. 403).

3. *NBR*, 125f. (pr. *BJ* 71 [1985]: 85) and 151f. (*BD* 2, no. 23., pp. 67f.).

4. *Die Thomasschule Leipzig zur Zeit Johann Sebastian Bachs. Ordnungen und Gesetzte: 1634, 1723, 1733*, facsimile edition with a commentary by Hans-Joachim Schulze (Leipzig: Zentral-Antiquariat der DDR, 1987), 27–32 (Caput IV: Von dem Amt des Wöchentlichen Inspectoris).

5. The Sanctus in D (BWV 238), *Magnificat* in E-flat (BWV 243a), and cantatas "Darzu ist erschienen der Sohn Gottes" (BWV 40), "Sehet, welch eine Liebe hat uns der Vater erzeiget" (BWV 64), "Singet dem Herrn ein neues Lied" (BWV 190), "Schau, lieber Gott, wie meine

Feind" (BWV 153), "Sie werden aus Saba alle kommen" (BWV 65), "Mein liebster Jesus ist verloren" (BWV 154).

6. The cantata "Christen, ätzet diesen Tag" (BWV 63).

7. Cf. Kirsten Beisswenger, *Johann Sebastian Bachs Notenbibliothek* (Kassel: Bärenreiter, 1992).

8. *NBR*, 366 (*BD* 3, no. 779, pp. 255f.).

9. *NBA*, 246 (*BD* 2, no. 614, p. 479).

10. *NBR*, 306 (*BD* 3, no. 666, p. 87).

11. *NBR*, 251f. (*BD* 2, no. 627, pp. 492f.).

12. *NBR*, 139 (*BD* 2, no. 260, p. 191).

13. *NBR*, 318 (*BD* 3, p. 649, no. 53b).

14. *NBR*, 318 (*BD* 3, no. 950, p. 476).

15. *NBR*, 152 (*BD* 1, no. 23, p. 68).

16. *NBR*, 199 (*BD* 2, no. 423, p. 325) and 209 (*BD* 2, no. 477, p. 384).

17. *NBR*, 209; German original in Evelin Odrich and Peter Wollny, eds., *Die Briefkonzepte des Johann Elias Bach* (Leipziger Beiträge zur Bach-Forschung, 3., erweiterte Neuausgabe/ expanded new edition; Leipzig: G. Olms, 2005), no. 54, p. 144.

18. *NBR*, 293 (*BD* 1, no. 184, p. 267).

19. *NBR*, 200 (*BD* 1, no. 42, p. 107).

20. See Hans-Joachim Schulze, commentary to facsimile edition of BWV 541 (Leipzig: Neue Bachgesellschaft, 1996).

21. For the genealogy see *NBR*, 281–94. For the "Old-Bach-Archive" see Marius Schneider, ed., *Altbachisches Archiv* in *Das Erbe deutscher Music*, ser. 1, i–ii (Leipzig, 1935) and Peter Wollny, "Alte-Bach-Funde," *BJ* 84 (1998), 137ff.

Bach in the Early Twenty-first Century

Hans-Joachim Schulze

In his dictionary of musicians, the Sondershausen court organist Ernst Ludwig Gerber, son of J. S. Bach's pupil Heinrich Nicolaus Gerber, made the apt comparison: ". . . this great artist [Bach]" has bequeathed to us "the following works in order to test our talent, just like the bow of Ulysses."[1] Gerber knew whereof he spoke: one of the printed copies of the *Clavierübung, Part III* (1739)—in the United States since the 1920s and now at the Eastman School of Music in Rochester, New York—was once in his possession and contains, in addition to the date 1765 (when Gerber presumably acquired it), comments entered between 1799 and 1814 that refer to his own performances of this *opus summum* of organ music. Strictly speaking, in comparing the challenge of playing Bach's music with that of drawing Odysseus's bow, Gerber should not only have had the measuring of talent/strength in mind, but also the testing of a special ability, for the twenty-first canto of Homer's epic describes in detail how it was not only a matter of the span of the bow but also of the skill to send the arrow through the upper metal loops of twelve carefully aligned battle axes. Therefore, talent here also includes ability to judge.

How are we today, early in the twenty-first century, able to judge, after two centuries of intense and occasionally extremely fruitful research activity, the life and works of the greatest of all Leipzig cantors of St. Thomas's Church. Gerber's remark that Bach left *works* behind for us must be taken literally: in spite of all patient searching, the documentary basis for Bach's biography remains despairingly small. Despite recent discoveries, we still know almost nothing about the man himself, little about circumstances accompanying his duties (at most only official things), again nearly nothing concerning the performance and resonance of his works during his lifetime.

Some recent scholarship, however, has not been deterred by this paucity of information. With sophisticated and Talmudic argumentation the body of documentation has been repeatedly probed and poked. Everything is looked at from every angle, scrutinized, questioned, and in cases of doubt also turned into its opposite; whether the writers of these historical documents and Bach himself in particular could possibly have foreseen such a process is not at all considered.

For certain exegetes, however, the lack of documents also has its advantages. Whenever the sources are silent about something, fantasy can roam. And so the numerous areas open to conjecture are thoroughly exploited, and increasingly so in recent times. Everything that cannot be absolutely contradicted is accepted, conjectured, assumed. Consequently, Bach the *musician* is sometimes pushed into the background as theologians, mathematicians, philosophers, physicists, rhetoricians, poets, art historians, and politicians seek to utilize him for their own purposes. As a result, an image of Bach has arisen that portrays him as a kind of hybrid of Leonardo, Newton, Leibniz, Goethe, Einstein, and some others, or even has him surpassing these. The disciples of this way of thinking are not aware of the embarrassing similarity of such a superhuman artistic figure to certain heroes whose doubtful adventures they must have eagerly read in their youth.

The uncritical deference accorded a "great artist"—which assumes that greatness is predetermined from birth and that one ought to consider not at all or only in the last instance chance happenings and personal shortcomings—is the starting point for many an adventurous hypothesis, problematic interpretation, and strange conclusion. But usually this premise only serves to mask absurdities, leaving weaknesses ignored.

This situation is by no means something new. Similar annoyances prompted Theodor Adorno to chide his fellow citizens a half century ago in his irate and at the same time apodictic essay, "Bach Defended Against His Admirers."[2] He objected to the notion of Bach merely as representative of a lost, safe world, as protector of medieval traditions, as representative of an artisan view of art. What was important to him was the ideal perfection he perceived in the compositions of Bach. He also saw in Bach a pathbreaker who anticipated, especially in his keyboard works, many tendencies of the *Empfindsamkeit*, the Classic period, and even early Romanticism.[3]

Adorno's grim contribution to the theme "culture and society" need not be followed in detail here. Nonetheless, the defense against the "admirers" who like to look at things through rose-tinted glasses remains at the beginning of a new century a timely issue for all concerned with the life and work of the Leipzig cantor of St. Thomas's. Earlier scholars may have sought the causes for Bach's inadequacies and conflicts in circumstances and contemporaries of Bach's time. Who hinders us, however, from casting a critical look also at the composer himself? Even if such criticism will have to be expressed, so to speak, only on one's knees (as the nineteenth-century cantor of St. Thomas's Moritz Hauptmann formulated it), it ought not be completely avoided.[4]

The Written Record: Problems of Interpretation

Bach's Style of Expression: The Entwurf of 1730

Let us consider briefly that relatively small body of available documents pertaining to Bach's life and in particular the few preserved letters handwritten and authored by Bach himself. We can determine that their language, with their customary mixture of German and Latin, and even on occasion French and Italian, is for the most part clear and intelligible, but not always grammatically perfect (something that understandably does not come across in published translations); moreover, we can see that Bach's language does not reflect Johann Christoph Gottsched's efforts to reform the German language. This is quite surprising, since Bach demonstrated—according to our present understanding—an excellent feeling for linguistic quality in his choice of texts for musical setting. His most comprehensive autograph document, the *Entwurff einer wohlbestallten Kirchen Music, nebst einigem unvorgreiflichen Bedencken von dem Verfall derselben* ["A sketch of a well-regulated church music program, with some impartial thoughts on its decline"], a kind of basic constitution of Leipzig church music, was, in the customary fashion of the time, apparently written down as a draft and then copied in a form appropriate for presentation.[5] In spite of this careful manner of proceeding, the fair copy handed over to the Leipzig city council contains a number of oddities, in particular the assertions concerning the number of necessary or lacking instrumentalists.[6] It remains uncertain whether Bach inadvertently let these inconsistencies stand, or viewed them as insignificant, or did not take the trouble to make unambiguous calculations, or regarded himself in situations like this as the only one competent to judge and therefore not to be challenged. Whatever the case, the ambiguities in the document have made it possible for modern scholars to argue vociferously for their opposing interpretations of it.[7]

Bach's Style of Oral Expression: Recollections of Kirnberger and Wilhelm Friedemann Bach

Bach's verbal utterances are known only in negligible quantity and, in any event, come to us second- or third-hand. Johann Friedrich Reichardt, former music director at the Prussian court, transmits in his *Musikalische Monatsschrift* of October 1792 a story about his teacher Johann Philipp Kirnberger (fig. 9.8a, p. 281), who while in his twenties in Leipzig ca. 1740 enjoyed Bach's teaching but worked so hard that he became sick for weeks. When Bach continued to instruct him at home and Kirnberger believed himself unable to show his gratitude, Bach allegedly replied:

Do not speak, my dear Kirnberger, of gratitude. I am pleased that you want to study the art of musical tones systematically. However, whether you will absorb the knowledge I have acquired will depend on you alone. I demand nothing of you except the assurance that you in turn want to transplant this modest body of knowledge in due time to other good people who are not satisfied with the usual *Lirumlarum*.[8]

From the point of view of its content, this report is absolutely credible—it reflects the attitude of someone, like Bach, who was largely self-taught and conscious of being a link in the chain of a tradition. But one also notes—insofar as it is not attributable to Kirnberger or Reichardt—the strangely old-fashioned German that the transmission has put in the mouth of Bach.

Along the same lines is a report, cited by Johann Nikolaus Forkel in his 1802 biography of Bach (fig. 10.1), that describes the scenario of Bach's visit to Potsdam in May 1747. At the insistent wish of Frederick the Great, the Leipzig cantor had decided on making this visit to the Prussian court (although the court report in the Berlin press of 1747 described the matter somewhat differently);[9] but Bach had hardly arrived at the home of his son Wilhelm Friedemann when he was *stante pede* summoned to the palace. As Forkel reports:

Wilhelm Friedemann, who accompanied his father, told me this story and I must say that still today I think with pleasure of the manner *how* he related it to me. In that era rather elaborate formalities still needed to be observed. The first appearance of Johann Sebastian Bach before such a great King, who did not even give him time to change his traveling clothes for a black cantor's robe, thus necessarily involved much apologizing. I do not wish to quote here the manner of these apologies, but will simply note that they constituted in Wilhelm Friedemann's mouth a ceremonious dialogue between the King and the apologizer.[10]

One can easily imagine how the worldly-wise, thirty-five-year-old King and the *galant homme* Wilhelm Friedemann Bach were amused by the awkward explanations of the old-fashioned "old Bach" for his offences against courtly etiquette. Thus, the beginning of this "historic" meeting between cantor and king, which put Bach for the first and only time of his life on the front page of a newspaper, had a comic aspect that Bach biographers have preferred to underplay. We do not know, of course, if Bach's awkward behavior was the result of his feeling under extreme pressure in the circumstances or whether the king, in his attempt to demonstrate affability, engaged in a practical joke. But we certainly do know that Frederick a few years earlier was himself in a similar situation, when he traveled through Leipzig; not being suitably dressed, he left the city just as he had arrived—incognito. However, *quod licet Jovi non licet bovi* (What is permitted to Jove is not to an ox).[11]

Polemical Writings: The Ernesti, Scheibe, and Biedermann-Schröter Controversies

Handwritten documents and printed polemical pamphlets dealing with controversies in the 1730s and 1740s reveal, after sober reflection, that Bach, who never attended a university, was no match for academically trained opponents in arguments; he therefore was inevitably forced to take the defensive. That was the case especially in the so-called "prefect controversy" that broke out in 1736–38, an argument between the rector Johann August Ernesti and the cantor Bach concerning the question of authority to give orders within St. Thomas's School, but more precisely having to do with the priority of academic or musical interests at the school.[12] Afterwards, there was the Scheibe-Birnbaum dispute, which lasted from 1737 to 1745 and began with a massive and fundamental criticism of Bach's manner of composing.[13] The cantor of St. Thomas's allowed—and had to allow—his interests to be represented after a fashion by a Leipzig academic, Johann Abraham Birnbaum, who was his friend. Finally, there is the controversy beginning in 1749 over an anti-music school curriculum of the Freiburg rector Johann Gottlieb Biedermann, opposed by Bach's distinguished organist colleague from Nordhausen, Christoph Gottlieb Schröter, who had lectured at the University of Jena and had publicly defended Bach in the Scheibe-Birnbaum

Figure 10.1. Johann Nikolaus Forkel, best known as the author of the first monograph on Bach (1802), had the advantage of communication with people who had firsthand knowledge of the composer, most importantly C. P. E. Bach, who corresponded extensively with Forkel. Under the title (here translated) "On Johann Sebastian Bach's life, genius, and works," the biography appeared in 1802 in the middle of the Napoleonic Wars, when feelings of nationalism and patriotism were running high. Therefore, Forkel, who felt that Bach was "the greatest musical poet and the greatest musical orator that ever existed," exhorted his fellow Germans to "Let his country be proud of him; let it be proud, but, at the same time, worthy of him!"

dispute.[14] This *querelle* concerned the interpretation of the phrase *musike vivere* as "living dissolutely," for Biedermann, basing himself on certain ancient writings, associated music with immorality and argued that it had no place in education. Bach, now in his last months of life, did not help things by getting involved in the controversy. Schröter's written-out argument, in which he pleads the cause of music by citing ancient writers, biblical witnesses, and scholarly publications of the time was, through Bach's unwise intervention, altered in various places; in particular, Schröter's case was not helped by the introduction of the following reasoning:

> And finally, to put it succinctly, the aforesaid program goes against national-princely regulations concerning church and entertainments. For if no one studies music any more (which the author would decry), what happens to church music? Where would the opera and instrumental musicians come from? And what would the ale- and wine-tax administration say about this?[15]

These are justified considerations without doubt, but unsuitable for a pamphlet with academic pretensions. Whether Bach himself had undertaken to write out changes of this sort or whether they are based on his spoken comments—noted in his presence and then added to the printed version of Schröter's program—cannot now be known. In any case, an objective observer must conclude that Bach was somehow at fault here—certainly the highly respected Schröter is reported to have been furious and demanded that Bach take public responsibility for the document.[16] Indeed, only death protected the cantor of St. Thomas's from further unpleasant confrontations.

Understanding Bach's Musical Legacy

Today it is not easy to understand the angry pen-wars that broke out so long ago. With or without a "prefect controversy," Bach's altogether unexciting biography—insofar as it is possible to document it at all—offers few opportunities for the attention-getting revelations that today's times, which are so much in the grip of sensationalistic journalism, seem to crave.

Therefore, inquiries seeking "sensational" findings have tended to focus on Bach's music rather than his life. Of successful attempts to master the bow of Odysseus, Bach's musical legacy, there is little to relate. Certainly no one questions the greatness and meaning of Bach's oeuvre, although so much has *not* survived that it is no exaggeration to speak of the greatest artistic-cultural loss of modern times. However, that we should proceed carefully precisely because of the very greatness and the limited quantity of Bach's output is an insight that is not so easy to implement in today's atmosphere, which promotes rather self-discovery, self-experience, self-representation, self-realization, and self-appreciation; hence we have the current vogue for "updating" and reinterpreting performable art works of the past rather than seeking to understand them in their own terms. Paul Hindemith, in his 1950 Hamburg Bach lecture, alleged that the established image of Bach had "impaired our view of the true stature of Bach, both of the man and of his work."[17] However, given current, modish tendencies to reduce everything to the ordinary level of the everyday, it might be good to revive an appreciation of that image.

Approaching the life's work of someone like the Leipzig cantor of St. Thomas's should be a large-scale, conceivably unending process. However, often this is not the case. But how then should one proceed? Schematic descriptions of some two hundred church cantatas—here a da capo aria, there a secco recitative, thereafter a fugue, finally a chorale composition with obbligato instruments—are of little use, if one does not reflect further on the music. At least it should be asked *with what justification* an utterance of the Lord or a prophet takes the form of a four-voice choral fugue, *why* a statement of religious dogma poured into rhyme produces as its musical corollary a densely worked-out quartet or quintet movement for voices and instruments, *why* a cantus firmus in a medieval church mode is embedded not in a modern concertato texture but rather in an old-fashioned motet movement. The continuing reflection on the "why so and not otherwise?" must normally follow on the heels of the analyzing question concerning the "how." The relatively little effort that is attached to these two steps will usually be rewarded with rich returns.

The Search for Hidden Meanings

These days, to be sure, the hunt for information *behind* the music draws more attention, especially when it involves an alleged deciphering of abstract numerical relationships concealed beneath the surface of the music. The intentional existence of such relationships can be refuted in any case through a time-consuming replication of the supposed compositional process. Still, it is questionable whether such an investment of time, especially today, is really justifiable, for not even the simplest number allegory can be shown to have a sound basis—at least in the work of Bach. Take the polyphonically rendered question of the disciples in the Last Supper scene of the St. Matthew Passion, "Herr, bin ichs?" (Master, is it I?) (BWV 244/9e). In 1937 Martin Jansen noted that this occurred eleven times—the number of disciples less one—concluding that the absence of a twelfth occurrence represented the silence of

Figure 10.2. This passage from the first version of Bach's St. Matthew Passion (1727; BWV 244¹) shows that Bach, at least originally, did not intend that the phrase "Herr, bin ichs? ("Lord, is it I?") be stated eleven times—as in the later, standard version—to represent symbolically the eleven faithful disciples. Although it is possible that Bach intended the eleven statements of the question in the later version to have that symbolic meaning, there is absolutely no proof of this. This is a good example of how difficult it is to establish with any confidence that Bach strove to incorporate number symbolism in his music.

the traitor Judas. This usage can, to be sure, be traced in various compositional pro-cedures back into the seventeenth century to Johann Theile and Heinrich Schütz.[18] However, a comparison between the early version of the St. Matthew Passion (BWV 244b, fig. 10.2) and its final version of 1736 shows that the number 11 in no way belongs to the original conception, but rather came about only by means of a later revision.

Another example of seeking meaning behind the surface of the music was the at-tempt, undertaken a few years ago, to interpret the sixth of the so-called Brandenburg Concertos (BWV 1051)—with its unusual demands on the (usually "underprivileged") violas and the demotion of the viola da gamba (a favorite instrument of aristocratic amateurs)—as candid criticism of the conditions at the Anhalt-Cöthen court.[19] But this sociopolitical inference was subsequently countered by evidence showing that Bach was merely perpetuating a scoring convention of the seventeenth century.[20] This, in turn, has led to a disillusionment with such types of interpretation.

Reconstructing Lost Works

The same criticism can apply to the various attempts and methods to close gaps in a composer's oeuvre by reconstructing lost works. This practice serves on the one hand to spread the name of the scholar involved and, on the other, to pander to the market of performers and audiences who thirst for novelty. Despite the fact that many of Bach's works have not survived, it is also true that a work allegedly lost may in fact never have existed. Nonetheless, some would prefer not to believe that a single composition required two or more stages of work or that a piece was written for special reasons in the idiom of another instrument (and hence is not a transcription of a lost work for that instrument). Accordingly, a version of the second Brandenburg Concerto (BWV 1047) without string ripieno has recently been proposed, and the well-known D Minor Toccata for Organ (BWV 565) has been proposed as a later version of "a lost original for violin solo" or "unauthentic, a work of another composer."[21]

The lost work most subjected to attempts at restoration is unquestionably the Passion of St. Mark of 1731 (BWV 247), of which only the text survives.[22] Despite the loss of Bach's music for this Passion, new versions (largely based on other works of Bach) are nonetheless constantly being presented, as if this guarantees us a third Passion from the pen of J. S. Bach. Some of the arias and choral parts were likely provided by the *Trauer-Ode* (BWV 198), which was performed in 1727 in memory of the Saxon electress Christiane Eberhardine, who never converted to Catholicism (fig. 0.19, p. 27); its somber solemnity made it an obvious model for the Passion setting. Therefore, incorporating parts of the *Trauer-Ode* into a reconstruction of the St. Mark Passion appears legitimate to some extent. But to adopt the reverse attitude and perform the completely extant and well-documented but infrequently performed *Trauer-Ode* apparently occurs only to a few. Admittedly, the Good Friday Passion deals with a subject and context generally familiar to modern audiences, whereas a memorial to a long-forgotten potentate has less obvious appeal today. However, when it concerns the person and work of a Johann Sebastian Bach, considerations other than contextual familiarity ought to apply. In fact, the unofficial memorial service in October 1727 to remember the electress immediately acquired—through the participation of the Leipzig council and the leadership of the university as well as other high personages—the status of an act of state such as Bach never experienced a second time in Leipzig. Therefore, a performance of the *Trauer-Ode*—seen in the context of its origins—would provide an impressive snapshot of that special moment in Bach's life and an essential insight into his career.

That one can hope for a performance of this kind has much to do with the developments of the last decades. For still in the 1950s, Bach's secular cantatas, among which the cited *Trauer-Ode* must also be reckoned, were rarely performed because it was felt that audiences could not relate to the texts, which celebrated birthdays and other occasions connected with princely and other personages or with events unrelated to twentieth-century life. Here much has changed, although the interest of audiences in such "historical snapshots" in general is not yet very pronounced. Nevertheless, it is better to perform authentic compositions rather than half-finished "reconstructions" either of instrumental movements or of vocal works with often displeasingly inferior text declamation (since reconstructors often do not fully grasp Bach's manner of composing).

Bach Performance Today

Bach's Music in Staged Interpretations

An expanded or complete canon of works, however, is of limited value, if it is not appropriately performed. It is in this realm that there is perhaps the greatest gap between scholarship and practice. Whereas scholarship attempts (or should attempt) to come as close as possible to understanding the factors that underlay original performances of this or that work and must not allow itself to be distracted from this goal, music performance is confronted with the demands of the public, or, in more general terms, of the market. Consequently, it is not always clear what will most influence the direction developments in performance will take. If the "Coffee" and "Peasant" cantatas (BWV 211 and 212) must be performed dramatically and their uncommonly gestural music experiences a superfluous doubling by histrionics introduced into performances of them, this reflects the apparently insufficient trust of the performers in the expressive power of the music (fig. 10.3). Moreover, what a dance interpretation or reinterpretation of cantatas, passion music, or the B Minor Mass can possibly contribute to the knowledge of a work or experience remains known only to the performer(s) or the choreographers, who are motivated by ego and artistic inclination. Apparently we also have here an obligatory tribute to the age of electronic media, in which an enjoyment of art without pictorial "background music" appears no longer thinkable or expected.

From here the next step is the total acceptance of the brazen, unwritten, and as yet unproven laws of the market, which effect a decline of a once-high culture in different realms of subcultures and can even cause the best works of a cultural heritage to degenerate into materials to be exploited for profit. Whether these and other unhealthy developments can be stopped or reversed is uncertain at present.

Issues of Performance Practice

Being near the moment of juncture between two centuries and two millennia offers an opportunity to look back and to evaluate the achievements of scholarship and practice on the one hand and, on the other, as occurred after the nineteenth century, to reject certain ideas and practices of the century just concluded. Thus, one could reject the tempos adopted so frequently in the performance of older music; these often give the critical listener the impression that the object is to get through the music as quickly as possible. A further criticism, having more to do with head than hands, would concern the widely held conviction that older music can only be performed in one way. Nonetheless, in spite of all the work invested and in spite of all pertinent inferences drawn from

Figure 10.3.The staging of musical works not specifically intended for the theater remains controversial. Illustrated is a scene from the recent production of the St. Matthew Passion (using an abridged version by Mendelssohn) that was premiered at Berlin's Deutsche Oper and continues to be performed elsewhere. Conceived and directed by the late Götz Friedrich, then the general manager of the Deutsche Oper, the production unfolds as a play within a play: a group of young people assemble to reflect on the Passion of Christ, and then act it out with Bach's music, resulting in what Friedrich called a "compendium of music-making enactment."

Quantz, Philipp Emanuel Bach, and others, the gaps of knowledge regarding Johann Sebastian Bach mentioned at the beginning of this essay also include wide realms of performance practices. Possibly the premise of total determinism mentioned at the beginning stands in the way, for some find it difficult or impossible to concede to Bach a pragmatic, empirical approach to his art.

Temperament

An appropriate example is the issue of temperament, i.e., of tuning and the size of intervals. Consider the title "The Well-Tempered [*Wohltemperierte*] Clavier" that Bach used for two volumes of prelude and fugue pairs in every key—forty-eight pairs in all. Was he referring by "well-tempered" to the eponymous theory known already in the seventeenth century, or was he using the word *wohl* in the non-technical sense of "well" or "good"? In any event, "well-tempered" temperament could not have been identical with "equal temperament" (in which the mathematical and acoustic distance between consecutive semitones is identical throughout).[23] Thus, Bach's meaning will always remain controversial[24] (fig. 10.4).

The documentary basis is small: in his published *Versuch über die musikalische Temperatur*, Friedrich Wilhelm Marpurg relies occasionally on a statement of Johann Philipp Kirnberger, who as student of J. S. Bach had to give the latter a helping hand in tuning the clavier, whereby Bach "demanded expressly that he make all major thirds sharp."[25] The argument between Bach and Gottfried Silbermann over the tuning of organs is legendary, but in fact is transmitted only in anecdotes: Silbermann reportedly alleged that he would temper organs according to his own ideas, and Bach retorted that he would play the organ in any key he wanted, whereupon he improvised in A-flat minor, causing Silbermann to run away in order not to have to hear the howling "wolf" on the fifth A-flat–E-flat.[26] The evidence suggests that Bach conquered the tuning problem pragmatically by ear and adapted himself to local conditions. It would be unthinkable that before organ concerts or at organ testings in Dresden, Altenburg, Kassel, and elsewhere he would have retuned several thousand organ pipes to his personal taste. On the other hand—contrary to his empirical way—several generations of contemporaries and pupils—from Werckmeister and Neidhardt through Sorge and Schröter to Mizler, Kirnberger, and Marpurg—concerned themselves with the mathematical and natural-scientific foundation of tuning, but without being able to puzzle out the "secret" of the practitioner Bach, who tuned without recourse to mathematics[27] (fig. 10.5). Thus, the extant calculations are notable not only for their abstract, mathematical precision but for the fact that this precision is virtually unattainable in actual practice. Beyond that there are continuing attempts to discover the secret of Bach's tuning procedures from measure counts, the number of beats in a prelude or a fugue, the letters of the title *Das wohltemperirte Clavier*, or other real or imaginary sources of information. What one should think of such attempts and what their likely outlook for success is can be inferred from comments above.

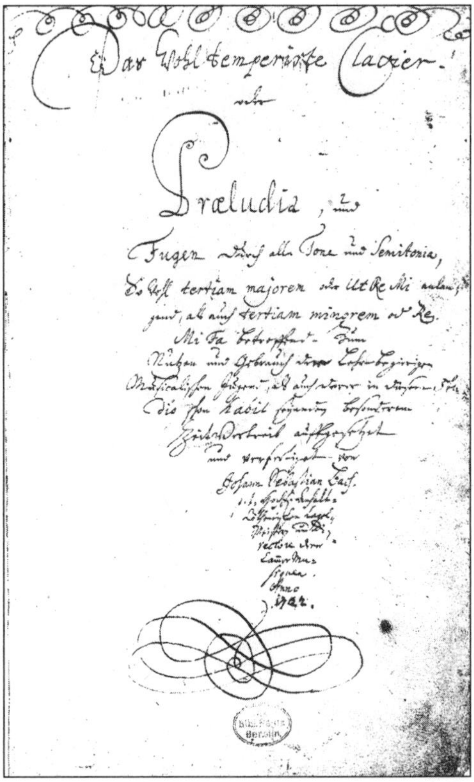

Figure 10.4. In 1722 Bach copied out the first volume of *The Well-Tempered Clavier* (BWV 846–69), with a prelude and fugue in every major and minor key (twenty-four in all). His point was to make the case for tuning methods that allowed music in every key to be acceptably in tune, for previous temperaments did not have that advantage, although they permitted music in certain keys to sound in more perfect tune than the newer, more flexible methods. (It is impossible to tune a keyboard so that every tonality will be perfectly in tune.) Today the most common tuning system is "equal temperament," whereby, in principle, the acoustic distance between every semitone is the same; the drawback is a certain homogeneity among keys as well as the fact that all keys are slightly out of tune. "Well-tempered" tunings from the Bach period included equal temperament but also others that produced acceptable results in all keys yet offered acoustic, and hence affective, distinctions between them.

Conclusion

A close collaboration of scholarship and practice appears advisable also for the coming age. To be sure, musical practice—adopting the methods of musicology—has up to now often made itself independent of scholarship and performers themselves now sometimes even have recourse to the source documents. Nonetheless, at least in connection with the work of Bach, musical practice has not yet made

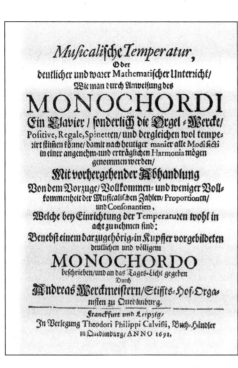

Figure 10.5. Andreas Werckmeister, while not the composer J. S. Bach would be, nonetheless shared many interests with him. Both were organists of broad intellectual interests who were well-known examiners of new or rebuilt instruments. Both were deeply religious, believing in music as a (mathematically expressible) reflection of divine order and purpose; thus, for Werckmeister (as also for Buttstett, see fig. 0.23, p. 35), the triad is a symbol of the Trinity. Werckmeister, moreover, adopted the astronomer Kepler's notion that the heavenly bodies produce a cosmic music. Both Werckmeister and Bach were also interested in the practical issues of tuning and temperament, with Werckmeister proposing, in his *Musikalische Temperatur,* "well-tempered" tuning systems to enable music in all keys to be composed and performed, as subsequently realized in Bach's *Well-Tempered Clavier.*

musicological scholarship superfluous. Therefore it would be best to maintain the "classical" division of labor, whereby music performance would have a certain sensitivity to the real or presumed demands of the market, and scholarship would enjoy a greater independence from them, so it can in fact exercise its corrective function, and not, as so often happened in the twentieth century, have to sanction historically unfounded, arbitrary activities of musical performers and the market.

This essay and translation was previously published in an almost identical version (but without illustrations) in Bach Studies from Dublin, *edd. Anne Leahy and Yo Tomita (Dublin: Four Courts Press, 2004). The editor is grateful to Four Courts Press for permission to republish the essay here. The footnotes were supplied by the editor-translator with the approval of the author.*

Notes

1. Ernst Ludwig Gerber, *Historisch-biographisches Lexikon der Tonkünstler* (Leipzig, 1790; repr. 2 vols., ed. Othmar Wessely, Graz: Akademische Druck und Verlagsanstalt, 1977) 1: col 90.
2. Theodor Wiesengrund-Adorno, "Bach gegen seine Liebhaber verteidigt," *Merkur. Deutsche Zeitschrift für europäisches Denken* 5 (1951): 535–46. Repr. In *Prismen. Kulturkritik und Gesellschaft* (Frankfurt a. M.: Suhrkamp Verlag, 1955, 1964). Eng. trans. as "Bach Defended

Against His Devotees," *Prisms*, tr. Samuel and Shierry Weber (Cambridge, MA: MIT Press, 1967), 135–46.

3. Thus Adorno, "Bach Defended Against His Devotees," 136f., in his characteristically confident yet opaque way asserts that Bach's work "embraces the entire sphere of the 'Galant,' not alone in stylistic models like the French Suites (BWV 812–17)—in which at times it seems as if the mighty hand has in advance given definite shape to the genre types of the nineteenth century—but also in the large, completely constructed works like the French Overtures, in which the moments of pleasure and organization are, in Bach's manner, no less present than in Viennese Classicism."

4. Moritz Hauptmann, "Über die Recitative in J. S. Bachs Matthäus-Passion," *Opuscula. Vermischte Aufsätze* (Leipzig: F. E. C. Leuckart, 1874), 116.

5. *NBR*, 145–51 (*BD* 1, no. 22, pp. 60–64).

6. *NBR*, 145–55 (*BD* 1, no. 22, pp. 60–64).

7. See the Introduction, n. 26.

8. German text in Friedrich Ludwig Aemilius Kunzen and Johann Friedrich Reichardt, *Studien für Tonkünstler und Musikfreunde* (Berlin, 1793), 112. Cf. also *NBR*, 322f. (*BD* 3, no. 975, pp. 523f.). The word *Lirumlarum* implies music on a very low level.

9. *NBR*, 224 (*BD* 2, no. 554, pp. 434f.). This report says nothing about Bach's dress and has him waiting in an anteroom for permission to hear the king's regular chamber music.

10. *Über Johann Sebastian Bachs Leben, Kunst und Kunstwerke* [Leipzig, 1802], ed. Walther Vetter (Kassel, etc.: Bärenreiter, 1970), 28. For English translations see Johann Nikolaus Forkel, *Johann Sebastian Bach. His Life, Art, and Work*, trans., with notes and appendices, by Charles Sanford Terry (London: Constable & Co., Ltd., 1920), 24f. and *NBR*, 429.

11. That is, the king was not bound to the rules governing ordinary people.

12. *NBR*, 172–85 and 189–96 (*BD* 1, nos. 32–35, pp. 82–96; and 39–41, pp. 95–106; *BD* 2, nos. 382f., pp. 268–76 and no. 406, p. 293; *BD* 3, no. 820, pp. 312–15).

13. *NBR*, 337–53 (*BD* 2, no. 400, pp.286f.; no. 409, pp. 296–305; no. 413, p. 309; no. 420, p. 322; no. 436, p. 336; no. 442, pp. 360–62; no. 552, pp. 432f. See also no. 441, pp. 340–60).

14. *NBR*, 352f. (*BD* 2, no. 552, pp. 432f.).

15. *BD* 1, no. 55, commentary, p. 125.

16. See *NBR*, 241–43 (*BD* 2, no. 592, pp. 461–64), for a third-party account of the matter as well as Philipp Spitta, *Johann Sebastian Bach*, tr. Clara Bell and J. A. Fuller-Maitland, 3: 255–60.

17. Paul Hindemith, *Johann Sebastian Bach. Heritage and Obligation* (London: Oxford University Press and New Haven: Yale University Press, 1952), 8. German original in Paul Hindemith, *Johann Sebastian Bach: ein verpflichtendes Erbe* (Frankfurt: Schott, 1950), 6.

18. Martin Jansen, "Bachs Zahlensymbolik, an seinen Passionen untersucht," *BJ* 34 (1937): 96–117, esp. 101f.

19. Michael Marissen, *The Social and Religious Designs of J. S. Bach's Brandenburg Concertos* (Princeton: Princeton University Press, 1995), 35–62.

20. Ares Rolf, "Die Besetzung des sechsten Brandenburgischen Konzerts, " *BJ* 84 (1998): 171–81.

21. Klaus Hofmann, "Zur Fassungsgeschichte des zweiten Brandenburgischen Konzerts," *Bachs Orchesterwerke. Bericht über das 1. Dortmunder Bach-Symposium 1996*, ed. Martin Geck with Werner Breig (Witten: Klangfarben Musikverlag, 1997), 185–92. On the D Minor Toccata BWV 565 see Peter Williams, "BWV 565: A Toccata in D Minor for Organ by J.S. Bach?" *Early Music* 9/3 (1981): 330–37, Rolf Dietrich Claus, *Zur Echtheit von Toccata und Fuge d-moll BWV 565*, 2nd ed. rev. (Köln: Dohr, 1998), and also Bernhard Billeter, "Bachs

Toccata und Fuge d-moll für Orgel BWV 545: Ein Cembalowerk?" *Die Musikforschung* 50/1 (1997): 77–80.

22. On this controversial question see Arnold Schering, "Zur Markus-Passion und zur 'vierten' Passion," *BJ* 36 (1939): 11–32; Friedrich Smend, "Bachs Markus Passion," *BJ* 37 (1940–48): 1–35, repr. in Smend, *Bach-Studien. Gesammelte Reden und Aufsätze*, ed. Christoph Wolff (Kassel, etc.: Bärenreiter, 1969), 110–36; Alfred Dürr, "Bachs Trauer-Ode und Markus-Passion," *Neue Zeitschrift für Musik* 124 (1963): 459–66, repr. in *Im Mittelpunkt Bach* (Kassel and New York: Bärenreiter, 1985), 115–25; *idem*, "Markus-Passion (BWV 247)," *Neue Bach Ausgabe* II/5, *Kritische Bericht* (Kassel, etc.: Bärenreiter, 1974), 248–66 (with facsimile of the libretto published 1731); Gustav Adolf Theill, *Die Markuspassion von Johann Sebastian Bach (BWV 247). Entstehung—Vergessen—Wiederentdeckung-Rekonstruktion* (Steinsfeld: Salvator-Verlag, 1978; 2nd, expanded ed. 1981); Klaus Häfner, *Aspekte des Parodieverfahrens bei Johann Sebastian Bach. Beiträge zur Wiederentdeckung verschollener Vokalwerke* (Laaber: Laaber-Verlag, 1987), 161–71; Hans-Joachim Schulze and Christoph Wolff, *Bach Compendium*, Vokalwerke Teil III (Leipzig: Peters, 1988), 1078–81; Andreas Glöckner, "Bachs Markus-Passion BWV 247—Chancen und Grenzen einer Rekonstruktion," *Bachwoche Ansbach, Offizieller Almanach* (1995), 77–81; Andor-Harvey Gomme and C. Schneider-Kliemt, "Ein neuer Versuch mit der Markus-Passion," *Musik und Kirche* 68 (1998): 30–38; and Alfred Dürr, "Bach—vermarktet" (review of Gomme, *op. cit.*), *Musik und Kirche* 68 (1998): 147f. with Gomme's response, 148f.

23. Thus, equal temperament is a species of well-tempered tuning.

24. The latest hypothesis regarding Bach's temperament is offered by Bradley Lehman, "Bach's Extraordinary Temperament: Our Rosetta Stone," *EM* 33/1–2 (2005): 3–23, 211–31. His theory is based on an interpretation of the series of decorative loops at the top of fig. 10.5.

25. *NBR*, 368 (*BD* 3, no.815, p. 304).

26. Edward John Hopkins, *The Organ* (London, 1855), 143, quoted in *NBR*, 410f. The "wolf" produced by certain systems of keyboard tuning is the result of the simple fact that it is impossible for all intervals to be "pure"—that if octaves are "pure" or "perfect," then fourths or fifths cannot be perfect (because a perfect fourth plus a perfect fifth, which nominally adds up to an octave, is actually slightly larger than a perfect octave). The wolf results when a keyboard is tuned such that most intervals are perfect or close to perfect—except one, the "wolf," which is badly out of tune in order that the other intervals may be better. The wolf can theoretically occur between any two notes, but normally involves pitches that are not likely to sound together.

27. On the issue of tuning generally, see Mark Lindley, "Temperaments," *New Grove*, 2nd edition (2000), 25: 248–68.

Notes on the Authors

RAYMOND ERICKSON, emeritus professor of music at Queens College and the Graduate Center, CUNY, is a scholar and performing artist with a deep commitment to liberal arts education. This has found particular expression in his conception and direction of thirteen cross-disciplinary Aston Magna Academies, funded by the National Endowment for the Humanities, which brought together hundreds of scholars and performing artists to consider music in cultural context. As harpsichordist and pianist, he has performed widely and given master classes in Bach interpretation in the U.S. and Europe, and participated in the first U.S. period-instrument recording of the Brandenburg Concertos. He has authored/edited three previous books, including *Schubert's Vienna* (1997).

ROBIN A. LEAVER is professor of sacred music at Westminster Choir College of Rider University and visiting professor at the Juilliard School in New York. A past president of the American Bach Society, he has published extensively on liturgy, church music, theology, and hymnology. He has made significant contributions to Luther, Schütz, and Bach studies, including four books on Bach as author or editor and chapters in *The Cambridge Bach Companion* (1998), *Die Quellen Johann Sebastian Bachs: Bachs Musik in Gottesdienst* (1998), and the *Oxford Composer Companions: J. S. Bach* (1999). His latest book is *Luther's Liturgical Music: Principles and Implications* (2007).

MEREDITH LITTLE received the Ph.D. (Stanford University, 1967) with a dissertation on the dance music of Jean-Baptiste Lully. She subsequently taught at several universities and has performed as a harpsichordist. Her publications include *La Danse Noble* (1990, with Carol Marsh), which inventories and describes the extant French court dances and their sources, and *Dance and the Music of J. S. Bach* (1991 and 2001, with Natalie Jenne), a descriptive and analytic study of Bach's dance pieces. She has published extensively in scholarly journals such as *Early Music, Recherches sur la musique française classique*, and *Journal of the American Musicological Society*, and authored twenty entries on baroque dances in the 1980 and 2000 editions of *The New Grove Dictionary of Music and Musicians*.

ROBERT L. MARSHALL, Sachar Professor of Music Emeritus at Brandeis University, is the author of *The Compositional Process of J. S. Bach* (1972, winner of the Otto Kinkeldey Prize of the American Musicological Society), *The Music of Johann Sebastian Bach: The Sources, the Style, the Significance* (1989, winner of the ASCAP-Deems Taylor Award), and *Mozart Speaks: Views on Music, Musicians, and the World* (1991). He is an honorary member of both the American Bach Society and the American Musicological Society. He is coeditor of *Variations on the Canon: Essays on Music from Bach to Boulez in Honor of Charles Rosen* (2008).

CHRISTIAN F. OTTO is professor of architecture at Cornell University. He finds particular fascination in the aesthetic and cultural condition of buildings, cities, and landscapes, especially in eighteenth-century Central Europe, and also studies the radical shift in approaches to urban design that occurred in the eighteenth century from Würzburg to Vienna under the influence of the Schönborn family. Another focus of his work is the twentieth century. His publications include *Space into Light: The Churches of Balthasar Neumann* and *Weissenhof 1927 and the Modern Movement in Architecture* (with Richard Pommer). He has served as editor of the *Journal of the Society of Architectural Historians*.

NORMAN RICH, emeritus professor of history at Brown University, is the author and editor of several books on modern German history, including *Friedrich von Holstein: Politics and Diplomacy in the Era of Bismarck and Wilhelm II*, *The Age of Nationalism and Reform*, *Hitler's War Aims*, *Why the Crimean War: A Cautionary Tale*, and *Great Power Diplomacy: 1814–1914*, and has contributed numerous articles and book reviews to American, Canadian, and European journals. The recipient of research awards from the Center of International Studies (Princeton), St. Antony's College (Oxford), the Guggenheim Foundation, and the Fulbright program, he received a Distinguished Teaching Award from Michigan State University.

STEPHEN ROSE is lecturer in music at Royal Holloway, University of London, having previously been a research fellow at Magdalene College, Cambridge. His research explores various aspects of German baroque music, including its social and economic contexts, music publishing, popular culture, and performance practice. He has published articles in *Early Music*, *Early Music History*, *Music & Letters*, and the *Journal of the Royal Musical Association*, and is currently the reviews editor (books and music) of *Early Music*. He is completing a monograph titled *The Musician-Narratives of the German Baroque*.

HANS-JOACHIM SCHULZE, a native of Leipzig, studied at the conservatory and university there before receiving his doctorate from the University of Rostock (1979). In 1990 he was made honorary lecturer at the Martin Luther University in Halle-Wittenberg and 1993 honorary professor at the conservatory for music and theater in Leipzig. He has been associated with the Leipzig Bach Archive since 1957, serving as acting director 1974–79 and, from 1990 until retirement in 2000, director and project leader of the New Bach Edition. He is the principal editor of the *Bach Dokumente* and coeditor, with Christoph Wolff, of the *Bach-Compendium* (1986–89) and the *Bach-Jahrbuch* (1975–2004). He is an honorary member of the American Bach Society as well as of the Neue Bachgesellschaft in Leipzig.

GEORGE B. STAUFFER is dean of the Mason Gross School of the Arts and professor of music at Rutgers University. He is author or editor of eight books on Bach and baroque music, including *J. S. Bach as Organist* (with Ernest May, Indiana University Press, 1986), *Bach: Mass in B Minor* (Yale University Press, 2003) and, most recently, *The World of Baroque Music* (Indiana University Press, 2006). He has held Guggenheim, Fulbright, ACLS, IREX, and Bogliasco fellowships and is a past president of the American Bach Society.

SIMON WILLIAMS is chair and professor in the Department of Theater and Dance at the University of California, Santa Barbara. He has published widely in the history of European theater and opera in the eighteenth and nineteenth centuries, with particular attention to the work of Richard Wagner. His books include *German Actors of the Eighteenth and Nineteenth Centuries* (1985), *Shakespeare on the German Stage* (1990), *Richard Wagner and the Festival Theater* (1994), and *Richard Wagner and the Romantic Hero* (2004). He is coeditor of *A History of German Theater* (2008) and is presently editing and partly writing an *Encyclopedia of Actors and Acting*. He is a regular reviewer for *Opera News*.

CHRISTOPH WOLFF is Adams University Professor at Harvard University. Born and educated (organ and musicology) in Germany, he taught the history of music at Erlangen, Toronto, Princeton, and Columbia Universities before joining the Harvard faculty in 1976. He currently serves as director of the Bach-Archiv in Leipzig and president of the Répertoire International des Sources Musicales. He has published widely on the history of music from the fifteenth to the twentieth centuries, especially on Bach and Mozart. His books include *Bach: Essays on His Life and Music* (1991), *The New Bach Reader* (1998), and *Johann Sebastian Bach: The Learned Musician* (2000). He is honorary professor at the University of Freiburg and is a member of the American Academy of Arts and Sciences and the American Philosophical Society.

Photo Credits

Grateful acknowledgment is made to the following for permission to reproduce both published and unpublished images as the figures and plates indicated.

Herzog Anton Ulrich-Museum Braunschweig, Kunstmuseum des Landes Niedersachsen (photos: Bernd Peter Keiser), 8.2, 8.5.

Historisches Museum und Bach-Gedenkstätte Köthen, 3.14 (photo: Jan William Howard), 1.12, pl. 11, pl. 12 (photos: Foto-Fritzsche).

Jörg Schöner, Fotodesign BFF (Dresden), pl. 20 (photo: Jörg Schöner).

Klassik-Stiftung-Weimar, Herzogin Anna Amalia Bibliothek, 1.9 (Sig. 10-166-378), 3.9 (Sig. KHz-1932), 3.10 (Sig. 10-165-231).

Kupferstich-Kabinett, Staatliche Kunstsammlungen Dresden, 0.27c, 1.2a, 1.4b, 3.27, 3.28a–b, 6.8b, 6.11, 8.14, 8.16.

Leipziger Städtische Bibliotheken, Musikbibliothek, 9.6b–c.

Mainfränkisches Museum Würzburg, 3.8.

Metropolitan Museum of Art (New York), The Elisha Whittelsey Collection, The Elisha Whittelsey Fund, 1960 (Acc. No. 60.632.21), 1.7. © The Metropolitan Museum of Art.

Museum für das Fürstentum-Lüneburg, 0.2, 0.3a, 0.4a–b, 0.28b, 3.3.

Museum für Hamburgische Geschichte, 8.4, 8.6.

Museum Schloss Ehrenstein (Ohrdruf), 0.12a–b.

Museum Schloss Neu-Augustusburg (Weissenfels), 0.27d, 2.12, 3.11a–b, 4.2, pl. 7 (photo: Gerhard Bach), pl. 8.

Neuberin-Museum Reichenbach im Vogtland, 5.1c, 5.3, 5.4, 5.5, 5.6, 5.7.

Rand McNally (Skokie, IL), pl. 2–3. Reproduced with permission from *The Rand McNally Historical Atlas of the World History*. © Rand McNally.

Ratsbücherei der Hansestadt Lüneburg, 0.3b (Sig. HL 27).

Schlossmuseum Arnstadt, 0.13a, 0.14.

SLUB Dresden / Deutsche Fotothek, Kartensammlung und Staatliche Kunstsammlungen Dresden, Kupferstich-Kabinett, 0.19, 0.27a, 1.2b, 1.3, 1.4a, 2.15, 3.6, 3.29, 5.1b, 8.12 (SLUB Kartensammlung, A 19531), 8.13, 8.17.

Staatliches Museum Schwerin, 1.4c.

Staatsarchiv Hamburg, 3.4.

Staatsbibliothek zu Berlin, Handschriftenabteilung, Porträtsammlung, 1.13 (Wadseck, Bd. 31,1 Nr. 72), 2.14 (Theologen).

Stadt- und Universitätsbibliothek Frankfurt am Main, 0.29 (Mus. Hs. 1538).

Stadtarchivs Mühlhausen, 3.7 (photo: E. Gerlach).

Stadtgeschichtliches Museum Leipzig, 0.18, 1.4d, 1.5, 1.14, 2.3, 3.1, 3.19, 3.20, 3.21, 3.23, 3.24, 3.25, 5.8, 8.1, 9.1a, 9.1b, 9.1c, 9.1d, 9.2, 9.3, 9.4a, 9.5, 9.6a, 9.10a, 9.10c, pl. 14.

Stadtgeschichtsmuseum Arnstadt "Haus zum Palmbaum," 0.13b, 3.5, pl. 5, pl. 6.

Stiftung Preußische Schlösser und Gärten Berlin-Brandenburg (Potsdam), 3.32b, 6.10.

Teri Noel Towe, pl. 1 (photo: Gregory Kitchen), © Teri Noel Towe. Weydenhammer portrait courtesy of Christina Neumann and Erika Norwood; Haussmann portrait courtesy of William H. Scheide (Princeton, NJ). http://www.npj.com/thefaceofbach/.

Thüringer Landesmuseum Heidecksburg (Rudolstadt), pl. 4 (Landkarte Schwarzburg-Rudolstadt 1791, Inv.-Nr. TL MH La 221, "Die Staaten der Fürsten zu Schwarzburg" Nr. 379).

Universitätsbibliothek Leipzig, 9.6d (Hyg. 1037).

Yale University (New Haven, CT), Beinecke Rare Book and Manuscript Library, 0.15, 0.17a–b, 0.20, 2.10, 2.11, 4.1, 4.3a–b, 4.4, 4.5, 4.6, 5.2.

Yale University, Irving S. Gilmore Music Library, 0.7, 0.23a–b, 2.6, 6.1, 7.2.

Yale University, Sterling Memorial Library, Map Division, 0.1, 0.9, 1.1, 3.15, 3.18. Courtesy of Map Collection, Yale University Library.

Every reasonable effort has been made to contact copyright holders and secure permissions. Omissions can be remedied in future editions.

Index of Cited Works by J. S. Bach

MISCELLANEOUS WORKS AND WORKS OF FALSE OR
DOUBTFUL ATTRIBUTION

General Index

For references to BWV numbers, see "Index of Cited Works by J. S. Bach," beginning on p. 315. For individuals named "Bach," familial relationships to Johann Sebastian Bach (1685–1750) are given in parentheses.